Irma Grese

Becoming The Hyena of Auschwitz

Judith A. Yates

ISBN: 979-8-218-48675-4

Published by:
Best True Crime Books, Games & Video LLC
POB 52
Adolphus, KY 42120
Website: www.BestTrueCrime.com
email: truecrimebook@yahoo.com
Ordering Information: Quantity sales. Special discounts are available on quantity purchases by corporations, associations, nonprofits, and others. For details, contact the publisher at the address above.
Printed in the United States of America
Cover design by Judith A. Yates
Cover – image of Irma Grese Imperial War Museum, © Crown Copyright IWM.
Cover art by Darasimi the Techartist. @bety_techartist on fiverr.com. Instagram – Darasimi arts.
No Artificial Imagery or/and AI – powered writing (AI) was used in this book.

NOTES ON IMAGES

I used images of the deceased in this book that are necessary to the narrative. Each of those bodies is a loved one; I do not include crime scenes in any book for that reason. We should never, ever forget what happened in the Holocaust, and it is imperative to remember the victims are people, not numbers.

Photos marked "Public Domain" are provided for illustrative purposes only and do not amplify the outlay of this book. Every effort was made to locate the original photographer and rights to images marked "Public Doman." Any misuse is purely unintentional. -JAY

The images from the Ray Cook collection, according to the United States Holocaust Memorial Museum Archives Department, "were taken by a committee of former Yugoslav prisoners for their records and then widely distributed to American soldiers. We regularly receive inquiries and offers from individuals who have prints from this series that their relative brought home from their service during the war …you find additional information about each image in the photo reference collection records… these images are not rare, nor would you be plagiarizing anyone by using them in your publication." (Kyra Schuster, Lead Acquisitions Curator, email dated February 24, 2025, to the author.)

In pre-publishing, a few of these images were advertised as "rare." (This book is the first time the Cook family has shared their collection.) The above information was received after publication and corrected. Every effort to correct this error has been made, and the author apologizes for any misunderstanding. -JAY

For Esther Litwin – Loeb (September 15, 1925 – May 5, 2011)

Holocaust survivor, activist, humanitarian, and my dear friend. I miss you so. *Shalom*.

In recognition and thank you to the following supporters:

Steven Gosse

Courtney Grace Campbell

Dave Moore & WW2CollectorsWorld.com

Michael Schucht

The Vogt Family

Dan Zupansky, Host of "True Murder"
www.truemurderpodcast.com

Contents

Images

There is only one good, knowledge, and one evil, ignorance.

-Socrates

Author's Note

I was the Director of a collegiate Criminal Justice Department when I made the telephone call that changed my life and, inadvertently, began this book.

I telephoned the Gordon Jewish Community Center in Nashville, Tennessee and asked for a guest speaker who was a Holocaust Survivor for my History of Criminal Justice class.

"I have the perfect person," I was told. "Her name is Esther Loeb. I don't know how she has maintained a sense of humor after what she has been through, but she does speaking engagements."

Esther was a tiny lady with a striking smile, curling silver hair, a sweet Yiddish accent, and a contagious laugh. Esther walked slowly but steadily. ("I'm come-ink, hah-nee!" She would call out while I waited for her.) She did public presentations about her life in Nazi Germany, her childhood spent in a Siberian forced labor camp, and life after the Holocaust. She also had a glib sense of humor. Esther was sharp, a sweetheart, but she knew when someone was BS-ing her. We became instant friends.

Esther Litwin was born in 1924, in Bydgoszcz, Poland. Her family consisted of her father, Joseph Litwin, who owned two prosperous shops, her mother, and her sister, Regina. (Later there would be a third child.) And then the Nazis invaded. Little Esther witnessed Jewish babies ripped from their mother's arms and bashed against walls by SS soldiers. She observed innocent people randomly yanked from the street, lined up and shot. Young girls were rounded up and sent away to be German troop "companions." The Litwins would attempt to flee but were eventually arrested and sent to a Siberian work camp. "It was so cold you had to have a wrap around your face, or your lips and tongue would freeze," Esther would say. She would tell of watching her beloved handsome father waste away and die from pneumonia. Then: "Have you ever been chased by a bear?" Esther would ask her audience, eyes sparkling. She told of picking berries, stepping around the bush, and suddenly there stood a huge bear!

In 1943, Esther, Regina, baby brother, and their mother, along with other Polish prisoners, were freed. But to go where? They had nothing. They lived on boiled grass. The sweet newborn brother starved to death in his mother's arms. The Litwins returned to Poland in 1945 to discover their entire family had been murdered, so they moved to a displaced persons camp. Esther volunteered in 1948 to go to Israel, where she fought in the army for two years. The family later moved to the United States, landing in Alabama, where she witnessed the discrimination of the late 1950s. Esther married a man who spoke no Yiddish, and she spoke no English. ("He was *very* cute" she would gush.) Together they moved to Nashville where she would initiate the building of the Nashville, Tennessee Holocaust Memorial. She began to do speaking engagements. Esther was a fiery, emotional, and educated speaker. But her PTSD would mean she had to rest for days after a presentation. I asked her once, after she experienced a frightening bout of pneumonia, "when are you going to slow down, stop doing speaking engagements?"

She became somber and said, very passionately, "Not until the last breath leaves my body!"

Sometimes I took her to lunch. I can still hear her ask me, "Do you vant to go to Vendy's, hah-nee?" Esther was so small, when she sat down there was a generous space between the soles of her shoes and the floor. We talked about everything – *everything*. How to meet a man (in a grocery store, she advised). The state of politics. She supervised a busload of elderly people on a monthly casino trip. The new class I was teaching. Challah bread. The definition of respect. Was I eating right? She was teaching Yiddish to young people. She had nightmares for a week after doing an hour's presentation. Her son, who worked at Vanderbilt Hospital, passed away. (His last words: "I love you, mama.") Was I dating? And always, always, giggling over something. Every time we parted, or hung up the phone, we ended with, "I love you."

"I'm proud of you, hah-nee," she would say.

Esther died on my birthday in 2011. She is with me daily; however, losing my friend Esther is a constant, deep, sorrow wrenching my heart with such force it takes my breath to darkness. Heartache is real.

I cannot fathom Esther's life as a child. How adults could be so driven to watch innocent people suffer so heinously based on a difference no one can even see. What made people so cruel they could beat, murder, torture people like my beloved friend, and then attend a party to eat blueberries and play music?

I began working on a manuscript that answered these questions. My years of research have been focused on female crime so I was most interested in Irma Grese (GRAY-*zuh*); she seemed to be the epitome of the "evil female Nazi." The manuscript went to the wayside as other projects took precedent.

Every time I watched Esther speak or we were together, I demanded of myself to learn more about the Nazi murderers: what caused people to twist into monsters and then back into people so easily? As a Holocaust survivor, Esther always maintained that if we stop remembering, it could happen again. As a criminologist, I always maintained we must understand how it happened so it will never happen again.

In 2023, my friend and colleague, Dr. Henry C. Lee, graciously invited me to China's 4th International Law, Forensics, Investigation, and Educational Conference. I submitted a paper entitled "Becoming The Hyena of Auschwitz: A Correlative Study of the Origins of Brutality in Irma Grese of Nazi, Germany." Unsatisfied with what I had, I wanted to go further. This book is the result.

What created Irma Grese remains a mystery as she was never interviewed by a criminologist or a psychologist. She was questioned about her crimes but not about her thoughts or feelings except legally, in the courts, but for a few sentences. Was she driven by an innate neurological process to kill? Were sadistic tendencies allowed to run amok in her work environment? Could she have been paying back, in some twisted fashion, those who emotionally harmed her?

Esther and I always agreed how Nazi Germany must be understood on a broad scale or the Holocaust could not be comprehended at all. Cruelty does not happen in a vacuum. Esther could recall being ostracized on the school playground long before her family was forced to flee their town. Thus, in this project, I purposely detail the world around Irma Grese. To understand Grese it is imperative to comprehend Nazi ideology, the people around Grese, and her environment. I explore why she was labeled "the Hyena of Auschwitz" with exception of offering several hypotheses. I mention ripostes to explicate Grese's behavior. Like all theories of criminal behavior, there is no "one" answer.

I do not want to rehash information, much of which seems to be supposition, repetition of rumors, or "possible" facts, on Grese. It is difficult as so much written on Grese's life is simply that: assumption or repetition. I dispel some myths and note what information was questionable to the best of my abilities as a researcher. If there is more than one version of an event, I attempt to offer all versions known. In no way do I condone her behavior; I approach it as a criminologist: unbiased and open-minded.

This book does not include the entirety of Nazi Germany nor the Holocaust. It highlights the incidents that are important to understanding Irma Grese. There will be errors – the retelling of history is fraught with error. What I have done is the best within my power to tell the story of Irma Grese and theorize what created the Hyena of Auschwitz. As I have reiterated to my students, "Theories are what criminologists argue poolside, drinks in hand, at cocktail parties."

Writing this book came with a cost. My depression would flare. I had nightmares: in one, I was a Nazi camp guard. A cat jumped into the razor wired, electric fence surrounding the camp. I pulled at the cat to rescue it and the animal came apart in my fingers. I awoke screaming and attempting to slap gore off my hands. Another nightmare took place in the mid-1940s; I was walking through a damp, murky, nighttime fog in Bergen-Belsen; people and things were slow-moving shadows. I kept peering through the grey, attempting to make sense of my purpose: was I SS? Was I a prisoner? What was my fate? And why was it so quiet and still? The shadows never took detail and never came any closer, no matter where I walked or how fast. In yet another nightmare, I was trying to interview a haughty Irma Grese, desperately searching for an ilk of humanity in her soul. I realized I was Jewish (which I am not) and an icy fear paralyzed my body: *she is going to know. She is going to know...* and in another, I was lying amongst hundreds of nude dead bodies in a camp's mass grave, writhing to escape through the waxy, putrid, skeletal corpses, wheezing, struggling to avoid the gaping mouths and empty eyes.

I hope this book gives us a better understanding of the "how" and "why" one of the fiercest females in the Holocaust committed such cruelty in just a few years of her young life. And I hope Esther is smiling down on me, saying, in that sweet Yiddish accent, "I'm proud of you, hah-nee."

Esher Litwin (in lighter scarf) with her sister Regina. This photo was taken at Landsberg Displaced Persons Camp in Germany after WWII. Esther, Regina, and their mother were the only people left of their entire families. They lost everything they had in the war, to include all family photographs. (Circa 1946? Photographer: unknown. Credit: United States Holocaust Memorial Museum Collection, Gift of Esther Loeb. Used with permission.)

Introduction

Female Missionary 'Nazi Bitch' Cult Serial Killers
by Peter Vronsky

Author of *Female Serial Killers, Sons of Cain* and *American Serial Killers*

Since the end of the Second World War, German women in the Third Reich were perceived as either "compliant bystanders" or "victims" of Nazi racial prerogatives that defined the primary function of females as birth-machines and enablers of their genocidal warrior husbands. Some wives did accompany their husbands to the killing fields and death camps, even bringing their children with them. These women did their matrimonial duty to wash and scrub the blood off their husbands' uniforms at the end of day of killing, while their murderous husband had supper prepared by her, read the paper, smoked his pipe and played with the kids, before going off to bed only to rise the next morning to do more killing. The slogan for women in Nazi Germany was *Kinder, Küche, and Kirche*—Children, Kitchen and Church.

Recent scholarship has revised that narrow viewpoint of women's place, in particular, Wendy Lower's, *Hitler's Furies: German Women in the Nazi Killing Fields* which partly explored the role of young single women teachers sent as 'colonial missionaries' into the eastern killing fields of conquered Poland, Russia and the Ukraine to educated enslaved conquered peoples to respect and obey their Third Reich masters and prepare local ethnic Germans for their new roles as overseers of *untermenschen* ("subhumans") slaves. Often these young women became witnesses and even accessories to the 'ethnic cleansing' of those who were unfit to work in territories being "Germanized." Scholarship has also identified the role of female nurses in the medical murder ("euthanasia") of disabled Germans who were classified as "life unworthy of life" and put to death in medical facilities.

There was, however, one segment and category of women in the Third Reich whose capture in the last months of the war, immediately exposed a category of female perpetrators: the female *SS-Aufseherinnen*--"supervisors" or" prison matrons" --found at some of the concentration camps being liberated. The SS, the *Schutzstaffel*, "protection units" which operated and staffed the death camps were the Nazi Party's notorious paramilitary elite which wore a deaths head skull and crossbones on their headdress and sported a double *sieg* (victory) rune "lightning SS" symbols on their collars, a familiar sinister symbol to this day.

The *SS-Aufseherinnen* wore a feminized version of the field-grey SS uniform tunic with a skirt and jackboots—much like old-school policewomen or prison matrons prior to the 1980s, but they were not sworn members of the SS—females were not allowed to join the "brotherhood." The *SS-Aufseherinnen* were not permitted to wear the deaths head or the SS *sieg* rune lightning flashes, nor were they permitted to wear sidearms like their male counterparts. The carrying of handguns was a jealously guarded male prerogative. Nonetheless, the women did wear on their left sleave, as did the male SS men, the Nazi imperial eagle clutching a swastika in its talons, as a symbol of their state service and did carry truncheons or riding-crops, as beating prisoners with bare hands or fists exposed them to being infected by one of the many diseases that inmates contracted in their state of deprivation.

As American and British troops liberated camps like Dachau and Bergen-Belson in Germany in the last weeks of the war in 1945, the battle-hardened soldiers were shocked by the sight of enormous piles of corpses that had accumulated in the last weeks of the chaos of the collapsing Third Reich and by the presence of female SS guards in the midst of the dead. At Bergen-Belson some 10,000 unburied corpses were found littering the camp grounds and an additional 13,000 inmates died in the immediate days *after* liberation.

The capture of female guards was caught on film and photographs, ranks of hard-faced and brutal women and their presence offended the soldiers' male sensibility of the era, in particular some of the younger and traditionally attractive women found on the guard staffs. They and their male counterparts were first put to work gathering thousands of emaciated corpses scattered on the campgrounds and carrying them to huge mass grave pits before being marched off into captivity and in some cases war crime prosecution and trial.

Toward the end of the war, in January 1945, the Nazi camp system consisted of 20 individual concentration camps or death camps (there was a difference) and 165 subsidiary or "satellite" camps with a registered inmate population of 714,211 inmates (511,537 males and 202,674 females.) Despite the fact that mass gassings were suspended in Auschwitz in November 1944 on Himmler's orders, approximately a third of the inmates still alive in January 1945 from that statistic, will die in the next remaining four months of the war, in forced 'death' marches, deprivation, starvation, disease and random brutality and criminal neglect at the hands of their guards and state custodians. Many will even tragically die in the days *after* being liberated; some, according to lore, died of intestinal shock when eating Hersey bars that American GI's routinely dispensed throughout the war to the starving from North Africa, Italy to France and into Germany.

Of the 40,000 or so SS camp guards, ten percent were women: 3,508 female *SS-Aufseherinnen* and 37,674 males of the *SS-Totenkopfverbände* (Death's Head Units) as the camp guard service division of the SS was designated. [1] Some historians have challenged the number of *SS-Aufseherinnen* assigned to actual supervision of inmates, arguing that the actual number was closer to 90 to 190 while the others served in secretarial and communications functions within the SS, beyond just the camp guard service. [2] The exact number will never be determined.

The *SS-Aufseherinnen* were indeed primarily recruited as support secretarial staff in both the SS headquarters in Berlin and in various of the many branches of the SS, including the camp system administrations and including as supervisors of female inmates, starting with the exclusively female concentration camp Ravensbrück, 90 km (56 mi) north of Berlin.

The *SS-Aufseherinnen* were classified as paid female employees of the SS—auxiliary workers—and not as enlisted members of the SS itself, an 'honor' reserved strictly for males. Regardless, they had the same authority and power over primarily female concentration camp inmates and males as well who might have fallen under their supervision, and many of them proved to be as sadistic.

All the *SS-Aufseherinnen* were required to sign declarations acknowledging they would be punished by death if caught stealing confiscated Jewish property, an oath of secrecy (non-disclosure agreement) on the "implementation of the evacuation of the

Jews"—the bureaucratic euphemism for genocidal killing—prohibiting them discussing what they witness even with their comrades. Some had to sign an additional 'declaration on dealing with prisoners' which prohibited private conversations with inmates, accepting gifts or other items, buying, selling or bartering items with prisoners, and an acknowledgement that the passing on of letters to or from inmates, would be treated as high treason. These were regulations that similarly male camp guards were subject to.

Young German women who proved themselves to be 'racially suitable' to work for the *SS-Aufseherinnen* were recruited from the *Bund Deutscher Mädel* (BDM, or the League of German Girls, a Nazi version of the Girl Scouts.) SS men were also encouraged to recommend their female relatives.

A former concentration camp survivor recalled the transformation of shy young German female civilian recruits into the formidable death-dealers that they would become:

> Before they received their field-grey uniforms, they all came in a body to see the chief supervisor. Most of them were plainly and rather poorly dressed, and stood shyly in the office, looking ill at ease and anxious; many did not know what to do with their hands. Langefeld [the chief supervisor] told them which houses they would live in, where to get their uniforms and when their duties would commence.... Then I often observed through the window how they would walk across the main square, nudging each other and staring with terrified eyes at groups of prisoners being marched past. In some you could see a transformation as soon as they were 'kitted out'. High leather boots already changed their manner; add a field cap cocked jauntily over one ear, and they started looking more self-confident. [3]

SS-Helferinnen earned approximately 185 RM (Reichsmark) monthly, in 1943 equivalent to $1,348 in 2024, substantially more than the 76 RM average wage of women of the same age in an unskilled factory job. [4]

The war crime trials following the war were scattered across Germany and the former occupied nations. Most of the murders took place in Eastern Europe, especially so in Poland and the Soviet Union and because of Cold War politics, we subsequently lost track of exactly how many perpetrators were put on trial, but it was a miniscule percentage, and female perpetrators were even a smaller percentage of that. At its very best, no more than a few dozen *SS-Aufseherinnen* were prosecuted and some of the worst offenders, like the subject of this book by Judith A. Yates, the 21-year-old Irmgard Ilse Ida Grese--Irma Grese--"Hyena of Auschwitz" ("*die Hyäne von Auschwitz*") and "Bitch of Belsen" were sentenced to death and executed.

The 'Sweats' and *Ilsa, She Wolf of the SS*

When World War Two - "the last good war" came to an end in August 1945, war crime trials of Nazi and Imperial Japanese perpetrators and the horrific accounts of depraved abuse and torture perpetrated by the defendants, spawned a torrent of articles in dozens of monthly postwar pulp 'men's adventure' magazines aimed at male American readers with titles like *Argosy, Saga, True, Stag, Male, Man's Adventure, True Adventure, Man's Action, True Men, Man's Story, Action for Men, Men in Conflict, Man's Combat, Man's*

Epic, Man's Book, New Man, World of Men, All Man, Showdown for Men, Man's Daring, Rage for Men, Rage: The Magazine for Real Men, Fury: Adventure for Men, All Man's Magazine, and *Man's Age.*

The entertainment staple for these magazines were the salaciously told accounts of wartime Nazi rape atrocities, tales of forced concentration camp brothel sex slavery and bizarre painful medical experiments. The magazine covers featured garish images of bound and battered women in states of undress with headlines like SOFT NUDES FOR THE NAZIS' DOKTOR HORROR; HITLER'S HIDEOUS HAREM OF AGONY; GRISLY RITES OF HITLER'S MONSTER FLESH STRIPPER; HOW THE NAZIS FED TANYA SEX DRUGS; BRIDES OF TORMENT FOR THE S.S. BEASTS; CHAINS OF AGONY FOR THE BOUND BEAUTIES OF NORWAY; DAMNED BEAUTIES FOR THE NAZI HORROR MUSEUM; STRIPPED VIRGINS FOR THE NAZIS' TORCH OF TORMENT; TORTURED BEAUTIES FOR THE NAZI BLOOD CULT.

These magazines were sold openly everywhere next to *Time Magazine*, *Life, New Yorker* and *Better Homes & Gardens*, and they became known as the "sweats" for the luridly coloured cover illustrations of predominately male torturers and female victims glistening with sweat, an effect enhanced by the casein paints and acrylics used by the cover artists.

These sensationalistic lurid pulp magazines featured not only a gamut of Nazi and Japanese World War II atrocities, but sweaty cannibal stories based in the South Seas and Africa; spicy Middle East harem rape scenarios; and contemporary Cold War, Korean War, Cuba and Vietnam War vice and torture themes. But Nazis with their cult-appeal, remained the central focus of this black hole in our global culture, and remain so to this very day at this writing in 2024. (More the reason, and the call, for Judith's book.)

Women in general, in these blatantly misogynistic publications, were portrayed in only two biblically paraphilic ways: either as captives bound and forced into sex against their will or as sexually aggressive, bare-shouldered or Nazi-uniformed females with a cigarette dangling from their lips, subject to inventible punishment or death for their evil-minded sexuality by the end of the story. In this paraphilic world of the 'sweats' women were either the proverbial sacred Madonna defiled or a profligate whore punished; there were no other options available.

The highly publicized postwar trials of female *SS-Aufseherinnen* with film and photos of the accused women in the prisoner dock, some of them elegantly dressed and made-up and lewd witness testimony of female Nazi sexual depravity and sadism spawned decades of a "Nazi Bitch" subculture and subgenre in the 'sweats' and in graphic arts that inevitably influenced a genre of cinema as well.

Reichsführer-SS Heinrich Himmler is featured on this cover of a "sweat" magazine. (Circa June 1946? Photographer: unknown. Courtesy Peter Vronsky. Used with permission.)

When the movie *Ilsa, She Wolf of the SS* was released in 1974, it reminded us of our misconceived belief that women did not kill or torture—unless they were Nazis (or black widow honeymoon killers.) This infamous exploitation movie made by Canadian producers was set in a Nazi slave labour camp (actually shot on the set of *Hogan's Heros.)* Ilsa (played by Dyanne Thorne) is the female camp commandant, a deranged sex-maniac-SS-mad scientist. She enjoys forcing male prisoners to have sex with her, castrating those who fail to satisfy her. She also conducts medical experiments designed to test whether women can withstand more pain than men, which of course involves lots of graphic footage of the torture of buxom naked women.

Ilsa, She Wolf of the SS was a sleazy B-movie, a staple of grindhouse theatres, but a year later the theme got 'classed up' by Italian film director Lina Wertmüller. Her film *Seven Beauties (Pasqualino Settebellezze),* with Shirley Stoler (who played female serial killer Martha Beck in *The Honeymoon Killers*) portraying a female SS camp commandant who demands sexual service from inmate Giancarlo Giannini, in a sequence that Internet's *IMDb*® claims "remains one of the most harrowing and fascinating scenes ever filmed." [5]

One can debate endlessly the meaning and subtext of the mostly male sexual fascination with beautiful blond Nazi killer bitches, and the "perform or face castration" dilemma (kind of like publish or perish in academia) but its narrative roots are indisputably founded in true historical events in Nazi Germany between 1933 and 1945.

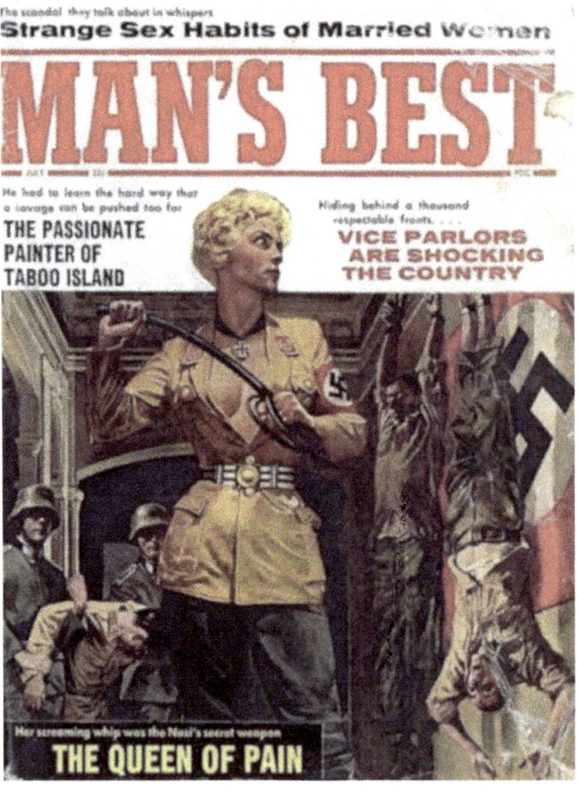

A blonde "Nazi" female – perhaps based on Irma Grese - is featured on this cover of a "sweat" magazine. (Circa July 1946? Photographer: unknown. Courtesy Peter Vronsky. Used with permission.)

State serial murder in the Third Reich and Perpetration-induced PTSD

By now we know that serial killers are neither exclusively male nor are they exclusively driven by sexual impulses. They include profit and power-control killers and mafia contract killers and although it would have been argued a few decades ago that the definition of a serial killer did not include military and genocidal killers, it especially includes them—and particularly those of the Third Reich. In fact, the Third Reich practiced state serial killing—serial mass murder—probably the first state in history to do so in the way it did.

In the twelve years that it existed, Nazi Germany murdered approximately twelve million people—that includes the Jews who made up nearly half of those victims. We are not talking here about people killed by aerial bombing, in sieges, by starvation or deprivation of occupied populations at home, or in urban battle crossfire—what we are talking about is one-on-one collective acts of murder—teams of killers firing single gunshots from small-arms to the back of victims' heads; hanging; beating to death; injections of phenol into the heart; stomping; burning alive; killing by medical experimentation and through so-called 'sport' killing and other individual acts of brutality. Towards the end the Nazis picked up the pace with mass killing in gas chambers, but those never really worked very well and broke down often but still, worked well enough to kill three million victims. But most of the remaining 9 million were murdered person-to-person by thousands of serial killers who killed day after day, victim by victim, one on one, shot by shot, until they could kill no more. There was even a name for these serial killing functionaries: *genickschussanspezialisten,* "nape of the neck shot specialists." Several thousand of these state-sponsored serial killers murdered literally millions of victims, one by one, one on one—not in firing squads—but each executioner shooting "his own" victim in the back of the neck as the victim kneeled, bending their head forward, exposing a trajectory that would result in a bullet entry at the neck that would traverse the victim's head through their brain—thus the 'nape-of-the-neck shot specialist' term.

For the longest time we believed in the Nazis' defence that they were "only following orders"—we did not forgive it, but we believed in it as an explanation, and that is one of the reasons that we have until recently excluded Nazi war criminals from the category of serial killer. We presumed they were not doing what they did by choice and that their victims were selected for them and the act of killing ordered at the pain of dire punishment if refused. Recent scholarship has completely put that notion to rest. We now know that direct participation in killing was in many cases an optional and voluntary choice and no German trooper was punished for refusing to shoot unarmed men, women, and children. If they refused, and some did, they were not shot themselves, they were not sent to a concentration camp, nor were they even sent to the Eastern Front. At worse, they were teased by their fellow-troopers for being "weak" and perhaps passed over for promotion.

Today we can categorize Nazi perpetrators as *missionary* type serial killers who are politically, morally, religiously or ideologically motivated to murder particular types of victims who they feel deserve to be eliminated from society. But in many cases, they did not commit these crimes because they were fanatical Nazis. Historian Christopher Browning studied a mobile killing unit that hunted down and killed thousands of men, women and children in eastern Polish country villages, shooting them into mass graves one by one. Browning discovered that the killers were mostly reserve police officers approaching middle-age, from the rank-and-file of which only 25 percent belonged to the Nazi Party. [6] This unit did not consist of indoctrinated elite, black-uniformed SS troops, security police units, specialized *Einsatzgruppen* killing commandos, or even vigilante Nazi fanatics; they were ordinary Hamburg traffic cops on temporary assignment in the Polish countryside behind German lines. Thus, Browning called his book on the subject, *Ordinary Men.*

What we are beginning to understand is that the Nazis were able to induce a type of temporary state of psychopathy in its citizenry, where ordinary sane "normal" people were made capable for brief periods of time to commit serial murder. Brief periods, because with time many began to have mental breakdowns, resorted to alcohol abuse, had nightmares, and even committed suicide, and developed what has been recently termed "perpetration-induced traumatic stress"—a type of post-traumatic stress disorder suffered by perpetrators of atrocities. [7] Thus the Nazis introduced the gas chambers in the winter of 1941-1942 not for more efficient killing necessarily, but for a less traumatic experience for the perpetrators. Gas was seen as a "humane" way to kill victims reducing the psychological toll on the killers who were murdering by the hundreds of thousands in the East. In fact, gas chambers as a "humane" method of killing were *re-introduced,* because they were first used by the Nazis in 1939 at home in the T-4 Operation (*Aktion T-4*) so-called "euthanasia" program to kill "humanely" their own disabled German babies and chronically ill adults, like unwanted pets in an animal shelter.

While we have come close to understanding how the Third Reich made ordinary men into serial killers, we have yet little information on the 'ordinary' women involved in the killing. And they did indeed exist in Nazi Germany, to some degree authentically reflected by the pulp fictional *Ilsa, She Wolf of the SS.*

The fictional Ilsa is inspired by a combination of two notorious real-life blond/redhead Nazi serial killing females, both products of the state: Ilse Koch, the "Bitch of Buchenwald" and the subject of this book, Irma Grese, the "Bitch of Belsen" (and "Hyena of Auschwitz.") Both these women were accused of taking personal pleasure in the sadistic torture and mutilation of concentration camp inmates beyond their call of duty. They were more than just state nurtured serial killers—they were free-lancing opportunist murderers who excelled in killing because they personally found pleasure in it. As such they would have been, and to some degrees were, condemned by the Nazis too. Yet it is doubtful whether Ilse Koch or Irma Grese would have committed the atrocities they did if they were not introduced and prepared for it by the German National Socialist state.

While Ilse Koch was not an SS-*Aufsehrin*, she is often painted with the same brush and her prosecution after the war speaks much on how female concentration camp perpetrators were perceived and prosecuted.

The Case of Ilse Koch—the Bitch of Buchenwald

Ilse Koch was a forty-one-year-old red-haired green-eyed buxomly woman when she was put on trial in 1947 for crimes committed in the Buchenwald concentration camp where some 50,000 inmates had died. Interestingly enough, Ilse was tried three times for different crimes in Buchenwald—by the Nazis in 1943, by the Americans in 1947, and again by the new West German government in 1950.

The charges laid against her in her trial by the Americans, the most famous of the three trials, were monstrously spectacular. It was alleged that Ilsa, who was the camp commandant's wife, would assemble newly arriving inmates and order that they remove their shirts. Ilse would then walk the ranks of the prisoners selecting those with tattoos she liked. She would then have them killed, skinned, and have household artifacts made from the cured tattooed skin like lampshades, photo album covers, handbags and gloves. Her house at the concentration camp was alleged to have light switches made from human thumb bones and furniture and decoration made from body parts and shrunken heads. It was alleged that she had murdered approximately forty inmates for this purpose. [8]

It was all incredibly creepy stuff and would ten years later inspire a real serial killer back in the USA, Ed Gein in 1957, who after reading too many men's pulp true adventure magazines, adopted Koch's reported decorating style by furnishing his own lonely Wisconsin farmhouse in the same way, using the body parts of women he killed or dug up from graves. [9]

That would make Ilse Koch a very unique serial killer—a *hedonist lust* type—a rare species among women—the only one known in modern times, a female killing to harvest body parts through some kind of compulsive sexual deviance. The closest thing to Ilse on the historical record is Elizabeth Báthory, some four centuries earlier.

There were other charges levelled against Ilse. There was a distinctly sexual edge to the charges—Ilsa was described as a "nymphomaniac" although her sexual indiscretions were confined to other SS staff at the camp and not with inmates. But the accusations that she collected human skin and had a tattooed skin lampshade made, distinguished her from the other thirty defendants from Buchenwald standing trial with her. The crimes were so depraved that they became a symbol of Nazis genocidal madness at its most evil and extreme. Newspapers and magazines reproduced photographs of leather-like patches of tattooed skin, one with a pair of clearly discernible nipples, shrunken heads and other artifacts, including lampshades, allegedly made of human skin and found in Buchenwald when US troops liberated the camp in 1945. There was newsreel footage in movie theatres.

Ilse Koch, The Bitch of Buchenwald, was sentenced to life imprisonment in 1947 but a year later American occupational authorities suddenly commuted her sentence to four year's imprisonment, to the shock of public opinion worldwide. Having served a year, she had three years remaining on her sentence, when public pressure resulted in her being put on trial again by West German authorities, who sentenced her to life imprisonment. Today Ilse Koch has a legion of defenders and not all of them are neo-Nazis or Holocaust deniers—and yes—you guessed it—some are feminists who portray Ilse as a victim of male inmates who slandered Ilse Koch for her "transgression of gender stereotypes." [10]

The feminist defence: the 'Ilse Koch phenomenon'

Ilse Koch was never an official functionary of the camp—she was the commandant's wife and while that gave her a tremendous degree of authority, it was entirely unofficial. Here, according to one German historian, Alexandra Przyrembel, was the first key to the vehemence with which Ilse was prosecuted after the war and the sexually depraved nature of the crimes she was accused of. According to this historian's feminist perspective, Ilse was prosecuted because she defied traditional gender roles and offended the male inmates' patriarchal sensibilities by doing so. Przyrembel argues that Ilse as a woman, offended the sensibilities of the "male society of inmates." She states:

> …. Ilse Koch appeared—in the perception of inmates—to have penetrated the domain of power reserved for the male members of the SS or at most certain *Kapos* (inmates who supervised inmate labor). This interaction between the (apparent) confirmation and transgression of gender stereotypes is, in my opinion, the root of the 'Ilse Koch phenomenon' after 1945. [14]

It appears that when it comes to women murderers, radical feminism has no bounds in its assertion that female serial killers are essentially a social construct of the oppressive and conspiring male patriarchy—even a patriarchy confined to a concentration camp. For radical feminism Ilse Koch is as much a victim of the patriarchy as Aileen Wuornos was.

"…kill them in a more decent way."

It was during this internal 1943 SS investigation that allegations were first made that Ilse Koch made human lampshades, an offense under the Nazi code-of-conduct which insisted that killing be conducted with decorum or "decency." Even the taking of photographs was a serious offense, despite the fact that thousands of perpetrators snapped pictures of themselves committing atrocities. SS-men were tried and imprisoned if they were caught taking photographs of atrocities or if they killed Jews without orders or killed them for depraved personal motives. [15] During one SS court-martial an SS private testified that the SS defendant had killed children by holding them up off the ground by the hair and shooting them. He testified, "After a while I just could not watch this anymore and I told him to stop. What I meant was he should not lift the children up the hair, he should kill them in a more decent way." [16]

The SS defendants ended up on trial because they were passing around photographs of the atrocities like trading cards while on leave in Germany. (Some sent photographs to their wives, girlfriends and mothers.) SS Chief Himmler was very vocal on the issue of killing with decorum, when he addressed a gathering of his senior SS killers, "Most of you know what it is like to see a hundred corpses laid out in a line, or five hundred or a thousand. To have stood fast through this and—except for cases of human weakness—to have stayed decent, has made us hard." [17]

In other words, when the tattoo skin artifacts were supposedly found in her former house at Buchenwald in 1945, she had not been living in it for two years and had been thoroughly investigated for it back in 1943. If indeed she had such fetishized trophies in her home, the SS investigators would have confiscated and destroyed them, and Ilse would have been severely punished for the offense—especially since she was not even a member of the SS but a civilian wife of an SS offender.

The tattooed skin collection

The specimens of tattooed skin were not a propaganda invention. They were indeed found in 1945 along with shrunken heads, perhaps at the house where Ilse once lived, or in the camp pathology department. In fact, such samples were indeed being collected but with official SS sanction. The culprit was an SS doctor, Erich Wagner, who had been writing a thesis on the links between criminality and the desire to be tattooed. Wagner photographed numerous inmates who had tattoos and apparently either upon their deaths or after ordering their deaths, detached pieces of their skin bearing the tattoos, cured and saved them not as decoration, but as academic specimens. According to historian Przyrembel, Ilse Koch did not attend the photographing and might not have even been aware of the existence of the tattoo project. [18]

A photograph of a lampshade allegedly made of human skin next to shrunken heads and samples of preserved tattooed skin was entered into evidence at her trial, but the actual lampshade itself apparently was misplaced. While forensic analysis definitively identified the skin samples as human, no test reports on the lampshade were entered into evidence.

Dr. Sitte, a PhD in physics, a former inmate, was one of the star witnesses against Ilse Koch. He had been confined in Buchenwald from September 1939 until the liberation in April 1945. He stated that he had worked in the camp's pathology department and that tattooed skin was stripped from the bodies of dead prisoners and "was often used to create lampshades, knife cases, and similar items for the SS." Sitte told the court that it was "common knowledge" that tattooed prisoners were taken away after Ilse Koch had selected their tattoos and they would be murdered and skinned for her.

But under cross-examination, Sitte admitted that he had never himself personally seen any of the lampshades allegedly made of human skin and that he had no personal knowledge of any prisoner who had been reported by Ilse Koch and was then killed so that his tattooed skin could be made into a lampshade. He also admitted that the lampshade that was on the display table in the photograph was not the lampshade made from human skin that he was referring to, allegedly delivered to Koch. Later in a 1948 letter to the New York Times after Ilse Koch's sentence had been commuted, Sitte further admitted that:

> I began to work in that pathology department only after the Koch era (Koch had been arrested for embezzlement and corruption) and by this time the SS leaders had abandoned their custom of displaying objects adorned with the tanned skin of tattooed prisoners. [19]

In his letter Sitte concluded, "This was not evidence against Ilse Koch, but against the SS officers in the camp, who killed prisoners for their tattooings."

But Sitte pleaded nevertheless against the reduction of Ilse Koch's sentence, "Is justice to the victims of Ilse Koch and her kind so much less important than technical justice to this pack of murderers?"

The US Military Governor of Germany, General Lucius D. Clay explained his decision to commute Koch's sentence. He stated that Koch "could not be proved guilty of the serious war crimes that had been initially cited against her by the evidence presented at her trial. Among the specific charges was that she had used tattooed human skin for lamp shades and other household articles." [20] The problem according to Clay was that US

Military Tribunal procedures allowed not only for hearsay evidence to be entered, but also for written affidavits without the defense being given opportunity to cross-examine the witnesses.
In 1976 Lucius Clay recalled:

> We tried Ilse Koch. ...She was sentenced to life imprisonment, and I commuted it to three years. [she had already served one year] And our press really didn't like that. She had been destroyed by the fact that an enterprising reporter who first went into her house had given her the beautiful name, the "Bitch of Buchenwald," and he had found some white lampshades in there which he wrote up as being made out of human flesh.

Well, it turned out actually that it was goat flesh. But at the trial it was still human flesh. It was almost impossible for her to have gotten a fair trial. [21]

None of this in any way mitigates Nazi atrocities nor the specific charge that inmates were murdered for the collection of their tattooed skins. Holocaust deniers make a big deal out of Clay's assertion that the lampshade turned out to be made of goatskin (and that it was never determined in a test for the US National Archives, where Ilse's photo albums are today stored, from what "animal" the suede covering the albums was made.) But there was never any doubt that some mad scientist at Buchenwald had collected those human tattoo skin specimens and shrunken heads. The inmates were unaware of the purpose, and assumed they were acts of personal depravity and laid them squarely on the doorstep of Ilse Koch, who they despised.

While this may clear Ilse from those specific charges, it does not exonerate her as a member of the Nazi party, a corrupt commandant's wife living on the grounds of a concentration camp and committing other offenses. The other charges against her, that she exploited inmate labor for her own purposes and vindictively reported prisoners resulting in their punishment and sometimes executions and had inmates who dared to glance at her punished or murdered for their "impudence" towards a German woman are entirely plausible and very likely. They are in fact, the very source of the inmates' hate for her—not her gender role transgressions. The senior SS staff had inmates working as servants, cooks, housekeepers and gardeners at their homes—the SS wives set the degree of discipline for slave domestics. Ilse was an old-time Nazi Party member, and one can easily imagine her attitude towards Jews and Communists and other "enemies of the state" confined in her husband's camp.

"Lampshade Ilse" as she was dubbed in the press, vehemently appealed her sentence claiming to be innocent of all the charges but in 1967 she gave up and committed suicide at the age of sixty-one by hanging herself in her cell.

Ilse was an evil and awful human being and got the end she deserved. But as far as the extraordinary charges of using human skin as household decoration for which Ilse Koch became so notorious, Ilse might have actually been innocent. The accusations are reminiscent of the myth around Elizabeth Báthory—of her bathing in victims' blood to preserve the youthful luster of her skin. But as the classic John Ford western, *The Man Who Shot Liberty Valance* declares, when there is a choice between printing the truth or the legend, the legend always wins out. As repulsive as historian Prsyrembel's feminist argument might be, that Ilse Koch was railroaded on those specific charges because she offended patriarchal sensibilities of the camp inmates, it is a charge one cannot completely dismiss as easily as one wishes. In one way or another, how we perceive and define female serial killers indeed is often defined by social constructs and politics, including those of gender stereotyping.

Anus Mundi: Irma Grese at Auschwitz

Turning to the subject of this book, Irma Grese who, unlike Ilse Koch, actually was an SS-*Aufsehrin,* there is context to where she deployed by the Nazi state. After a year's service at Ravensbrück concentration camp in Germany, Irma was sent in March 1943 to what some SS doctors bitterly called "*Anus Mundi*"—the "asshole of the world"—a swampy hellhole the size of about forty American city blocks—the Auschwitz-Birkenau mega death camp in Poland.

There were "generations" of camps in the twelve-year history of the Third Reich, with different functions, and distinctions between a first-generation "concentration camp" (*Konzentrationslager, KZ*) in Germany like Dachau and Ravensbrück, and a second-generation death camp or "annihilation camp" (*Vernichtungslager)* in occupied Poland. Concentration camps in Germany were sources for the rental of slaves to German corporations, and while they were brutal and had a high death rate from deprivation and abuse, they were not used for systematic killing and did not have gas chambers. The second-generation annihilation camps were all located in Poland and were purposed for the express objective of killing everybody who arrived there and were fitted out with an early type of gas chambers that used a mounted tank engine to produce carbon monoxide that would kill the victims.

There was also a bureaucratic distinction. The concentration camps were administrated by the SS Main Economic and Administrative Office (*WVHA, SS-Wirtschafts und Verwaltungshauptamt)* the mandate of which was the economic exploitation of slaves. But the annihilation camps came under the administration of Reinhard Heydrich's SS-Reich Security Main Office – (*RSHA, Reichssicherheitshauptamt*). Two different bureaucratic mandates and cultures; the WVHA was about exploiting living slave labor; the RSHA was about killing all the "sub-humans."

Auschwitz was an anomalous and late-developed third generation camp combining a forced labor concentration camp with a huge annihilation facility, under the administration of the WVHA. The RSHA arrested and transported the inmates; but at the end of the line, the WVHA took custody of them. Double railway spurs snaked directly into the camp with packed cargo trains backed up along the line attempting to unload thousands of Jewish deportees daily from the most distant towns and cities of occupied Europe—places like Greece, Rumania, Hungary, Italy, Yugoslavia. (The Jews of Germany, Poland, Russia and northern and central Europe had already been mostly murdered by shooting on location and in the second-generation annihilation camps.)
They would be forced off the train on "the ramp" and they would undergo "selection"—those to live sent in one direction and those to die sent in another, towards four huge combination crematoria-gas chambers the size of railway stations. Unlike the previous slow-killing carbon-monoxide gas chambers, these chambers used a form of quick-acting industrial pesticide cyanide gas. One can see in aerial photographs from 1944 taken by

passing USAF bombers on the way to targets in the vicinity and can easily compare the immense size of these killing facilities next to train cars in the photo parked nearby on the spur. Two of the huge underground gas chambers could accommodate 1,200-1,500 victims each. (The other, later two were built above ground.)

SS doctors on the ramp "selected" the very old, the very young, the weak, the sick, or the infirm to walk about a five-minute distance from the arrival ramp to the nearest gas chamber. Of course, one did not need a medical degree to tell who was fit for slave labor—any one of us could do that easily without attending medical school. And ordinary SS-men performed that selection at the other camps previously. But by their "selection" of who lived or died, the physicians were now assigned by the state to take the responsibility and burden and guilt unto themselves for the killing—rendering murder into the realm of a medical procedure ordered by a doctor. As Victor Brack, chief of Germany's medical murder "euthanasia" program said, "the syringe belongs in the hand of the physician."

Those "ordinary" men—the cops who after three months of blowing out the little brains of children and their screaming mothers one by one—ended up as mental cases. The Nazis discovered they can synthesize psychopathy temporarily, but they couldn't make it persist—the majority of killers were bothered by what they were doing. At Auschwitz they *medicalized* and assembly-lined the killing procedure—it was no longer murder, no more than a surgeon plunging a razor-sharp instrument in a patient's body is assault—it was "racial hygiene" practiced and supervised by professional physicians—they were healing the German race by destroying the Jewish bacillus infecting it. There were always physicians on the ramp—with a second shift of physicians on standby in case the first needed to be relieved. [22]

Again, we see a type of state induced "artificial psychopathy"—a psuedo-scientific medical rationalization for serial killing. One survivor, a scientist himself, stated the ramp physicians began using a medical term, *therapia magna** as a joke at first but then seriously:

> They considered themselves performing *Therapia Magna Auschwitzciense.* They would even use the initials TM. At first it was mockingly and ironically, but gradually they began to use them simply to mean the gas chambers. So that whenever you see the initials T. M., that's what it means. The phrase was invented by Schumann who fancied himself an academic intellectual among the intelligentsia of Auschwitz doctors. [23]

The physicians "selected" mostly old and middle-aged men and women and children under fourteen to die. Healthy young men and women and those with needed skills were sent to work, unless the young woman was carrying an infant in her arms, in which case she was selected to die with her child—somebody had to carry the infant into the gas chamber.

Occasionally trustee inmates working on the ramps would discreetly whisper to a young mother to give her child to an elderly relative to carry when approaching the selection, assuring the mother that her child and grandmother would be assigned to a "soft labor" section of the camp. This would save the young mother's life—but not that of her infant. Other mothers understated their child's age hoping to save them from hard labor, unwittingly condemning their own child to death in the gas chamber.

Those "selected" by the physicians would become walking dead, sent directly from the ramp to the gas chambers. They would be ushered into huge subsurface undressing rooms to prepare for a "shower." There they would be told to hang their clothing carefully on numbered pegs and reminded to tie their shoes together by the laces so they would not get lost. (It made it easier to sort the victims' clothing afterwards if it was already sized and the shoes paired.) They would be told to hurry along into the shower in the next room before the hot water ran out or before the coffee and breakfast that awaited them grew cold. And off they went.

Once packed into the huge concrete chamber with dummy shower heads, the airtight door would be suddenly slammed shut behind them, the lights turned off and cyanide gas pellets would be poured 'under doctors' orders' by SS medical orderlies from the roof into four vented metal mesh columns dispersed along the length of the chamber. The cyanide gas was a commercial product which was released from the pellets once exposed to warm air. Called *Zyclone-B* (Cyclone B) it was designed to kill rats in granaries by gas so as not to contaminate the grain or storage facility with pesticides. The SS demanded that the manufacturer produce special batches of the gas without the "irritant" warning odor intended to alert people of its presence. The manufacturer balked, claiming it would endanger the patent they held on *Zyclone-B* if they did that. The SS insisted. Special custom-made batches were delivered without the irritant. The gas was odorless and painless to the victims, killing them through rapid respiratory and cardiac arrest and oxygen depletion in the blood. Victims did not "choke" on the gas, they just dropped dead with seizures. But it was a horrible death, nonetheless, with victims packed tight among naked dying strangers in pitch-black dark, clawing on each other in respiratory and cardiac paralysis in ever gradually expanding circles from the mesh columns.

The four crematoria-gas chambers were capable of easily killing approximately 10,000 people a day—*each.* The problem was not killing but disposing of the bodies—at maximum capacity the crematoriums combined together could only burn 5,000 bodies every 24 hours. But furnaces frequently broke down forcing corpses to be burned in huge hellish smoking open-air pits at the camps perimeter. Bones and ash would be ground to dust and hauled away in dump trucks for disposal in the nearby river. Somewhere between 1.1 and 1.5 million people were killed this way at Auschwitz, mostly Jews but Gypsies, Poles, Russians and other "subhumans" as well.

The Auschwitz camp and its satellites was like a small slave kingdom, with the registered number-tattooed inmate population totaling 155,000 at its maximum. These inmates were put to work in "processing" the corpses, emptying the gas chambers, extracting the gold teeth, sorting the belongings of the dead to be shipped back to Germany for profit, or working in the kitchens, gardens, warehouses, clinics and artisan shops which supported the enterprise of death, or on construction gangs expanding the already huge camp perimeter to accommodate more and more victims to gas and burn, day in day out, trainload by trainload.

"Sport"

So it was here at Auschwitz, that little blonde Irma Grese at tender age of nineteen, the former Nazi girl scout and wannabe nurse, was assigned to supervise a camp section with 30,000 female inmates—those chosen from the ramp to temporarily live a little longer—

as long as they did not get sick or collapse, could do the work assigned to them, committed no infraction real or imagined and were lucky not to have encountered some idle SS-man or female SS-*Aufsehrin* like Irma in a bad mood swing looking to "sport" with inmates.

To "sport." It was a guards' term, meaning to idly brutalize prisoners for no reason other than to relieve the boredom, technically an offense but as long as it did not "get out of hand" the authorities looked the other way.

One surviving inmate testified that when Irma arrived at Auschwitz she appeared to be "a young girl in my eyes about 18-19, with a round full face and two long braids." The inmate was transferred to another section and did not see Ilse for several months. When she saw her again, she was stunned by the dramatic transformation. She had "slimmed down, her hair was up in a bun, the uniform immaculate and she had a cap over her head and on her waist was a belt and a pistol."

With her stunning blonde good looks, the teenage Irma had become the center of attention. Some sources allege she became the lover of the notorious Dr. Joseph Mengele, a handsome wounded war hero physician who worked on the ramp in an immaculately tailored uniform and conducted in his spare time horrific medical experiments on dwarfs and child twins. One of his experiments consisted of attempting to change eye color by injecting dyes directly into the iris. Mengele, nicknamed the "Angel of Death," would whistle Schumann tunes as he "selected" on the ramp or scrapped bone marrow samples without an anesthetic from screaming children. Witnesses placed Irma on the ramp when Mengele was there. She brutally beat and kicked people attempting to bypass the selection or to switch lines afterwards.

An inmate physician testified that Irma had a fixation on women with large breasts and would inevitably whip their breasts to the point that they would become infected. She would always make a point of being present when the physician treated the painful infection "swaying back and forth with a glassy eyed look" as the inmate cried in pain.

As the testimony accumulated, it became more lurid and condemning.

Irma carried a special lightweight cellophane whip which was particularly painful and cutting and which she had custom made in one of the camp workshops. She kept prisoners standing for hours during roll call, mercilessly beating and stomping any inmate who collapsed. She forced prisoners to kneel for hours, killing anyone who keeled over. She rode around the camp on a bicycle, shooting prisoners with her handgun, according to one eyewitness account, which of course illustrates the problem that historians (and police today) have with eyewitness court testimony, as *SS-Aufseherinnen* supposedly did not carry sidearms.

It is hard to sort some of the testimony between fact and fiction. One witness testified that Irma was accompanied by a German shepherd, trained by her to bite the breasts of female inmates which she would unleash on prisoners who fell behind in convoys, but this is unlikely as specially trained dog handlers (*Hundesstaffel*) were in charge of the animals, each paired with its handler. One could not just "borrow" a guard dog.

It was said that Mengele broke-up with Irma when he learned that she was having lesbian affairs with other inmates, something strictly prohibited by not only camp regulations but German law as well. Again, the portrayal of the female defendant as somehow sexually depraved, is reminiscent of the charges leveled against Ilsa Koch. Now the witnesses against her were mostly female and accusations of Irma's lesbianism might be reflective of the taboos of the era, if we follow historian Przyrembel's logic.

When Auschwitz was closed down as the Red Army approached in December 1945, Irma accompanied female prisoner transfers back to Ravensbrück and then to the temporary transit camp of Bergen Belsen, which was never officially a concentration camp. By then the Third Reich was collapsing and the camp administration basically ignored the needs of the overcrowded, sick and starving camp population. The thousands of corpses littering the campgrounds were not how the Nazi maintained concentration camps, but became a dramatic visual icon of the Holocaust; factually inaccurate but symbolically true.

Irma Grese was sentenced to death and executed by hanging on December 10, 1945—the youngest woman hung by the British in the 20th century.

The making of state serial killers

Irma Grese was not "following orders" when she beat and murdered her victims. She was clearly freelancing—to the point that the SS themselves thought excessive and had her transferred from perimeter duty after one too many "sport" killings of inmates.

Both male and female guards in Nazi concentration camps were conditioned in a way to suppress any empathy they may have with the inmates, a primary characteristic of psychopathy. They were trained to strip the inmates in their perception of any identity other than the generic "enemy of the state." No private communication was allowed between the prisoners and guards. Auschwitz was a murderous kingdom where killing was the norm. How could Irma Grese be anything but what she was in an environment like that with the conditioning she had?*

Nazism was to a great extent a cult but its ideology seemed to play almost no role in the crimes of Ilse Koch and Irma Grese; nor did "following orders" appear to have much to do with it in the two women's cases since they were acting mostly on their own initiative. Historians, sociologists and psychologists have been struggling to explain how so many "ordinary" people in Germany ended up serially murdering so many victims. We are not talking about the "banality of evil" bureaucrats who killed from behind their desks never actually seeing their victims, but of the thousands of people who were killing one on one, with blood splashing into their faces—all serial killers.

One of the earliest theories, suggested by Theodor Adorno, was that there was a type of testable 'Authoritarian Personality Type" that could be scored on a so-called F-scale. Some of the personality feature consisted of:

- Rigid adherence to conventional values
- Submissiveness to authority figures
- Aggressiveness toward out groups
- Opposition to introspection, reflection and creativity
- Preoccupation with power and "toughness"
- Destructiveness and cynicism
  an exaggerated concern with sexuality
- Projectivity – a disposition to believe that dangerous conspiratorial things go on in the world

Some of these characteristics are reminiscent of some of the psychopathology found among serial killers. According to Adorno, fascist cult movements encourage such a personality to express itself in cruel and violent ways against ideologically targeted out groups. [25]

This approach has come under severe criticism. Historian Zygmunt Bauman dismissed it, arguing that it was as if saying: "Nazism was cruel because Nazis were cruel; and Nazis were cruel because cruel people tended to become Nazis." Bauman rejected Adorno's 'authoritarian personality type' because it implied that ordinary people did not commit atrocities. [26]

John Steiner suggested a version of the 'authoritarian personality type', the so-called "sleeper," a personality prone to violence that is unleashed by circumstance by something like the latent violent subculture of the Nazi movement. [27]

Ervin Staub accepts Steiner's idea that people can be latently violent but believes that the so-called "sleeper" is a very common trait to most people—that all human beings have a primary capacity for violence. There is a little bit of a serial killer in all of us. Staub says, "Evil that arises out of ordinary thinking and is committed by ordinary people is the norm, not the exception." [28]

Bauman disagrees. He argues that most people slip into the roles society provides them, and he is very critical of the "faulty personality" as a cause behind cruelty. Evil is situational, according to Bauman. Serial killers are made.

There is some evidence for this. Philip Zimbardo at Stanford University conducted an experiment where he set up a mock prison and using personality tests filtered out sadistic personality types among those volunteering as guards. Yet within six days, volunteers who did not test for sadistic traits began to devise rapidly escalating brutal and cruel methods to control and deal with the volunteer prisoners. Zimbardo concluded that the prison situation alone was a sufficient condition to produce aberrant, anti-social behavior.

Zimbardo discovered that a third of the eleven guards emerged as cruel and tough—constantly inventing new ways to torment their prisoners; that a middle group tended to be tough but fair, played by the rules, even if they were cruel but did not exceed the cruelty on their own initiative and only two actually went out of their way not to be cruel or showed acts of kindness to the prisoners.

If brutality and serial killing can be situational, then before we go dismissing Irma Grese as a Nazi bitch, we need to take a closer look into the face of the former Kentucky born and bred chicken factory worker and IGA cashier Lynndie Rana England, who at the age twenty-one found herself photographed tormenting and abusing naked prisoners as a reservist in a military police company in Iraq assigned to the notorious Abu Ghraib prison. Lynndie never killed anybody but is that the difference between her and Grese? How far did Lynndie have left to go? How many of us have a serial killer inside ready to be unleashed in the right situation? Is the process of how becoming a serial killer much more simple and easier than we suspect?

In conclusion, when I wrote my study of female predators, *Female Serial Killers: How and Why Women Become Monster,* I concluded that women serial murderers, although they expressed themselves differently from male serial killers, all killed more or less for the exact same motive: power and control. It's all about the power and the control, and the Third Reich was the power and control cult utopia for state-sponsored serial killers, women included.

Sources:

* *therapia sterilisans magna* -- treatment of infectious disease by the administration of large doses of a specific remedy for the destruction of the infectious agent in the body without doing serious harm to the patient.
* The more extensive story of female serial killers in Nazi Germany, beyond the scope of this introduction, is about the hundreds of nurses who participated in the medical murder of at least 150,000 mentally and physically handicapped German children and adults in a medical killing campaign disguised as euthanasia.

[1] Katharina von Kellenbach. *The Mark of Cain: Guilt and Denial in the Post-War Lives of Nazi Perpetrators,* Oxford University Press, 2013. p.102.
[2] Rachel Century, *Female Administrators of the Third Reich*, Palgrave Macmillan, 2017. p. 68.
[3] Margarete Buber-Neumann, *Als Gefangenebei Stalin und Hitler. Eine Welt im Dunkel*, Berlin: Ullstein, 1949. (*Under Two Dictators: Prisoner of Stalin and Hitler*, trans. Edward Fitzgerald, London: Pimlico, 2008. p. 321
[4] https://time.com/3915391/the-forgotten-brutality-of-female-nazi-concentration-camp-guards/
[5] http://www.imdb.com/name/nm0831471/bio
[6] Christopher Browning, *Ordinary Men: Reserve Police Battalion 101 and the Final Solution in Poland,* (2nd Edition), New York: HarperPerennial, 1998. p. 48.
[7] Rachel MacNair, "Psychological reverberations for the killers: preliminary historical evidence for perpetration-induced traumatic stress", *Journal of Genocide Research* Vol. 3, No. 2, 2001. pp. 273-282
[8] "Information on the Infamous Concentration Camp at Buchenwald", 14 February 1945, in US vs. Josias Prince zu Waldeck, *et al.,* War Crimes Case No. 12-390 (The Buchenwald Case), War Crimes Office, National Archives and Records Service, 1976, Record Group 153, Records of the Judge Advocate General, National Archives, (Washington, D.C.) [cited as Buchenwald Case]
[9] Peter Vronsky, Serial Killers: The Method and Madness of Monsters, New York: Berkley, 2004. (2020 Second Edition), pp. 185-186.
[10] Alexandra Przyrembel, "Transfixed by an Image: Ilse Koch, the 'Kommandeuse of Buchenwald'", *German History* Vol. 19, No. 3. (2001) pp. 369-399.
[11] Michael Kater, *The Nazi Party,* Cambridge, Mass: Harvard University Press, 1983. pp. 148ff and 254.
[12] http://yad-vashem.org.il/odot_pdf/Microsoft%20Word%20-%206088.pdf
[13] See: Christopher Browning, *The Origins of the Final Solution: The Evolution of Nazi Jewish Policy, September 1939-March 1942,* Lincoln, Nebraska/Jerusalem: University of Nebraska Press/Yad Vashem, 2004.
[14] Alexandra Przyrembel, p. 376 and p. 386-387.
[15] Yehoshua R. Buchler, "'Unworthy Behavior': The Case of SS Officer Max Taubner", *Holocaust and Genocide Studies*, Vol 17, No. 3, Winter 2003, pp. 409-429
[16] Ernst Klee, Willi Dressen, Volker Riess, *"Those Were the Days": The Holocaust as Seen by the Perpetrators and Bystanders,* London: Hamish Hamilton, 1991. p. 197
[17] PS-1919, *International Military Tribunal,* Volume 29, 1948. p. 145
[18] Alexandra Przyrembel, pp. 383-384
[19] K. Sitte Letter to the Editor, *New York Times,* , October 18, 1948 pg. 22

[20] "Clay Stands Firm In Ilse Koch Case" *New York Times,* October 22, 1948
[21] George C. Marshall Research Foundation, Virgina. Videotaped interview with General Luscious Clay, cited by http://www.nizkor.org/features/denial-of-science/clay-koch-03.html
[22] See Robert Jay Lifton, *The Nazi Doctors: Medical Killing and the Psychology of Genocide,* New York: HarperCollins, 1986.
[23] Robert Jay Lifton, p. 208
[24] Raymond Phillips, *Trial of Joseph Kramer and Forty-Four Others (The Belsen Trial)*, London: William Hodge and Company, 1949. p. 706
[25] Theodor Adorno, *The Authoritarian Personality,* New York: Harper & Row, 1950.
[26] Zygmunt Bauman, *Modernity and the Holocaust,* Ithaca: Cornell University Press, 1989.
[27] John M. Steiner, "The SS Yesterday and Today: A Sociopsychological View", in Joel E. Dimsdale (ed), *Survivors, Victims, and perpetrators: Essays on the Nazi Holocaust,* Washington DC: 1980
[28] Ervin Staub, *The Roots of Evil: The Origins of Genocide and Other Group Violence,* Cambridge: University of Harvard Press, 1989. p. 1

PART ONE

Into the Hyena's Den

"The female killers stood out in survivor's memories, in their actions and appearance."
-W. Lower, *Hitler's Furies*

"Don't you get it? Human fanatics are more monster than any of the Lore."
- K. Cole, *Immortals After Dark*

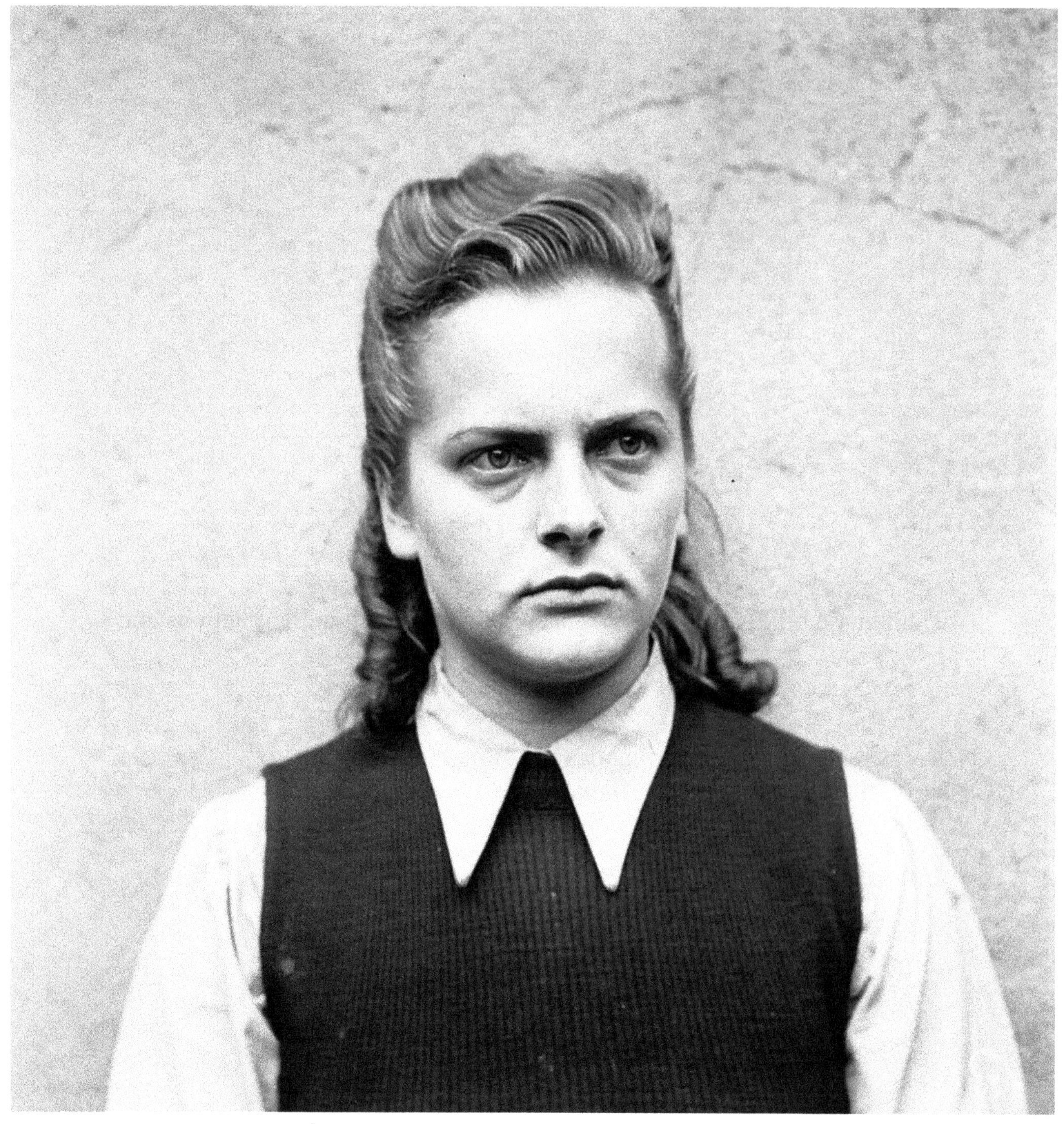

Irma Grese is considered one of "two of the more violent case studies within Holocaust historiography." (Long, 2021, p. 14)

Irma Grese's mugshot at Celle. She purposely changed her hairstyle for the trial. Note the marked difference in appearance between photos taken prior to her working in the concentration camps and after a few years in service. (Circa August 1945. Photographer: unknown. Courtesy Imperial War Museum. Used with permission.)

CHAPTER 1
Summary

Irma Grese was barely 20 years of age when she became a high-profile threat during the European genocide of at least 30 million people between 1941 to 1945. Grese trained to be a Nazi camp guard at Ravensbrück and rose quickly through the ranks at Bergen-Belsen and Auschwitz. She would be arrested and prosecuted in the 1945 Belsen Trial, [1] found guilty of war crimes, and executed by hanging. Grese is the youngest of Nazi female guards to receive the death sentence and the youngest woman to die judicially under British law in the 20th century. Irma Grese's tenure in the camps was marked by extreme ruthlessness earning her the moniker "The Hyena of Auschwitz" where her Nazis comrades had to curtail her sadism. There are various theories that may explain Grese's legacy of extreme brutality.

Three potential theories are discussed in this book to ascertain the foundation of Irma Grese's abhorrent behavior: the Spectrum of Ability to Murder (humankind's natural ability), the probability of Grese having a paraphilic disorder, and narcissistic injuries. Utilizing triangulation and cross checking, Grese's life is discussed while considering the impact of tremulous childhoods on adults, the Nazi-created environment of prejudice and patriotic obligation, and the juxtaposition of Nazi rule versus reality. Results will show how all these factors may have created The Hyena of Auschwitz.

This book is based on documentation from reputable sources to cross-check and verify facts. Very little material is available on Irma Grese's life; much of the documentation stems from family interviews, Holocaust survivors, self-report, and court room testimony. Grese herself was not forthcoming and, apart from the arrest interrogations and Belsen Trials, was never interviewed. Most witnesses are deceased. The case occurred in Germany during WWII. When it became clear Germany was losing the war, thousands of camp documents were destroyed. Post WWII, many wanted to forget and move on.

So much of Irma Grese's life story is now dependent on repetition and assumption; so many books, papers, and documentaries repeat this information and label it fact. As one example, one biographer has Holocaust survivor Ilona Stein testifying at the Belsen Trials as "… the most prominent one because … she spoke of various sexual encounters she had with Grese…" [2] Ilona Stein would testify on September 26, 1945, of surviving the Holocaust at the Bergen-Belsen Trials; at no time did she discuss any sexual encounter with Grese. An author states Grese stood up in court in response to cross examination and shouted "Heil Hitler!" [3] This incident does not appear anywhere in the entirety of the Bergen-Belsen court transcripts. Records reveal this was not Grese nor did it occur in the Belsen trial.

Rumors, fallacies, and myths have persisted regarding Irma Grese for decades. Even her last name is often mispronounced in videos and documentaries as "*Grease,*" "*Graze,*" "*Greasy,*" "*Grah-zay.*" There are images circulating labeled as "Irma Grese" that

---

[1] Officially titled the "Trial of Josef Kramer and 44 others," for this book it will be called "The Belsen Trials."

[2] Jennings, p. 54.

[3] Ibid., p.55

are of other female camp guards, or photographs of movie actresses. [4] Grese has also been identified as a "prison warden" or "Nazi Commander" (she was neither). Another myth which has persisted is Grese using soap made of prisoner body parts and lampshades composed of the tattooed skins of murdered Jewish men. She has been depicted in skin-tight polished black leather uniforms detailed with Nazi insignias, a dominatrix.

This book is the closest existing biography of Irma Grese and the environment that shaped her. It will finally dispel many rumors surrounding Grese.

[4] The most popular misidentified photo is actress Aleksandra Śląska from the 1963 movie "The Passenger" identified as Irma Grese, still currently sold on eBay and other online marketplaces.

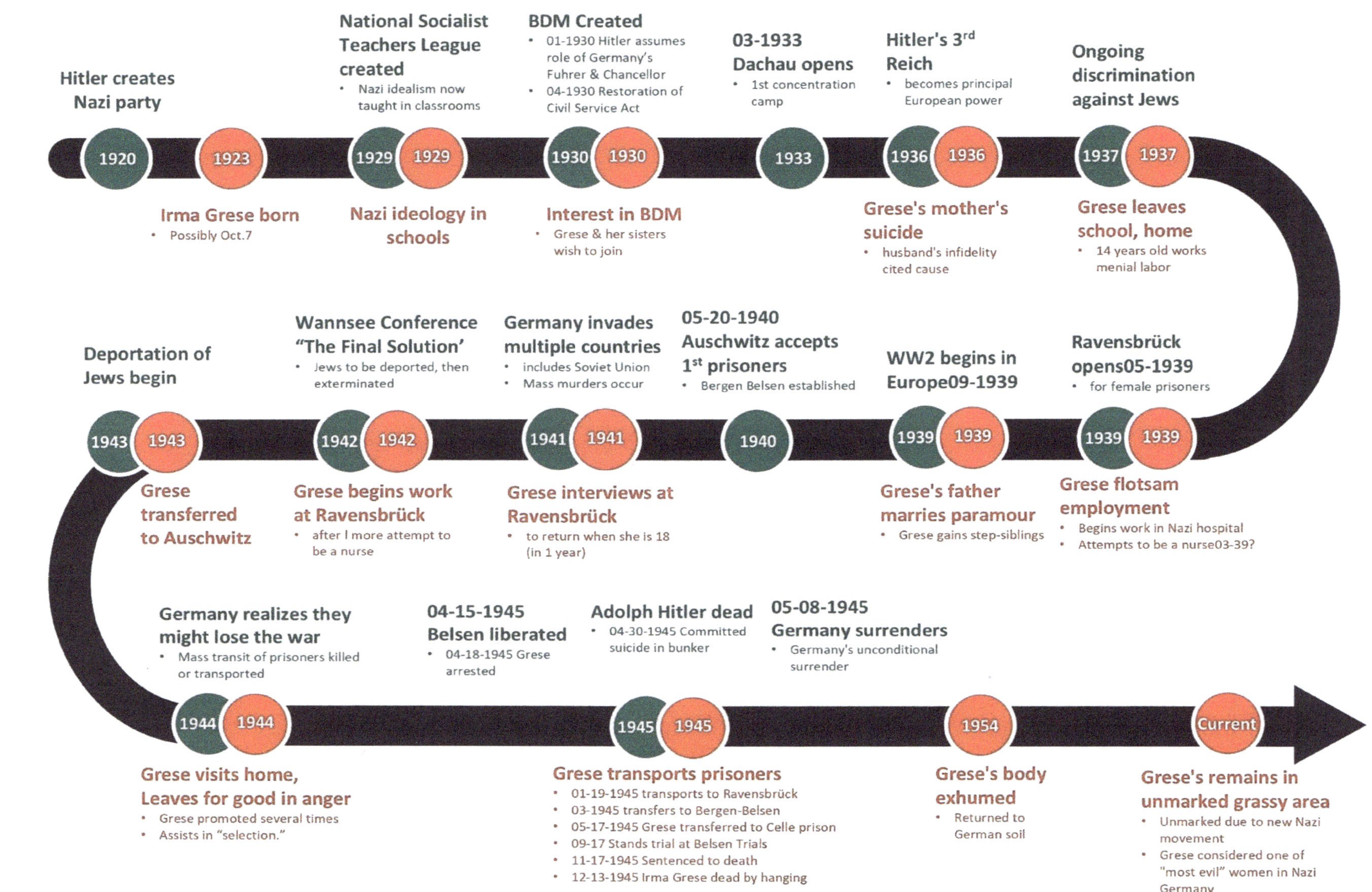
TIMELINE
1920
Hitler creates Nazi party
1923
Irma Grese born
• Possibly Oct.7
1929
National Socialist Teachers League created
• Nazi idealism now taught in classrooms
1929
Nazi ideology in schools
1930
BDM Created
• 01-1930 Hitler assumes role of Germany's Fuhrer & Chancellor
• 04-1930 Restoration of Civil Service Act
1930
Interest in BDM
• Grese & her sisters wish to join
1933
03-1933 Dachau opens
• 1st concentration camp
1936
Hitler's 3rd Reich
• becomes principal European power
1936
Grese's mother's suicide
• husband's infidelity cited cause
1937
Ongoing discrimination against Jews
1937
Grese leaves school, home
• 14 years old works menial labor
1939
Ravensbrück opens05-1939
• for female prisoners
1939
Grese flotsam employment
• Begins work in Nazi hospital
• Attempts to be a nurse03-39?
1939
WW2 begins in Europe09-1939
1939
Grese's father marries paramour
• Grese gains step-siblings
1940
05-20-1940 Auschwitz accepts 1st prisoners
• Bergen Belsen established
1941
Germany invades multiple countries
• includes Soviet Union
• Mass murders occur
1941
Grese interviews at Ravensbrück
• to return when she is 18 (in 1 year)
1942
Wannsee Conference "The Final Solution'
• Jews to be deported, then exterminated
1942
Grese begins work at Ravensbrück
• after I more attempt to be a nurse
1943
Deportation of Jews begin
1943
Grese transferred to Auschwitz
1944
Germany realizes they might lose the war
• Mass transit of prisoners killed or transported
1944
Grese visits home, Leaves for good in anger
• Grese promoted several times
• Assists in "selection."
1945
04-15-1945 Belsen liberated
• 04-18-1945 Grese arrested
Adolph Hitler dead
• 04-30-1945 Committed suicide in bunker
05-08-1945 Germany surrenders
• Germany's unconditional surrender
1945
Grese transports prisoners
• 01-19-1945 transports to Ravensbrück
• 03-1945 transfers to Bergen-Belsen
• 05-17-1945 Grese transferred to Celle prison
• 09-17 Stands trial at Belsen Trials
• 11-17-1945 Sentenced to death
• 12-13-1945 Irma Grese dead by hanging
1954
Grese's body exhumed
• Returned to German soil
Current
Grese's remains in unmarked grassy area
• Unmarked due to new Nazi movement
• Grese considered one of "most evil" women in Nazi Germany

CHAPTER 2
The Hyena's Path

She was 22 years old on December 13, 1945, when she stepped onto the chalk "X" marking the trap door of the new Hamelin Prison gallows. "Do you have anything to say?" She was reportedly asked. The pretty blonde with striking blue eyes replied in a lazy voice, "*Schnell.*" ("Quickly.") Executioner Albert Pierrepoint placed a white hood over her head, secured the hangman's noose, then stepped back to pull the lever, releasing the trap marked by the "X." The young woman dropped to her death. She was pronounced dead at 10:04 a.m., and was left to hang for 20 minutes before being cut down. [5] Thus, a bloody, atrocious career ended for Irmgard Ilese Ida Grese, AKA Irma Grese, AKA The Hyena of Auschwitz. Grese is one of many high-profile Nazis found guilty of war crimes in the 1945 Belsen Trial, where the public initially met those partially responsible for the genocide of at least 30 million people between 1941 to 1945. At least half of the victims came from interwar Poland. And it was here, in Poland, where Irna Grese became known as one of the most sadistic women in the history of Nazi Germany.

She wasn't always the feared executioner who supervising Nazis had to punish for being "too cruel" to prisoners. She was a tow-headed schoolgirl. She possessed a lovely singing voice. Irma loved cats and had a talent for turning a sparse home into a pleasant place to live. She could be kind and soft-hearted, particularly when discussing sisterhood. She apologized to some inmates for her brutality at the height of her most sadistic activity.

Yet, Grese admired the Nazi party from youth, being raised on dogged Nazi propaganda. Before she was twenty years old, she was trained and employed in concentration camps, gleefully torturing, murdering, and sexually assaulting prisoners. She was an arrogant show-off, drunk with power and openly broke the limitations of abuse against prisoners on a lark. Grese was defiant to the end of her short life, happily singing Nazi songs the night before her execution, remaining stoic and angry on the gallows until she dropped to her death. Irma Grese became The Hyena.

What creates a "monster" so early in a young woman's life? How did Irma Grese become so cruel at such an early age up to her death? What collective factors caused a schoolgirl, who bolted from schoolyard confrontations and cried when her brother was injured, to become one of the most frightening symbols in a Nazi death camp?

Grese is not the sole female sadist employed in the concentration camps. There are others, including Maria Mandl, Elizabeth Vokentra, and Juana Bormann, also executed for particularly cruel behavior in war crimes. But Irma Grese is perhaps the most notorious of the females. She would become the youngest and most quickly promoted to Nazi Germany's SS-*Helferin* guard. And she is most recognized as being esthetically pleasing, even to those she tortured and reigned over in her short but brutal career. Irma Grese's popularity is the juxtaposition of evil and beauty.

[5] Pierrepoint, A. (1974), p. 150

Definitions

It is impossible to completely understand the development of Grese's sadistic tendencies without examining the environment and situations from whence she arose and survived. A complete overview of World War II, the rise and fall of the Third Reich, and a detailed explanation of the concentration camps would digress from this book; however, it is imperative to include an overview of the environment which caused a frightened schoolgirl to become a "state serial killer." [6]

Germany After World War I

To understand Irma Grese, we must understand why Nazism succeeded; what seeds were planted in her psyche even before she was born. After World War I, Germany was left in a financial, sociological, and emotional turmoil without solid leadership. German pride, which had always been fierce, became nearly nonexistent. Men who did come home from the war were fragmented and overwhelmed. With fathers being traditionally the head of household, WWI created "broken" homes, or homes left without the patriarchal leadership. Germany was not included in creation of The Treaty of Versailles (1919) between France, the United States, and Britain. Clause 231 the "War Guilt Clause" determined Germany was to accept complete responsibility for the war, lose 13% of land, and 48% of Germany's iron and coal production. Germany was to pay repartitions. Both resulted in an economic tailspin. Then there was the continued blocking of shipments into the country, creating a shortage and price hike in food and supplies. As a result, revolutions began to occur cross-country.

Leadership became fragmented. Germany has historically held that, rather than leaders representing the people (as in the United States), the people represent their government. Without a strong leader to hear and follow, society became disjointed.

Every group requires an enemy; it is a cause and measure of a group's success. With an enemy comes the scapegoating, identifying a cause for all things adverse: financial, sociological, and emotional. Jews and "undesirables" were an easy target due to history, religion, and group personality. For example, homosexuality was targeted as far back as The Novels of Justinian, Novella 77 in AD538. Gay men, it stated, caused earthquakes, starvation, and plagues. The practice was condemned by God and considered blasphemous. Homosexuals (or suspected) could be put to death from 1532 to 1806 in the Holy Roman Empire. The German Critical Code (1871) made homosexual acts between men a crime in Paragraph 175, associating it with bestiality, prostitution, or child sex abuse. Homosexuals have been the "enemy" for religious groups up to present time. Purportedly, Irma Grese was a bisexual and sent to the gas chambers anyone who observed or participated (albeit unwillingly) in her same-sex interactions. Her same-sex attraction was reportedly the downfall of one of her affairs with a high-profile Nazi, and a measure of her persecution in her trial and up to modern times. To label someone a homosexual was to instantly paint them as the enemy: immoral, illegal, and mentally unstable.

---

[6] Serial mass murder, as discussed by criminologist Vronsky, P. (2007). pp. 370-372

Irma's Heroes

Adolph Hitler

Adolph Hitler (1889 – 1945) was a frustrated artist who utilized illegal and illicit means to rise to power as the Nazi Party leader. He initiated WWII in Europe and was central to the genocide of millions of people. He committed suicide as he realized Germany lost the war. Hitler's name is forever associated with evil. (Circa? Photographer unknown. Public domain.)

Henrich Himmler

Heinrich Himmler (1900 – 1945) oversaw the genocidal programs. He was rabidly devoted to Hitler; fellow Nazi leaders joked of his loyalty. A sickly child and failed soldier but a bookish intellectual, Himmler had a keen interest in the occult and mysticism which he incorporated into the Nazi Party. He was captured after the war but committed suicide by cyanide tablet. He is considered the architect of the Holocaust, yet upon seeing his first mass shooting he became physically ill. (Circa: 1942. Photographer: Unknown. Bundesarchiv, Bild 183-S72707 / CC-BY-SA 3.0)

Karl Gebhardt

Karl Gebhardt (1897 – 1948) a defendant in the Medical Case Trial at Nuremberg. He was brilliant, according to Irma Grese. He was a noted medical doctor before Nazi Germany, then performed experiments on female prisoners causing much horrific suffering and death. Gebhardt may have been responsible for assisting Grese obtain work at Ravensbrück. He would be tried and hanged after the war. (Circa 1947. Credit: USHMM, courtesy of Hedwig Wachenheimer Epstein Copyright: USHMM. Public Domain)

World War II

The Axis powers (Germany, Italy, and Japan) fought the Allies (Great Britain, France, the Soviet Union, and the United States) in a war that affected every part of the globe.

Irma Grese was about six years old when World War II began in Europe on September 1, 1939, when Germany invaded Poland. Great Britain and France responded by declaring war on Germany days later on September 3. The war between the U.S.S.R. and Germany began on June 22, 1941. The war in the Pacific began on December 7/8, 1941, when Japan attacked the American Naval base at Pearl Harbor and other American, Dutch, and British military installations throughout Asia. [7]

The Allies who fought were considered heroes in their own countries, supermen who conquered true evil, for the evil was tangible in this war - dictators whose irrational dogma was broadcast and printed, ideologies foreign to God-fearing countries who believed and practiced freedom and democracy. Besides being bloody and cruel, this was a highly emotional war. The Axis powers fought the Allies for ideals as much as power. Very few people were left unscathed by these emotions.

"Sixty to eighty million people, or 3 percent of the world's entire population, predominantly women and children, were killed…between the invasion of China by Japan in 1937 and the fall of Nazi Germany and Imperial Japan in 1945 … the enemies (were) far more sadistic than… the Taliban, al-Qaida, or ISIS." [8] The most accurate estimate is eleven million European people (six million of whom were Jews) were murdered by Nazis and Nazi allies. One historian and expert on WWII states "Thirty thousand people a day, for six years" lost their life during WWII. [9] In between, entire villages were destroyed, cities were bombed, farmlands obliterated, along with innocent civilians and their businesses, some of which were generational.

As occurs in wartime, the axis powers were collectively considered to be mad men by the Allies, regardless of whether they followed the Nazi regime. The Allies, in turn, were painted as bitter enemies by the Axis powers, and some acted as such; as an example, Allied soldiers raping and assaulting innocent females to punish the "enemy" armies. [10] Thus there was talk of the Allies' brutality– so many innocent people were caught between the Nazi powers and those set to destroy them.

The Lebendiges Museum Online (LEMO) notes, "it was clear to many Germans that the pact between the 'mortal enemies' of many years could mean that war was imminent. However, the use of the term 'war' was expressly forbidden by the Nazi regime after the invasion of Poland on September 1, 1939." [11]

Nazism

"Nazi" is an acronym for The National Socialist German Workers' Party (NSDAP). From *Hitler and the Collapse of the Weimar Republic*:

---

[7] Hughes, et. al.
[8] Vronsky (2018). P. 310
[9] Interview with David Moore, WWII historian, April 16, 2024.
[10] Study on rape by American soldiers in WWII cited in Vronsky, p. 320-3
[11] https://www.dhm.de/lemo/kapitel/zweiter-weltkrieg

> [Al]most all essential elements of ... Nazi ideology were to be found in the radical positions of ideological protest movements [in pre-1914 Germany]. These were: a virulent anti-Semitism, a blood-and-soil ideology, the notion of a master race, [and] the idea of territorial acquisition and settlement in the East. These ideas were embedded in a popular nationalism which was vigorously anti-modernist, anti-humanist and pseudo-religious.[12]

Not everyone in Germany supported the Nazi party. This political party was formed in 1919, after the Treaty of Versailles was signed. But the Nazi party was declining in 1928, and in the parliamentary elections of 1930, the party raised only about 18 percent of votes. The Nazi party rose to 37 percent of the national vote in 1932. Hindenberg named former opponent Adolph Hitler as Chancellor and with the 1933 burning of the Reichstag (the parliamentary building), which Hitler blamed on Communists. The Nazi party rose to power. [13] It is a myth that Grese's hero Adolph Hitler was elected to any station by "the people." [14] Nazism was declared as Germany's sole legal political party in July 1933, shortly after the launching of Dachau (the first concentration camp). Eventually, to not pledge allegiance to the party meant suspicion and possible imprisonment. The Nazi regime would collapse in 1945.

Irma Grese would become a reverent believer in the ideals of Nazism:

- The superiority of the Aryan race, "white supremacy."
- Antisemitic and racist themes in literature, education, and daily living.
- The expansion of territory, to be taken by treaty or by force.
- An obsession of agrarian production (due to the global economy).
- Maintaining "pure" bloodlines in Germans by prevention of "race mixing" in any form (sexual, social, economic, etc.).
- Sacrifice of self for the "greater good" (the country) and the plans of Adolf Hitler.
- The major role of females was to produce "perfect" children of "pure blood" for Germany.
- Extermination of homosexuals, Jews, and other "undesirables."
- Endorsement of "Positive Christianity" and eradication of other religions
- Adolph Hitler was the savior, the leader, and the response to Germany's problems.

Hitler was the central apex of the Nazi movement, on whose shoulders the entire movement rested. "National Socialism was not primarily an ideological and programmatic, but a charismatic movement," historian Martin Broszat explains, "whose ideology was incorporated in the Führer, Hitler, and which would have lost all its power to integrate

---

[12] Broszat (1987). *"Hitler and the Collapse..."* p. 38

[13] Hamilton, R.F. (2014)

[14] For an excellent resource on the background of the voting and political movement of the Nazi party, see Hamilton, R.F. (2014) "Who Voted for Hitler?"

without him. ... [T]he abstract, utopian and vague National Socialistic ideology only achieved what reality and certainty it had through the medium of Hitler." [15] Hitler was the product of a damaged childhood, seeking solace and validity. He was also seeking power and control (the basis for all crime). Hitler's ideas did not just appear or emerge from a broken mind; historically, the Jews have always been victims of persecution.

Hitler did not persecute Jews solely because he hated Jews. He plucked some idealism from history. The Synod of Elvira (the provincial Council of Elvira) in 306 listed intermarriage and carnal knowledge between Christian and Jews. In 535, The Synod of Claremont forbid Jews from having authority over Christians to include holding a government position. Jews were to wear a "mark" on their clothing per the Fourth Lateral Council (1215), followed by archdiocese in Mainz (Germany) of 1259 ordering Jews to wear yellow badges. By decree of mostly the church, Jews were ostracized and rendered powerless in business and government. Adolph Hitler and the Nazi party utilized a history of discrimination to continue the prejudice and persecution. Hitler sought power and Germans sought a powerful leader. Hitler needed Germany as much as Germany needed Hitler.

Irma Grese's chance to attend university (college) was nil; the new government now limited female applicants to university. Jobs once open to women now closed doors or limited applications to females (doctors as one example). The war needed secretarial staff and nurses, so women could remain – and were hired – for these positions. Irma Grese dreamed of being a nurse; at least two of her sisters would become nurses. Women were needed (and rewarded) to fulfill the Nazi dream: the Nazi mother who supported her Nazi man and bore his pure Aryan children to populate the world. Working in the concentration camp initially was a "man's job" until the lingering war demanded men at the front.

The Nazi red and white flag, emblazoned with the black swastika, was being raised ubiquitously over Nazi-occupied areas, eventually replacing all official flags. As Germany expanded, more flags occupied more territory.

Teachers and professors would receive new curriculums. While some teachers embraced these curriculums of rewritten history, patriotic songs, and loyalty to the Führer, some instructors continued to teach the usual curriculum under threat of exposure (the consequence being investigated, and possibly imprisoned) while those "in the middle" regrettably adopted the rewritten curriculums - because to disobey meant loss of work, wages, and life: the SS not only arrested and/or murdered the offender, but the offender's family and friends lives were also under threat. In fear, anger, or disgust, people who once broke bread together were now suspiciously scrutinizing everyone around them; anyone – children included - could turn in their friends, families, coworkers, or classmates with charges of being unpatriotic. Children could report adults. Reporting was rewarded.

Hitler believed wholeheartedly in reshaping the mind of the child. He understood the power of reprograming, and he did so, beginning in the classroom. Holocaust survivor Dorothy Fleming recalls in her childhood "(our) teacher spoke very seriously... 'at home I want you to keep your eyes and ears open and listen carefully to what your (family and friends) are saying. If you hear them saying anything nasty or critical about our new system, you are to report it to me.'" [16] Little Dorothy knew, as did her classmates, to *not* report was just as serious an infraction as "nasty or critical" opinions of Nazi doctrine.

[15] T*he Hitler State* (1981)

[16] Cited in HolocaustCentUK (n.d.)

Author Erika Mann observed the Nazi dictatorship firsthand and notes:

> The German child is a Nazi child, and nothing else. He attends a Nazi school; he belongs to a Nazi youth organization; The movies he is allowed to see are Nazi films. His whole life, without any reservation, belongs to the Nazi state. That the Führers best bet lay, from the very beginning, in the inexperience and easily credulity of youth. [17]

Mann describes a first-hand account of the Nazi child walking to school under rows of Nazi flags, reading or hearing the propaganda (that has replaced all media) denouncing Jews / "undesirables;" noticing placards prohibiting Jewish entry into businesses, places of leisure, and certain city and town zones. By law, the child and those around them must use the greeting "Heil Hitler!" in replacement of usual greetings such as "good morning" and "hello." "'Heil' actually means salvation (and) used to be applied to relations between man and his God." (p. 21). Adults and children will be, by law, eventually ordered to attend Nazi organizations to include the Hitler Youth. At ten years of age, boys join the *Jungvolk* and at 14 years old promoted to Hitler Youth. For females there was the League of German Girls. Regardless of sex or age, there was a group for all youth. Little Irma Grese would yearn to join.

Youth Groups

Schwesternschaften der Hitler-Jugend (Sisterhood of the Hitler Youth) had been growing since early 1920s. And in 1930, it became the *Bund Deutscher Mädel*, (also known as BDM, "Band of German Maidens"). One year later the BDM was the female branch of the Hitler Youth. And by 1933, it boasted a mass following, in part because there were no other organizations for young girls, and it was compulsory (All social organizations for youth were either dissolved or integrated into the Hitler youth groups by law.) BDM separated members by age: Girls between 10 and 14 years old were in the Young Girl's League (*Jungmädelbund*). For girls 14 to 18 there was the *Bund Deutscher Mädel* (BDM) proper. A third, Faith and Beauty (*Glaube und Schönheit*) for young women 17 – 21 years of age, was created when Irma Grese was five years old. The latter branch was voluntary – though it was wise to join – and the members learned the arts of being a loyal Nazi wife and parent to loyal Nazi children. There were focuses on education and employment for the women - who should have been married - by this age group. Members bonded over cooking and sewing classes, cookouts, sports activities, marching, holiday trips – all steeped in the bogus, rewritten history created by propaganda, which also recreated the Führer as a savior, a knight on a white horse. Children as young as six were taught to rebel against parental advice deemed erroneous by the Nazi party, to include speaking against Hitler or having Jewish friends. Giving birth to future German soldiers, holding the Aryan race superior, and the importance of being a fit Aryan wife and mother were the goals of BDM. Self-sacrifice was considered a most important attribute. To "think German and act

[17] Mann (1938). P. 19

German" was the Führer's goal. "They will never be free again, not in their whole lives." [18] Ironically, the same could be said about so many prisoners condemned to the prisoner camps of Nazi Germany. [19]

[18] Von der Grun (1980), pp. 118-19

[19] I use the term "camp" loosely; there was nothing camp-like about these places, for they were places where people did not want to go. From the first camp onward these "camps" encompassed people were held against their will, terrible food and housing, and (eventually) with the goal of murdering innocents. Because the word "camp" is universally used, I choose this term – the author.

Symbols of the New World Order

Insignias are an important part of organizations. Symbols unify and identify; they also discriminate by separating members from nonmembers. Nazi symbolism was an important part of creating the Third Reich. The symbols of the New World order were not new, but based on ancient art and historical organizations. Thus, history and lore combined with new ideations became a modern display of power by creating both pride and fear.

The Swastika (*Hakenkreuz*)

The broken cross symbol was discovered in a burial ground in ancient Troy by a German archeologist. Far-right nationalists adopted the Swastika after World War I to symbolize a racially "purity" and the Nazi Party adopted the symbol in 1920. In *Mein Kamph,* Hitler wrote of the flag he envisioned using the swastika. The swastika is not a symbol for evil unless utilized for such. Even the name "Swastika" is Sanskrit (*svastika*) for "good fortune." Its first use was possibly in Eurasia, remaining a sacred symbol in certain religions, including Buddhism.
As a member of the League of German Girls, Irma Grese would have worn a Swastika pin or patch on her uniform, a red and white rhombus with the black swastika in the center.

The Double Lightning Bolts

The double lightning bolts were pseudo-runes utilized by the Nazi Party and became an SS emblem in 1933. Besides the initials "SS" the bolts also stood for "Victory! Victory!" German typewriters were outfitted with extra keys of the double symbol allowing the typing of the logo with one tap of the key. As a female, Irma Grese could not officially join the Nazi Party.

Skull and Crossbones Emblem (*Totenkopf*)

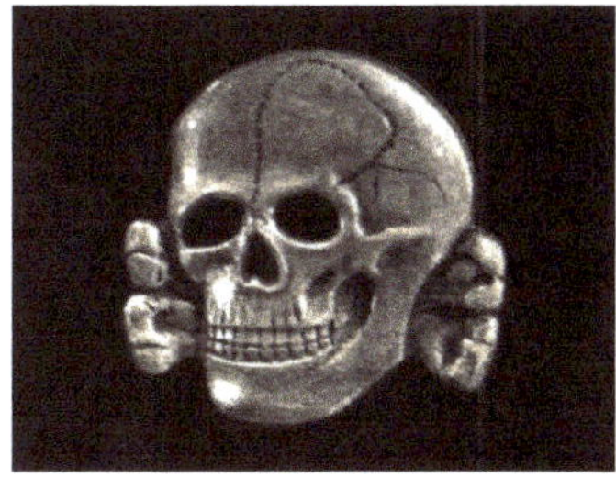

Another ancient symbol resurrected by the Nazi party, the skull and crossbones symbol has been utilized throughout history by many groups. Its general purpose has always been to strike fear, and in Nazi Germany, this was no different. It was utilized, according to Heinrich Himmler, to remind those who wore it to put themselves at risk for their country. Irma Grese would never have donned the black Nazi soldier uniforms or anything resembling the uniforms.

In the name of the *Furor*

Not all Germans or persons in German – occupied territory supported the Nazi party as did Irma Grese. This included enlisted men, some of whom initially saw the military as the best choice and most successful way of making a living. Some of the men were forced into military service.
Like Irma Grese, some embraced their military standing with fervor. Others, like Irma Grese's father, took advantage of what was offered with membership. And there were those who, like Josef Goebbels, would rather commit suicide and familicide before living without the Nazi Party.
(This group of photographs: circa 1940s. Photographers: unknown. Photos courtesy the private collection of Ray Cook. Used with permission. These photos have been minimally altered for clarity to remain true to the original photographs. This is the first time the family has shared these photographs.

Left – the original photograph obtained by Ray Cook, Sr.
Right – altered photograph to reveal uniform details. The uniform indicates he is a German Army 2nd Lieutenant.

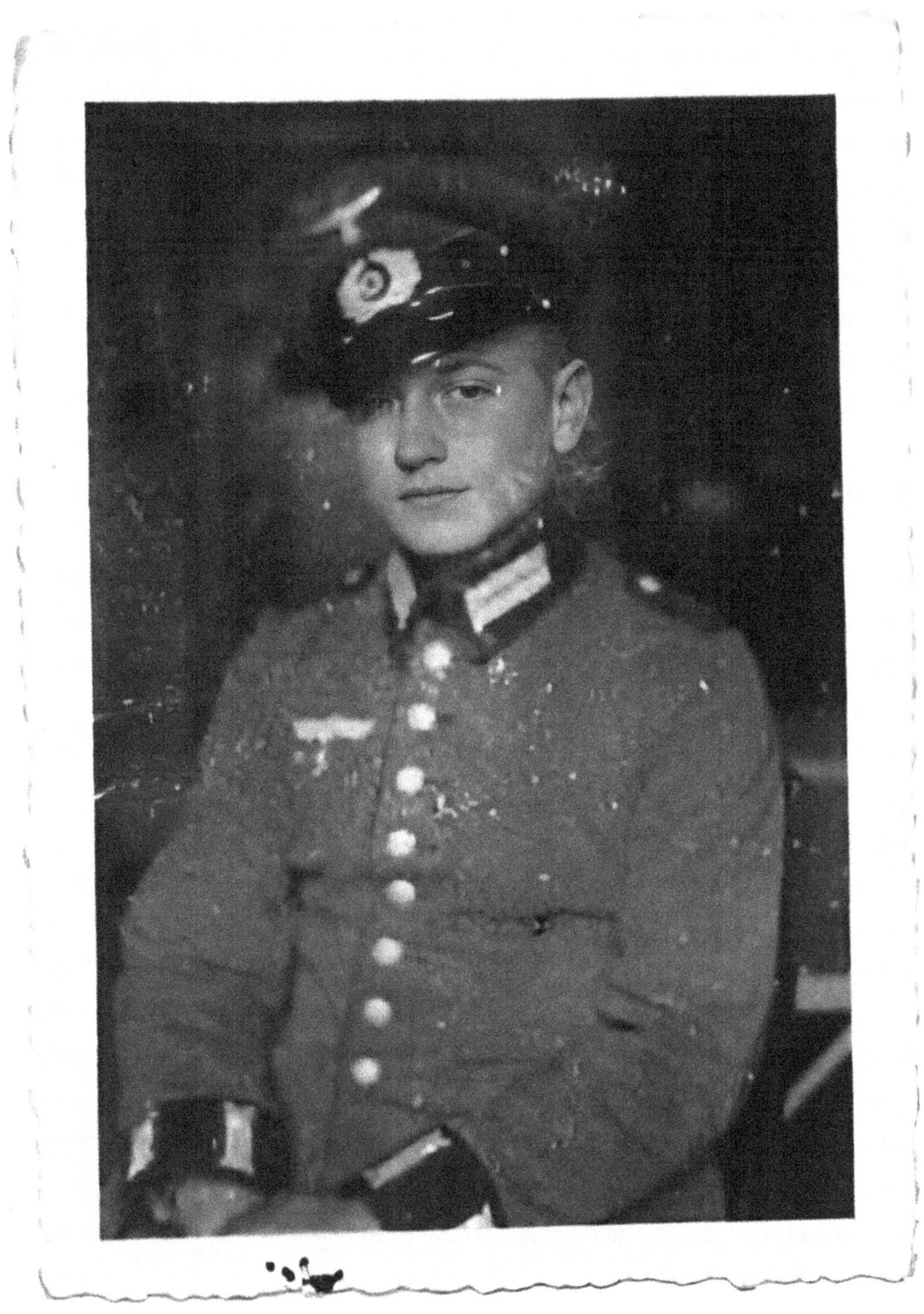

German Army newly enlisted soldier in dress tunic. Note the cockiness of the tilted hat.

German Army Officer Trainees (circa 1944).

Marching German Army, possibly pre-WWII.

A German Army Enlisted Soldier.

Guard tower possibly at a POW camp or an early concentration camp tower, location unknown

The Pogroms

Opposite page: Jewish woman chased by a Ukrainian crowd during the pogrom. She has been stripped to her underwear, and has a bloodied face. A "death dealer's" left leg can be observed immediately behind her. Note the boy who is assisting with a club. Irma Grese would have supported such actions, being a fanatic for the Nazi Party.
The original image is on film, **"**Lvov Pogrom, Jews rounded up, beatings." USHM: "The film was seized by the U.S. Army in an SS barracks near Augsburg, Germany, and was delivered … to the U.S. Chief of Counsel for Prosecution of Major European War Criminals. The film was introduced as evidence (USA Exhibit 280) at the International Military Tribunal trial of war criminals at Nuremberg."
From the United States Holocaust Memorial Museum: "Germany invaded the Soviet Union on June 22, 1941, occupying Lvov within a week. Ukrainian mobs went on a rampage against Jews. They stripped and beat Jewish women and men in the streets of Lvov. Ukrainian partisans supported by German authorities killed about 4,000 Jews in Lvov during this pogrom."
This film was shot about the time Irma Grese was applying to be an *Aufseherin* at Ravensbrück. She would have been acutely aware of such incidents.
It is unknown if the woman in the photograph survived the attack. (Circa July 1, 1941. Photographer unknown. Yad Vashem Photo Collection, 80DO2. Public Domain of Ukraine.)

Chapter 3
The *Schutzstaffel* (SS)

To detail the SS - its components, history, and entire purpose - would digress from the story of Irma Grese. However, some information is imperative to understand what, in part, created The Hyena of Auschwitz. The SS impacted all of WWII. This included Irma Grese and those around her.

To ensure German loyalty to the Nazi party, the *Schutzstaffel* (SS) was created. [20] Initially a small sentry of volunteers acting as Hitler's bodyguards, time and necessity now produced a larger organization that created a police state within Nazi Germany. By the time Nazis came into power (1933), membership of the Nazi party was at 52,000, [21] by 1944, the membership totaled about 800,000. [22] The SS agency now controlled security, mass surveillance, and state terrorism in Nazi Germany and German – occupied Europe. The SS would eventually be broken into smaller units and individual offices (still under command of the SS) called SS-*Sonderkommandos.* These smaller units were given "specialized assignments."

Not all SS were made killers or fanatics. Nor were they Third Reich humanoids, and they were not all completely duped. The SS was a fascinating system for all the havoc wreaked and irreversible damage done.

The Treaty of Versailles limited numbers in the German army; thus, men who wanted to fight in WWII were not able. The SS became the obvious choice. Those attracted to the military structure, engrossed in the idea of fighting for their county, and men drawn to power and prestige, clamored to join the SS. The SS encompassed many types of men and provided them with what they were seeking: work, validation, purpose, ego, opportunity, power and control. [23]

Females were not allowed to join the SS, but would be allowed to volunteer for "helper" positions, to include, eventually, guard positions at the camps. These female "helpers" would be trained at Ravensbrück.

Like all organizations – including Irma Grese's training program at Ravensbrück – the SS began with strict membership codes; as the war began, then the longer it continued, those codes were placed aside to increase membership. Few people expected WWII to last as long as it did, and with close to 6,000,000 German military deaths by war's end, [24] bodies were needed at the front. Some of the SS served in the military. Many others, not on the front line, made life a living hell for minorities.

The SS consisted of degreed and professional men, religious leaders, and field experts, but most were uneducated – even illiterate. Some Holocaust survivors recall the ignorance of guards in the camps, some of whom could not even count or ruminate over complex decisions. As will be discussed, substance abuse ran rampant with camp guards. Many were corrupt, just as their brothers on the outside. It was a paramilitary structure

[20] Not all components of the Nazi regime will be discussed in this book. There were many departments of the Party.

[21] McNab (2009)

[22] Laquer, W. et. al. (2001)

[23] Ervin Straub's excellent book, "The Roots of Evil" (University Press, 1989) describes the SS in great detail, to include the psychological factors.

[24] Multiple resources, including The National WWII Museum of New Orleans.

which, according to Nazi leaders, was the epitome of the perfect man and based on honor. Eventually the SS was given free rein to act without fear of the law. With this power came corruption.

The SS were men who could do as they pleased without repercussion. From publicly cutting off the Payot of Hasidic Jewish men to rape, assault, theft and destruction of property, the SS had ultimate power on the streets and in the camps.

The SS men were clad in uniforms that still today strike a chord in people with fear, uneasiness, and sobriety. The uniforms were purposely tailored to not only strike terror, but accentuate these "perfect" embodiments of true Aryan specimens. Copies of these uniforms are worn today by zealots who subscribe to "white power" and discrimination.

The SS was created utilizing both the military model and mysticism, making the organization and its members even more powerful and enticing. In part, SS history encompassed:

- Direct perpetration of genocide.
- A lifestyle versus a membership.
- The idea of being "racially pure," to include the "perfect" height and weight.
- Complete subordination to the Naz ideology.
- National Socialism.
- An organization of only the elite.
- The weeding out of those who could not "make it" in the group, considered "not good enough."
- The appearance of a brotherhood of educated men.
- Creedence to the attitude that the SS brotherhood was more important than family.
- Rewards (emotionally, monetarily) of identity and superiority.

Irma Grese surely lapped up this dogma, judging by her work behavior and court testimony.

If an SS stopped someone on the street, they could detain the individual, beat, or kill them, imprison them without charge, or give any order regardless. They could barge into a Jewish household and "procure" any item. SS men painted warnings on Jewish shops, and then punished anyone who disobeyed the orders to abuse or refute the owners.

Not all SS men were brutal or self-absorbed. There was a scale, from those who refused to murder to those who enjoyed killing. Some became wanton killers upon membership or longevity in the SS. Irma Grese would become one of these murderers.

The mass murders did not occur in a vacuum. Jews were shot on sight or beaten to death on individual basis, but the mass killing began with firing squads of lining up people – sometimes over a large pit – and shooting them dead. While this ridded Nazi – occupied territory of "undesirables" or "enemies of the people," it did not work fast enough, and it caused much anguish for many of those pointing the gun. Next came the loading of people into a closed truck bed, directing the vehicle's carbon monoxide into the sealed bed, and driving some miles until the people were dead. The drivers had to remove the dead bodies and deal with the fumes, so this, too, would become a burden to the psyches of the killers. Finally, the idea of extermination camps to murder *en masse* became, in the Nazi mind, a far more effective way to complete the annellation of a people. Jews and other "enemies" could be loaded into cattle cars by the thousands, dropped off at the camps, and be murdered in the gas chambers within hours of arrival. Others could be starved, worked to death, murdered in the camps, and all other means by people like Irma Grese and her comrades.

Not only did Irma Grese believe wholeheartedly in Nazism, but felt she was extirpated from direct responsibility of murder. She would embrace the personal pleasure of murder only later.

The SS was a movement, an ideal, like most of the Third Reich, embracing and creating killers. Those who fell to the wayside for personal or professional reasons gained power by other means. There was no power for those civilians approached by an SS uniform. Irma Grese observed this on the streets, and then lived it firsthand.

CHAPTER 4
Into The Flames

Holocaust

The word means "to be consumed by fire" or "a sacrifice … a thorough destruction involving extensive loss of life especially through fire." It is used to describe a "mass slaughter of people" to include the Jews by Nazis in WWII. [25] The first known use is the 13th century. It comes from the Latin word *holocaustum*: "a sacrifice consumed by fire." In modern Hebrew "Shoah" ("catastrophe") [26]

Dead bodies (and some living persons) of concentration camp victims were burned in the crematoria, although not all camps had crematoria. The most well-known camp would be Auschwitz, known then and still as a symbol of grief, terror, and mass killing. Auschwitz was a complex of over 40 camps. Of at least 1.3 million total, an estimated 1.1 million Jews, Poles, Romani, Soviet POWs, homosexuals, Gypsies, and other "undesirables" lost their life here. [27] Some of these people lost their lives directly because of Irma Grese; it is impossible to know how many.

"From its rise to power in 1933, the Nazi regime built a series of incarceration sites to imprison and eliminate real and perceived 'enemies of the state.'" [28] Dachau was the first, and such a success that Hitler would assign SS Chief, Heinrich Himmler to supervise the building of a camp system. Beginning 1934, SS officers oversaw the camps. By 1944, 30 main camps and numerous smaller camps existed throughout Germany and German-occupied Europe.

The "camps"

Not all camps were death camps. Sites of incarceration ("camps") included:

Concentration camps – Labeled "concentration" camps because of the concentration of types of prisoners, and the camp itself served various purposes. These camps detained civilians deemed real or perceived enemies. "Enemy" ranged from a person who was perceived to be a spy, or someone deemed an unemployable addict. There was no trial, just arrest and imprisonment. (Recall how children could report family and friends who said anything negative regarding the Nazi system; the information the children gave could result in an arrest.) Eventually, after exploitation by labor, the prisoners would be murdered.

Forced labor camps –created for the purpose of brutal exploitation of prisoner labor for economic gain. Prisoners were literally worked to death creating or operating goods for the German government. German businesses gained free labor, and goods, such as munitions, were produced faster.

[25] Merriam-Webster's Collegiate Dictionary, 2023
[26] First known use: 1967
[27] In comparison, at this writing Dallas, Texas has a population of 1.3 million; San Jose, California about 1.1 million.
[28] United States Holocaust Memorial Museum, Washington, DC

Transit camps –temporary holding facilities for Jews awaiting deportation to other camps. The conditions here were no better than other camps.

Prisoner-of-war camps – to detain Allied prisoners of war. The POW's camp maintenance was to meet the conditions set forth by the Geneva Condition.

Killing centers - exclusively for the assembly - line style murder of large number of persons immediately upon their arrival. [29]

The man placed in the position of superintending the genocide was a bespeckled mystic occultist, clandestinely jeered at for his slathering devotion to Adolph Hitler: Heinrich Luitpold Himmler (1900 –1945), who aspired to eventually replace Hitler as leader of the Reich. One of Himmler's first jobs before becoming a high-profile Nazi was a short stint in a company manufacturing fertilizer. He moved up the ranks once he joined the Nazi Party. Like Hitler, Himmler's strict standards for SS membership requirements did not meet his own physicality: he was neither physically strong, blonde, blue-eyed, or a warrior of any type. Still, Himmler created numerous programs to maintain the Aryan prototype. In March 1933, he appointed a convicted felon, and zealous Nazi, to oversee the first official concentration camp (Dachau). By the end of 1934, Himmler was overseer of the entire camp system. This one-time unsuccessful chicken farmer became one of the most feared men in Germany. There were thousands of camps by the time the Allies won the war.

Irma Grese and Heinrich Himmler's paths were woven together; they crossed career paths several times, this former farm girl and one of the most powerful men in Germany. Given Grese's penchant for the Nazi dream, she was most likely in awe of the small, arrogant leader. Being a teenager, whose heroes were Nazi leaders, there is no doubt she would have at least been impressed.

For this book, this author lists only the camps that employed Irma Grese.

The camps in Irma Grese's Life

Ravensbrück

Located near the picturesque town of Ravensbrück, the largest female concentration camp in the German Reich housed over 120,000 females [30] – political prisoners, sex workers, homeless, Jews, females from across Europe who were deemed "unfit" or "undesirable." This was the first prison camp specifically for females, and it is where female guards were trained. At least 30,000 prisoners were killed by starvation, disease, gassing, or at the hands of staff. Ground was broken to build in November 1938. It would become terribly overcrowded, forcing over 1,000 prisoners to live in a space built for around 100. Toward its end, Ravensbrück was marred by disease, including typhus, due to overcrowding. [31] Overcrowding led to food shortages, lack of waste management, and lack of supplies (such as medication). A gas chamber was built in February 1945 and was constantly in motion,

[29] US Holocaust Museum "Nazi Camps."
[30] Ravensbrück did hold some male prisoners.
[31] It would be necessary to burn the camp to the ground upon liberation to stop the spread of typhus.

with at least 5,000 females walking into the chambers and none leaving alive. Ravensbrück was liberated by Soviet troops in April 1945.

Bergen-Belsen

Established in 1943, about 11 miles north of Celle, Germany, Bergen-Belsen was a section of Auschwitz and built to hold male Jewish hostages. It was made up of five satellite camps. Males were sent to "convalesce" at Bergen-Belsen from other camps only to end up dead from disease, starvation, or/and exhaustion. Females lodged here for a short time, then were transferred elsewhere. Initially, the camp was considered to have better conditions than some, until camps near the front line were evacuated and the prisoners were sent by train car or forced march to this center; then it became overcrowded and rife with disease. When the loss of the war became imminent, officials burned every document possible and attempted to cover their crimes. Following negotiations, British troops liberated Bergen-Belsen on April 15, 1945. Irma Grese then became a prisoner.

Auschwitz

Irma Grese knew Auschwitz was the ultimate killing machine, where an estimated 5,000 people could be executed and burned within 24 hours, given all machines functioned properly. Auschwitz, located in Poland, was a city unto itself, encompassing over 40 extermination and concentration camps and included:

Auschwitz I (the first and main camp, Oswiecim) - used as the Soviet and Polish POW camp.

Auschwitz II (Birkenau) - the extermination camp

Auschwitz III (Buna / Monowitz) - the slave labor camp

There were smaller camps in between the major ones. Auschwitz served three purposes: Extermination, forced labor, and concentration. The killing of prisoners was committed with cold, careful process. Detainees were taken off the railroad cars that had transported them from their lives into death, with the trains rolling straight into the camp.

Auschwitz II – Birkenau

In 1941, the slave labor who built Birkenau created a camp initially for 125,000 prisoners of war. This branch of the Auschwitz system opened officially in March 1942. Birkenau would become the killing center; 90% of Auschwitz victims perished in Birkenau. [32] The female guard staff was overwhelmingly underrepresented. At its highest peak in population there was approximately one female staff member for every 789 female prisoners, and one female staff member for every 2,110 total prisoners.

[32] Numerous sources.

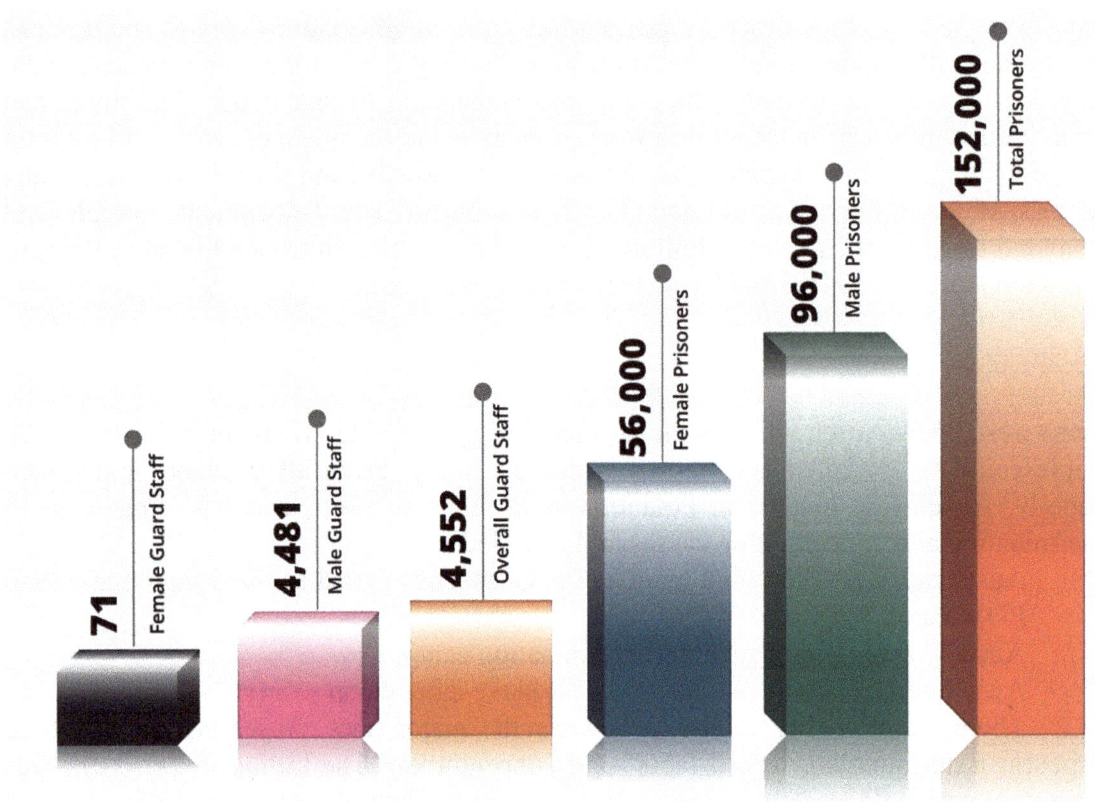

Birkenau population at its highest peak (August 1944)

(Numbers are estimated; it is not possible to know the exact amount of people involved in the operations of a concentration camp. Victim numbers are always estimated. Design by Fareesa, @design_perfect)

Officers were there, waiting, shouting instructions over the bustle of humanity, barking guard dogs, and the sounds of the train. Goggle-eyed adults, children and elderly poured out of the boxcars where they had ridden for days, without food or water, without a proper toilet, leaving sick and dead bodies behind. The exiting population were split into the two lines – one group to die immediately, the other to be imprisoned - but not told of the death that awaited. Many were gassed within the hour and their bodies burned in the crematorium. The operation of movement functioned just as the crematorium operated: all parts progressed correctly and synchronized. And Irma Grese willingly took part of this system, called "selection."

While the camps were in operation, propaganda films had been released to the German public showing happy, healthy prisoners who only suffered slight inconveniences while being incarcerated. At war's end, Nazis attempted to destroy any semblance of brutality or negative behavior towards the prisoners. This included forcing prisoners to exhume the putrid dead to smash the bodies and spread the remains. Some records and evidence exist; it was impossible to destroy it all. And the surviving prisoners testified, including tales of sadistic tortures and murders, in several trials. This included much testimony against Irma Grese.

Camp Supervision Tiers

Each camp had an individual hierarchy. These leaders were selected with care; strength of character, brutality, loyalty to the Nazi party, and mindset were more essential than experience or education. Utilizing this system, the Nazi party selected intimidators to supervise operations. Brute strength overrode communication skills. There was no room for kindness or humanity.

Not all Nazi camp employees were brutal; some even hated their work and assisted prisoners furtively. Irma Grese was one of the roughly ten percent of the guards who were brutal oppressors. To display any feelings for prisoners or to not display toughness was considered as weak, disloyal to Germany, and traitorous. Survivors recall many of their oppressors being alcoholics and/or drug addicts, illiterate, lacking in common sense and skillsets. (After the war, it was revealed many Nazi soldiers operating the camp did so under the influence of alcohol and/or drugs. Reportedly, officers who removed prisoners from train cars were intoxicated during this work.) Like any military operation, camps functioned through people of all behaviors and personality types.

However, the harsh did rise to the top quickly. These are the Nazis who created an inferno in the hell of the camps, the ones who eventually were tried in court and who made the history books. [33] Irma Grese was one of them.

Positions for women in camps were limited. From highest position to lowest as discussed in this book:

Job Titles

Per the Auschwitz – Birkenau Memorial and Museum these are the positions in the German Nazi concentration camps and extermination centers:

[33] It should be noted very few of the brutal SS went to court or were charged. Most went to lead "normal" lives after the war, some still believing in the ideology of Nazism, some shedding the beliefs to never discuss again.

Kapos were prisoners selected as work supervisors for other prisoners in the camps.

Oberaufseherin [34] – the senior supervisor, the second highest ranking a woman could obtain. Irma Grese obtained this rank in Auschwitz-Birkenau.

Lagerführerin – female commander of a camp or camp section, "camp leader." (Basically, it is the same as *Oberaufseherin* - which appears in some documents.)

Rapportführerin – ("Report Leader") – oversaw sections of *Blockführerin*. In this role, Irma Grese beat prisoners and abused her powers.

SS Aufseherin – plural: *Aufseherinnen* (translation: "overseer") – female guard in the camp. They eventually replaced many men in the camp so the men could move into combat positions on the front lines. This was Irma Grese's first title, but she moved up quickly through the ranks.

SS–Gefolge – female civilian employees of the *Schutzstaffel* (SS).

Blockführerin – ("block leader") – guard supervisor over individual blocks in the camps.

Blockalteste – usually a prisoner chosen as block leader.

Departments

Camps were divided into five departments, each with a specific duty:
Commandant's Offices – leadership
Political Department – registering incoming prisoners, the prison, and crematoriums.
Protective Custody – the prisoner's complex.
Administration - including maintenance and facilities.
Medical – supervised by a camp physician.

A building in a concentration camp was often a "hut" or "barrack" in camp parlance.

---

[34] "Aufseherin" pronounced *Auf-seh-rin*.

***Aufseherin* identification card of Luzie Halata.** It is allowing her to carry firearms (Date: unknown. Photographer: unknown. Courtesy *Das Bundesarchiv*. BArch, NS 4-LU/6. Permission to use.)

Translation:
Concentration camp of the Waffen-SS Lublin ID Number 316
Of SS – Aufseherin
Luzie Halata
DOB 5.10.1910
is a member of the command staff of the Lublin concentration camp. She is entitled to carry firearms in service.

Irma Grese would have received such a card upon being hired as an *Aufseherin.* Grese's card is lost to time; there are still some ID cards surviving liberation. Some solely exist in photocopy form.

267

Konzentrationslager der Waffen-SS Lublin

Ausweis Nr. 316

die SS-Aufseherin
Luzie Halata
geb. 5.10.1910
ist Angehörige des Kommandantur-Stabes des Konzentrationslagers Lublin. Sie ist berechtigt, im Dienst Schusswaffen zu tragen.

Luzie Halata

Lublin

SS-Sturmbannführer
und Lagerkommandant

PART II

Meet The Hyena

Major Cranfield (Representing defendant Grese): If you had your ears boxed, would you call that a beating?

Ilona Stein (Holocaust survivor & witness): I would call that nothing at all compared with the way how she used to beat people.

- Witness testimony against Irma Grese, The Belsen Trials, September 25, 1945.

Irmgard Ilese Ida Grese, AKA Irma Grese, AKA "The Hyena of Auschwitz" was born around October 7, 1923, in Wrechen (Neubrandenburg County), North Germany. She attended a one-room school with classes taught by a single teacher. She is seen here, age about 12 years old. (Circa 1935. Location: unknown, possibly Wrechen. Photographer: unknown. Public domain) Right: Artist's rendering of Irma Grese as a child (Circa: 2023. Art by Nobe Studio, @nobeststudio. Used with permission. © J. A. Yates)

CHAPTER 5
Birth – 10 Years Old

Towheaded Irmgard Ilese Ida Grese opened her blue eyes for the first time on or about October 7, 1923, [35] in Wrechen [36] (Neubrandenburg County), North Germany. The Grese children were raised here in the peaceful, rural Prussian province of Mecklenburg, situated south of the Baltic Sea, and about 90 miles north of Berlin. City dwellers from Berlin would drive to Irma's birthplace to enjoy peaceful weekends on the lakes, forests, and picturesque farmlands. Not much later, Nazi Germany would hold the land and those who worked it as sacred, a return to the rural lifestyle that built the country. The big landowners of Mecklenburg prospered. The youth programs that would mold Irma Grese and her peers would reflect this ideology.

When Irma was born there were 175 inhabitants in Wrechen.[37] It was home to old – fashioned conservatives who enjoyed traditions, relished simplicity, and had no use for major change. Decades later, Wrechen would remain largely unchanged; the town continues to sport brick- laid winding paths and chickens who cluck and scratch freely. Modernization has moved the town forward with paved roads and fresh signs for visitors. The homeowners whose houses sported the Nazi insignias have plastered over the old symbols cemented above their front doors to signify new ideals and warm welcomes. Solar panels are installed on selected red clay roof tiles. Still, it maintains much of the old-world feel, with picturesque beauty at every turn. There are quaint vacation homes and bed & breakfast stays boasting gardens bursting with color and unique personalities. There is not a food chain or neon sign around. Wrechen remains full of thick green shrubbery and quaint architecture, long – held secrets, and old stories in its history.

Irma's father Alfred Anton Albert Grese (1899 -?) grew up in an area near Göhren, then a farming and fishing village, near Wrechen. Mother Bertha Wilhelmine Auguste Grese (née Winkler, or Winter, depending on the source, 1902 or 1904 - 1936) hailed from either Göhren or from Warbende, Mecklenburg-Stelitz, Germany. Alfred and Bertha met, married, and settled in Wrechen.

Their first child was Alfred (b.?). Next would come Lieschen, the oldest sister (b. 1921) who would grow up to become a nurse. Irma would be born in 1923, then Helene (who went by the nickname "Leni," 1926-2016), and finally Otto (1929 -?).

On January 30, 1933, a transformation in Germany would alter history's course across the world: Adolph Hitler became the German Chancellor. Nine-year-old Irma Grese was unaware how this date would mark her life from this time forward.

The family worked, like most in this part of Germany, in agriculture. Most historians and authors have Alfred Grese working as a farmer or owning a dairy. Alfred worked as a "dairy farmer … oversee(ing) an estate (where) he became the 'supervising milker' (with) two subordinates and a few cows." Berta's responsibilities included "…looking after the family garden and limited livestock (3 pigs, geese, and chickens")." [38]

---

[35] According to the German Federal Archives (*Bundesarchiv*) Irma Grese's birthday is November 7, 1923.

[36] Pronounced "*Vreck-en*"

[37] Noks (2014)

[38] Brown, D. P. (2002) p.12

Above: One of the few period photographs of Wrechen (Neubrandenburg County), North Germany, Irma Grese's birthplace. When Irma was born there were 175 inhabitants in Wrechen, a farming community. A portion of the town sits on the edge of the Wrechener See Lake. The white house still stands; construction began in 1842 when a six-year-old worker laid the first stone. (Circa 1900. Photographer unknown. Source: https://docplayer.nl/56515477-Houttuinen-11-purmerend.html. Public domain.)

Below: A rare 1902 postcard of Göhren on Rügen. Irma's father Alfred grew up near Göhren. Mother Bertha probably hailed from Göhren. This postcard was mailed the year Alfred was three years old; Bertha was probably born the same year. (Circa 1902. Photographer unknown. Copyright Judith A. Yates)

The Grese lives were marked by the difficulties that arise with farming and raising children, without much indulgence.

The Grese household was not a wealthy family. The Grese children slept two to a bed on straw mattresses and wore hand-me-downs from older siblings or donated clothing. The village children attended a one-room school with classes taught by a single teacher; a Mr. Göbel led the Grese children and their peers through various educational endeavors. Most historians have the Grese children attending school in Wrechen. One historian who visited the town states, "there is no school. I think that Irma went to school in the Furstenhagen village (where) there was also a Nazi group of BDM." [39] One dog-eared school photograph exists of Irma and her classmates: thirty-plus, many blonde, youngsters ranging in ages and sizes. Irma is wearing two long braids and grinning directly into the camera.

Irma Grese reportedly suffered childhood trauma from an early age. Some accounts record her parents as fighting mightily: their five children living in fear and conflict, directly affected by the parents' anger and abuse. Some records have her father as a brutal drunk. Others paint him as stern, taciturn, a man of the church who rarely drank and raised his children to be obedient and respectful. He was reportedly quiet and hard-working.

One biographer notes Irma Grese was "starved for attention" and Berta "was a submissive and meek woman" while Irma's father "provided a strict upbringing to his children." Irma would have an interest in politics from an early age while her academic interests waned. This biographer has Irma Grese joining the Young Girl's League (*Jungmädelbund*) at ten years' old. [40]

Helene Grese granted an interview to journalist Peter Wieble on May 23, 1987, in Vechta, Germany. The interview would consume three cassette tapes, only a portion of this interview is available at this writing. Helene would paint an idealist picture of the Grese childhood. "We children knew no hardship, but were raised to be frugal," she told Wieble.

Helene discussed how the children worked, walking from the village to the farm to "fetch milk," of eating turnips as a snack, how it was the children's responsibility to care for the cows, pigs, ducks, geese, and chickens, collect grass and nettles; it was the responsibility of the children to take lunch to their fathers in the fields, fetch a parent who spent too long at the local pub, chop and stack wood for the winter, fish, do the laundry, "just do all sorts of things." Helene spoke of her sister Irma with admiration and love. According to Helene, theirs was a typical life for low-income farming families in small communities.

Although Alfred Grese did not support Nazi Germany, he joined the Nazi party as a local group leader in 1937. Irma would later tell he was "very religious and conservative and did not believe in Nazism." [41] Alfred may have joined for practical reasons - to stay off the SS radar or to reap any rewards. He understood Nazi Germany protected and revered the farming community.

Alfred's official title would have been *Blockleiter* (Block Warden, or block leader). Originally established in 1930, and then revised in 1933, a *Blockleiter's* duties would involve reporting to his authorities any anti-Nazi activity of a neighborhood. Alfred Grese

---

[39] Interview via email of Joanna Czopowitcz, https://ssaufseherin.blogspot.com. (July 2, 2024)
[40] Jennings, R. (2015). P. 26
[41] Hellinger (2021)

would be expected to take part in the propaganda machine. It is unknown if Alfred kept files on each family, reported anyone who spoke against Nazism or Hitler, or spied on his neighbors. Did he have information on each household, their political opinions, and personal relationships? Alfred did not hold any political rank. He surely wore a uniform during his official "duties." There were monetary and other rewards to be had by contacting the Gestapo and turning in anyone who balked at the Nazi party. By the end of the war Alfred was one of almost half a million Block Wardens. [42]

If Alfred Grese did in fact take seriously his duties as a Block Leader, a young teenaged Irma Grese would have noticed. The sleek uniform, the command of respect, the rewards would have been an obvious sign of power.

Helene Grese would allude to Alfred's strict, authoritarian personality. "When we went to bed, the slippers had to be right in front of us." Alfred would whistle for the children when it was dinner time. "Because of his whistle, we children had to show up for dinner as quickly as possible; he attached great importance to punctuality." [43] The children were beaten [44] for disciplinary purposes; perhaps this was foreshadowing for Irma's future.

Helene may have been concealing family abuse, for each time she discusses a negative in her interview with Wieble, she adds a positive. For example, she explains, "father used to go to the small inn that was attached to the blacksmith shop to play scat. If a man was absent (from home) a child would come running to get his father." Then adds of her own father, "He drank beer very sparingly." Of punishment Helene explains, "If we were naughty we would get hit with a stick, but otherwise it was fine." (It is unclear if she is discussing school or home life.) Rather than discuss her mother's suicide, Helene states simply, "mother died in 1936." [45]

Multiple studies "have demonstrated that experiencing child abuse can lead to a range of internalizing and externalizing behavior problems… abused children can exhibit a variety of psychological problems, including anxiety and depression… Exposure to domestic violence in childhood has been linked to … low self-esteem, social withdrawal, depression, and anxiety." [46] Narcissistic personality disorder may develop from "childhood environments characterized by excessive deviations from ideal rearing…" [47] Supposing Alfred Grese was abusive, and depending on Helene's role in the family dynamic, she may have been concealing the truth, or recalling the past as she remembers. If their childhood was one of bliss with some turmoil, as she did tell, it remains problematic to prove. Given Irma Grese's behavior as an adult it is difficult to believe serious trauma was nonexistent.

A. Gonzalez and D. Mosquera (2011) note narcissistic features may develop from "'too much' attention … the child will not be seen as an individual … (they) will be born to fulfill an adult's needs." (p. 5) The parent is living vicariously through the child; no physical abuse occurs. As examples: the parents choose what activities the child will participate in, the clothing, the social network. The child is raised to believe they are grander than others, more talented, and special. Once the child leaves the home and realizes they are the proverbial "small fish in the big pond," the child (now older) may be traumatized, angry, and appears as a "snob" or "lofty." They have poor socialization skills

[42] Nazi Conspiracy and Aggression (1946). P.449
[43] Wieble (1987)
[44] To what extent this punishment extended, Helene did not say
[45] Ibid
[46] Herrenkohl, et. al. (2010)
[47] Gabbard (1989) cited in Gonzalez, et. al. (2011). P. 4

as a result. If Irma Grese was raised to believe she was highly intelligent, better than other children, and sure to be successful based on who she was, it would have had just as damaging an effect as physical abuse.

Still, Irma experienced joy as a child. She and her sister Lieschen were considered superior singers and loved singing school songs and harmonizing for the family at home. Irma was an animal lover and enjoyed playing with cats as there always seemed to be a cat around – most are excellent mousers, handy in rural living. It was said when her brothers teased one of the kittens, Irma cried over the cruelty. She would play games with her siblings, wade in the neighboring creeks with the sun bearing down on her blonde head. Irma would chop up the fish that Helene and Otto used as fishing bait or as food for the farm ducks. She had an artistic side, decorating their plain living space with what little they had, and her natural gift for decorating made Helene a bit jealous.

A wealthy family named Seibt resided in the village, and the Grese children delivered Sunday papers to them, to earn a few cents, which they saved. The Grese children knew they were far removed socially, but they played with the Seibt family's son, Karl, who owned actual toys. The Seibt family would occasionally pass down clothing to the Grese family.

The Grese family was the first in Wrechen to own a radio; perhaps this is the first time the outside Nazi world entered their lives. Helene reported she did not remember when news of the party ever entered their daily discussions.

10-year-old Irma Grese's Germany was taken over by Nazis. Now the Grese children's education would be steeped in Nazi rhetoric.

In 1929, The National Socialist Teachers League was created to educate and control teachers. The League oversaw the Nazi training course for educators, a mandatory month of training where the instructors were told what to teach (Nazism), where, and how. Teachers who did not follow or who questioned the curriculum could be reported to the authorities – to include reports by students – and imprisoned. The Restoration of the Professional Civil Service Act of April 7, 1933, dismissed civil service employees belonging to certain groups: professors and teachers who were Jewish, communist (or suspected) or any other "undesirables" were removed from the education system. Remaining teachers were forced to become members of the Nazi Party. Grese would be educated by non-Jewish teachers, in a classroom closed to Jews, surrounded by posters of Hitler as a savior and eminent leader adorning the classroom walls. Little Irma would join in class songs that included lyrics like "Hitler is our god." Schoolgirl Irma would learn to read from books such as "A is for Adolph" decorated with children in Nazi uniforms giving the Nazi raised – arm salute. They read *Der Giftpilz* ("The Poison Mushroom") warning children of the dangerous Jew. The Nazis' plans to "de-intellectualize" education - preventing introspection and contemplation - was aided by releasing "approved" textbooks; science was revised to favor the Aryans, and sports would become majority of the curriculum. It was a strategy to produce soldiers and women dedicated to the ideal. Irma Grese, from an early age, was, as author Erika Mann described, "the Nazi child":

> No German group was more stringently affected by the changes of the dictatorship than the children. The German child is a Nazi child, and nothing else. He attends a Nazi school; he belongs to a Nazi youth organization; the

> movies he is allowed to see are Nazi films. His whole life, without any reservation, belongs to the Nazi state. The young have no individual interest; they know nothing of another world, with another rule. [48]

And there was the passing of the Enabling Act of March 23, 1933. Intimidation and control of political parties ensured votes to pass the act which gave Hitler carte blanche to now enact laws without interference from the parliament; it was to be legal for four years. Germany was now a dictatorship and Adolph Hitler was at the helm, just as he had been plotting.

By the time Irma Grese was of age to make friends outside of family and schoolmates, the *Bund Deutscher Mädel* (Band of German Maidens, or BDM) was there to determine a German girl's social calendar. There were summer camps with hiking and swimming, comrades to share stories around a campfire, good food and marching and singing. Helene would later explain she and Irma wanted to join the BDM. Alfred forbade his daughter's membership; either because the closest group was in Furstenhagen or because he was against the ideal. [49] Both girls were still in school, membership was not yet mandatory, and it was a long ride - five hours by car – and Irma would be on a bicycle. Yet in 1936, while Irma and her sisters were still attending school, membership into BDM became mandatory. One author notes that Wrechen, in 1933, hosted "flourishing branches of the Nazi youth organizations." [50]

Perhaps Alfred forbade his daughters because the expense was too high for a farmer's meager salary. The BDM uniforms had to be purchased by the members. Some families sewed the uniforms using a pattern purchased at stores such as ABC Schnitt (a sewing pattern book) or Lutterloh, a small business established in 1935 specializing in books of sewing patterns. [51] Each carried instructions to ensure the clothing was to regulation, to include material type. If they had the money the family would purchase uniforms at the *Brauner Laden.* The official uniform blouses and skirts sold here included insignia imprinted on the white buttons: "BDM," tiny oak leaves, and "JM." [52] A plain white blouse and dark blue skirt pulled from a girl's closet would also suffice for the uniform.

Uniforms purchased through official outlets sported the Nazi insignias and reminders in every form possible, from tags to buttons. When a girl was buttoning her shirt, pulling on her stockings, or sliding into her jacket, she was reminded – even subconsciously - that she was a proud BDM member.

The BDM group, to most German girls, *belonged* - they were perfect German specimens, according to the Nazi regime; they must have appeared so inviting to girls with their full blue skirts, white midi blouses and dark ties. The BDM members sported polished, black heavy boots, perfect for marching, hiking, and working child-bearing muscles. Members appeared to readily accept one another and had a place in the world – one of honor. Not belonging to the BDM may have been another strike against the lonely child Irma Grese. The BDM was soon the largest female youth organization boasting over 4.5

---

[48] Mann (1938) p.19

[49] Helene made this admission in 1987; she could have been distancing her family from any Nazi-related activity.

[50] Playfair, G. & Sington, D. (1957) p. 166

[51] Both businesses exist still. They are no longer affiliated with any Nazi activities.

[52] For a detailed explanation and examples of the BDM clothing, see bdmhistory.com "Uniforms" tab.

million members. [53] If Grese was bullied and ostracized in school, she no doubt observed other girls wearing the special uniforms, a sorority of exclusives, the sole organization for females her age, and rewarded for their new patriotism by adults (including teachers). Today the BDM would be dubbed "the cool kids."

Irma's sister Helene would later testify in Irma's defense during the Belsen Trials. In primary school, Helene would insist, when "girls were quarreling and fighting, (Irma) never had the courage to fight, but ... ran away." [54] As a little boy, Grese's brother Otto once split his lip open. It was Irma who sobbed that Otto was in pain. Years later, this childhood tender-heartedness would be recalled in a vain effort to save her life.

[53] Pine, L (2010)

[54] The Belsen Trial, Helene Grese testimony, October 16, 1945

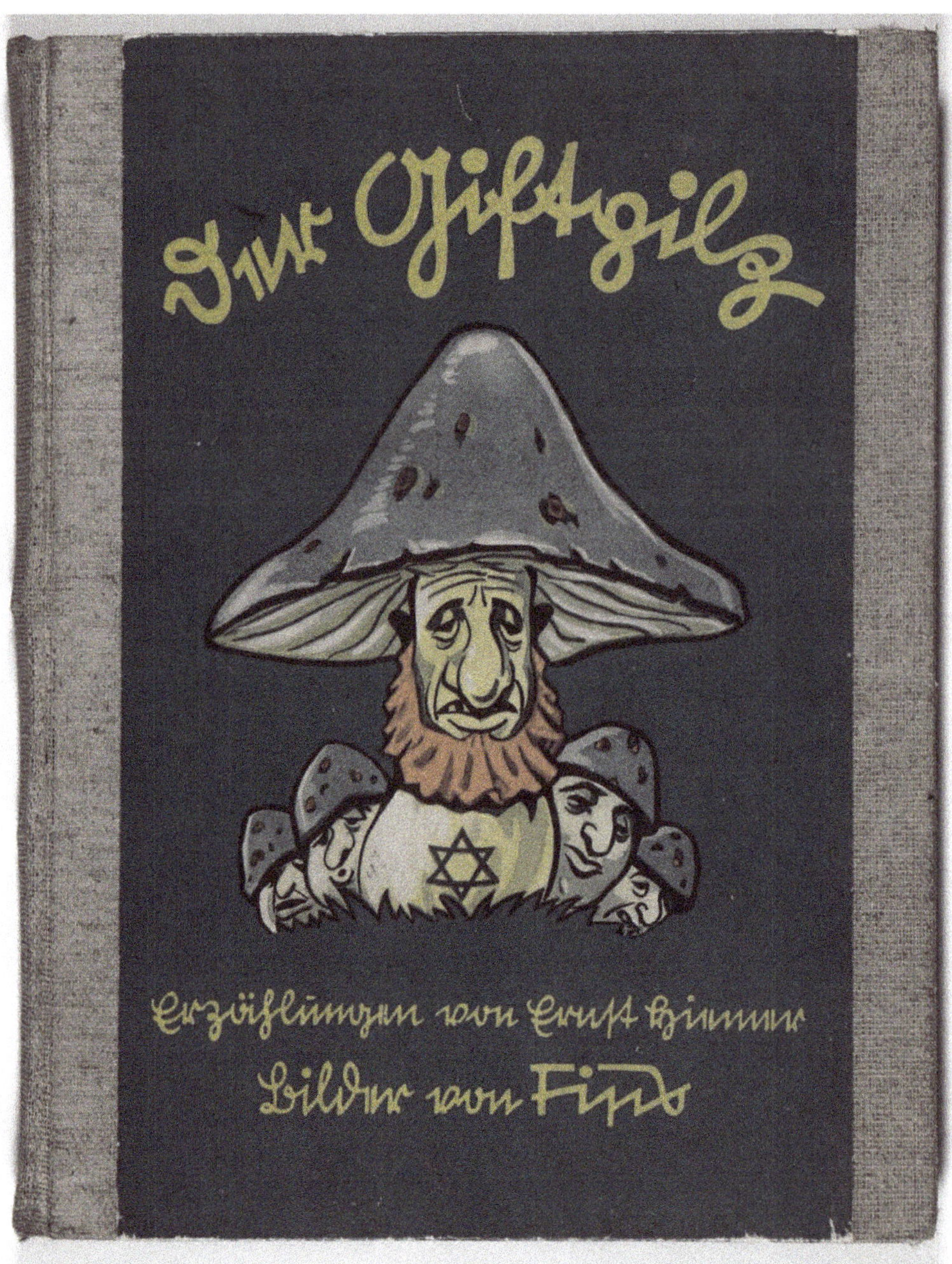

A child's storybook that Irma Grese and her classmates probably read in class; the publication was widespread. The anti-Semitic *Der Giftpilz* ("The Poison Mushroom"), written by Ernst Hiemer with illustrations by Philipp Rupprecht was popular. This blatantly discriminatory children's book was published by anti-Semitic publisher Julius Streicher in 1938.

The book contained short stories with color artwork. Jews were depicted as black – clothed and unattractive, preying on the young and beautiful blonde, blue-eyed children as they go about their innocent day. The Jewish characters lured children, counted money they gained through deception, and plotted against the innocent.

At the end of the war, American soldiers destroyed as many of these books as possible; a few still exist and fetch a hefty price by collectors. (Circa 1938, Source unknown, Public Domain.)

CHAPTER 6
Teen Years

In 1936, when Grese was 13 years old, Berta discovered Alfred was an adulterer; his unfaithfulness to the marriage is said to be the cause of Berta committing suicide. Some historians have her downing a glass of hydrochloric acid. This is questionable.

Science author Brian Clegg explains, “It’s very unlikely that concentrated hydrochloric acid (it would probably have been called muriatic acid in 1936) would have been available for domestic use.” Clegg, who is an award-winning British science author, explains that a farmer in a 1936 rural village would not have access to a stronger, pure form, which would have been highly caustic and only available “from a chemical supplies company.” Should the hydrochloric acid truly been used for cleaning, “it would have been in a diluted form, as it still is in some cleaning products (e.g. some toilet cleaners), typically 10-15% concentration.” Berta would have used water to dilute this product, which would have been dangerous. She most likely purchased muriatic acid “over the counter as a cleaning product for domestic use” and pre-mixed in a glass bottle. [55]

An American label of muriatic acid from the same period features the word POISON under the product name with skull and crossbones and an antidote.

Perhaps it was attention – seeking behavior; Berta may have believed it was harmless. She would have learned differently on the first sip. This chemical would not reach the throat due to the pain of the lips and tongue.

Dr. Richard Adler holds a PhD in Organic Chemistry and is a Doctor of Internal Medicine. He explains muriatic acid would have been a common household item in 1936, saying, “I’m sure it was readily available. (People) used caustic chemicals around the house for all kinds of things” without understanding the toxicity. An example, “to keep storm windows from frosting up, they laid sulfuric acid around the windowpanes.” Dr. Adler explains Berta Grese must have been in an emotionally difficult situation; “just starting to drink (hydrochloric acid) would sting your eyes” and cause much physical pain before ingesting it. In his expert opinion, Dr. Adler finds it difficult to believe Berta was not aware of its toxicity. [56]

The chemical cleaned the surfaces of the home, but ingested, Berta’s mouth and throat would burn along with severe chest pains. She would be drooling and vomiting blood, gasping for air.

Reportedly, Berta Grese drank the chemical after forming a careful plan.

Berta first ordered the children to clean the house, scrubbing the floors, dusting, and washing thoroughly. She then directed them to run to the local pub and fetch their father. The family would come home to find Berta on the bed.

Her husband and children would see her body going into shock as Berta’s blood pressure plummeted and sweat poured out of her body. It would have been a terrible, painful experience for the family.

---

[55] Interview with Brian Clegg, March 3-6, 2024

[56] Interview, Dr. Richard Adler, March 9, 2024

Berta Grese was rushed to the hospital but did not survive. She is buried in the tiny cemetery where the wealthy Seibt family mausoleum is located. [57] Berta's stone inscription:

> You left your loved ones too soon, who are standing here at the grave and crying. [58]

The general explanation given for her suicide is Alfred's affair with the local pub owner's daughter, a widow. [59] It was also local gossip that Berta was unstable: she was not a good provider, and she was a troubled soul. Berta's death left Alfred to care for his brood. He was reportedly ambivalent to his wife's death. He married the pub owner's daughter in 1939, moving her into the Grese home. This widow brought with her four children. Eventually she and Alfred would have a daughter together. Again, accounts vary as to the treatment of her stepchildren and Irma's reception to her stepmother.

Generally, Irma Grese's negative adult behavior is linked to her mother's suicide; although noted author and Professor of Psychology Ervin Staub notates several interesting studies about German children. Results include:

- Reluctance to deviate from adult standards under peer influence.
- Fewer German infants (than other nationalities) securely attach to their mothers.
- German mothers allow less autonomy to their children.
- German children are more likely to trust authorities.
- German children advocate strong leadership.
- From the seventieth to the twentieth century, children were considered evil, and their willful personalities should be "broken down."
- Obedience to parents (or higher authority figure) has high value and is to be gained by any means necessary.
- Individuals owed complete alliance to the state, a training instilled in children.
- Bureaucratization and militarization contribute to respect for authority. It would become a learned behavior by children in the household. [60]

In a traditional German household, Irma Grese would have understood she was to be obedient to authority (particularly a strong leader). Her personality and freedom were restricted. Thus, her mother's suicide may not have played as large a role in her future behavior as previously believed.

---

[57] Berta's gravestone no longer exists. An expert on Irma Grese explains, "I was on the cemetery in Wrechen, but I have not seen any grave with this name. Possibly it was destroyed." (Interview via email of Joanna Czopowitcz, https://ssaufseherin.blogspot.com. July 2, 2024)

[58] Wieble (1987), translated from German

[59] If this was the same pub where he played Skat, it most likely caused quite the scandal in a small, Catholic German town.

[60] Staub, E. (1989) pp. 108-11.

Irma Grese either followed the rules and expectations without question or chafed for the need of individuality and self-expression. An archetypal German household during the time of her formidable years would have quashed the latter. While this is not the sole factor in becoming an adamant supporter of the Nazi party, it would certainly play a role in her life.

Following this period in Irma Grese's life, biographer Brown's interview notes from an anonymous person adds: "it was common knowledge in the village that (Irma Grese) begin to withdraw more into herself; she would stand on a hill and whistle like some boy, always kept whistling, and didn't [do] much as far as the other children were concerned, and didn't care for them at all." [61]

One journalist has Grese joining the *Bund Deutscher Mädel* (BDM) proper; "she was a bossy little girl, liking her tunic and her medal and her little authority." She preyed on the "lazy and absent – minded little girls." This is where, according to an interview with her family, Irma Grese "struck" someone, a fellow BDM member. "She was applauded for the deed." [62]

As a member of the BDM, Irma Grese would have thumbed open the pages of the Youth Leadership pamphlet to read what was expected of her as the *Jungmaedel*, "The *Jungmaedel* Service." The organization focused on two dynamics: the government expected her to be a team member and completely loyal to the party. "You, too, belong to our leader" the instructions read. "Aside from your duties at home and in school, service in the *Jungmaedel* now also asks you to do your part voluntarily and joyfully." BDM events demanded a girl do her best. The *Jungmaedel* warned Irma Grese of being "too proud and too open to lie to your comrades or suck up to your leaders!" [63]

Criminologist Dr. Lee Mellor is a noted author and expert on sexual psychopathy and assists in cases as a professional consultant. Based on decades of analysis, Dr. Mellor states "sexual sadism (begins) in early puberty, with general sadism being a precursor in childhood." He likens Grese to serial killer Rose West (b. November 29, 1953), who assisted her husband Fred West with the torture, sexual assault, and murder of at least ten young females between 1973 and 1987. Based on Grese's behavior later in life, Dr. Mellor believes Irma Grese was, like West, "a girl whose self-esteem was utterly crushed through social exclusion during her childhood and teenage years. I think it is likely (Grese) was sexually abused. This led her to develop a pathological need for her to assert power over those weaker than her in order to feel in control of her own mind/emotions, thereby enabling her sexually." [64] Dr. Mellor believes Irma Grese had demons resting in her psyche that would explode when given the opportunity: the right environment, and victims who could not fight. These demons were born in her childhood.

And then World War II was launched in September 1939. It was called "the bloodiest war in history." Not one family remained unaffected, including the Grese family.

As discussed, there is no exact date and records are nonexistent of when Irma Grese did join the *Bund Deutscher Mädel*, (BDM), but membership for all girls would eventually become mandatory; she joined at some time. Grese took the organization with staunch,

---

[61] Brown, D. P. p.17
[62] Holt, P. (16 November 1945). P.2
[63] "The *Jungmaedel* Service." Cited in Sandon, C. A. https://bdmhistory.com
[64] Interviews with Dr. Mellor, August 19 – 24, 2023

serious devotion. "She was quite proud of (joining) because the organization was only open to 'genuine' Aryans, and she became very enthusiastic about the 'mission' of the Nazis and the 'dangers' of race 'pollution.'" [65] She became so overzealous that her grades, never very high, began to slip.

By now, Adolph Hitler would be ingrained in all of Germany's minds and hearts-for better or worse. A young Irma Grese took it for better, and greeted others with zest, "Heil Hitler!" She had become enthralled with the Nazi party, had been inundated with the salute that inflicted all:

> Every child says "Heil Hitler!" from 50 to 150 times a day, immeasurably more often than the old neutral greetings. The formula is required by law; if you meet a friend on the way to school, you say it; study periods are open and closed with "Heil Hitler!" "Heil Hitler!" says the postman, the streetcar conductor, the girl who sells your notebooks in the stationary store, and if your parents first words when you come home to lunch are not "Heil Hitler!" they have been guilty of a punishable offense, and can be denounced. [66]

Most biographers have Irma Grese saying "Heil Hitler!" with much pride and gusto by this time in her life.

This is what is known of Irma Grese's early childhood. The hyena was within, pacing to get out.

[65] Hellinger

[66] Mann, p. 21

A Young Hyena's BDM

Sources vary on Irma Grese's membership into the BDM (*Bund Deutscher Mädel*) What is known, according to her sister Helena, is that the Grese girls begged their father to allow them to join. BDM was akin to today's Girl Scouts of America but with a much darker agenda.

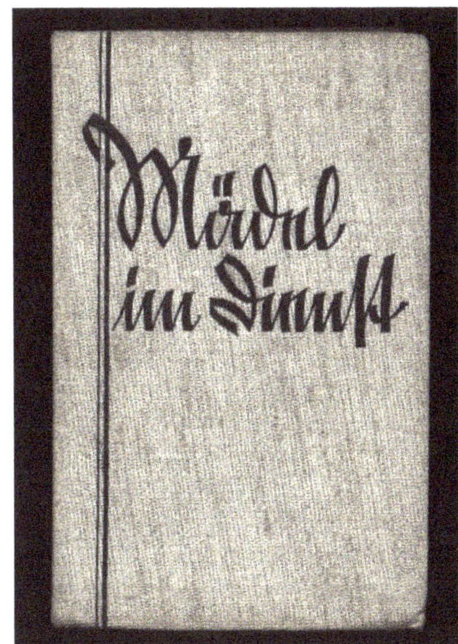

The BDM Handbook *Mädel im Dienst* (Girl on Duty) demanded a girl's alliance with Hitler and National Socialism, to serve their country sincerely, and to happily do their duty as young girls and women for Germany. (Circa: unknown. BDM History website authored by Chris Crawford and Stephan Hansen, Copyright (c) 2008 – 2015 Cynthia A. Sandor/BDMhistory.com. Used with permission.)

A 1943 postage stamp promoting the BDM. "Duty of Youth Day" a "holiday was something of a rite of passage, on which new members were often admitted to the Nazi Party." [67] The act of mailing a letter or even adding a stamp was engrossed in rhetoric. (Circa: 1943. Source: unknown. Public Domain.)

[67] Bytwerk, R. (n.d.)

The BDM Gear. When Irma Grese joined BDM, the family was expected to purchase the gear and clothing. If a family could not afford to purchase the clothing the shirts and blouses could be handmade; still, there was strict criteria. The brown jacket is a *Kletterjacke*, or "climbing jacket." (Circa unknown. BDM History website authored by Chris Crawford and Stephan Hansen, Copyright (c) 2008 – 2015 Cynthia A. Sandor/BDMhistory.com. Used with permission.)

A group of unidentified girls pose proudly in their BDM summer uniforms. (Circa unknown. BDM History website authored by Chris Crawford and Stephan Hansen, Copyright (c) 2008 – 2015 Cynthia A. Sandor/BDMhistory.com. Used with permission.)

Left: The BDM winter uniform. "Wearing your uniform outside of special occasions was originally not allowed, but it soon became commonplace … to wear their uniforms to school. Some teachers who were party members often preferred girls who were active in the BDM over their other students and gave them better grades, while they admonished girls who weren't members or were not very active in their service." [68] (Circa unknown. BDM History website authored by Chris Crawford and Stephan Hansen, Copyright (c) 2008 – 2015 Cynthia A. Sandor/BDMhistory.com. Used with permission.)

[68] BDMHistory.com

Examples of propaganda posters used to entice women and little girls to join the BDM. Irma Grese was no doubt aware of these posters appearing across Germany and German – occupied territories. The girl in the left poster is wearing one of the BDM "sporting outfits." The blonde girl in the second poster is clad in her summer uniform, with the tie and knot given to her upon membership. Irma Grese most likely saw herself as the little blonde girl: a perfect Aryan specimen. (Circa unknown. BDM History website authored by Chris Crawford and Stephan Hansen, Copyright (c) 2008 – 2015 Cynthia A. Sandor/BDMhistory.com. Used with permission.)

This poster was utilized for the annual Nazi Nuremberg Rally which began in 1923. Participation would eventually reach half a million people and usually occurred near the Autumn Equinox. The fictional girl is a ideal member of the *Bund Deutscher Mädel*. (BDM, "Band of German Maidens.") By 1933, *Bund Deutscher Mädel* boasted a mass following, in part because there were no other organizations for young girls, and because it was compulsory. BDM separated members by age: Girls10 -14 years old were in the Young Girl's League (*Jungmädelbund*). Girls 14 - 18 the *Bund Deutscher Mädel* (BDM) proper. Faith and Beauty (*Glaube und Schönheit*), for 17 – 21 years of age, was created when Irma Grese was five years old. (Circa 1933. Artist unknown. Public domain)

CHAPTER 7
Into the World

Grese dropped out of school around 1938 at about 14-15 years of age. There is no documented intention. Perhaps it was treatment at school and at home: persecution from other students, failure to pass classes, constant inferior grades, and a strict, even abusive, father. It may have been the norm; only eight years of education was compulsory. [69] Children were needed in the household or on the farm more so than in the school room.

Helene Grese, Irma's sister, would testify years later how Irma worked from six to twelve months "on the farm of a peasant." [70] Grese kept this job from spring to winter in 1938. Coming from a village of farmers, Irma must have been drawn to what she knew. She had little education and limited experience in employment.

Next, Grese accepted employment in a shop in Lychen (*Loo-shun*), a town in the Uckermark district, Brandenburg. She reportedly sold dairy products. This clerk job lasted another six months.

The same year Irma Grese was leaving formal education behind, Heinrich Himmler was masterminding a Corp of what would be called *Aufseherinnen, (Auf-seh-nen)* a female auxiliary group hired to "discharge men for tasks not directly related to combat." [71] Himmler looked to the Finnish women's group *Lottas-Svärd* as a model organization for *Aufseherinnen*. Himmler also foresaw a better and more productive German militia by creating a female auxiliary.

Lotta- Svärd had been in operation for about five years when Irma Grese was born. Initially associated with the White Guard [72] in the Finnish Civil War of 1918, *Lotta- Svärd* would become a volunteer organization that grew to become the "largest volunteer auxiliary organization in the world," with 60,000 members in 1930 and 242,000 in 1941, roughly six percent of Finland's population. [73] Initially, only Christian Finnish women were allowed to be members of *Lotta- Svärd* if they had two references from reliable sources, and then passing rigorous training. As the war lagged these criteria were abandoned. Women had to fill in for any man who was needed on the Finnish Civil War frontline. *Lotta- Svärd* were unarmed auxiliary who worked on the front lines, auxiliary posts (including air raid warning bunkers) and hospitals, and like *Aufseherinnen* filled in for men at home as the war lagged on.

The *Aufseherinnen* uniform style was borrowed from the *Lotta- Svärd:* a long-sleeved, knee length grey dress buttoned to the throat with black buttons over a long-sleeved white blouse featuring arrow collars. Another uniform consisted of a short-skirted, sleeveless smock that buttoned over one shoulder. Both featured the blue Swastika-like symbol, completed with a hat featuring flaps to unbutton for inclement weather and safety. Little dolls would soon be available in these uniforms for play and display.

One source has Irma Grese signing up for the Reich Labor Force (*Reichsarbeitsdienst;* RAD) at this time, which may have sent her to the "peasant's

[69] Mailänder (2015). P.3
[70] The Belsen Trial, Helene Grese testimony, October 16, 1945
[71] Cline, S. (2014). P.2.
[72] An anti-socialist voluntary militia that fought the socialist Red Guard in the Finnish Civil War.
[73] Nevala-Nurmi, S., & Nevala, S.-L. (2006). P.3.

farm"and then to the clerk job in Lychen. RAD was a state labor source that had been formed in 1934 to provide labor for agricultural work and civic organizations; it provided jobs for the unemployed (unemployment being a serious problem in Germany after WWI). RAD was a paramilitary organization, ensuring that while their independent male and female troops practiced drills, worked fields, built roads, and raised buildings, they understood the importance of National Socialism. Grese's work on the farm may have been part of the *HJ-Landjahr*, a program that sent youth to work in the countryside. *HJ-Landjahr* was split into a boy's division and a girl's division. The largest majority were males.

Another resource notes "before her 17th birthday, (Grese) moved to the SS Female Helpers' training base, which was located near Ravensbrück, the all-female concentration camp." [74] Ravensbrück was near her birthplace. Feasibly Irma Grese did join the BDM, enter the Reich Labor Force, complete her *HJ-Landjahr,* and move into the base. It would have been the best choice for a full-fledged female in becoming as close to a Nazi as possible. She continued to be a staunch supporter of Hitler; her father, the head of household, emotionally remained anti-Nazi. Irma would have been fully aware of this. She also would have recognized Alfred as block leader. It is interesting that she never reported him, particularly after what would occur between them in the future, for he could have been arrested and taken to jail.

As a reverent Nazi party supporter, Irma Grese most likely attended Nazi Party Rallies. Her entry fee and Nazi party dues paid for these events. The biggest Rallies were held annually in Nuremberg 1933 – 1938 and lasted up to a week. The Party Rally Department of the City of Nuremberg was the event planning committee. There would be about 450 miles between Grese's hometown area and Nuremburg, but if she was unable to travel to Nuremburg there were smaller rallies she could attend. Rallies in Nuremburg gathered thousands of people together; the smaller rallies were almost as popular. Both featured shows of support for the party, support of WWII, and the sharing of information and excitement. The Hitler youth groups would march, speeches were made, and propaganda would be spread to further the cause. Irma Grese would have strolled under the red, black, and white flags. She would have eyed the smart uniforms of the SS men, listened to the presentations about Germany's golden future, controlling Jews and other undesirables, and perhaps partaking in dancing and local food. She may have marched with a female organization; all the groups were represented: the SS, the SA, the Wehrmacht, and the Hitler Youth Groups. She would have met new people; attendees would travel cross-country for rallies. There were parades and presentations. It is easy to picture the lovely blonde girl, eyes wide at the size and depth of the event in a real city, slowly walking through the crowd. The number of people in her hometown could have fit in a larger local pub or restaurant. It must have been dizzying, intimidating, and electrifying to see all these people, and all of them toasting her beloved Germany and the National Socialists. To watch a muster of females who all fit together as they marched proudly and professionally. To a girl seeking answers it all would have been so enticing.

The Reich had already opened "Labor Exchanges" in all occupied towns to ensure every able-bodied German was doing their best for the country. As proof of employment, Irma Grese would have been carrying a "Workbook" (Labor Pass) which listed her employers. By 1938, even housewives were required to carry Labor Passes. Irma Grese

[74] Kater, (2006), p. 70

dreamed of having "nurse" listed in her Labor Pass. To establish her career, she found employment in 1939 at Hohenluchen [75] SS Sanitorium for German soldiers, hoping to be offered a nursing apprenticeship. The sanitorium was just north of Berlin, about twenty miles from her birthplace, and treated injured SS men. Under the Nazi regime it became a place of much more sinister doing.

Initially Hohenluchen was a sanatorium for tuberculosis (TB) patients, built by the Red Cross in 1904 for those suffering from "consumption" as TB was labeled. At this stage the cause of tuberculosis was unknown, and the hospital was in a humid area, the worse place for TB patients. When the Nazis took over Hohenluchen the question of TB patients convalescing in this humidity was questioned by experts, but ignored.

SS - *Gruppenführer* Doctor Karl Gebhardt had become Medical Superintendent in 1935; he created Germany's first sports medical clinic here, a sports program for the disabled, and was Berlin's first professor of sport's medicine. Gebhardt was also an old pal of Himmler, having known him in childhood, and had begun following Hitler from the beginning. Hohenluchen sported a swimming pool and state-of-the-art facilities used to train 1936 Olympians. Irma Grese spent two years working at Hohenluchen. She was in awe of Doctor Karl Gebhardt. He was a Nazi "superstar;" and a young, impressionable girl who was in awe of the organization would have been excited to be in the company of such a man. She no doubt was aware of Heinrich Himmler, Adolph Hitler, and other Nazi officials frequently visiting the sanitorium, sometimes hosting high-ranking officials from other countries. It is unknown if Grese ever spoke to these notable men, or crossed paths. There is a rumor that Hitler used the swimming pool to take relaxing laps.

If Grese did see or speak to her *Furor*, it would have been the only time she encountered the worshipped Hitler. Adolph Hitler never visited the concentration camps. While he was certainly aware of camp activities, he stayed away from the murders, tortures, and brutal existence.

Karl Gebhardt conducted experiments to treat war wounds. Ravensbrück prisoners would eventually provide live specimens for experiments on bone graft, nerves, sulfa drugs, and gangrene; the information could be used to assist and save Nazi soldiers. If one of the "specimens" should die or an experiment went wrong, there were plenty more from where than one came. There are no records of Grese's work at Hohenluchen but it's probable Grese "was exposed to vivisection performed on prisoners from Ravensbrück." [76] Thus, she observed and understood the nature of Ravensbrück and its treatment of prisoners prior to being hired.

By 1940, the concentration camp jobs were not being filled fast enough to meet desired prisoner – to – guard ratios. For example, Birkenau was built for 20,000 but would swell to 30,000 prisoners; its "female guard staff never exceeded 71." [77] So, the guard jobs were filled via Labor Exchange "… the Nazis had to use compulsory orders to fill the vacancies." [78]

At about the age of sixteen, Irma Grese reportedly packed her belongings and moved into the SS female helper's training base. It was near home and near Ravensbrück.

[75] Also spelled *Hohenlychen*
[76] Adele-Marie (2019) p.110
[77] Auschwitz 1940-1945, 172-175. Cited in Cline, p. 52
[78] Brown, cited in Lewis, I (2018). P.43

This may have been in anticipation of working at Ravensbrück; it may have been because she was so dedicated to the cause. Or it was a financial decision.

Sometime around 1940, Heinrich Himmler was photographed as he inspected Ravensbrück. A photograph reveals the female guard staff standing at attention in their caps, long jackets and skirts, stiff white arrow collared blouses outside of the jackets. Himmler, in long coat, hat, and holding his gloves, approaches, eying the group. Some of the women eye him; some of them stare forward. Snow dusts the ground and the tiled rooftops. Irma Grese had missed this inspection; but, as the architect of the camps and commander of the camp system, Heinrich Himmler would soon constantly loom over her life.

While Himmler visited the camps and Irma Grese was still dreaming of becoming a nurse, a new program began for female guards that would figure largely into Irma Grese's future. A number of *Aufseherinnen* were sent to Berlin to be trained in guard dog handling and training. The dogs were used to guard and to assist in prisoner discipline. Guards who graduated from this program became *Hundeführerins*, or dog handlers. Once they returned to their workstations in the camps *Hundeführerins* would be responsible for their dog's upkeep. The dogs were usually working outside of the camp perimeter on outside work details. These dogs, usually German shepherds, were highly trained. The dogs would prove lethal.

Opposite page: Uniform of an SS-Aufseherin Ravensbrück dog-handler Gertrud Rabestein (1903-1974). Rabestein, whose name tag is sewn in the skirt, was a notoriously cruel *Aufseherin*. Rabestein was a dog handler from 1939 to 1942, at Ravensbrück, the year Grese was hired. This is a winter uniform as it is composed of wool. The back of the tunic appears altered to fit, just as Irma Grese would have her tunic altered to fit her body. Grese also had her skirt altered to fit her attractively. It is highly probable Grese also had her name sewn into her uniforms to keep them separated in a wash. The sewing was done by prisoner labor, and Irma Grese demanded perfection. (Circa 1940. Location: unknown. Photography of card by Alexander Historical Auctions. Courtesy Alexander Historical Auctions. Used with permission.)

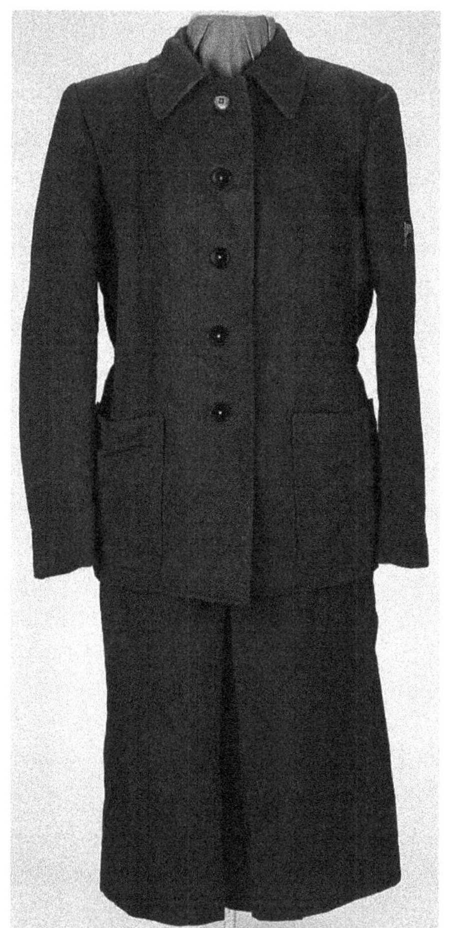

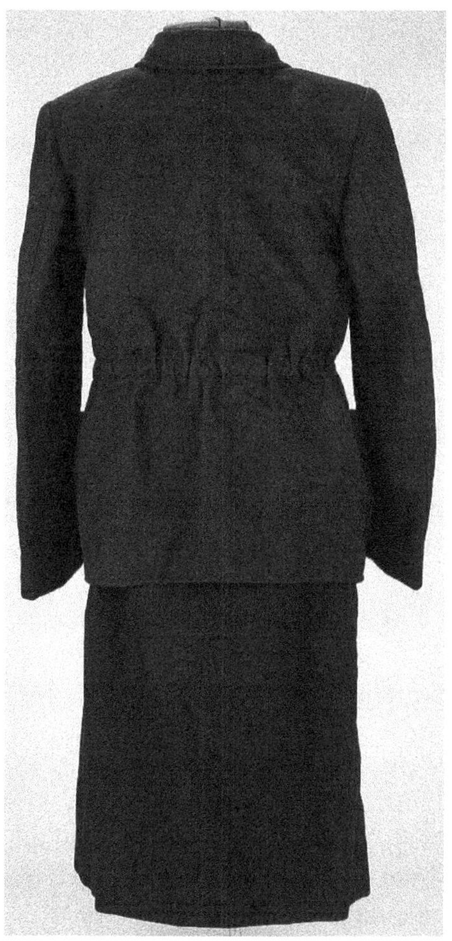

SS-Aufseherin
Gertrud Rabestein
K.L. Ravensbrück

Grese was dreaming of an apprenticeship that would assist her in getting into nursing school, but low grades, lack of education, or the government kept her from obtaining that apprenticeship at Hohenluchen. Regardless, her nursing career was not destined to move forward. "According to her own statements, she worked (at Hohenluchen) as an auxiliary nurse," one author explains, "according to the sanatorium's personnel book, however, she was employed there as a chambermaid." [79]

Grese had heard positive things from the government about working in the concentration camps, she would later tell a prisoner. With limited skills, little education, and - like many young people growing up in wartime, the desire for more in life – employment in the SS camps appeared easy and financially appealing.

Most likely, Grese perused the public job description:

> You only have to watch over prisoners, consequently, applicants, who should be between the ages of 21 and 45, don't need professional training [sic]. The salary of hired *Aufseherinnen*, who become employees of the Reich, is determined by (schedule) TOA IX and a step raise will be given after a three-month probationary period. Community food allotment as well as a "well-furnished official residence" and service clothes (fabric and fatigue uniforms) are assured. [80]

There are at least two theories on how Irma Grese became a trainee at Ravensbrück.

One theory is that Grese was referred to Ravensbrück by the Labor Office. She believed it was a step towards a nursing career. During her 1945 testimony at the Belsen trial Irma Grese testified the Labor Exchange would not allow her to continue training at Hohenluchen. Grese would testify:

> "In July 1942, I again tried to become a nurse, but the Labor Exchange sent me to Ravensbrück Concentration Camp, although I protested against it. I stayed there until March 1943, when I went to Birkenau Camp in Auschwitz. I remained in Auschwitz until January 1945." [81]

Several newspaper reporters place Irma Grese at home in October 1940, celebrating birthday number seventeen, "her last birthday to spend at home," singing, dancing, and enjoying a huge meal. [82] This is when Irma told her family she had been "discharged from her job as a probationer nurse (nobody seems to know why) and she had been drafted under Nazi labor laws to be a trainee concentration camp guard … in Auschwitz." [83]

Another theory is that, in 1941, Grese voluntarily interviewed for a position in the SS female concentration camp service with a "recommendation from her supervisor" at Hohenluchen. [84] SS - *Gruppenführer* Doctor Karl Gebhardt suggested Grese apply for a

---

[79] Cited in Muller, J. M. (2024). P. 9

[80] From *"Das FrauenkonzentrationLager Ravensbrück"* cited in Adele-Marie, Appendix I

[81] Kater, p. 70.

[82] Holt, P. (18 November, 1945). P.4

[83] Holt, P. (16 November 1945), unknown page

[84] Brown, D. P. (1996), p. 25

position with the Nazi concentration camp, Ravensbrück. [85] He would put in a good word for her. So, some time before March 1941, a seventeen - year - old Grese voluntarily left Hohenluchen to apply. [86]

There were three groups of female employment in the concentration camps. The largest group was the female supervisors who oversaw the female prisoners. The radio and telephone operators and the office employees created the second group. Grese set her cap for the third group: the nursing staff.

Regardless of how she landed in the application office, whoever interviewed Grese advised her to return when she was 18.

It might have been The Labor Exchange that assigned Grese work as a machinist at a Furstenberg dairy farm [87] from March 1941 to June 1942. She made a salary of 40 to 60 marks per month. [88]

She did not return to Ravensbrück immediately upon turning 18. Grese again attempted to obtain an apprenticeship at Hohenluchen for the last time; again, she was unsuccessful. Irma Grese was never going to become a nurse.

Heinrich Himmler, in his creation of the *SS - Helferinnekorps* (the voluntary auxiliary service), believed females could not be Nazis, but they could be supporters. Thus, the *SS – Helferinnekorps* were considered members of the *Waffen -SS,* [89] paid by the SS and would have a uniform with the SS runes (lightning bolts). They were to meet the same standards but would never be commanders of an entire camp. They could carry weapons but there would be strict criteria. There would, eventually, be two ways to be employed in the camps. One would be a "volunteer": the *SS – Helferinnekorps*. The other by compulsory orders by the Labor Exchange – a group classified as *SS – Kriegshelferinnen* ("war auxiliaries").

Being voluntary, the *SS – Helferinnekorps* held more influence than *SS - Kriegshelferinnen*. An eighteen-year-old Grese would return to volunteer for employment at Ravensbrück as part of the *SS – Helferinnekorps*.

By the time Irma Grese was accepted into training, every woman between 17 – 50 years of age was legally bound to register with the Labor Exchange to work as the war raged and took more men – unless the woman was pregnant or was mother to two or more children (under age 14). "By 1943 the majority of women working in the various concentration camps were conscripts, which means that they did not willingly choose a job that would put them in the position of becoming a perpetrator." [90]

Finally, at the age of 18, on June 1, 1942, Irma Grese was hired. Either she was still interested in nursing, or her goal was to become one of some 3,500 female guards at a concentration camp. Regardless of motive, *SS – Helferinnekorp* Irma Grese was hired. She was on her way to becoming a proud *Aufseherinen*. It would mean death and destruction for so many.

---

[85] Some accounts state a nurse suggested Grese apply at Ravensbrück. Others have Grese losing her job at the hospital and not quitting by choice.

[86] Another source reports Grese was fired from the hospital, but gives no citations to this event except that there was an interview with Grese's family. This may be where this information originated. It is possible Grese told her family she was "let go." Grese changed stories often with her family, and did not always tell the truth.

[87] According to Helene Grese's testimony at The Belsen Trial, October 16, 1945, Irma worked at a Furstenberg small shop to assist in a "butter shop, a small dairy." (p. 19)

[88] Irma Grese, testimony, The Belsen Trial, October 16, 1945

[89] *Waffen-SS* ("armed") was the combat branch of the SS, considered far more fanatical and ruthless.

[90] Lewis, I. (2018) p.43

Job announcement for camp "supervisors"

These two pages: This letter from the Ravensbrück commandant's office was sent to job agencies and newspapers. It was used to advertise jobs in the concentration camps. Irma Grese would have had to complete "the personnel questionnaire attached to the appendix." (Circa: unknown. No date. Location: originally Ravensbrück. Credit: courtesy Magdalena Chomitkowska. Public domain.)

Translation:

Copy
Ravensbrück Concentration Camp
Ravensbrück, den.......
Commander's Office
I/ AZ.: 260/ - Ha.-
Re: Application as a supervisor
Reference:
Appendix:
On the basis of your application for employment as a supervisor, you will be briefly informed of the task you are to be entrusted with here.
In the Ravensbrück concentration camp, women are imprisoned who have committed some kind of violations against the Volksgemeinschaft and now have to be isolated in order to prevent further damage. These women are to be supervised during their work assignments inside and outside the camp. So they do not need to have any professional knowledge for this work, since it is only a matter of guarding the prisoners.
The female overseers are Reich employees and are paid according to the TO.A. (Collective Bargaining Regulations for Employees). You will receive Group IX as an entry level and Group VIII after a probationary service period of 3 months. For example, a single supervisor at the age of 25 receives a gross salary of 185.68 RM and, after deduction of social security contributions, taxes, as well as other statutory contributions and costs of food and accommodation, a salary of 105.10 RM per month. They also receive communal catering (troop catering) in the camp [sic], which is charged at 1.20 RM per day. Service clothing, such as cloth and drill uniforms as well as some underwear will be provided free of charge. Houses with service apartments are available for accommodation, which are well furnished.
If you are suitable and have the appropriate activity, there is the possibility of being deployed as a camp leader in one of the subcamps of the Ravensbrück concentration camp and the possibility of promotion up to salary group VI.
Their activity is recognized as a war effort. They also belong to the entourage of the Waffen-SS. The prerequisite for employment is therefore that you are unpunished and physically healthy. You are therefore asked to submit the following documents first:
Police clearance certificate,
curriculum vitae,
photograph,
medical health certificate,
referral from the responsible employment office.
You want to return the personnel questionnaire attached to the appendix and fill it out carefully. You will then receive [illegible] notification. However, the final dismissal depends in any case on the examination findings of the local site doctor. Employment can take place on the next 1st or 15th if the conditions of employment are met.

Abschrift!

Konzentrationslager Ravensbrück
Kommandantur
I/ Az.: 260/ - Ha. -

Ravensbrück, den ....

Betr.: Bewerbung als Aufseherin.
Bezug:
Anlg.:

Auf Grund Ihrer Bewerbung um Einstellung als Aufseherin wird Ihnen kurz mitgeteilt, mit welcher Aufgabe Sie hier betraut werden sollen.

Im Konz.-Lager Ravensbrück sitzen Frauen ein, die irgendwelche Verstöße gegen die Volksgemeinschaft begangen haben und nun, um weiteren Schaden zu verhindern, isoliert werden müssen. Diese Frauen sind bei ihrem Arbeitseinsatz innerhalb und außerhalb des Lagers zu beaufsichtigen. Sie brauchen für diese Arbeit also keine beruflichen Kenntnisse zu besitzen, da es sich ja lediglich um die Bewachung der Häftlinge handelt.

(Margin: …er: … – 45 Jahre)

Die Aufseherinnen sind Reichsangestellte und werden nach der TO.A. (Tarifordnung für Angestellte) besoldet. Als Eingangsstufe erhalten Sie Gruppe IX und nach einer Probedienstzeit von 3 Monaten Gruppe VIII. Eine ledige Aufseherin im Alter von 25 Jahren erhält z.B. brutto 135,68 RM und nach Abzug der Sozialversicherungsbeiträge Steuern, sowie sonstiger gesetzlicher Abgaben und Kosten der Verpflegung und Wohnung monatlich 105,10 RM Gehalt. Sie erhalten ferner im Lager im Lager Gemeinschaftsverpflegung (Truppenverpflegung) die mit täglich 1,20 RM berechnet wird. Dienstbekleidung, wie Tuch- u.Drillichuniform sowie teilweise Unterwäsche wird Ihnen kostenlos gestellt. Zur Unterbringung stehen hier Häuser mit Dienstwohnungen zur Verfügung, die gut eingerichtet sind.
Bei entsprechender Eignung und Tätigkeit besteht die Möglichkeit, als Lagerführerin in einem der Außenlager des KL Ravensbrück eingesetzt zu werden und Aufrückungsmöglichkeit bis Gehaltsgruppe VI.

Ihre Tätigkeit wird als Kriegseinsatz anerkannt. Sie gehören auch zum Gefolge der Waffen-SS. Voraussetzung für die Einstellung ist daher, daß Sie unbestraft und körperlich gesund sind. Sie werden daher gebeten, nachstehende Unterlagen zunächst einzureichen:

Polizeiliches Führungszeugnis,
Lebenslauf,
Lichtbild,
Ärztliches Gesundheitszeugnis,
Zuweisung des zuständigen Arbeitsamtes.

Den in der Anlage beigefügten Personalfragebogen wollen Sie sorgfältig ausgefüllt zurückreichen. Sie erhalten dann weiteren Bescheid. Die endgültige Einstellung hängt allerdings in jedem Falle von dem Untersuchungsbefund des hiesigen Standortarztes ab. Einstellung kann bei Vorliegen der Einstellungsbedingungen zum nächsten 1. oder 15. erfolgen.

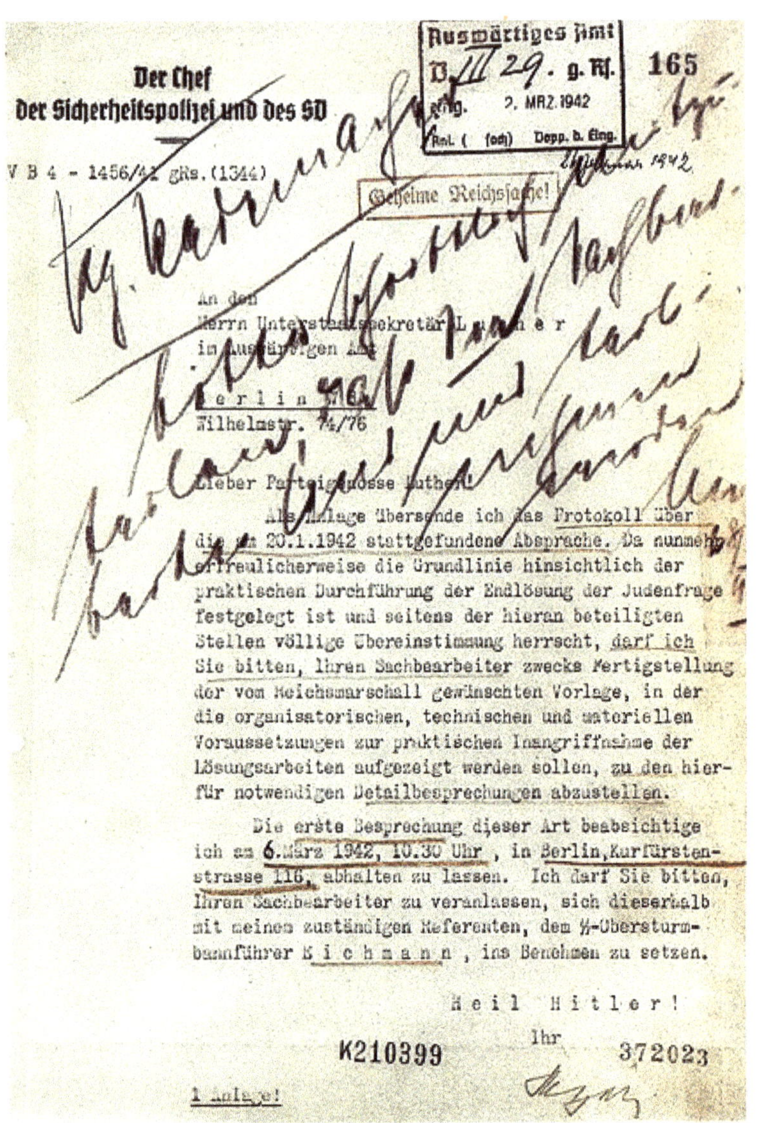

Ausmärtiges Amt
D III 29. g. Rs. 165
Eing. 2. MRZ 1942

Der Chef
der Sicherheitspolizei und des SD

V B 4 - 1456/42 gRs.(1344)

Geheime Reichssache!

An den
Herrn Unterstaatssekretär L u t h e r
im Auswärtigen Amt

B e r l i n W 8
Wilhelmstr. 74/76

Lieber Parteigenosse Luther!

Als Anlage übersende ich das Protokoll über die am 20.1.1942 stattgefundene Absprache. Da nunmehr erfreulicherweise die Grundlinie hinsichtlich der praktischen Durchführung der Endlösung der Judenfrage festgelegt ist und seitens der hieran beteiligten Stellen völlige Übereinstimmung herrscht, darf ich Sie bitten, Ihren Sachbearbeiter zwecks Fertigstellung der vom Reichsmarschall gewünschten Vorlage, in der die organisatorischen, technischen und materiellen Voraussetzungen zur praktischen Inangriffnahme der Lösungsarbeiten aufgezeigt werden sollen, zu den hierfür notwendigen Detailbesprechungen abzustellen.

Die erste Besprechung dieser Art beabsichtige ich am 6.März 1942, 10.30 Uhr, in Berlin, Kurfürstenstrasse 116, abhalten zu lassen. Ich darf Sie bitten, Ihren Sachbearbeiter zu veranlassen, sich dieserhalb mit meinem zuständigen Referenten, dem SS-Obersturmbannführer E i c h m a n n , ins Benehmen zu setzen.

H e i l H i t l e r !

Ihr

K210399 372023

1 Anlage!

Translation of body of letter:
Enclosed I am sending you the minutes of the proceedings that took place on January 20, 1942. Since the basic position regarding the practical execution of the final solution of the Jewish question has fortunately been established by now, and since there is a full agreement on the part of all agencies involved. I would like to ask you at the request of the Reich Marshal to make one of your specialist officials available for the necessary discussion of details in connection with the completion of the draft that shows the organizational, technical and material prerequisites bearing on the actual starting point of the projected solutions.

I want to schedule the first discussion along these lines for 10:30 a.m. on March 6, 1942, at 116 Kurfürstenstrasse, Berlin. I therefore ask you that for this purpose your specialist official contact my functionary in charge there, SS-Obersturmbannführer Eichmann.
Heil Hitler!
Yours, Heydrich

Preparing for mass murder
A letter dated February 26, 1942, from to SS Foreign Minister Martin Luther from Reinhard Heydrich (considered the "main architect" of the Holocaust Genocide.) Written after the Wannsee Conference, Heydrich is moving to the next step for the "Final Solution of the Jewish Question." Irma Grese was probably ruminating over returning to Ravensbrück for work; as she labored at the Furstenberg dairy farm, the plans for mass murder of millions was underway. (Circa February 26, 1942. Location: unknown. Public Domain. Translator: Not listed in original translation.)

CHAPTER 8
The Hyena and the Final Solution

While Irma Grese toiled at the dairy farm in Furstenberg, she most likely attended a celebration for the new year of 1942. And as she contemplated returning to apply at Ravensbrück or endeavoring again to become a nurse, a shift in her future occurred at the far away Wannsee Conference that first month in 1942.

Grese and her fellow Germans were already living in an antisemitic world, where the rights of Jewish citizens – from owning domestic pets to imprisonment without jury – were slowly being taken. Irma Grese and others read of these decrees and surveyed the destruction of civil rights dissipate for their Jewish neighbors, family, and friends.

Some important dates in Grese's life include:

1933 –
Jews excluded from employment in any legal profession and any civil service.
Restriction number of Jewish students at German schools and universities.
1934 –
Jewish actors not allowed to perform on the stage or in movies.
Jews no longer allowed to slaughter animals (effecting Kosher diets).
1935-
Marriage and extramarital affairs between Jews and non-Jews prohibited.
German court judges must refrain from legal commentaries or opinions written by Jews.
Jewish officers expelled from the army.
Jews were not allowed to take doctoral exams.
1936-
Jews now forbidden to be tax consultants, veterinarians, and teachers.
1937-
Jewish children banned from public schools.
Jewish doctors could not treat non-Jews.
Jew's passports were required to carry a stamp of "J."
1938-
Jews were banned from all schools, leisure activities (parks, cinemas, sports events/clubs, health spas).
Jews could not enter certain areas of the cities.
Jews could not own guns.
Jews must register their property.
Any Jew with a "non-Jewish" first name had to change their name to Sara (females) and Israel (males).
1939-
Jews were to turn in all valuables, to include gold and silver, without compensation.
1941-
Germany declares war on the United States.

Hitler meets with officials to discuss the elimination of all Jews, a plan that has been ongoing. Hitler had intended the extermination after German's victory, but the war does not end as quickly as he planned.
1942-
Jews were to surrender all pets (from livestock to goldfish) to officials for euthanizing. The pets could not be handed off to anyone outside of the euthanizing centers.
January 20 -The Wannsee Conference sealed the fate with "The Final Solution to the Jewish Question." [91]

Despite their best efforts, the SS was not murdering enough Jews to obliterate them from existence. The September 1939 invasion of Poland meant extermination of Jews *en masse;* German-occupied Polish Jews were rounded up and murdered in extermination camps. The invasion of the Soviet Union in June 1941 accelerated the attempt. Jews were to be deported to ghettos, then to concentration camps to be exterminated. In The Wannsee Conference's ninety minutes, a select group of German leaders came to an agreement: Germany and German-occupied areas were to be rid of *all* Jews, from unborn to terminally ill, including Jews who fought for the Germans at war, learned educators and scientists, noted artists and authors, and doctors who had assisted German society.

While Irma Grese and other "true Germans" worked and played, the attendees of The Wannsee Conference determined the "why and how" millions of Jewish persons were to be murdered. It was an official follow-up to a conversation between Hitler and Himmler on December 18, 1941. "Jewish question/to be destroyed as partisans" Himmler had written in his calendar. [92]

[91] An untold number of Jews had already been murdered, for varying reasons, by this time.
[92] Dederichs, M. (2009)

The Young Hyena

Photos of Irma Grese prior to becoming an *Aufseherin*; she was 17-18 years old. This author believes there is a possibility Grese had these made for identification cards. Notice the stark difference between these photographs and the photograph of Grese in her August 1945 mugshot at Celle. (Circa 1940. Locations: unknown. Photographers: unknown. Sources: unknown. Public domain)

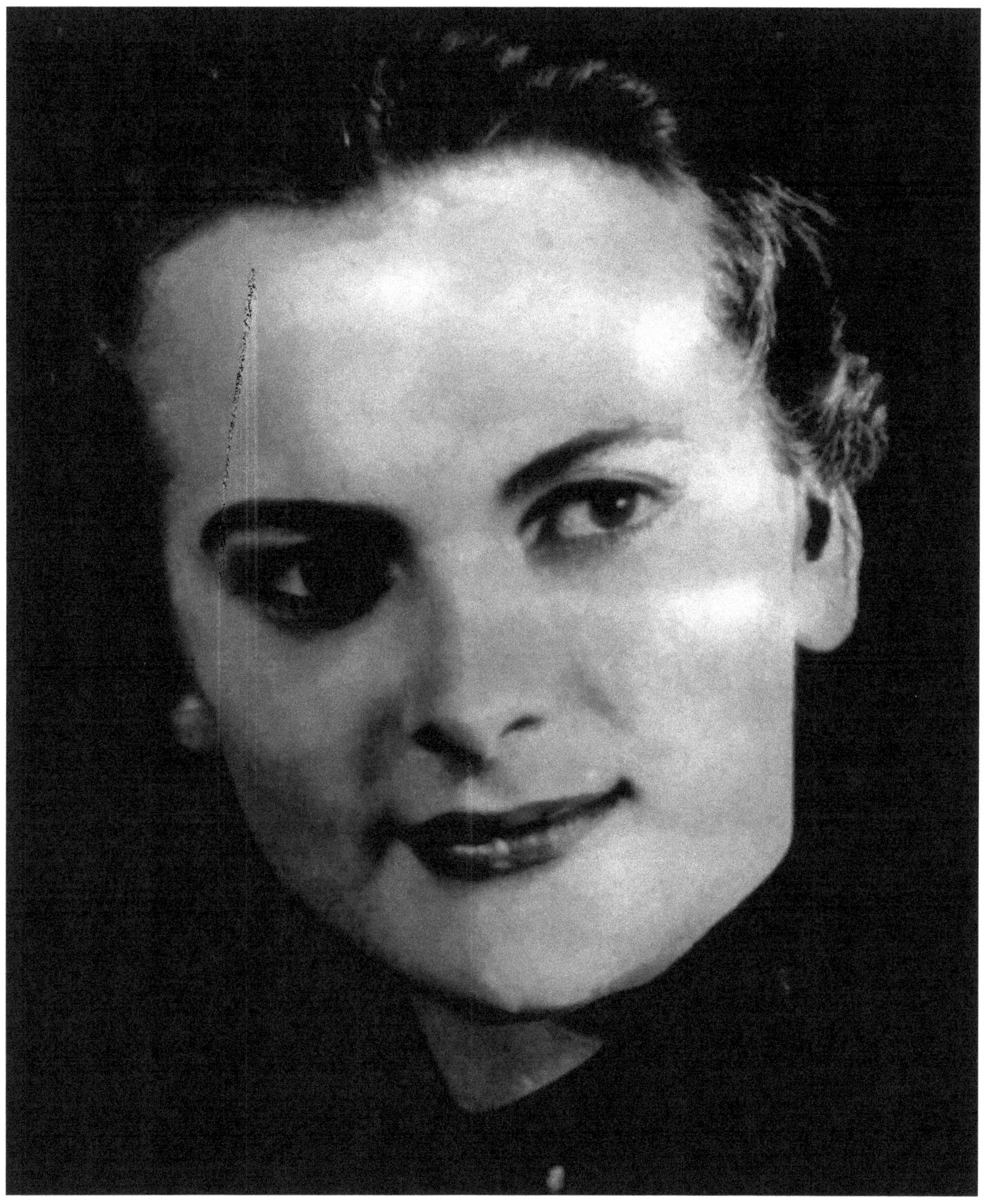

"Irma Grese was very beautiful. And she was extremely evil."

- R.J. Noks, Holocaust survivor.

Opposite page: A rare image of Irma Grese with an unidentified man. This may have been a propaganda photograph.

The stamp on the back reads:

Rudolph Stansky
A.i.r. Ausbildungsstelle Ravensbrück
Irma Grese
Bild Nr. 1.
Aufn. Dat. 9/40

"*Ausbildungsstelle*" translates into "apprenticeship place" or a place to train people. "*Aufn*" translation to English is "Rec" ("received")
There is a debate regarding the identity of Irma Grese in the photograph, and the photo's origin. The team at Ravensbrück Memorial Foundation's photo library has noted "We don't think this is in Ravensbrück. Grese was working at the sanatorium in Hohenlychen. The stamp on the back was probably applied later. The letter "ü" is missing: Ravensbrück, (it is not spelled) Ravensbruck. Women were trained as guards in Ravensbrück from around 1942." [93]

If the date stamp of September 1940 is correct, Irma Grese would have been about the age of seventeen and residing in the SS female helper's training base near Ravensbrück concentration camp. She did not begin training at Ravensbrück until June 1942:

1938/1939
Grese employed in Lychen for six months.
1939
One source has Irma Grese signing up for the Reich Labor Force (*Reichsarbeitsdienst*).
1939
(May) first Lichtenburg group of female prisoners and female staff brought to Ravensbrück.
1939
Grese begin employment at Hohenluchen.
1939 (September 1)
World War II begins in Europe, Germany invades Poland.
1940
(?) Grese moves into SS female helper's training base near Ravensbrück. She is about 16.
1940
(October) Grese visits home for 17th birthday (according to newspapers).
1942 (June 1)

[93] Communications April 8-9, 2024.

Irma Grese hired at Ravensbrück at 18. 4-week training
1941 (June 22)
War declared between the U.S.S.R. and Germany. More men are needed at the front.

The photograph was shared with a quality control expert who, after careful perusing, believes the woman is Irma Grese. [94]
Regarding the man in the photograph, another source explains:

The "V" on the right shoulder indicates he is an 'Old Fighter,' one of the first Nazi party members in the 1920s. The "winkel (Ehrenwinkel)" or Honor Chevron for the Old Guard on the right arm is symbolic of joining any party organization before January 30, 1933, … a mark of distinction only awarded to members who had served during "the years of struggle" and could be seen on uniforms of all ranks. (The insignias) indicate the man is an SS *Rottenfuhrer* assigned to the Education Center. The man is an NCO … if he belonged to the SD, he would also have the rank chart in the rays. [95]

This author believes the woman is Irma Grese posing for a publicity photograph. The misspelling of "Ravensbruck" could indicate the stamp is not of European descent (there is no "ü" in the English language.) Because Grese was attractive and the epitome of "German female," she modeled for a propaganda photograph with an NCO from the Education Center. The photo was transferred to Ravensbrück, the training camp, where it was received on 09/1940, in the hopes of recruiting female guards.

(Image courtesy anonymous donor "K" and property of "K." *To copy this photo is an infringement of copyright*)

[94] Interview with "M.G." March 26-27, 2024
[95] Discussion, January 4 – March 22, 2024. AxisHistory.com

Part III

The Hyena Emerges

"Always Accuse Your Enemies of Your Own Sins."

- Attributed to Joseph Goebbels, Hitler's Minister for Public Enlightenment and Propaganda

“I have beaten prisoners, but I have not ill-treated them... it has nothing to do with being vicious.”

- Irma Grese, testifying at the Belsen Trial.

Ravensbrück Women's Camp. It was here where Irma Grese trained. This was the foundation of Grese's career in the concentration camps – and where the horror would have begun. (Circa 1945. Location: Ravensbrück Women's Camp. Photographers: unknown. Courtesy: The Archive of The State Museum Auschwitz-Birkenau in Oświęcim. Used with permission)

CHAPTER 9
Ravensbrück

Ravensbrück was not the first concentration camp for female prisoners, but it would become the largest. The incarceration of females began around 1933. The "Decree of the Reich President for the Protection of People and State" had abolished civil rights previously protected by the Constitution of The Weimar Republic. Now the SS could arrest and hold anyone, including people suspected of speaking against the Third Reich, including "political prisoners." This was a broad term that would be liberally applied without proof, resulting in imprisonment without trial, as was "prostitute," "communist," and "criminal."

In June 1933, KL Moringen [96] concentration camp begins to hold female prisoners. That October it was converted to a female – only camp. The SS female guards *Aufseherinnen* would replace male SS guards. It was a move created in part to prevent male SS guards from sexual activity with prisoners.

At the end of 1937, female prisoners would be transferred to a prison housed in a castle, Lichtenburg. For two years this became the central concentration camp for female prisoners. These women were to be treated as nondiscriminatory but unsympathetic, with no beatings. Female guards were now being recruited to apply. Maria Mandl was a guard at Lichtenburg for a year starting 1938, until she was transferred to a supervisory position as an *Oberaufseherin* – a senior guard – to Auschwitz. This simple transfer would be a huge conversion in Irma Grese's future.

Lichtenburg became overcrowded as more alleged female political prisoners, communists, and criminals were arrested. The large, rectangular buildings with smooth exterior walls and steep gabled roofs could no longer keep the population of females being led into its prison. Germany's invasion of Poland on September 1, 1939, meant the number of prisoners would be ramped up as more arrests were made in the streets. A new facility was required for female prisoners.

The village of Ravensbrück, near Fürstenberg, within reasonable distance from Berlin, proved to be an excellent site to build a camp. Fürstenberg was a popular destination as a health resort. There were three lakes, including lake Schwedt, next to the camp. A sanatorium was in the town. This was a place for people to unwind and leave the bustling city on a holiday. But now the name "Ravensbrück" would become synonymous with horror.

Most residents of Fürstenberg and in the area supported the Nazi party and were privy to the Ravensbrück camp activities. The camp brought jobs to the area and provided slave labor by farming out the prisoners. Fürstenberg residents would become familiar with seeing the prisoners marched to and from work sites away from the camps.

The first Lichtenburg group of female prisoners and female staff approached the entry gates in May of 1939. The concentration camp was still under construction. By 1942, Ravensbrück would be the sole camp for all female prisoners and boasted the most female guards of all camps. Two years later all female guards would be trained here. The camp was in a constant state of construction, so the first female guards were housed in existing buildings. By this time new female recruits attended standardized training.

---

[96] "KL" and "KZ" are abbreviations for *KonzentrationsLager*, "concentration camps."

When Irma Grese arrived at Ravensbrück ready to work for the Third Reich, the camp would have been training future female guards with a standard program since March 1942. The camp itself stretched out like a city unto itself in front of the new recruits, many from small villages like Wrechen. There were 18 barracks, in rows, and included a poorly supplied *Revier*, or camp hospital. Heinrich Himmler would establish brothels in many Nazi concentration camps; prisoners from this all-female camp would supply the women. (The exception was Auschwitz, which used their own female prisoners.) [97] Several in-house factories were located at Ravensbrück. The kitchen was a popular place for prisoners to work, though heavily guarded to prevent theft. There was a "punishment bunker" where a camp doctor would be required to observe all prisoner punishments while a fellow prisoner would carry out the beatings for extra rations. (Himmler had ordered whippings for infractions beginning April 1942.) The prisoner's camp latrine was barely large enough to accommodate the growing number of prisoners.

Grese would learn that Ravensbrück's 34 satellite camps housed Social Democrats, Communists, German anti-fascists, Gypsies, Poles, prostitutes, drug addicts, Russians, mentally ill, Ukrainians, Jews, Jehovah's Witnesses, Austrians, British, homosexuals, Americans – all women considered "inappropriate" – and a multitude of languages floated through the air. Color-coded triangles were sewn onto their clothing to distinguish a prisoner's infraction; the most commonly recognized is the yellow star of David for Jews.

As time went on, and Ravensbrück population grew, these triangles were re-sewn onto increasingly filthy rags of clothing, and eventually prisoners would survive on barely enough calories to keep their skeletal bodies functioning, living minute to minute. But that would take a few years. In the beginning, there were beautiful gardens and an aviary. A salon for *Aufseherinnen* would be established. These luxuries were maintained by prisoners who could be beaten or killed for any small discretion. Death would eventually become the norm for prisoners.

The Ravensbrück camp, when initially opened, was hygienic and clean. Still, it was a prison with a strict regime and encompassed slave labor. Roll call, or *appell*, would be at 2:00 A.M. or 2:30 A.M. depending on the season. All prisoners – including the deathly ill - were lined up and silently counted. Some women fell dead or fainted; those around them dared not speak, look around, or move. Sometimes roll call lasted a few hours, depending on who was counting and the prisoner's health. Interrupting roll call meant a severe beating, sometimes to death, depending on the officer in charge. Irma Grese was destined to be one that prisoners avoided.

After count, women went to work twelve-hour days at the nearby Siemens Electric Company, the tailor shop, the carpet shop, or on construction and roadwork. There were camp administrative jobs, cleaning positions, and some women even knitted items for the war effort. Each job required supervision; the job fell to *Aufseherinnen* like Irma Grese.

About 6:00 A.M. (depending on the length of roll call) the prisoners were given work assignments. Breakfast, when it was available, was a weak cup of liquid passed off as coffee and a small piece of black bread. Noon meals were no better. These were the only two meals unless one could secure a stolen piece of food at the risk of death. Prisoners were forbidden to stop working or they received beatings. The noon meal was the sole break from a 12-hour workday. Latrines filling to overflow made washing

[97] Irma Grese would send female prisoners to the brothels as punishments later in her career.

nearly impossible; prisoners did as best they could prior to the first roll call and upon returning to camp after work. They often stepped over the dead to do so.

Working at Ravensbrück were the *Aufseherinnen,* who learned to punish prisoners for any infraction – real or imagined – with slaps, punches, whips, and boots. The most brutal seemed to be the ones who were promoted.

It would be in Ravensbrück where the Hyena was released.

Next page: **Honorary Obligation** that every supervisor had to sign when taking up duty. Note the official photograph attached.
(Circa: 1940s-? Image source: unknown, possibly MGR/StBG, KL/11-11. Not dated. Appears in *"Anwerbung und Ausbild von SS-Aufsehreinnen."*
"Recruitment and training of SS guards." Pp. 13-14. Public Domain.)

Translation:

<u>Honorary obligation</u>
Furor decides whether an enemy of the state lives or dies
No nationalist is therefore entitled to lay hands on an opponent of the state or to physically mistreat him.
I hereby declare, relying on my word of authority, that I will faithfully follow the furor's instructions in all situations, which I express with my signature.

Ravensbruck, aen (?)

____

Ehrenwörtliche Verpflichtung.

Über Leben und Tod eines Staatsfeindes entscheidet der Führer.

Kein Nationalsozialist ist daher berechtigt, Hand an einen Staatsgegner zu legen oder ihn körperlich zu mißhandeln.

Ich erkläre hiermit unter Berufung auf mein Ehrenwort, daß ich die Weisung des Führers in allen Lagen treu befolgen werde, was ich mit meiner Unterschrift zum Ausdruck bringe.

Ravensbrück, den ____________

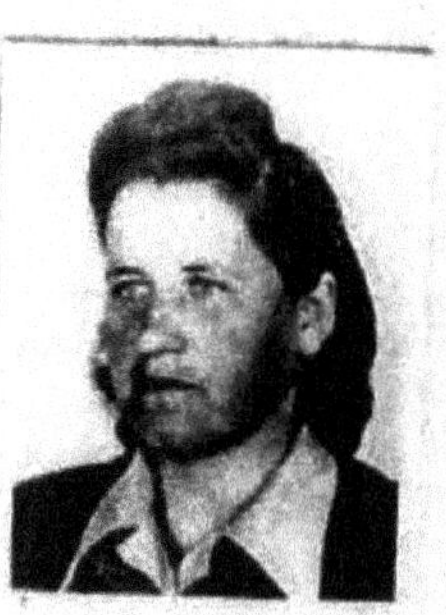

____
(Unterschrift)

____
(Dienstgrad)

CHAPTER 10
Birth of the Hyena

In 1939, Irma Grese's *alma mater* the *Bund Deutscher Mädel* (BDM) would adjust its focus to supporting the war effort. Membership for all girls remained mandatory. The indoctrination continued preparation for motherhood and marriage. Followers could purchase prints and postcards of Adolph Hitler at many stores. The girls plastered campaign posters on their own walls and ensured their uniforms and specialized outfits were perfect. Irma Grese most likely looked back fondly on the memories, and how she had begged her father to allow her to join before she had to enlist. The BDM continued in ensuring girls would support National Socialism just as the SS ensured women were supportive.

The SS preferred to recruit women for camp work between the ages of twenty-one and forty-five years old "with no specific vocational background or skills." Long (2021) lists four ways "female guards were recruited: active recruitment by the employment office (*Arbeitsamt*), recruitment by armaments companies that employed concentration camp inmates, recruitment from groups of female factory workers by the SS, and … (the job seekers) submitting a written application." [98]

This meant numerous women of lower socioeconomic status who were single and/or supporting a family were applying. Like Irma Grese, many of these women came from rural areas with little education. Most (over 75%) were unmarried, some of them with children. Others were recruited from factories or labor positions and farms. Also, like Grese, some had turbulent home lives as children. They came from varied backgrounds; for example, the 6'3" Herta Bothe was studying to be a nurse; Juana Bormann a deeply religious missionary, before they became infamous brutal guards.

These new trainees learned of the guard jobs in the same manner anyone hears of a custody job: word of mouth, recruiters, flyers, or an advertisement as seen in a German newspaper:

> "Healthy, female workers between the ages of 20 and 40 wanted
> for a military site (Good wages and free board, accommodation and clothing) [99]

When recruiting, the "military site" offered easy work, simple living, with excellent pay, lovely housing, and outstanding benefits. Only the best were selected and then only the best people would be hired. It was not called a concentration camp or a prison; it was, as seen above, "a military site." The potential recruits would observe images of smiling, beautiful female employees enjoying luxuries like cups of fresh fruit and leisure time by the lake. While making the job appear enjoyable and coveted, such advertising also began the psychological effect of creating "gratitude and loyalty of (the) willing and tractable recruits." [100]

As Irma Grese was contemplating her next place of employment, SS Officer Edmund Bräuning was leading additional recruitment drives to hire more female guards.

---

[98] P. 6
[99] Cited in McGuinness (2021) [*sic*]
[100] Mailänder, p.4.

He focused on businesses whose employees were mainly women. Bräuning would ask management to call all the females together, then expound on the wonderful job opportunities that awaited them in the "rehabilitation centers" as camps were also called. His lectures on plentiful food and easy work drew in the women who were working under harsh conditions and going home to war-torn cities, hoping they could scrounge up decent meals. Factory work was problematic. Bräuning never failed to recruit groups of women eager to sign up at Ravensbrück. [101]

There was another way to ensure female indoctrination. Factories utilizing slave labor from the nearby concentration camps ordered their female supervisors to complete *Aufseherinnen* training to comply with the new German laws. "Their job and its venue did not change, only the job title." [102]

When Irma Grese finally returned to Ravensbrück at eighteen, she had to undergo a series of tests before she was allowed to move forward. The process would take about four weeks. First, an SS-approved doctor gave Grese a physical exam. She had to prove she was not pregnant and was physically fit for duty. Working for years on a dairy farm most likely gave Grese the strength and substantial capacity to handle any labor that was required. She also had to list any illnesses in her lifetime along with her height (5'5") weight (about 120 pounds) and her physical appearance (blonde hair, blue eyes). She had to swear she did not come from Jewish heritage. Another physical exam, measuring such body parts such the distance across her temple and shape of her nose, would ensure she was Aryan, according to Nazi medical experts.

When Grese was accepted into employment, she would have been handed a stack of papers to complete, applications, decrees, and general information. As with most applications, she would be obliged to give her employment, criminal history, military duty history, and educational level. Applicants could not have a criminal record. She would have to list any communist or Jewish ties, to include that of her parents, list the addresses where she had lived, and give every detail of information on herself possible. Grese was one of the few applicants with a medical background in her work history.

Next, Irma Grese and her fellow *SS – Helferinnekorp* would take a written exam. Questions included:

1. When did the Russian Campaign begin?
2. When did the first German train line begin operation and on what stretch did it connect?
3. What is the meaning of the abbreviation SS?
4. 1⁄2 divided by 1⁄4 =?
5. When and where was the Führer born?
6. What is the purpose of the sterilization law?
7. Which hereditary diseases do you know?
8. How heavy is a kilogram of iron?
9. Who discovered printing?
10. What is race?
11. 46,131 – 13,794 divided by 9 x 2 + (3/4 + 0.10) divided by (3/9 divided by 1/27) – 999.15=?

---

[101] Bräuning would later become the lover of Dorothea Binz, one of the sadistic officers and supervisors at Ravensbrück.
[102] Cline, S. (2014). P. 19.

12. Where did Adolf Hitler write the book *Mein Kampf*?
13. When did the Russian Campaign begin?
14. What are the names of the peninsulas in the south of Europe?
15. What is the name of the island on which Napoleon was exiled the second time?
16. Which countries have a border on the Mediterranean Sea?
17. What was the darkest day of the movement?
18. Where does the Danube begin and end?
19. Who is the military commander of the Native German Army?
20. Which seas does the Suez Canal connect to?
21. What does *Weltanschauung* mean? [103]

While most of these questions seem strange today, children growing up and being raised on Nazi indoctrination would have known the answers. Note it tested common sense, some mathematical skills, but mostly patronage.

If Grese and her fellow applicants passed this test, background examinations were conducted by the gestapo. And she would sign an oath:

> The Führer decides the life and death of a public enemy. No Nazi is entitled to strike or physically abuse an opponent of the state. I hereby give my word of honor that I will obey the instruction of the Führer in all levels, to that I give my signature. [104]

All recruits understood their "word of honor" to not "strike or physically abuse" a prisoner was binding. [105] Punishment was approved; vengeance or abuse was not permitted. A firearm could *only* be used in the event of an escape or a physical assault. Only a superior could decide death of a prisoner. Maltreatment was forbidden. This came from the desk of Heinrich Himmler himself. Irma Grese's signature appears on these documents.

Now it was a "hurry up and wait" game. If they passed the background, they became trainees. Irma Grese passed the background to begin her four weeks of training, followed by a probationary period.

Irma Grese would have signed oaths to Hitler and to Germany, revealed secrets, answered questions regarding her patriotism, and signed contracts. She would swear to not reveal any information about her work inside the camps; she agreed to remain at the station assigned. Official business was to be discussed among officials and not the prisoners, nor were prisoners allowed to view any official documentation. Any violation could result in severe punishment.

Grese would receive a copy of the *SS Disziplinarstraf und* Beschwerdeordnung (Disciplinary and Penal Code, SS-DOB) which explained to the trainees how SS discipline operated. The codes applied to the female guards although they could not be members of the SS. Inside the 63 pages, they were advised punishment was

[103] BDC-National Archives II, 235- 237 cited in Cline, p.21-2
[104] Hildegard Krüger, Erklarung, 9 September 1944, KL Ravensbrück cited in Cline, p. 23.
[105] Hildegard Krüger, Ehrenwörtliche Verpflichtung, 13 December 1944, KL Ravensbrück. Cited in Cline, p.22

to be fair and impartial. Infractions were listed. Punishments included verbal warnings, written reports, expulsion, and beheading.

She would also thumb through the *Lagerordung*, an outdated manual on prisoner punishment. It was originally written for Dachau, but by now was questionable due to the ongoing changes in the prisoner system. Irma Grese learned she was to make a report of each time she used punishment and to have several noted witnesses. Still, much of this manual was vague and lacking.

The SS men employed in the camps had been ordered to treat females as equals in this system – they were all considered officers. Trainees who were to be *Aufseherinnens* were told the same: they were not second citizens; they were comrades here. It must have been a welcome environment to woman coming from abusive or tyrannical relationships at the hands of males, a home like the Grese family. But under the command of Rudolph Höss, [106] who hated the idea of females working in the camps, sexism occurred in a trickle-down effect. Höss would not discipline SS males who badly treated their female coworkers.

Grese and the women who sat in the training rooms were in a precarious situation in this new employment. Like the SS males, the females were Reich employees who enjoyed the same status. Yet they were still considered "women auxiliaries"/ civil employees in a paramilitary organization. Nazism remained a man's world, created and supervised by men only. Females still could never be true members of the SS. Males were now not allowed to work one to one in the camps with female prisoners (for fear of developing intimacy). They were placed as perimeter guards with guns and had orders to shoot escapees on sight. Murder was not the norm for females, according to the Nazi plan. Those females issued guns were to remove guns from holsters only in rare instances. The firing of a gun was a man's job, unless it was an emergency. Females would not engage in victim selection - and would rarely guard persons selected - for gas chambers. Not one female is known to have administered the Zyklon B used to murder in the gas chambers. Directly murdering inmates – shooting, stabbing, beating - was not considered a "female" enterprise. A scant few would challenge that thought process; Irma Grese was certainly one of them. So was another blonde German woman named Dorothea Binz.

[106] Sometimes spelled "Hess."

Irma Grese's Coworkers of Note

Maria Mandl (1912 -1948) utilized a whip and boots to torture, punish, and murder. Maria Mandl was abominably cruel, ripping children from mother's arms and trouncing the parents who protested. She created the Women's Orchestra of Auschwitz, forcing them to play flawlessly while witnessing neighbors, friends and relatives die. Maria Mandl would be hanged on January 24, 1948. (Mugshot from Montelupich Prison, Poland. Circa 1946. Location: Montelupich Prison. Photographer from The Archival Collection of the State Museum Auschwitz-Birkenau, Oswiecim. Public domain.)

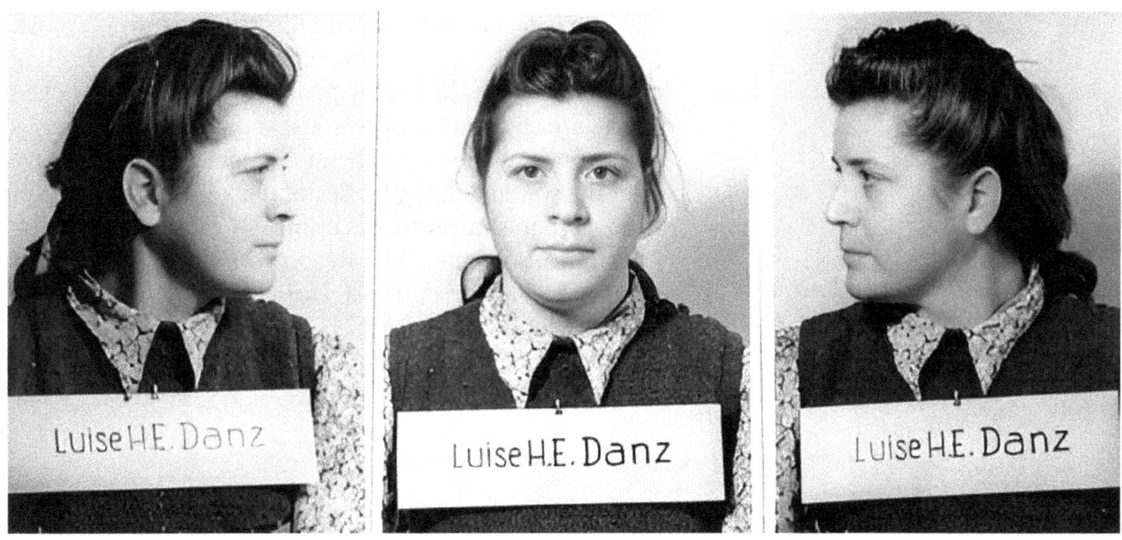

Luise Danz (1917 – 2009) another of the ten percent of the abusive guards employed in the camps. She had worked at several camps before landing in Auschwitz. Danz was arrested in 1945, was tried, and sentenced to life imprisonment serving 10 years. She was tried again in 1996; charges were dropped due to her age. (Circa 1945. Location: unknown, probably Lützow. Photo by lekcjaImmediat. Public Domain.).

Left: Artist's rendering of *Rapportführerin* Margot Drechsel (1908 – 1945). She was Irma Grese's supervisor at one point in Grese's career. She was described as ugly, tall, thin, rangy, and vulgar. Drechsel would sometimes dress as a doctor, though she did not have the ranking. She was an office worker prior to training at Ravensbrück. She moved somewhat quickly through the ranks between Auschwitz II – Birkenau, Auschwitz I, and Ravensbrück. Margot Drechsel was another woman who established herself with inherent cruelty. She was hanged in 1945 by the Soviets. This image is often mislabeled as "Irma Grese." (Circa: unknown. Location: unknown, probably Auschwitz. Artist: unknown. Public Domain.)

Josef Mengele (1911-1979) was rumored to have an affair with Irma Grese. Mengele was a highly trained and respected physician prior to the war. In 1943, he was transferred to Auschwitz where he performed tests and experiments on prisoners with no scientific value. Mengele would send prisoners to death while whistling classical music. He sliced, maimed, removed, switched limbs, injected dyes and poisons, and conduced surgeries on prisoners without anesthetic. Mengele fled the country after the war and died of a heart attack in 1979. He never received punishment for his crimes. (Circa July 29, 1944. Location: Solahütte SS Resort. Photographer: either Bernhard Walther or Ernst Hofmann or Karl-Friedrich Höcker. Public Domain)

Rudolf Höss (1894–1987) fought in WWI and was educated in the family business, attending the *École supérieure de commerce.* From a wealthy family, he was an early member of the Nazi party and worshipped Hitler. His interests included music, reading, and the occult. He was a stalwart Nazi until his death. (Circa: 1935. Photographer: Unknown. (By Bundesarchiv, Bild 183-1987-0313-507 / CC-BY-SA 3.0, CC BY-SA 3.0 e, https://commons.wikimedia.org/w/index.php?curid=134662507.)

Above: Josef Kramer's (1906- 1945) driver's license dated July 1942. According to rumor, Irma Grese was having an affair with Kramer. Kramer was a sexist, an only child of a strict Catholic upbringing. Prior to becoming a Nazi in 1931, he held few jobs. His wife and Leni Grese would become friends during and after their loved one's trial. ((Photo: Circa 1942. Location: unknown. Photographer: unknown. Public Domain)

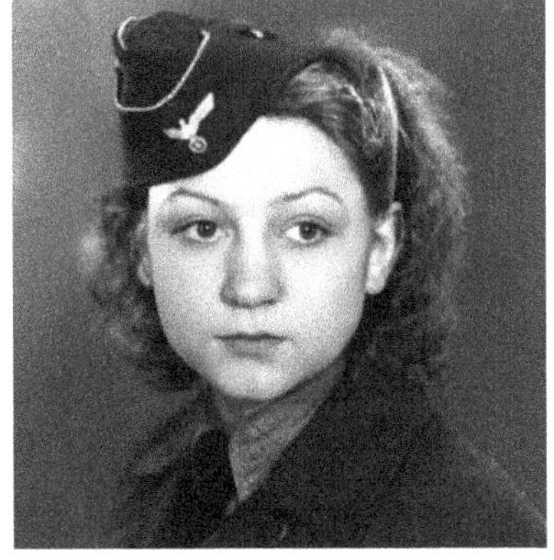

Early photo of Dorothea Binz (1920–1947) the primary trainer of new recruits including Grese. She had been promoted quickly, and would be about 20 years old when Irma Grese stepped into the facility. Like Irma Grese, Binz enjoyed torture and was probably a sadist. Binz once murdered a prisoner with a pickax, used the dead woman's skirt to clean her boots, then rode off on her bicycle. Some prisoners retaliated by knocking her to the ground; one dropped a bucket over Binz's head. She was hanged at Hamelin Prison by Albert Pierrepoint, the same man who hung Grese. Her last words: "I hope you won't think that we were all evil people." (Circa unknown. Location:
unknown. Photographer unknown. Public domain)

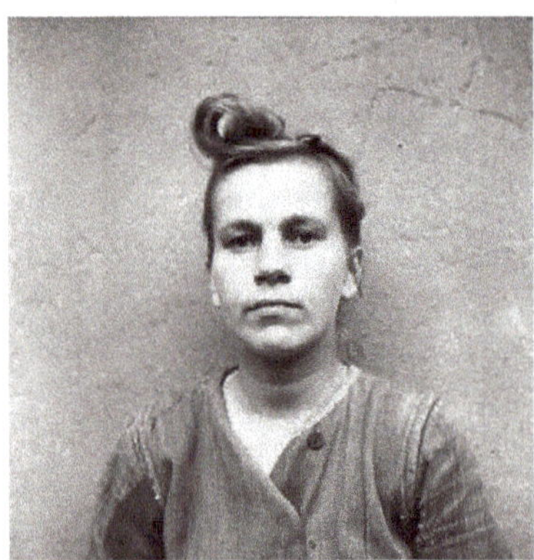

Elisabeth Volkenrath (1919– 1945) like Grese, was an unskilled worker who volunteered for service in the concentration camps and trained under Dorothea Binz at Ravensbrück. She worked at Birkenau, promoted to *Oberaufseherin* in 1944. Volkenrath was considered one of the most hated and feared staff members in the camps. She was sentenced to death in the Belsen trials. (Circa August 1945. Photo by Silverside (Sgt) No 5 Army Film Photographic Unit - Imperial War Museum collection as BU 9689, Public Domain, https://commons.wikimedia.org/w/index.php?curid=4364842)

Below: Irma Grese and her coworkers walked past dead bodies daily. The piles of bodies became higher as the war lingered. This is an unfiltered photograph obtained during WWII. While it was illegal to do so, many Germans in the war collected and traded these types of photographs; some sent them home to loved ones. The below photo has never been viewed publicly until now. (Circa 1945. Location: unknown, possibly Dachau. Photographer: unknown. Photo courtesy the private collection of Ray Cook. Used with permission.)

CHAPTER 11
Trained by The Beast

A few female staff made it their personal mission to create extreme suffering for prisoners, including one woman named Dorothea Binz.

Dorothea Binz (1920 – 1947) was the primary trainer of new recruits. She had been promoted quickly and would have been about 20 years old when Irma Grese stepped into the facility. Binz, a maid before Hitler took over Germany, began her new career at Ravensbrück and stayed; thus, her knowledge of the camp was complete. Binz, like all female trainers, did not train men. Binz used the Nazi – created curriculum of lectures, films, discussion on ideology, and booklets to instruct her class. Irma Grese and the other recruits would have sat through the long discussion on prisoner movement. Prisoner treatment was another extended lecture. There would be viewings of rhetoric-filled films. After the training, Binz would explain it was pertinent the trainees sign forms stating they understood the procedures taught to them. This included the teaching of the use of force and violence, two subjects rarely mentioned in existing training materials. Irma Grese would eventually ignore instruction in either.

Prisoners would gossip and discuss the new recruits. They bestowed monikers for guards, including "The Beast" for Binz. They took bets on who would last, the length of time before sweet faces became sinister, and which of their oppressors would become the most callous and abusive. On average, it took about a week of working around prisoners for the new guards to become tormenters. Some, like Irma Grese, seemed to mirror Dorothea Binz by taking it further than harsh words and a few slashes with a leather whip. Dorothea Binz was one of the extremes used to gauge cruelty in the camps.

The probationers would have already heard about their trainer; gossip travels fast in such a small community, and Binz was already legendary at Ravensbrück for her cruelty and quick rise through the ranks. Binz and Grese had much in common. Both were from a lower middle-class family, both had left school early, and both had volunteered to work in the camp against a father's wishes. Binz had tuberculosis as a teen and thus stigmatized, banned from many jobs. She was 19 years old when she began work in the Nazi camps in August 1939, was promoted to *Aufseherin* within a month, "the true star of the camp," one author recognizes Binz. Binz became so powerful "(the) chief guard was completely overshadowed by deputy (Binz)." [107] Binz grew up imbedded in Nazi propaganda and was a rabid supporter.

Biographers believe Binz supervised a bunker used for torture and murder. She was most likely employed as director of a cell block in the summer of 1942 when she began mentoring Grese.

Dorothea Binz was ruthlessly cruel. She continuously abused prisoners with her boots, fists, and whip; she shot and beat random prisoners on a whim. French ethnologist Germaine Tillion testified how Binz had assisted in beating a nude female prisoner until the woman was a bloody heap, then stood on the woman's thighs until blood oozed over Binz's boots. Dorothea Binz once observed a female prisoner on a roadside crew who, in

[107] Erpel, S. (2007). P. 60

her eyes, was not working as hard as she felt was necessary. Binz dismounted her bicycle, took away the woman's pickaxe, and chopped the woman to a bloody, dead heap. Binz used the woman's skirt to clean blood off her shining boots, returned to her bicycle, and pedaled off without expression. She led a German Shepard dog on a leash, continually threatening to let it loose on inmates. (Yet, Binz had a smaller pet dog she adored. When the dog died, Binz deeply mourned the dog's death with a special grave and flowers.) She savored watching inmates being killed. She would select inmates for death without motive. Dorothea Binz lived with SS officer Edmund Bräuning in a home outside of camp. Witnesses reported the couple enjoyed romantic strolls though the camps, stopping to observe inmate torture as amusement.

Unlike Grese, she was not considered such a beauty by the prisoners nor the press. Square shoulders, with a pear-shaped, plain face, she was blonde and blue-eyed and thick. What Binz lacked in grace or femininity she made up for in brutality; she became a feared figure in the camps, the epitome of power.

Irma Grese and the other probationers would have understood everything about this new occupation encompassing power. The uniform, the gun, a job where your presence alone strikes fear, the money, the ability to walk through a town and instantly command respect. These women, who before had little or nothing, who came from farms, factories, or menial jobs, now had power and control. They knew there were promotions and status once again within their reach. The new Germany had taken away a woman's status; they could no longer be judges, lawyers, doctors; they could not attend college. Nazi Germany had told them they were needed at home to have babies and take care of their German man. Women did have status because they could bear children; they were rewarded by the Third Reich simply for this fact. This new power and control were both a motivator for employment and a motive behind their brutality.

Once they had been employed for a length of time, subtle changes occurred in the power structure. Perhaps it was the work conditions, the job becoming the opposite of what was promised. There were the prisoner conditions in camps: stench of unwashed bodies, foul food, poor sanitation. There were long hours and male chauvinism. Brutality was the norm. For a simple girl this was a foreign planet. Rules she swore to uphold and laws she swore to follow were upended for so many: guards drank, women smoked cigarettes, and many of them were having sex – including same-sex liaisons - outside of marriage. Grese had been taught all along the Jew and other undesirables were to be treated as "subhuman;" soon, she was reveling in brutality and sexual deviancy and some of it with these "subhumans." According to W. Lower, "there is general agreement among scientists that the environment is the most important factor in determining whether one will become a perpetrator of genocide."

Lower's theory is further proven in the camps considering, in the outside world, this "negotiation of power relations" was "not possible" nor was it proper. [108] Most people in the outside world did not simply walk up to others, beat them down with a whip, a slap, or boots and not expect retaliation or arrest. [109] There was no "perpetrator-victim relation" in the camps. In the world of concentration camps, Irma Grese had the legal right to abuse – it gained respect, it was accepted, and she utilized it to impress fellow officers and

[108] (2013)

[109] The exception being, during this period, Germans against civilian "non-Germans."

supervisors. Besides looking resplendent, she also behaved in an exemplary manner. Grese's behavior also established, for probably the first time, her identity.

Grese was at an impressionable age – and emotionally immature – so learned identity was established by behavior here; specifically, cruel behavior. She noted Dorothea Binz had an identity, one that was revered in this world. Binz was high in the ranks and high in esteem. Grese was currently a lowly trainee. Grese would later go one step further than Binz.

However, not all guards were brutal or dangerous. Auschwitz survivor Ella Lingens – Reiter is cited as explaining "no more than five or 10% were criminals by nature…" the rest being "perfectly normal … fully alive to good and evil." [110] Some were compassionate, albeit clandestinely. A few might slip gifts – such as toothbrushes and bits of food – to prisoners. Some were severely affected by what they saw and did what little they could to ease the burdens of the prisoners. And a few fell in love with those they took an oath to destroy.

Dogs were used by some of the guards, including Irma Grese. Heinrich Himmler deemed the use of dogs as excellent intimidation for prisoners; he believed this intimidation process worked best on female prisoners. A kennel of well-trained guard dogs existed at Ravensbrück. The kennel was located near the entrance. They had been built almost immediately when construction of Ravensbrück began, and dogs were added as soon as the kennels were ready. Irma Grese would learn the dogs were used on outside details. They were to be picked up at the gate, and then taken to their kennels after the outside work detail came in. Dogs were trained to chase down escapees on command and then to hold down their prey to bite in three places starting with the foot, then shoulder, and, as a last resource, the throat.

Like so many training programs in employment, teaching was quite different from real-world work. For example, counting inmates at *appell*. In theory, the business was stress-free – until there were over a thousand prisoners to count, their language barriers caused issues in giving and receiving orders, and the ignorance of some guards. The use of unnecessary force was still strictly prohibited; but probationers viewed seasoned guards beating prisoners for the most random of infractions or by spite. Classroom training had focused on the mechanics of the work. It must have been a shock to the systems of many new guards as they entered the workplace in their new uniforms and fresh faces.

Irma Grese's workdays followed a strict routine: each morning they awoke to the sound of reveille, there was a morning muster, then roll calls for both staff and prisoners. The end of the workday meant (regulated) leisure time. The employees worked either day or night shifts.

If a trainee or even an A*ufseherin* on probationary period discovered this was not a career to pursue, she was free to leave; the Nazis wanted no doubters in the midst. It was inevitable recruits would learn most prisoners were not criminals, as originally advertised. Most recruits stayed on, lured by both the job perks and group pressure. Some historians explain it was easy to leave the work; the trainee turned in a letter, packed up and departed. Other historiographers explain it was difficult to quit the job. The ease of leaving probably also depended on the time, the institution, the mode of arrival ("volunteer" or compulsory orders), and the location of the camp. Irma Grese stayed.

[110] Prisoners of Fear (1948). No p. #

Should a trainee determine they wanted to leave, she was first to speak with a supervisor, who ordered her to report to the camp director, a position of dominance. Thus the "quitter" was placed in a position to "shame" herself. The "quitter" would be forced to ruminate how she would return to a menial job explaining why she was not good enough for the Nazi Party. She would become an outcast by the team. She would lose the women who by now had become her substitute family and only friends. The "quitter" would lose the good pay, nice residence, healthy food, clothing allowance, and high status to return to a war – torn city and a menial job selected by the Labor Exchange. Others might view her as lazy, weak, or ignorant. Nonetheless, the trainee could leave at any time.

Political prisoner Margarete Buber-Neumann, housed at Ravensbrück, watched as recruits filed in for training. She would later explain the process from a first-hand account. "During the first week almost half of them would come weeping to Frau Langefeld (the senior camp supervisor) and ask to be allowed to go home." Langefeld would explain only the Commandant could release the recruits and any requests must be addressed to him. "Very few of them had sufficient courage" to go before an SS officer, "…so the great majority of them stayed on and got used to the new profession." Margarete observed how donning a uniform create a transformation, "a feeling of confidence and superiority." She penned in a memoir that not all the recruits changed so drastically: by day they shadowed the cruelest of female guards, and during free time these women were with SS men. There were no outside influences. "There were, of course, exceptions, but not many." [111] Grese, who had already been influenced by the environment at Hohenluchen and, with a desire to work for the Nazis, was not one of those who went weeping to a supervisor.

And some did weep. French anthropologist Germaine Tillion was imprisoned at Ravensbrück. In her memoir, Germaine recalls a new *Aufseherin* who said "excuse me" when walking in front of a prisoner. [112] This small, twenty-year-old guard would take less than a week to become acclimated to "proper" behavior towards prisoners. [113] Germaine would recall about 50% of the female guards adhering to brutal behavior, and at least one *Aufseherin* who wept, often at a workstation. The guard did not last long and was either transferred to a job away from prisoners or released from duties.

Initially, the training lasted about four weeks in Ravensbrück. Irma Grese would work and listened intently as she was taught basic secretarial skills, how to operate the camp telephone switchboard, storekeeping, postal and kitchen supervision skills. Grese and her classmates would be taught to handle any threats against their person. After training, there was her three months' probation.

This initial training was careful and concise. But, as the war lingered, and the camps gained prisoners as more people were arrested and sent to them. Entire villages were emptied. All the Jews in a town or village would be removed. The training for camp guards became haphazard. Training would decrease from a few intense weeks of acclimating to work and viewing propaganda films, to simply following a senior officer about for several days. As train carloads of thousands arrived at the camps, trainees received quick previews before working alone. The lack of manpower demanded some of the recruits be drafted to

---

[111] (2008) pp. 232-3

[112] Tillion, G. (1988). P. 6.

[113] Often biographers declare this unidentified guard is Irma Grese, though given her history it is doubtful.

other camps for education. Irma Grese did receive the prolonged class; she would later be moved to different camps.

Irma Grese and her classmates would be trained in a two-part program of "theory" and "practice." These young women were schooled in regulations, rules, and punishments in the camps.

Camp education mirrored the Nazi principles. Behavior was dictated to these trainees; their independence morphed into conformity. The workplace utilized the same doctrine Grese had received all her life, directly or indirectly:

- "We" versus "them" – the persons held in the camps were the enemy.
- The prisoners were not humans and were not to be treated as such.
- Pity, mercy, kindness, or any emotions remotely humane are signs of weakness.
- Punishment was meted out systematically where each guard had a clearly defined role.
- Staff worked as a team, which kept personal emotions and feelings at bay.
- The hierarchy of punishment ensured guards did not develop feelings for prisoners.
- Brutality gave a person clout and esteem.
- Everything was part of the "greater good" for country.
- Staff had a clearly defined role with no questions and no deviations.
- Physical contact between guard and prisoner was strictly prohibited unless it was for punishment, such as punching or kicking.

Lessons included paperwork, procedures, awareness of sabotage, correcting work slowdowns, and appropriate punishment procedures. The latter was carefully explained throughout training and probation.

An unnamed camp survivor reported one "Ravensbrück training session … fifty prisoners were brought before the trainees, who were ordered to beat them." Three of the trainees asked why the prisoners were to be beaten and one refused. The trainees who refused "was imprisoned." [114] Grese learned the rules of punishment included whipping: twenty-five strokes to the bare buttocks for a minor infraction were the minimum that could be doled out. A Nazi doctor should be on standby to ensure the punisher was safe. If a prisoner could not take all the blows, the beating would stop, and the remainder blows be administered the following day. Grese was told she would not be doing the beating; she would assign another guard to do the hitting for her. She could order a prisoner to do the beating and reward them with extra food. All staff had to participate; she could not refuse if another guard ordered her to strike a prisoner for any infraction. This ensured discipline was never personal, never sadistic and there was no emotional investment.

New trainees were taught how to supervise a work crew of prisoners, how to conduct *appell.* Trainers stressed how *Appell*, or count,[115] was the most important part of daily camp routine where prisoners were lined up in rows to be counted.

---

[114] McRae, S. T. (2016). P.11

[115] Both the English and German word will be used intermittently in this text.

The new employees would again be grilled on their political personal beliefs and tested on their knowledge of camp regulations, leadership, and understanding of punishment. If they passed this test, the group moved on to hands-on learning. Here, the women went into the camp to learn operations and supervisory jobs, what was expected, what was allowed, and what they would be doing.

Grese would learn how prisoners could write home once a month. She would assist in monitoring these letters. Prisoners wrote careful letters without discussing details. Grese and her comrades were unaware the women wrote between the lines in invisible ink – their urine. Receivers would iron or hold the letters to heat and be able to read the truth about Ravensbrück.

Irma Grese passed training with enthusiasm. She repeated the oath to serve Hitler along with her fellow inductees, then received an identification card bearing her photo. In July 1942, Irma Grese began her three-month probationary period at Ravensbrück as Auxiliary Female SS Guard (*Hilfsaufseherin*). She was paired with an established guard for a probationary period to became one of the estimated 41,182 guards and 8.5% of female guards working in the camps. [116] Grese was 19 years old and went from classroom to a "boots on the ground" career. If she failed to show proficiency in a task, she would be ordered to repeat a portion of training.

When Grese completed this training, she signed three principal forms which stated:

- She would be punished for becoming personal with prisoners, including the taking of prisoner property.
- She would adhere to the rules for guards, including punctuality and following procedures learned in training.
- She had received instructions for working with the prisoners.

And once her signature appeared on these documents, Grese officially became an *Aufseherin*. Her first job was to oversee *Arbeitskommandos* (prisoner work details). She most likely beamed with pride when receiving her sports kit, [117] a summer and winter uniform (grey) which included a coat, two pairs of heavy black boots, a sweater, five pairs of socks, stockings, gloves, and a cap. "The uniform was of a denim type material … The jacket bore the 'Eagle' [118] on the left arm and a proficiency motif denoting any special skills like radio/telephone/signals/ dog handling, etc. Badge(s) were sewn on the lower left sleeve. The (guards) were also issued with a sidearm 9mm Luther pistol and light dog whip [sic]." [119] Himmler had introduced these uniforms in 1940, and careful consideration had gone into the appearance. A uniform for these unskilled, low-income laborers, for women formally regulated to few plain dresses, must have looked, and felt, dashing and powerful, just as the uniforms did for the young men who had signed up for the SS. Stylists at Hugo Boss AG put much consideration into the design for the SS.

---

[116] Sofsky (1999)

[117] This may have been a box to hold food and a whistle. They were also issued a bread box.

[118] Women, not being "official SS," were not allowed to wear the Runes or Death's head.

[119] Dixon, I. (1992)

Hugo Boss [120] AG is a German clothing company founded in 1924. Boss created clothing such as suits and jackets. Beginning in the 1930s, Boss began producing all Nazi uniforms as designed by SS members artist Karl Diebitsch and graphic designer Walter Heck.

The Reich had already created uniforms for Irma Grese's coveted BDM, the German female children's organization. Now the uniforms worn so proudly by Grese, the SA, the SS, Hitler Youth, the Wehrmacht, and several other organizations were sewn by female, French POWs and Polish prisoners forced laborers working for Hugo Boss AG during the Nazi reign. [121] These workers received no pay, lived in squalor, and many were worked to death; the Boss company reaped the profits and flourished. [122]

The female guard uniforms were the epitome of Hitler's vision of dress for women.

Hitler's love for animals reflected in his fashion ideas. Lipstick was forbidden (Hitler told people it was created from animal waste) as were furs. To maintain true Germanic expectations of the Reich, Grese would have never dyed her hair, polished her nails, plucked her brows, or smoked a cigarette. [123] Skirts and dresses were to be large enough to accentuate those child-bearing hips, so trousers and slinky dresses for women were not *de rigueur*. Anything not German made or touched by Germanic hands – Parisian fashions, for example – with its own "German made" label was preferred. A "true Aryan" like Irma Grese wore clothing with a label from the newly formed clothing union of Association of German Aryan Clothing Manufacturers (ADEFA). ADEFA's name was sewn into the cloth, assuring the wearer it was untouched by foreign hands and made in Germany.

A German Fashion Bureau was established because, Hitler announced, German women must dress to reflect their pride of country, and be the best dressed in all of Europe. The German Fashion Bureau would be dubbed *Deutsches Modeamt*. Magda Goebbels was made honorary president of The German Fashion Institute (her husband, Joseph, was Nazi Propaganda Minister). Never mind Magda loved clothing created by French and Jewish designers (a true fashionista, Magda changed outfits several times daily) and was constantly smoking cigarettes. She also wore heavy makeup and perfume.

As a result of design and demand, the female guard uniforms were an amalgam of Hitler's fashion demands and work practicality. The skirts were past the knee with a single long pleat worn over practical jackboots or simple black shoes. The jackets were plain with straight, military style lines, and the blouses had stiff, pointed collars. Coats were just as plain: thick for German winters, hanging just past the knee. They did not come close to the pomp and style of the male's uniform. The women were not allowed jewelry or purses when in uniform. The women's uniforms were anything but feminine and there was nothing sexualized about them. Irma Grese was one of the few female guards who had her uniforms tailored to fit, flattering her femininity. She did her best to look attractive. Eventually, she would take it to extremes.

Did Irma Grese immediately set her goals to advance as far as a woman could go? Given what is known of her personality, Grese most likely desired advancement along with the dominance and pay grade accompanying such a position. She understood a

[120] Founder Boss had joined the Nazi party in 1931. The current company has no ties to the Boss family.
[121] Koester, R. (2011)
[122] The company has since made formal apologies and has no ties to any Nazi-styled organizations.
[123] Adolph Hitler hated cigarettes and banned them from his properties.

male *Kommandant* oversaw the camp and ultimately determined her advancement and capabilities. An *Oberaufseherin* (senior female guard) supervised the female section, and never the male prisoners, reporting all issues involving women to the male section department head (S*chutzhaftLagerführer*). Conflict occurred often between male and female supervisors. Life at the camps remained a man's world.

Grese would have considered a promotion to female report leader (*Rapportführerin*), a station just below the *Oberaufseherin* in the hierarchy. As a report leader she would be invaluable to a block leader supervisor (*Blockführerin*). The report leader would supervise and discipline the prisoners, mete out punishment, oversee the roll call, and, at Auschwitz, take part in "selections" where prisoners were sorted out to be sent to the gas chamber. It was the latter in which Irma Grese would later excel.

Before she could advance, Grese was employed in one of two groups. "Technical guards" supervised specific departments such as the kitchens. Grese could also be posted as a guard overseeing a work group of prisoners as the group cleaned, planted, built, or maintained a section of camp.

Whatever position Irma Grese held she learned quickly, like her fellow employees, she would learn every position held some type of absolute power over people.

Elissa Mailänder's excellent book "Female SS Guards and Workaday Violence: The Majdanek Concentration Camp 1942 – 1944" (2015) provides a detailed description of housing, socialization, and expectations from female officers employed at the camps. Like the buildings where they resided, these female officers were comparable in style. The area reserved for the camp employees resembled a military garrison. These women – the former nurses, secretaries, shop keeps, maids, laborers, factory workers, farmers like Irma Grese – were now immersed in the military lifestyle.

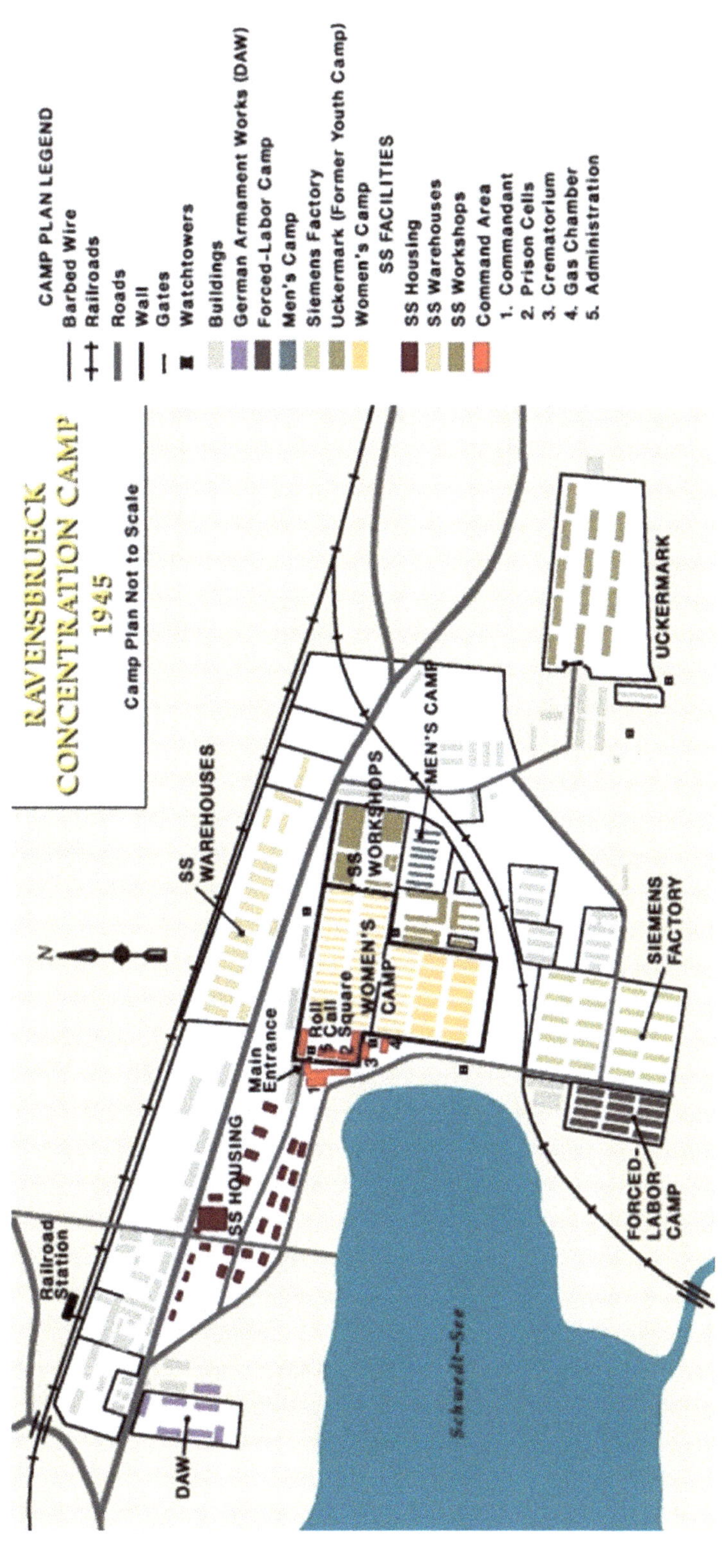
RAVENSBRUECK
CONCENTRATION CAMP
1945
Camp Plan Not to Scale
CAMP PLAN LEGEND
Barbed Wire
Railroads
Roads
Wall
Gates
Watchtowers
Buildings
German Armament Works (DAW)
Forced-Labor Camp
Men's Camp
Siemens Factory
Uckermark (Former Youth Camp)
Women's Camp
SS FACILITIES
SS Housing
SS Warehouses
SS Workshops
Command Area
1. Commandant
2. Prison Cells
3. Crematorium
4. Gas Chamber
5. Administration
N
SS WAREHOUSES
SS WORKSHOPS
MEN'S CAMP
UCKERMARK
WOMEN'S CAMP
Roll Call Square
Main Entrance
SS HOUSING
Railroad Station
DAW
SIEMENS FACTORY
FORCED-LABOR CAMP
Schwedt-See

CHAPTER 12
Life in Ravensbrück

Everything about employment in the camps encompassed power, including prisoners who supervised other prisoners. The groundwork to the architecture to the daily lives of guards and their superiors was a hierarchy. Forced labor built the groundworks of the complex, female prisoners hacking at the soil with picks and shovels, dragging carts of earth from the scene.

There were four villas for the SS officers and their families, commonly known as *"Führerhäuser."* The houses were handsome, a nod to old-world German style, with plenty of windows, stone porches, and steep roofs. High ceilings and a winding staircase accented the interior. The senior officer's quarters were built on a rise, giving the impression the lower staff were "looked down upon" and constantly observed. The female housing units, for example, "the arrangement and architectural style of the houses express the self-concept of the SS. They reflect the ideological frame and life world inhabited by the SS personnel." [124] The women's barracks were plain, boxlike buildings with steep pointed roofs, with shutters and balconies in two rows. There was a square to walk across in the center, the lake within strolling distance, a road on either side of the housing units. Irma Grese would initially have a room in one of these eight houses alongside other female recruits. She would have climbed the stairs holding on to a polished dark wooden handrail, her footsteps echoing on the solid wooden stairs along the plain walls. A few steps to a short landing, a turn, and a few more steps to the second floor would put her into a short hallway. Grese's room would be one of the ten studio rooms that occupied one of two floors, or she may have had to carry her items up to one of the four smaller attic rooms.

There have been various descriptions of the rooms. A former guard describes pretty curtains around the window in the room where she lived, sparse but quality furnishings, and shared dresser and wardrobe. Two to three women shared a room, and some had a single room, depending on the population. The inhabitants shared a washbasin. The rooms boasted thick carpeting. Decorations and niceties – linens, utensils, etcetera – were procured from the homes left behind when families were deported. There was a community toilet and tub down the hall for all the women living on the same floor. A kitchenette was on each floor.

Irma Grese may have enjoyed two rooms in her apartment. The single door led into a living room, with a tiny foyer for her coats and jackets. The rooms came furnished with accessories taken from homes in the local village, usually a sideboard, small table with chairs, and a cabinet. A doorway led to a washbasin in the corner, with white, squared tiles decorating these walls. The bedroom area was just large enough to hold a single bed with a shelf above. Wallpaper made it cozy, and the women would decorate their apartments to suit them. Grese lived in an 80' x 99' [125] sized room.

---

[124] Eschenbach (1997), cited in Mailänder, p. 6.

[125] Mailänder, p.6

This is a view of the SS housing estate - houses for the female guards, around 1940. Photos from the SS album of the women's concentration camp Ravensbrück 1940 to 1941/42: Starting in 1940, the Inspector of the Concentration Camps and the SS Budget and Construction Main Office had photographic documentary books compiled. The photographs were supposed to show the expansion of the camps, particular buildings and the 'productive use' of prisoners at their workplaces. The 92 images from the Ravensbrück album convey an impression of orderliness and efficiency. (The photograph was taken from the roof of the *Kommandantur*) (Circa: 1940s. Photographer unknown, Memorial Ravensbrück, Ph-Nr. 1639. Used with permission.)

Wartime photograph of a guard's room used by SS men. Irma Grese's room would have been comparable until she was promoted to supervisor; subsequently she would have a private room. While sparse, the rooms would be much nicer than what most of the women had back home. Irma Grese, for example, had slept on a mattress full of straw. (Circa 1941. Photographer unknown. Courtesy Auschwitz – Birkenau Memorial and Museum. Used with permission.)

There were sewing rooms and places to sit and knit or read in a common area. There was a piano that one of the senior guards loved to play and her playing was exquisite; she would lose herself in the rapturous notes. (Her name: Maria Mandl.)

Grese's room had a window in its door so anyone walking by could peer into her living space. There was an overseer for each building, the role was a rotating shift so the trainees – or employees – supervised one another, creating a precarious trust system. For Irma Grese, coming from a large, chaotic family and sharing a bed with her siblings, it was surely a welcomed change.

Meals were served canteen style and cooked by prisoners, but officers did not mingle with nonofficers. There was foodstuff not available to the outside world, and always fresh and plentiful. Prisoners cooked and cleaned so, for once in most of their lives, not one of these female officers were forced to scrub a cookpot or fret over dishpan hands.

Grese's clothing and behavior were regulated. Social time – including curfew – was monitored: there was one exit out of the garrison and a pass, closely inspected, had to be presented before passing through this exit. Only then could Grese and her fellow employees take the easy walk or bicycle ride to Fürstenberg, where they could shop, have a leisurely dinner, and – until one was added to the camp itself – visit a hair salon. Grese and her fellow workers received perks that made the jobs inside the concentration camp even more alluring. Grese could travel to Fürstenberg and show her ticket at the Fürstenberg cinema to take in a propaganda – filled, heavily censored free movie; staff received free passes. (Playhouses would shut down in 1944, but the cinemas would stay open until her treasured Germany lost the war.) Films played an important role in Germany society. Irma Grese was ensured she would not be sitting next to a Jew in the cinema.

Berlin, capital of Nazi Germany, was not too far away for a weekend getaway to a big city. Many civilians would look at Grese's uniform in awe; sometimes, the uniform gave access to free or discounted meals and items. The Ravensbrück staff could boat, swim, ski, and skate on nearby Lake Schwedt.

For a woman who had been working in the family home since she was old enough to lift a dust cloth or cut a vegetable, leisure time was a treasured concept.

Vacation leave and transfers were available. Supervised prisoners did all the domestic work for the Ravensbrück staff. (Grese would eventually have her own tailor.) For women who had been saddled with these chores since they were old enough to lift a dust rag or drag a mop, this was a luxury. It was free maid service, and the cost was to supervise – an easy task.

A female guard could view the lake and forest from her balcony; she could also view work crews of prisoners and – later - the crematorium belching out the dead from the opposite side of the building. [126] Few of the women brought their children to live with them. Like Grese, most of these female trainees were young, with little education and from poor families. A nice place to live, healthy and delicious food, and free clothing on above average wages was a far better opportunity than munitions factory work, one of the few jobs available for single females. The pay was double what factory workers were taking home. Room and board were low cost. Still, living expenses were much less costly than rent or mortgage and groceries (if available in war-torn Europe, where so many foods were rationed or unavailable). When Irma Grese reviewed her paystub, she would see mandatory fees taken out of her salary for Nazi Labor Front membership and a disability and illness

[126] Ravensbrück had a crematorium, but did not have a gas chamber until 1945.

fund. Grese's paycheck was 54 (Reichs)marks monthly starting salary because she was 18. [127] Once she turned 25, and if she were single, she would receive close to 186 Marks gross per month. Having a child meant a supplement of 20 marks per child. [128]

Unmarried and with no children, Grese would eventually earn 186.65 Reichsmarks monthly plus 35 Reichsmarks overtime premium (working over 300 hours a month). She would be paid a bonus of 100 Marks if she were working a post where it was considered a "hazardous condition." It was far better than a factory worker's salary at 76 Reichsmarks monthly. [129]

Irma Grese learned that her personal life in this new world was controlled – act professionally, keep a tidy room, dress neatly, and be loyal to the Nazi party. To be part of this life demanded a one hundred percent dedication; she was a female guard at a concentration camp twenty four hours a day, seven days a week. The Nazis owned the individual, and the individual now became the group. Any activity or behavior not the norm had to be explained and was subject to reprimands, including dismissal. Some guard trainees were released shortly after they were hired because they would be considered bad candidates. At least one woman was fired for having gonorrhea. At least one trainee from Grese's class was dismissed because she was too kind to prisoners. Irma Grese stayed, much to the horror of so many prisoners.

Irma Grese started out as a fresh-faced recruit in braids. What she became is a headline story. She would eventually break many of the rules she had sworn to uphold but was disciplined only once. Many of her infractions involved torture and murder of prisoners. For example, to whip and beat prisoners, Grese had a special whip made in one of the camp's factories. "It was cellophane paper plaited like a pigtail. It was translucent like white glass" she explained later. The *Commandant* ordered her to get rid of this whip and exchange it for one the other guards were using. She blatantly ignored the order. [130] Using this whip that cut and bruised, Grese whipped many prisoners, some did not survive the beating, and most taken to the camp infirmary.

She admitted to doing so while on the stand at the 1945 Belsen trial for her crimes (prosecution in bold):

Did the other *Aufseherinnen* (female officers) have these whips made too?

No

It was just your bright idea?

Yes

In *Lager* "C" you used to carry a walking stick too, and sometimes you beat people with the whip and sometimes with the stick?

Yes

[127] Irma Grese testimony, The Belsen Trial, October 17, 1945
[128] During WWII, the Reichsmark's rate was approximately 1 mark to $2.50 USD
[129] capitalpunishmentUK.org
[130] Irma Grese testimony, The Belsen Trial, October 17, 1945

.

Were you allowed to beat people?

No

So, it was not a question of having orders from your Superiors to do it. You did this against orders, did you?

Yes

Were you the only person who beat prisoners against regulations?

I do not know.

Did you ever see anyone else beat prisoners?

Yes

Did you sometimes get orders to do so?

No

Did you give orders to other *Aufseherinnen* working under you to beat prisoners?

Yes

Had you the right to give such authorisation?

No [131]

Irma Grese had found her calling in the concentration camps of the Holocaust. Gone was the pigtailed little girl who grinned at the photographer in a class photograph. Here now was The Hyena.

[131] Ibid.

Name: Ahrens Elvira
SS-Nr. Eingestellt am: 1.9.44
geb. 10.10.20 zu Burgdorf
Einheit: KL Neuengamme

Einstellung genehmigt am
ausgeschieden am:
Entlassungsgrund:
Bestell-Nr. W SS 4382 Metten & Co. Berlin SW 61

Neuengamme concentration camp personnel card

Irma Grese would have her own personnel card similar to the above concentration camp personnel card for Elvira Ahrens of KL Neuengamme. Neuengamme was the largest Northwest Germany concentration camp, the main camp with over 80 satellite camps.

Translation:

Name: Ahrens, Elvira
Set # 1.9.44
Date of birth 10.10.20 in Burgdorf
Unit: KL Neuengamme
retired on: ________________
Reason for dismissal:____________

(Date: circa 1940s. Photographer: Unknown. Source: *"Anwerbung und Ausbild von SS-Aufsehreinnen."* Public Domain.)

PART IV

Cutting Fangs at Ravensbrück

Major Cranfield: I suggest to you that you gloried in your jackboots and your pistol and your whip?

Irma Grese: Gloried? I could not say no.

Major Cranfield: When these people were parading, they were very often paraded naked and inspected like cattle to see whether they fit to work or fit to die, were they not?

Irma Grese: Not like cattle.

- Irma Grese, examined by Major Cranfield during the 1945 Belsen Trials

Aufseherinnen at Play

Women who wished to escape the lower–paying jobs during World War II applied for the job of *Aufseherin* at the concentration camps. Nazi employees received considerable perks, nutritious meals, inexpensive housing, and a chance to hold rank.

The job attracted younger women who had little education. Only a few *Aufseherinnen* were as dangerous and brutal as Irma Grese. Survivors reported that some female staff members were kind and helpful. The majority disappeared into obscurity after the war.

To be an *Aufseherin* also meant social time, sisterhood, identification, power, control, and membership. The young women who were once maids, farmer's daughters, factory workers, and laborers at other low-paying, low-skilled jobs now had a title with (usually) unchecked power. Drab clothing was replaced with a dashing uniform.

The women in these photographs have not been identified. Clearly, they are proud of themselves and happy to pose in their uniforms. Note they are smiling and posing only a few yards from the prisoner camp. These images are a rare glimpse of the *Aufseherinnen's* private life.

(Circa 1943? Photographer: Unknown. Credit: BArch, MfS, HA IX/11, ZM, Nr. 1630, Folder 1, Page 16; BArch, MfS, HA IX/11, ZM, Nr. 1630, Folder 1, Page 17. Used with permission with exceptional appreciation to Christian Carlsen of the Bundesarchiv.)

CHAPTER 13
Aufseherin

As discussed, the Ravensbrück of 1943 was not the same camp as the Ravensbrück before Irma Grese arrived there to interview as a seventeen-year-old hopeful. One author explains, "In the beginning, (SS commander) Heinrich Himmler used (Ravensbrück) as a show camp. There were flowers in the window boxes, birdcages and a beautiful road lined with trees. Himmler would show it to the International Red Cross to prove (he was) supposedly treating the prisoners well." [132]

Heinrich Himmler did inspect Ravensbrück often. His mistress lived less than ten miles away.

By 1943, there were 18 barracks/huts to include sickbays for prisoners and warehouses, two of each. Three tiered wooden bunks provided sleeping spaces in the inmate barracks with washrooms and toilets in each barrack. Female inmates began to flow in: Jews, Jehovah's Witnesses, gypsies, criminals, those labeled "work shy" and "race defilers." Soon, there were women from over 30 countries, most from Poland, the Soviet Union, with the smallest number from Yugoslavia. When 1942 morphed into 1943, Ravensbrück held an estimated 10,000 prisoners. Food was becoming scarce and of poor quality. The sanitation was horrific at best. Prisoners became so filthy that the overseers were loath to touch them; their winter gloves found use during all seasons. Inmates too sick or old to work, mentally ill, handicapped, or physically disabled were sent away to be gassed. [133]

Grese initially worked in Ravensbrück for seven months. All new *Aufseherinnen* had to work outside of the camp supervising a work detail as a first assignment. Once allowed to work inside, one of her positions was as a telephone operator for 54 Reichsmarks a month. [134] Other positions open to *SS Aufseherinnen* besides camp guard included typing, filing, and mail room operations. Eventually, Grese would be overseer of work details, supervising women in various jobs across the compounds. Grese would become one of 110 supervisors for every 5,300 to 6,600 prisoners on average. [135] Whatever job the prisoners were slaving at, whatever the weather, Grese insured she appeared flawless, from hair setting to uniform. She began to stand out among her peers for her good looks and her fastidious clothing.

She would begin to spend a great deal of time on her appearance. Despite her age she was quickly recognizable as promotional material. She looked the part of the Nazi female: blonde, blue eyed, stout, maniacally devoted to the Reich and young enough to never question her leaders. She must have metamorphosed into the militant lifestyle quickly, for she rose through the ranks faster than her peers. Grese was "one of the youngest of all the *Aufseherinnen* with status, authority, and relative autonomy as compared to other women who worked for the SS." [136] Supervisors increased Grese's task load and soon she would oversee "over eighteen thousand prisoners. It was her cruelty… (and) resolute, almost devotionally juvenile commitment to Nazi tenets that made her notorious" among

[132] Dawson (2016)
[133] United States Holocaust Museum (n.d.)
[134] Adele-Marie, p. 112
[135] Stebel (2003) p. 51, 180 cited in Mailänder, p. 10-11.
[136] Ibid. pp. 113

staff and prisoners. [137] Grese became one of the approximate 10% of female overseers in an estimated 37,000 SS guards in Nazi concentration camps. [138] It was not just her cruelty and devotion to ideology that brought Irma Grese to the forefront. She appeared to be loyal to no others except superiors. This was proven with an incident involving an *Aufseherin* named Buchhalter, who had been kind toward a prisoner.

The camps were rife with tipsters, prisoners who would give information on other prisoners' wrongdoings to staff for favors: an extra portion of food, new clothing, anything to make life a bit tolerable. It was discovered that Buchhalter was having an affair with a prisoner; she was also mailing out prisoner's unofficial mail to their families outside of the camps.

One version: Heinrich Himmler was inspecting the camp when he discovered Buchhalter's transgressions. Himmler stated Buchhalter would receive twenty-five lashes for the offense. Grese and the others were forced to watch Himmler deliver twenty-three lashes to the offender's buttocks. Himmler ordered Grese to deliver the last two lashes and complete the punishment. She delivered the blows without question or hesitancy.

The other version – and probably the truth – was discussed in the Belsen trials. Former *Aufseherin* Elisabeth Volkenrath testified she recalled *Aufseherin* Buchhalter "being punished," and "the punishment took place at the house where we lived in the dining room in the evening, and we had all to parade. Grese was also present …the punishment was 25 lashes with a whip, which had to be administered by the *Aufseherin*. (The *Kommandant*, Höss) came and read out the judgment and said to all the *Aufseherinnen* that this woman was being punished by order of *Reichsfuhrer* Himmler." [139] During the same trial, on October 16, 1945, Grese would also testify she was twenty years old when *Kommandant* Höss would order her to deliver the last two lashes to punish *Aufseherin* Buchhalter. Neither Volkenrath nor Grese said who delivered the majority of the blows. Regardless of the truth, Irma Grese beat a fellow comrade without hesitation for breaking the rules.

Heinrich Himmler was not one for hands-on punishment, and he had already proven he did not have the stomach for murder. Himmler had never seen a dead body prior to Minsk in 1941, where he ordered one hundred prison inmates to be shot in a mass grave. Himmler leaned over the pit to watch the mass execution; as the roar of bullets sounded, a victim's brain matter splashed on his coat. Himmler's liaison officer would later recall Himmler's turning green, then pale, heaving as if to vomit, almost fainting, and had to be helped to walk away.

The whipping of Ms. Buchhalter was typical of Nazi punishment during WWII's Nazi regime. "Although insubordination was taken seriously, excuses that soldiers had 'just been obeying orders' when they participated in Holocaust atrocities weren't entirely true." [140] Research has revealed while Nazi soldiers received beatings and threats for refusing to harm prisoners and hostages, no records exist of any being executed for disobeying an order to take part in the murders or tortures. After the war, one of the central defense arguments was "I was just following orders" - under threat of death. Irma Grese and her

[137] Ibid.
[138] Willmott (2015)
[139] Testimony of Elisabeth Volkenrath, Belsen Trials, Friday, 12th October, 1945
[140] Blakemore (2019)

comrades knew they would not be executed by her beloved Nazis should they ever refuse to kill or harm the enemy. Chastised, yes; disciplined, obviously.

As discussed, 0ne of Irma Grese's initial jobs was supervising *Aussenkommandos* ("outside squads") outside of the compound. Grese understood she was to observe prisoners as they cleared weeds, picked herbs, cleared brush, and shaped and cleaned roads. One survivor remembers:

> Each squad had its own *Aufseherin*. I got to know Irma Grese in the *Kräuter-Kommando* (weeds-squad). There we picked nettles, and our hands were bleeding because we did not get gloves. She gave us very high baskets and she stamped in the baskets with her boots. If the baskets were not filled up, she would beat us on the head left and right.
> Irma Grese was very beautiful. And she was extremely evil. [141]

As an *Aufseherin*, Grese would attend a 4am guard staff roll call where she would listen attentively to her *Oberaufseherin*. Then Grese would arrive at the roll call for prisoners. Prisoners were to line up, so many to a line front to back, in rows of ten, and stand motionless to be counted. The procedure was usually chaotic for Grese, for many prisoners did not speak the same language, often inmates wandered, some were missing, and it became the norm for prisoners to collapse, or even die, in place. It all caused the rows of ten to shift. Some of the officers could not count. They would ask prisoners to assist, and some prisoners could not count. At times just taking roll would last all day, causing some prisoners to faint. Adding to the issue was the need for an *Aufseherin* to prove her worth.

Another *Aufseherin* would have the same issues: prisoners unsure of the rules, or getting sick and fainting, prisoners dying in their tracks, the inability to count, an inept system ran by inept people. Then enter Irma Grese to "assist" in the *appell*. Her response to the issue was to beat and torture inmates who either innocently caused problems or appeared to cause problems.

At times, Irma Grese would be so frustrated with the count she would force prisoners to hold heavy rocks (or bricks) over their heads for hours. Anyone who fell would receive a beating.

Auschwitz survivor Magda Blau recalls Irma Grese breaking one of the foremost rules. She wrote the incident occurred in Auschwitz "around July 1942" (although Grese did not move to Auschwitz until March 1943. It is possible the dates were crossed. Keeping track of dates was not a priority nor was it easy for prisoners.) Magda Blau recalls the *Aufseherin* as being youthful, between eighteen or nineteen, "quite wide eyed, with a pretty, slightly chubby face and long plaites. She had only been here for a few days [sic] but I had noticed her because she was chatty with the other guards in the way of a young girl." This *Aufseherin* introduced herself "I'm Irma" and asked the prisoner her first name, using it to address the prisoner. She began casually speaking to Magda, even telling her, "I admire you" for the prisoner's fair work ethic. [142]

[141] Noks (2014)
[142] Hellinger & Lee (2021). Pp. 62-4.

"She looked a chubby woman, young woman," Magda Blau would recall, years later. "… about eighteen, nineteen, with long blonde plaits … plaits, chubby. And she didn't even have the (uniform) hat on." [143]

Irma was chatty, sharing personal information. Later, Magda felt Grese was "deceiving" her. "I was living in a small place," Grese told Magda about how she came to work for the SS, "And suddenly they asked for volunteers. But I didn't know where they were taking me. So, I volunteered, and here I am." [144]

Grese would also discuss with Magda the secret plans of building on to Auschwitz and even the in-depth psychological development that went into the planning. Magda was shocked but kept a calm demeanor, speaking kindly but carefully to the future Hyena of Auschwitz.

Magda Blau would later cross paths with Grese "in April 1943" in Birkenau. The prisoner did not recognize Grese- the guard had lost her naïve expression, shed some weight, and her uniform had been tailored to fit. She wore her uniform crisp and neat, much different than other *Aufseherinnen*. Grese's belt and boots were shined to a high gloss, with a revolver in the belt and a whip sticking out of one boot. Gone were the plaits; Grese's hair was up and tight around her skull. Magda ensured they were alone, for to speak to a guard could mean death. "Irma, you look like a real SS woman now," she observed.

Grese greeted her with a "hello, Magda."

"I hope you never become as brutal as the others." [145]

Grese did not respond or stop to chat. She continued down the road, and the prisoner continued to walk in the opposite direction.

Ravensbrück *Oberaufseherin* Maria Mandl was Grese's supervisor. Mandl (1912 - 1948) was attractive but did not possess the feminine good looks Grese enjoyed. With her triangular face and her dirty blonde hair piled on her head, Mandl utilized a whip and boots to torture and punish. Mandl began her career at the Nazi concentration camp Lichtenburg but was sent to Ravensbrück when it opened in 1939. [146]

December of 1941 would be Maria Mandl's third Christmas spent at Ravensbrück. Christmas is a much-loved celebration in German culture. (The traditional Christmas tree is credited as originating in 16th century Germany.) As the norm, prisoners would decorate Mandl's apartment, the living spaces for staff, and the general areas for the SS and their families. It was not a "Christmas" celebration but more of a "yuletide season" festival with parties for the staff and their families throughout the month. A decorated tree was placed in the center of the prisoner camp, as if prisoners would enjoy this festive reminder. If there was any shred of happiness from the decoration it was quickly snuffed out when an escaped Roma teenaged prisoner was caught, then beaten to death by guards in front of this Christmas tree. Mandl is rumored to be one of these killers.

Maria Mandl moved quickly through the ranks to *SS-Oberaufseherin* in April 1942. One of Mandl's assignments was supervision of punishments. In the Third Reich she would never outrank a man, but Mandl would become *SS-Lagerführerin* over Auschwitz-Birkenau and have command over the female prisoners and staff, including Irma

[143] An infraction that Grese would later pay for. Perhaps she felt it unattractive or the hats mussed her hair?
[144] Blau, Magda (1990)
[145] Hellinger & Lee. pp. 95-6.
[146] For an excellent account on Mandl, see Eischeid, S. (2023). "Mistress of Life and Death: The Dark Journey of Maria Mandl, Head Overseer of the Women's Camp at Auschwitz-Birkenau."

Grese. Maria Mandl was abominably cruel, beating, kicking, and thrashing prisoners, sentencing them to death or prolonged suffering, ripping children from mother's arms and trouncing the parents who protested, and purposely creating conditions of suffering. Mandl would befriend child prisoners then personally lead them to their death. She created the Women's Orchestra of Auschwitz, composed of prisoners who had been musicians on the outside. This orchestra was forced to accompany selections for gas chambers, "welcome" transportation arrivals, and roll calls. Sometimes, prisoners were forced to march in time to their music and anyone who failed was beaten or murdered. The Women's Orchestra had to play flawlessly while observing friends and relatives die. Maria Mandl's moniker would become "The Beast." [147]

So, in Ravensbrück, supported by some of the cruelest women in the Nazi killing machine, the beautiful, impeccably dressed Irma Grese rose through the ranks until she was supervising over eighteen thousand prisoners. Did her mentors and trainers have any influence over Irma Grese? Grese's behavior certainly came to mirror that of Binz and Mandl. Though when she supervised Grese later, Mandl found The Hyaena somewhat difficult to control.

In hindsight, it was said cruelty and sadistic behavior seemed natural to Grese, and her mentors had no effect on her bloodlust nor her viciousness. Numerous survivors also recount how females were much more brutal than male officers, to their surprise, so it is possible that these females were all naturally cruel without instigation.

The use of brutality and power was a tactic to establish one's place in the world throughout the SS – to prove one's mettle. Females, in particular, had to prove they belonged in this fierce world. And females had to prove themselves to each other, "one-upping" in capabilities. On the streets of Berlin or any other city, ladies had preened in pretty dresses and flashy hairstyles, or played the sufficient roles to prove their worth, the target being an employer, a man, a situation involving authority. In the grey world of concentration camps, the women clad in the identical, sexless guard's uniform had little to use except what was considered a talent, a coveted strength: brutality and power. Brutality had shock value. Power held worth. Numerous survivors recalled some *Aufseherin*'s punishments or acts of violence intensified when a male guard was in the immediate area. Inevitably, Irma Grese understood this dynamic.

Significant works exist documenting the "cycle of violence" where criminal – or "bad"- behavior is learned in the home as either a means of survival or individual behavior (where the victim becomes the perpetrator). Studies have revealed children from abusive homes do not all become violent adults. Neurobiology, environment, personality, psychopathy - a myriad of factors exist that can either carry on a legacy of abuse or stop the cycle. Now, in the concentration camp vocation, Irma Grese was isolated from the world she knew previously, surrounded by violence and despair, in a place where ferocity was rewarded. (Still, she had few friends in her life.) Suddenly, she was being recognized as a person of status. The ignorant, youthful girl with little life experience was perfect clay for this profession. Irma Grese was becoming The Hyena and she was cutting her fangs at Ravensbrück.

---

[147] Mandl would be arrested and tried by the Supreme National Tribunal at the Auschwitz Trial, found guilty, and hanged on January 24, 1948.

The Hyena's Uniform

Upon being hired as a guard at Ravensbrück, Irma Grese would have been issued a sports kit, a summer and winter uniform (grey) which included a coat, two pairs of heavy black boots, a sweater, five pairs of socks, stockings, gloves, and a cap.
Irma Grese was one of the few guards who had her uniforms tailored to fit, flattering her femininity. Gerda "Jane" Bernigau (1908 – 1992) was an SS *Oberaufseherin* who was employed at the Lichtenburg, Gross-Rosen, Mauthausen, and Ravensbrück concentration camps. She was also a trainer of new guards at Sankt Lambrecht. Bernigau would write a book about her work in the SS. She was never prosecuted for her crimes.

Next pages: Uniform of an SS helper, attributed to the overseer Jane Bernigau with jacket, skirt, blouse and cap. The skirt and jacket bear the name tag "Bernigau. KL Groß-Rosen," and the skirt also bears a label from the *Reichszeugmeisterei* in Munich (RZM). The RZM controlled the production and sale of uniforms for the NSDAP and its organisations, including the SS. (Note the SS detail on the skirt inseam.) Although Jane Bernigau was a senior guard at the Groß-Rosen concentration camp, she was not a member of the SS. It is therefore questionable whether she wore an SS uniform as a concentration camp guard. (Circa 2023. Location: Ravensbrück Memorial. Photographer: Britta Pawelke, Memorial Ravensbrück, V3240 A3. Used with permission.)

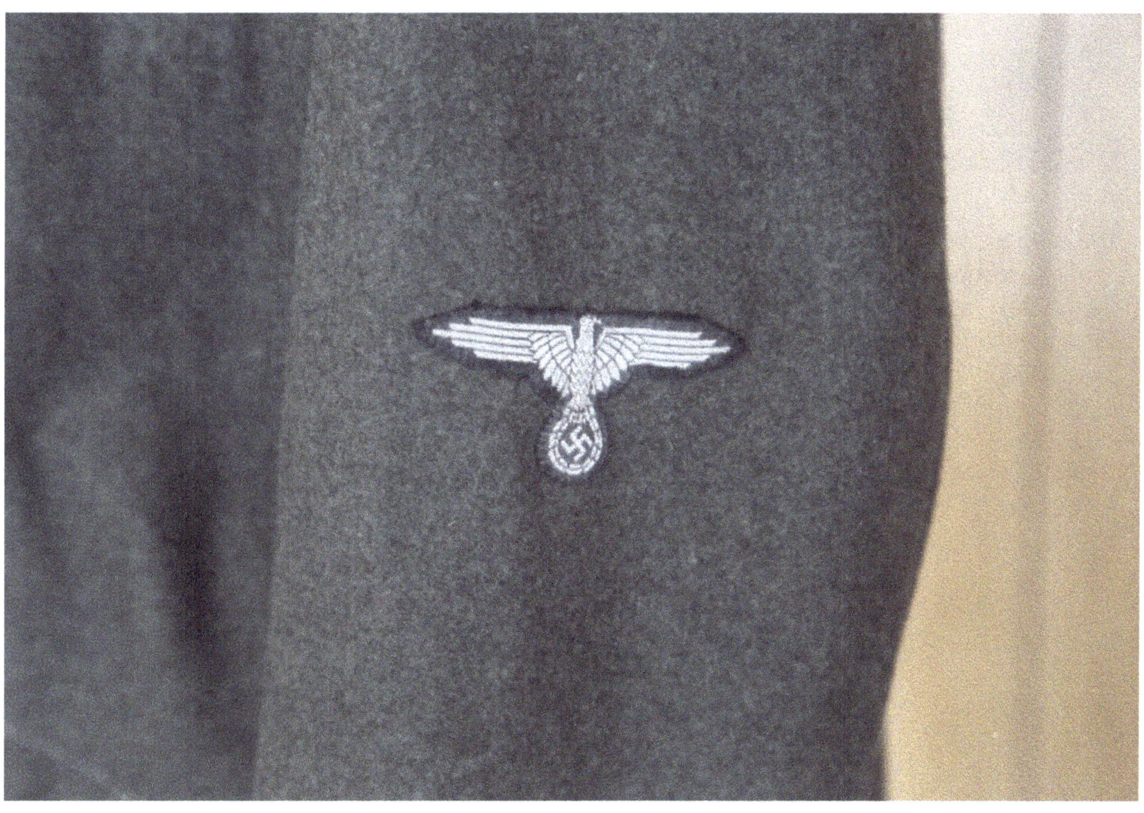

Housing at Auschwitz - Staff building (*Stabsgebäude*). "Little information has been preserved about how supervisors serving at KL Auschwitz spent their free time and where they were staying. Every day, after completing all their duties, they went to rest in the headquarters building (*Stabsgebäude*), where there were quarters for unmarried female guards. The supervisors' rooms were located on the first floor. They also had a common dining room at their disposal. The basement of this building housed the SS laundry and sewing room, and women assigned to cleaning the supervisors' rooms were also accommodated."
Irma Grese, being an unmarried female, would have roomed in this building while employed at Auschwitz. (Circa 1945. Photographer: unknown. Courtesy The Archive of The State Museum Auschwitz-Birkenau in Oświęcim. Used with permission)

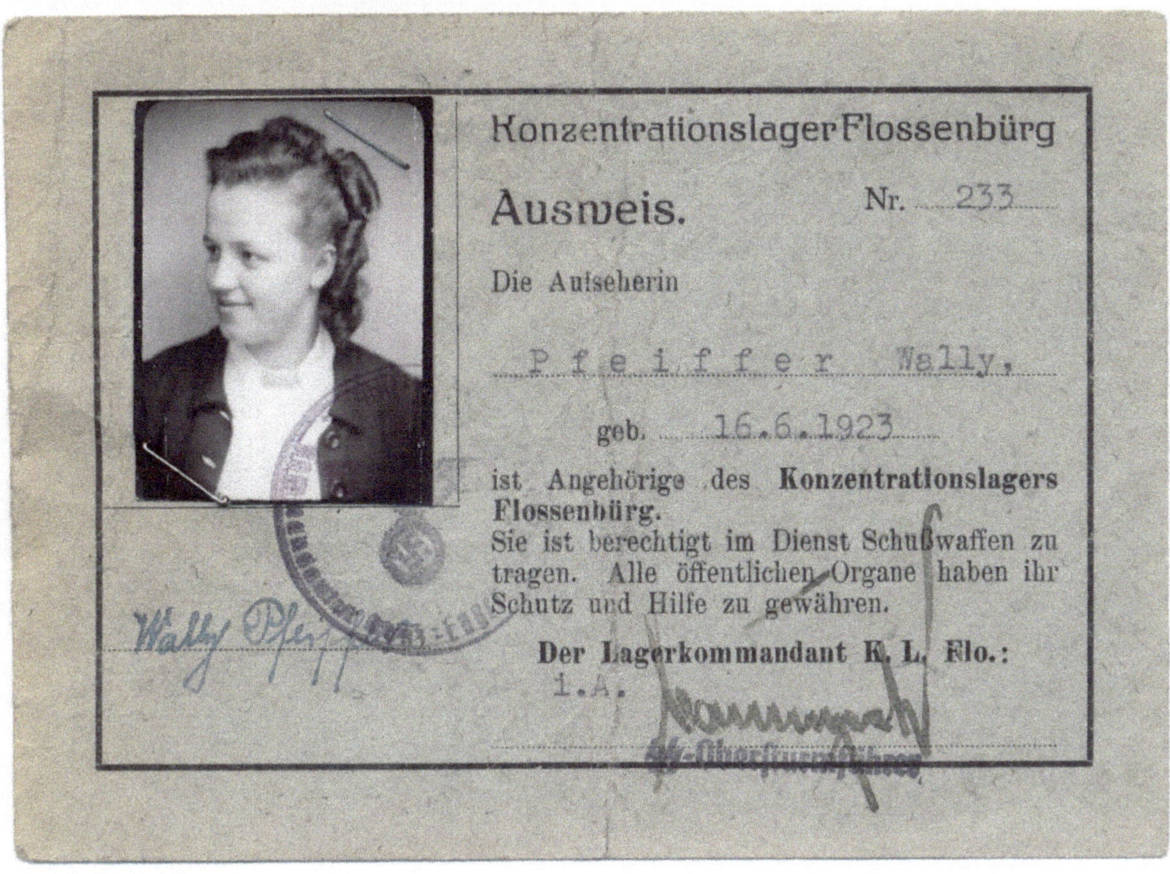

Konzentrationslager Flossenbürg

Ausweis. Nr. 233

Die Aufseherin

Pfeiffer Wally,

geb. 16.6.1923

ist Angehörige des **Konzentrationslagers Flossenbürg.**
Sie ist berechtigt im Dienst Schußwaffen zu tragen. Alle öffentlichen Organe haben ihr Schutz und Hilfe zu gewähren.

Wally Pfeiffer

Der Lagerkommandant K. L. Flo.:
i.A.

SS-Obersturmführer

An excessively rare female *SS-Helferin* identity card (*ausweis*) issued by Flossenburg concentration camp (1938-1945). These pale green cards measured 5.75 x 4 in. Translation: "Nr. 233, the helper Wally Pfeiffer, born June 16, 1923, is a member of Concentration Camp Flossenburg. She is permitted to carry a gun while on duty. All public organizations must ensure their protection and help..." Pfeiffer signed the card beneath her photograph which is marked with the camp's official stamp. The card, which was intended to be signed by the camp commandant, was signed by SS-*Obersturmführer* Ludwig Baumgartner (1909-1953), adjutant of the camp commandant at both Flossenbürg and Auschwitz concentration camps.
Irma Grese would have carried such a card. Grese's card has been lost in time, and very few *Helferin* identity cards remain. (Circa 1940. Location: Flossenburg concentration camp. Photography of card by Alexander Historical Auctions. Courtesy Alexander Historical Auctions. Used with permission.)

CHAPTER 14
Auschwitz-Birkenau
March 1943 - January 1945

"For those who endured it, violence caused pain and fear. For those who exercised and performed it, violence brought a feeling of power and, in many cases, lust."
- Lüdtk, cited in Kozlov (2010), p. 32

Auschwitz is the most familiar camp in the entire Nazi concentration camp system, in part because of its size and the fact it became the largest extermination camp. "Auschwitz" was actually a group of camps located in the same proximity.

While Irma Grese worked at Hohenluchen, Auschwitz was established in 1940, in Oświęcim, Poland, 40 miles west of Kraków. Kraków was a beautifully older city; the second – largest city in Poland and rich in history. Rich with culture and art, rife with academia and commerce, *Stołeczne Królewskie Miasto Kraków* (Royal Capital City of Kraków) boasted gothic architecture, with a Renaissance – styled influence and Baroque construction peeping through. Kraków was thriving, picturesque, and an imperative part of Poland. Thus, Adolph Hitler wanted Kraków.

Nazi Germany invaded Kraków in September of 1939. It went from a proud, Polish city to Germany's capitol for general government, with Nazi flags constantly waving in the breeze and SS uniformed soldiers at every turn. Drastic changes now, including the rounding up of Jews to force them into the Warsaw Jewish Ghetto, walled off from the city of which they were once so proud. From the ghetto, these people were stuffed into cattle cars and taken to various extermination camps, including Auschwitz.

Auschwitz I was created in Spring 1940. The Polish Army had abandoned army barracks near Oświęcim, and the SS commandeered these empty buildings. The buildings were surrounded by forest and marsh, with a main railroad hub. The Nazi party carefully selected this area. There was a reason and method for all they did.

"Political prisoners" were transported into the camp in the summer of 1940.

Auschwitz I was the epicenter of nearby camps, with departments established for a Gestapo camp, garrison, main employment office, warehouses for main supplies, and workshops creating goods for the SS. Forced prisoner labor worked these warehouses with guards overseeing the labor. It was initially an all-male camp. In March 1942, the camp became housing for the overflow of Ravensbrück female prisoners. Initially, only a wall separated the all - female blocks from the males until August when the women were moved to Birkenau. Birkenau, in the beginning, was nothing more than a hastily created subdivision. It would determine Irma Grese's fate.

In 1940, the Nazis took over a faction of huts near the Belsen military base in Northwest Germany. The camp was dubbed "Bergen-Belsen" and initially consisted of the few huts and shelters made from earth and trees. Half of these buildings were constructed of brick and the remaining buildings were the original horse stables. The camp of 60 wooden huts would eventually expand to just under a mile long and 400 yards wide. Irma Grese and her fellow guards were using 15 huts. There were five compounds (two for women) at Bergen-Belsen and the first transport arrived in 1941. [148] It was in Auschwitz II – Birkenau where Irma Grese blossomed into a beautiful but poisonous flower.

Bergen-Belsen is not located near Auschwitz I, but the two are commonly linked together; after the war, defendants of both camps – including Grese - were tried together at the "Belsen trial (1945)."

Auschwitz II-Birkenau was also built by prisoner slave labor, with work beginning in October 1941. Birkenau was a massive camp divided into ten sections encased in barbed wire fencing. The sole purpose of Birkenau was to murder. Experiments in killing were carried out until the "best" solution became Zyklon B dropped through the ceiling of an enclosed room.

The city of Oświęcim was renamed "Auschwitz," and was four miles from Auschwitz II.

Grese no doubt observed prisoners being transported and dropped off, herded into the "disrobing area" to strip, and then locked into the gas chamber believing they were taking a hot shower prior to a good meal. Their bodies were then carried to the crematory. Smoke chugged from all chimneys constantly unless something in the system broke down. "Up the chimney" the living prisoners would dub this death.

Auschwitz II served two purposes: extermination and concentration.

Auschwitz III would also be known as Buna, a slave labor camp, and established near the main camp in 1943. The exhausted and starving prisioners were a source of free labor, sent to toil away in the local factories. These factories then paid the Germans for the labor. Had she been on foot at Auschwitz I, Irma Grese would head west to make a four hour walk to this camp.

In 1944, Auschwitz I and II would be combined under the name "Auschwitz." Auschwitz III would include nearby sub-camps and be renamed "Monowitz."

From 1942 – 1944, prisoner labor built numerous sub-camps in the area. Any Poles living nearby with a home and land were forcibly removed by Nazis and their homes and goods confiscated. When a camp guard married, she received many gifts – all confiscated items the Polish families were forced to leave behind: dishes, linens, furniture, anything one needed to set up housekeeping. Irma Grese and her comrades would benefit greatly from this looting.

Grese set her bags down on the floor of her new home in March of 1943: Auschwitz-Birkenau. She worked as a postal clerk, answered telephones, and would quickly be moving up the hierarchy. One documentary reports Grese was made to supervise a group on prisoners working to build roads and tending gardens. "She received this punishment because she did not wear her caps." [149]

Survivor Luba Triszinska was assigned to an A*rbeitskommando* Grese supervised. The already frail women were forced to march almost seventeen miles to pick herbs. Grese rode along on her bicycle, a thick wooden stick in hand, with her dog trotting next to her. Prisoners who fell behind would hear Grese shout orders to her dog to attack them. Then came the inevitable beating with the stick. The weaker ones had to be carried by the

[148] Discussed throughout the Belsen Trial between September 17 – November 12, 1945

[149] Commentator unknown. (n.d.). World History's Execution of Irma Grese - The Hyena of Auschwitz - Nazi Guard at Auschwitz & Bergen-Belsen - WW2

stronger prisoners to the work site and back. Grese would order these women, dead or no, be placed in Block 25: the last stop until the gas chamber. A truck would arrive to load the women in. Luba witnessed Grese "chasing and driving out of their hiding places women internees who were trying to avoid being sent to the gas chamber. She would beat and pull them. I have also seen Grese at Block 25 assisting and using force to load the women into the lorries which were taking them to the gas chamber." [150]

As she settled into her new role, Irma Grese did not forget her family. After her induction into the SS world, Irma would see her sister, Helene, at least twice. Grese would travel on leave to visit her father sometime in 1943. She told her family, including 16-year-old Helene, she was working for the Concentration Camp Services and her work entailed supervising prisoners on work details and prevention of escape. Her family quizzed her on the purpose of imprisoning these people, and pressed for details of the prisoner diet. Their Irma was vague, saying only she was forbidden to speak with the prisoners and was not involved in meal preparation. She either did not want her family members to know, or she recalled the oath she had signed upon hiring.

Several Wrechen villagers recalled seeing Irma Grese on the road during this family visit. Grese either refused to acknowledge greetings or told the villagers she did not know them. It was as if she had returned to a hamlet of strangers, although these people had watched her grow for at least 14 years. Some of the people who greeted her had grown up alongside Irma Grese, sitting in the same classroom and sharing the same chores. In only a few years they became strangers to her.

One historian's account has Irma's father, Alfred Grese, initially impressed with his middle daughter. She looked well, her uniform was impeccable, and she seemed to have found herself. That evening, Alfred made his usual trek to the pub.

Upon Alfred's return, he came home to a crying daughter (from his second marriage). Irma had torn the limbs from the girl's doll. Irma's younger brother had slipped her revolver out of its holster and jokingly pointed it at Alfred. Alfred snatched the gun from the boy and used it to strike Irma. Irma hurried to her room to pack her suitcase. She left the house in anger. It was the last time she ever stepped foot in the home.

Another version has Irma and her father quarreling about her working for the SS. He was angered about her involvement and belief in the Nazi party; while Alfred joined because of intimidation or because the party offered him more than what he had, his thoughts on the party remained negative. This version has him thrashing her, then expelling her, forbidding her to return to her childhood home.

Whatever the truth, Irma Grese never saw her childhood home or her father again.

Long after the war, Helene would say "We in Wrechen were completely removed from world events." [151] She would say she had no idea of the war, no idea of what was going on in Germany until Alfred donned a soldier's uniform. If this was true, her sister coming home in her own uniform would have been big news. Irma, so proud of her official attire, left bruised (at the least, emotionally) and shamed.

Still, at some time there was a Nazi flag hanging behind the Grese family door. By 1945, when the Grese family was fleeing the Allies, it was still in place.

Irma Grese was now 20 years old. She was entering a world unlike Ravensbrück, where most of the staff (and prisoners) were female. In Birkenau, Grese was one of a small

[150] Deposition of Luba Triszinska, paragraph 2, The Belsen Trials

[151] Weibke (1987)

percentage of staff, and even less percentage of female staff. Despite the growth of Auschwitz and its satellite camps, the female guard staff remained at about 71 (less than 1 percent of overall guard staff); male staff would grow to at least 4,481. [152]

By the time Irma Grese unpacked her things that March 1943, Auschwitz had become the most feared concentration camp in the system. As in many camps, former criminals were recruited from the prisoner population to be part of the *Kapos* at Birkenau. Discrimination between prisoners – often against the Jews, prostitutes, and lesbians - was commonplace within much of the camp, as discussed in survivor's memoirs. The will to survive brought people to low standards they would never have considered in their former life. It also brought women together; some females banded together to survive.

Employee corruption was rampant at Auschwitz, with bribery, theft, embezzlement, and relationships with prisoners. Several officials would be sent to the camp to investigate the problems.

Grese would eventually be promoted. The *Kommandant* was the sexist SS Captain Rudolph Franz Ferdinand Höss (1900-1947). [153] Höss was the first *Kommandant* of Bergen-Belsen. A rumor filtered through the camp that Grese and Höss were lovers.

No woman, Höss would declare, would ever perform as well as a man in any position. This included Irma Grese. He blamed all operational problems – from poor sanitation to the spread of typhus - on the female staff. Rudolph Höss had enough to worry about, he would snarl, then to oversee a bunch of silly, stupid women. He was also aware the "final solution" was soon to take place.

Höss hailed from Baden-Baden in southwest Germany. He was training for the priesthood when the beginning rumblings of WWII sounded. He became a decorated soldier. Höss denounced Catholicism and joined the Nazi party. Rudolph Höss had moved through several concentration camps as he rose through the SS hierarchy. Finally, he made *Kommandant* in Auschwitz in 1940. It was Höss who turned Auschwitz I into an extermination camp after learning of "The Final Solution" (in May 1941).

Initially, sulfuric acid was used to kill the Jews. In an early visit in 1942 by Nazi leader Adolph Eichmann, Höss would demonstrate to his superior officer how Jews were packed into a room and the doors locked. Round wool filters, soaked with sulfuric acid, were tossed into the room. Instant, quick death, Höss would explain pragmatically. Corpses would be dragged out using devices that resembled ice tongs. The dead would be burned in a shallow ditch. The smell permeated everything. By mid-1942, Zyklon-B was being used to gas victims. Eichmann would don a gas mask to visit Block 11, the detention cell block, and view the number of victims stuffed into cells. He later observed how the Zyklon-B was tossed in and death taking between 3-15 minutes. Eichmann was satisfied. It was important to know the quickest system to carry out the killing of thousands.

Höss did so well at his job, he would be made chief inspector of the concentration camps in 1943. Irma Grese would understand the procedure upon entering Bergen-Belsen, having full knowledge of how the system of mass killing worked. Prisoners in satellite camps - like Belsen - were chosen in "selection" and taken away in trucks to the gas chamber. It would be impossible to know how many people died by gas chamber; it is estimated 2.5 million persons were murdered in Auschwitz in part by gassing.

---

[152] Auschwitz 1940-1945, pp 172-175. Cited in Cline, S. (2014). pp. 52-3.

[153] Also spelled "Hass" or "Höss ."

Irma Grese's Auschwitz would become known as the ultimate killing machine.

A portion of the camp continued to employ ex-convicts and known criminals as low-level supervisors ("*Kapos*"). One reporter has German serial killer Peter Kürten ("The Vampire of Düsseldorf") employed at Dachau first as a "trustee and then guard(s)." [154] Further research reveals this is not possible; Dachau was the first concentration camp opening March 20, 1933. Auschwitz's first prisoners arrived May 20, 1940. Peter Kürten was arrested on May 23, 1930, imprisoned, tried, and put to death on July 1, 1931.

[154] Holt, P (16 November 1, 1945) no pg.

A cell door in Auschwitz I, Block 11, the detention cell block. The brick building was the dreaded "punishment block." Executions, torture, and punishments were meted out here. The "Death Wall" for executions was between Block 10 and Block 11. Irma Grese sent prisoners here for extreme punishments, such as forcing four prisoners into a cell so small they were forced to stand for twenty nights; these prisoners went involuntarily to work when not in the cells. The cells were just over 10 square feet with a tiny hole for breathing. (Circa August 23, 2008. Location: Auschwitz I, Block 11. Photograph by and courtesy of Jill Anne McCracken. Used with permission.)

Brick barracks in Birkenau, section B1a. (Circa: 1942. Photographer: unknown. Courtesy: The Archive of The State Museum Auschwitz-Birkenau in Oświęcim. Used with permission)

Auschwitz camp office where Grese would have worked. (Date unknown. Photographer: unknown. Courtesy Auschwitz – Birkenau Memorial and Museum. Used with permission.)

CHAPTER 15
die Hyäne von Auschwitz

The time in Auschwitz-Birkenau was counted by the sound of alarms, prisoner movement, and shiftwork. Irma Grese's prisoner work crews would awake at various times when the bell sounded across the compound. Depending on the season – 4:30 AM in the summer, one hour later in winter – they cleaned their bunk areas, washed as best as possible, and drank a breakfast of putrid water (labeled as "coffee" or "tea"). The second bell of the day indicated it was time for roll call, where thousands of prisoners would scramble into place. They were counted twice to ensure the numbers were correct. Should roll call go without issue, work groups formed, and the 11-hour workdays began. Break time began at noon; labor resumed at 1:00 pm. Another roll call was held at 7:00 p.m. If a prisoner died during work, their corpse could be dragged into place for count. Dinner was usually a watered – down soup of subpar vegetables and a small piece of bread. There was "free time" until a bell sounded at 9:00 pm for sleep and silence.

Sundays and holidays meant days off from work for the camp population. This was a time to freshen up, or take part in an activity, such as attending a concert; the prisoner orchestra played every other weekend. Prisoners might write letters or open packages they received from the outside. Author and historian Piotr Setkiewicz, Ph.D., the director of Centre for Research at the Auschwitz-Birkenau State Museum explains, "non-Jewish prisoners could receive food parcels from their families since the autumn of 1942." He adds, "Such a parcel warehouse - *Paketstelle* - was situated in the women's camp in Birkenau BIb, block number 5, and about a dozen women prisoners supervised … *Aufseherin* (Elisabeth) Volkenrath worked there." [155]

September 1943 brought change to the war and Germany was now placing every available man into a soldier's uniform and sending them to the front of battle. Italy, a chief member of Germany's allegiance, surrendered to the West Allies. News traveled to Grese and her comrades at the camps, but those who believed in the Reich trusted their beloved Germany would pull through. Losing the war to the Allies was not feasible.

Irma Grese's life became Auschwitz-Birkenau. It was here where someone – the legend is, it was a prisoner – bestowed upon Grese the nickname *die Hyäne von Auschwitz* – The Hyena of Auschwitz.

Perhaps the moniker derived from the movement of the wild animal – slinking, teeth bared, running down its prey and snapping the bones in its frothing jaws. In some ethnic groups the hyena is a symbol of bad luck, evil, or a bad omen. Within some cultures the hyena represents stupidity, the unclean, vampires. The animal has been known to attack and kill humans without provocation; their expressions are never friendly, and they always appear wary. Or there may be a more mystical reasoning.

By the time Irma Grese had arrived in Auschwitz, Jews encompassed most of the prisoner population. There exists an ancient Hebrew story in the Talmud involving a shape-shifting hyena. The dog-like creature turns into a bat, which eventually turns into a smaller bat, morphing into a thorny weed; in several years it becomes a thorn and finally a demon. The translation:

---

[155] Personal interview with Piotr Setkiewicz, Ph.D., March 19-20, 2024

> "The hyena is a creature symbolic of scavenging, known for its tendency to move in on what others have achieved through their own hard and patient efforts, and snatch it away from them. This is Hyena's story, its nature, how its script was written at the time before time when God thought 'Hyena.'" Morphing into a bat, now the Hyena's scavenging has changed …to "blood-sucking tendencies" and "smaller, more accessible meals, and with greater expediency." As a weed, the creature now "can just stay put where it is and usurp the nutrients intended for others." [156]

An 1858 publication *Die Zoologie des Talmuds*, (a reproduction of the original artifact) cites rabbinical law and teachings, lists three names for the hyena: "bardales," "napraza," and "appa." This text refers to the Talmud's explanation that "this variety of names has its counterpart in a variety of metamorphoses, each lasting seven years, through which the male hyena passes, namely, of a bat, an "'arpad" (*i.e.*, some other form of bat), a nettle, a thistle, and lastly an evil spirit." [157]

Monikers were given to many Nazi notables during the incarceration of prisoners in the camps; some epithets were bestowed by the press covering the trials. These names were fear based ("The Beast," "The Dog Woman"), involving deities of death ("The White Angel"). While Irma Grese was labeled "The Beast" in the media, and the prisoners called her "The Grey Mouse" on occasion, she is most often identified as "The Hyena."

Conceivably, whoever labeled Irma Grese "The Hyena" observed in Grese more than a vicious animal. They peered deeper and found a girl whose soul was gobbling up everything she could, yet remained unfulfilled. Beating prisoners did not fulfill Grese. Torturing or "making sport" only filled whatever space for a short time. The scavenging grew to include physical and mental tortures, small personal bites of power, like forcing a prisoner to give up a bit of cloth or telling individual prisoners they were doomed. There were thousands of prisoners in Auschwitz, and Irma Grese had power, so it was imaginable – but unlikely – she would fill whatever was missing in her psyche. Maybe Irma Grese was that symbolic scavenger who never grew tired of unscrupulous theft, the theft of nutrients like hope, happiness, safety.

Grese had a vast environment to roam and practice her craft regardless of how the moniker was born. Once completed, Auschwitz would become the size of 6,000 football fields. The three main camps were Auschwitz I at 15,44 square miles, [158] Auschwitz II-Birkenau ("the killing center") which held four crematoriums, and Auschwitz III (Auschwitz – Monowitz, or Buna). Discipline was lax, underground black markets existed for both staff and prisoners, and alcohol was plentiful. (There is no written record of Irma Grese joining in on the copious amounts of drinking. It is probably safe to say she did imbibe.)

The chauvinist Rudolf Höss [159] served as Irma Grese's *Kommandant* until the end of the year 1944.

---

[156] Winkler (2014)
[157] Lewysohn, L. (2018) p. 76
[158] Overview of Auschwitz and Cehei Ghetto
[159] The rumors of Grese bedding Höss cannot be proven.

Under Höss' command most male SS officers seemed to forget the rule that female officers were to be treated equal, and female officers felt this resentment. It remained akin to a "good old boys club" where women were inferior and not to be taken seriously; they were neither ladies nor officers, only objects. They were called "whores" and "bitches." Irma Grese would have understood how Höss blamed the women for everything bad, from problems with weather and sanitation to issues with roll call; it was no secret he did not want to supervise women. Would he have used her for sex? Certainly. Did they actually have a relationship? Neither admitted if they did.

Holocaust expert and historian Jill McCracken writes, "Birkenau was a death camp by design, far larger than Auschwitz I or II. It had inmate workers, which helped facilitate the process if death, as did the other death camps." [160]

As discussed, it was Höss who had perfected the techniques of mass murder now utilized in Auschwitz. "Technically [it] wasn't so hard" he would explain. "The killing itself took the least time. You could dispose of 2,000 head in half an hour, but it was the burning that took all the time. The killing was easy." [161]

Höss, was ousted in Autumn 1943 for having a sexual affair with a political prisoner, resulting in an abortion at a camp hospital. Had a Nazi female been caught having such an affair, or having an abortion, the repercussions would have been severe. As punishment, Rudolf Höss was transferred to a desk job away from the camp. He returned to Auschwitz, in early May of 1944, for a special assignment. [162] Rudolf Höss' family welcomed him home to their house on the camp property; they had stayed living there because they enjoyed the nice, large home.

Höss was another example, comparable to Irma Grese, of a concentration camp hypocrite in the system of power. On March 21, 1947, witness Tadeusz Pietrzykowski would testify:

> Then, while working in the Stabsgebaude as an orderly, I came into contact with female SS officers, including Grese, Drechsler, Lokauer, Volkenrath, Borman, Weniger. I heard from them that when SS men of various kinds were intimate with Blockführers and Rapportführers, Höss ordered them to finish off the (prisoner) women. [163]

SS Captain Josef Kramer replaced Höss at the end of 1944, when Höss was transferred to Ravensbrück.

This was the environment Irma Grese entered at Birkenau.

Irma Grese would later testify during her trial that her first position at Auschwitz (Birkenau) was as an overseer of a road construction crew. Holocaust survivors recalled how Grese, in this position, would strike fear in these 20,000 to 30,000 Hungarian Jewish women prisoners. It was Birkenau where she allegedly earned another nickname, "The

---

[160] Personal interview with Jill McCracken, May 26, 2024

[161] Gilbert (1995). Pp. 249-50

[162] Höss would be arrested after liberation, tried, and hanged in 1947, at Auschwitz with some former prisoners witnessing.

[163] Testimony of Tadeusz Pietrzykowski against Rudolph Höss. In a twist of irony, Höss was found guilty and hanged in April 1945 next to the former gas chamber where he sent so many innocent souls to die.

Beautiful Beast." [164] Records also reveal she was given this moniker by journalists during her trial, along with other names. She may have earned this moniker due to rumors of her affair with the "Beast of Belsen" Josef Kramer.

After her shift was done, Grese would return to her living quarters, by now a dormitory outside the gates of the camp at Auschwitz. She would share a room with another *Aufseherin* at a cost of five Reichsmarks a month; if she secured a private room, she would pay 15 Reichsmarks. Some of the roommates became close friends. Irma Grese did not.

As Irma Grese worked, outside of the camp and on the outskirts of Auschwitz, Polish families were continually forcibly removed from their homes, their homes given to the higher-ranking officers or married couples. While the Polish families left with whatever possessions they were able to carry, the higher-ranking male Nazis and their families who moved in now used their beds, plates, chairs, and whatever else was left ... all while cursing the Poles as unworthy and subhuman.

Females did not live in these local houses unless they were married to a high-ranking official. Irma Grese's room would always have furniture taken from the homes of those exiled Polish families. Grese and her comrades also procured items stolen from the belongings brought by the camp's prisoners.

When forced from their homes, Jews and other exiles grabbed valuables: money, jewelry, tools of their trade, heirlooms. [165] These new camp arrivals were forced to abandon their belongings as they exited the train cars, tricked into thinking they would later retrieve the parcels, backpacks, suitcases and boxes. Designated prisoners interned in the camp would gather these precious belongings and carry them to the warehouse called "Kanada" [166] to be sorted out and packaged. Kanada had sections for clothing, eyeglasses, precious metal, alcohol, food, tools, shoes ... Clothing was taken apart to inspect the seams, should valuables be carefully hidden from sight. Prisoners who worked in Kanada (the *Aufräumungskommando,* or "cleaning-up commando") knew this was one of the best jobs in the camp: one could smuggle out goods to barter, find extra food, or even needed medication.

Prisoners knew they could be searched at any time. Holding contraband was a dangerous practice. Irma Grese was one of many who enjoyed stopping prisoners for random searches. If so much as a crumb was found, Grese set to beating the guilty party with her truncheon. She would destroy or keep the item.

It was illegal for Irma Grese and her fellow coworkers to sort through these items and select what they wanted – clothing, jewelry, home décor - so they would order prisoners to search for them – "organizing" it was dubbed. Auschwitz prisoners were already cleaning, washing laundry, cooking, mending, sewing, and other such tasks for camp staff, just as they performed at Ravensbrück. If there was a tear in a uniform it would be skillfully repaired by a seamstress prisoner; a stubborn stain on a rug could be removed by a prisoner doing the cleaning. If staff clothing did not fit correctly, it would be tailored. Linens would be clean and crisp. "Organizing" items from discarded luggage was just another forced duty.

---

[164] DEGOB

[165] They were allowed to take up to 100 pounds when leaving their home to be "resettled."

[166] This was a slang term. Canada was believed to be "land of plenty."

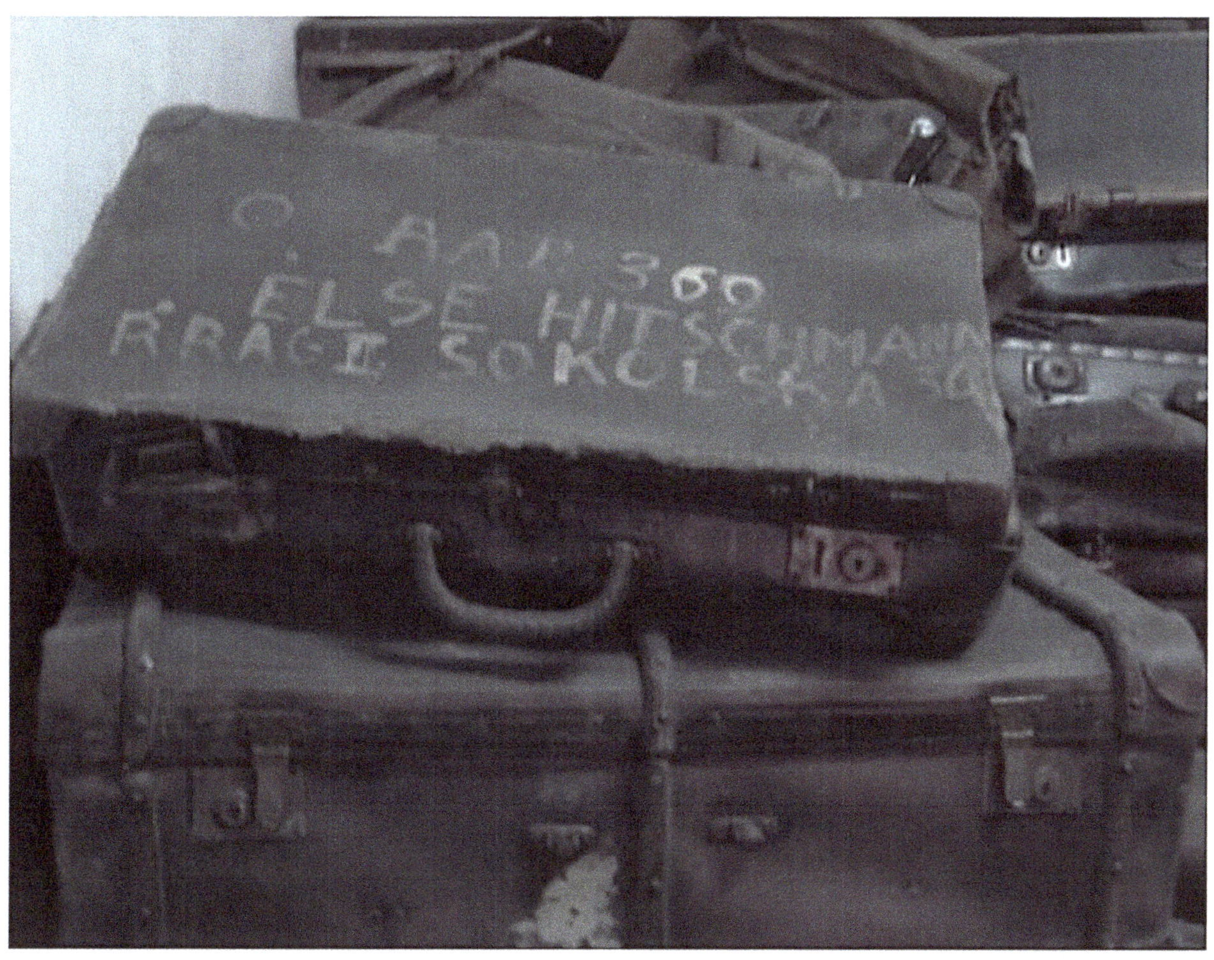

Suitcases confiscated from new prisoners arriving at Auschwitz I. This suitcase would have been sent to a camp section dubbed *Kanada* for emptying and sorting. Although not allowed, concentration camp staff pilfered items in *Kanada*. Irma Grese would own nice dresses, jewelry, apartment décor, and other items courtesy the theft, called "organizing" by staff and prisoners. Note how the prisoners had carefully written their identification on the cases; they were told, upon arrival at the camps, they would be retrieving their belongings. (Circa August 23, 2008. Location: Auschwitz Memorial. Photograph by and courtesy of Jill Anne McCracken. Used with permission.)

Interior of concentration camp hut for prisoners. Irma Grese walking through the door into prisoner huts, like those above, would strike terror. Grese often pulled women from their bunk area to be sent to the gas chamber, or she would beat women for the slightest infraction. (Circa August 23, 2008. Location: Auschwitz Memorial. Photograph by and courtesy of Jill Anne McCracken. Used with permission.)

Irma Grese called the headquarters building (*Stabsgebäude*) her home. As an unmarried female, she would have a room on the first floor. She could take her meals in the common dining hall. Her laundry and sewing were done in the basement by the prisoners who worked as maids and lived in the basement.

Grese and her fellow workers could stroll to *Haus 7*, Auschwitz's shop for the SS, and find luxuries that were always well-stocked: meat, milk, vegetables - food that people had to scrounge for outside of the camp in the increasingly war-torn country. They would return to their rooms, laughingly carrying the goods, chattering together. Outside of this world, had they not taken this job, these women would most likely been married with children and struggling to survive, a hand-to-mouth existence. The men would probably be sent to war. Irma Grese would no longer have to munch on raw turnips as a snack as she did back in Wrechen. As a camp guard she had a selection of treats.

There were organized trips to the SS holiday resort *SS Hütte Sole-Tal* (cottage "Sola Valley") in Porąbka. A bus would carry the revelers, gazing out the large side windows, to this nice resort where attendees would disembark to relax, sun, join their comrades for special treats, stroll the beautiful surrounding forest, enjoy music and sing-alongs, and be far away from the drudgery of work and Auschwitz.

Grese was disciplined for some unknown infraction and, as penalty, oversaw a punishment detail. (Grese would testify it lasted two days. A Holocaust survivor testified it was for seven months.) The punishment detail involved prisoners who were paying penance for some infraction. In Grese's detail, prisoners were forced to carry heavy loads of rocks from one area to another at rapid speeds; anyone who could not keep up the pace was beaten into the ground - "light punishment" Grese would later testify in trial. She did her duty and ensured those who fell behind were beaten severely.

In fall of 1943, Grese oversaw a gardening crew. That December, she was moved to mail censor, taking Elizabeth Volkenrath's job. Typically, this job would have never been assigned to a woman; but by this time all able-bodied men were being filtered to fight. And the death tolls inside the camps were increasing. With the frantic realization Germany might not win the war, the attempt to "purify" Germany ramped up, the line of the condemned into the gas chambers grew longer, and mass camp graves grew deeper.

Christmas remained a celebration for the concentration camp staff. Celebrations featuring good food and plenty of alcohol took place at each camp. Arthur Liebehenschel – a Nazi party member since 1932 - succeeded Höss as Auschwitz *Kommandant* on December 1, 1943. [167] He would approve a holiday tradition, but with a change: for three years the SS had set up a Christmas tree on the square where roll call was taken. Its electric lights blinked through the inclement weather. For three years the "gift" to the camp prisoners was murdering prisoners and stacking the bodies around this tree in a display. While Irma Grese worked as a mail censor, Liebehenschel halted the practice of murder and macabre display. Birkenau female prisoners were even allowed to make makeshift toys for the incarcerated children in the hospital.

Maria Mandl was here at Auschwitz, supervising Grese and associate female staff. Grese was one of the youngest charges, with most of the women being around twenty-eight years of age. Mandl had also left school when the same age as Grese, but she had received further education in private school. The educated Maria Mandl was supervising mostly uneducated rural class females. Her charges took bribes, were sexually promiscuous,

[167] Other sources have him arriving in November 1943.

imbibed in too much alcohol, feared Mandl, yet pandered to her in the hopes of promotion, and understood Mandl was there to bring order to the female staff. Maria Mandl, with her education, work experience, and dedication to ethics, was surely exasperated.

Turpentine was applied to external surfaces to treat lice, and is still used as an additive for cleaning and sanitation. Since the mid-1800s, turpentine had become a cleaning solvent in Europe: the clothes were soaked in a tub with the mixture then hung to dry in a warmer area. It became known as "French Cleaning" and later "dry cleaning." Thus, Irma Grese would have known turpentine was the best substance for immaculate boots and uniforms, protected her from insects, and it most likely helped mask the stench of the environment. Grese's obsession for perfection in appearance demanded that she hoard the much-coveted turpentine, causing fellow officers to complain to supervisors. "Mandl tried with varying degrees of success to rein in Grese and moderate her various requests for 'perks'" Maria Mandl's biographer writes. [168] Mandl was forced to now evaluate all *Aufseherinnen* requests on a personal basis, putting an end to Grese's hoarding and ending the complaints against her. Maria Mandl found Irma Grese was a difficult individual to control.

Not all of Birkenau found Irma Grese to be attractive. "When she walked through the camp with a whip in her hand," one survivor recalled, "she reeked with the smell of cheap perfume." [169]

There were the local social diversions where Irma Grese and her comrades could escape the drudgery of their work. Auschwitz, like a small city, provided entertainment for its people who worked there. They could join a sports club. Grese could walk to the canteen that sold foodstuff, including bones for cooking soup, and prepare a meal to cook for herself. She could stop by the canteen and then, if the show was something she was interested in, walk to the cinema. There were plenty of get-togethers for staff, including dances, games, and parties. Mandl's beloved female prisoner's orchestra would play at some of the gatherings. Sporting matches were held; some of the matches were prisoner against SS staff. Prisoners would perform in the small theatre or drinking halls if they had special talents - singing, acting, dancing, gymnastics - and outside performers sometimes came into the camps to give a show. Irma Grese must have attended the latter as they were mandatory for the SS. There would be copious amounts of alcohol and food; dinners sometimes comprised of fat, sizzling sausages, and deep mugs of beer. Women were not constrained by social standards. Irma Grese could wear her beautiful clothing and jewelry that had been "organized." And to escape even further away there was always *Solahütte*.

Solahütte was a Nazi resort, a short drive from Auschwitz, built by prisoner hands and boasted a sun deck, multiple cabins, hiking trails, hunting, and picturesque mountain views. The food was delicious and boasted delicacies not available to the public for some time, like chocolate and fresh fruit. Some of the SS staff who could play music brought their accordions, guitars, and the like, to play for the group, and photos have surfaced of female staff enjoying fresh blueberries and pretending to cry because their cups are empty.

Less than twenty miles away thousands of people were being herded into the gas chamber, their dead bodies dragged out with hooks, hair shorn, gold teeth ripped out with

[168] Eischeid (2024) p.114
[169] Cited in Morris, F. (2011). P. 64-5.

plyers, then stuffed into the crematoriums. The stench of the job added to the misery. The officers overseeing this daily routine received *schnapps* for the day's work.

The camp employees became one another's social circle, each other's family. Friends and family from the outside might visit, but only for a short time. Akin to law enforcement, military, and any government organization, the camp employees understood that no one "outside" comprehended their work; besides, they had all taken the oath and had been sworn to secrecy. Gossip ran amok as did relationships. Friendships and sexual relationships were made, damaged, and repaired or exchanged. Bonds were forged.

Perhaps this is why Irma Grese would become so touched by any discussion of sisterhood between female prisoners. She had her share of men or women, if rumor is to be believed, but she had no female friends as she self-reported. Her beloved sisters were far away, physically and socially. Or there was a more sinister motive.

Aufseherin Irma Grese's career was going well in the midst of this systematic killing. She received a promotion to *Rapportführerin*, "Report Leader." A survivor would recall this occurred about May 1944. Now, Grese was responsible for prison population records, the roll calls, and overseeing the *Blockführerin.* Just like the camp's function, her level of brutality was about to escalate.

Hungarian Jews began arriving at the female camp in May 1944. They were not given numbers, tattooed, or even registered. Thousands of these people came into the camp, carrying meager belongings that were immediately confiscated and taken to "Kanada." Those not gassed moved into the overcrowded *C-Lager* (Camp C), formerly labeled sector B-IIc. Initially, old horse stalls were turned into beds for over 5,000 women. The camp, at eight hundred yards length by two hundred yards wide, would swell to 30,000 female prisoners. Close to 400,000 total prisoners were gassed that summer. Many dropped dead from hunger, fatigue, or disease. Overseeing this camp was the newly appointed *Lagerführerin* [170] Irma Grese.

---

[170] Also called an *Oberaufseherin* ("Senior SS Maiden").

Work Schedule for Auschwitz II - Birkenau

The following three pages are an *Aufseherinnen* work assignment schedule for Auschwitz II - Birkenau, dated October 10, 1944.
Note on page 1 that #12, Irma Grese, is assigned to Block (*Blockpersonal*) BIIc with two (three?) other guards. There are 26 workers *(fach. Arb.)* and 29 auxiliary workers *(hilfs.arb.)*.
The third page is signed off by the "SS-Obersturmführer" (first lieutenant). Note the runic SS. Many German typewriters featured the special key.

Construction for Birkenau began in October 1941. Birkenau would become the largest of camps and sub-camps in the Auschwitz compound. Soviet soldiers liberated Auschwitz-Birkenau on January 27, 1945.

When this schedule was typed up and distributed,

- Irma Grese was reportedly assisting Josef Mengele in "selections" for the gas chamber. Around 90% (one million) of Auschwitz prisoners died in Birkenau.

- Grese was promoted several times.

- The Nazi party membership totaled about 800,000.

- Höss had returned to Auschwitz May of that year to supervise "Operation Höss": an estimated 430,000 Hungarian Jews were transported to the camp and killed in 56 days.

- Remaining Hungarian Jewish prisoners in Auschwitz were sent by the thousands for slave labor in various factories owned by the Reich. Certain businesses in the outside world flourished and prospered while the Hungarian Jews worked, some to death.

- BIIc would eventually be changed to Camp C (*C-Lager*).

(The three-page report, circa October 1944, Courtesy of The Archive of The State Museum Auschwitz-Birkenau in Oświęcim.Used with permission)

346a

Frauen-Lager,KL. u.II
Abte.III/aBIa-b/B.II b.g.c/ Birkenau,den 8.1o. 1944

Arbeitseinsatz des F.L.Birkenau,den 8.1o. 1944

Kdo. Nr.	Arbeitskommando:	Arbeitsort:	Kdo.Fhr.:	Aufs.	Kdof.	GP.	Fach, arb.	Hilfs. arb.	Gesamt: FA.	HA.
	Lagerzwecke:			2						
5.	Häftl.-Küchen	Lager	Franz,Pritzkoleit				1o	12o		
	Häftl.-Küchen	BII b.c	Mayer,Stiwitz	2			1o6	4o		
	Häftl.-Kantine	Lager	Seidel	1			3	2	119	162
6.	Kartoffelschälk.	Lager	Bienek	1				15o		
	Kartoffelschälk.	BIIb-c	Beck	1				3o9		459
7.	Schneiderei	Lager-BIIb					1oo	336	1oo	336
9.	Effektenkammer	Lager	Janda	1			3o	36	3o	36
1o.	Häftl.-Bekl.Kammer	Lage.BIIbgc	Gralka	1			3	2o3		
	Unterkunftskammer	Lag.BIIbc					41	62	44	265
11.	Pflegepersonal:									
	Krankenpfl.	Lager					65	141		
	Krankenpfl.Ärzt-	BIIb.c					68	13		
	Ärzt-Lab.Apoth.	Lager					47			
	Sauna-Bad	Lager	Roolofs,Pampel	2			4o	113	22o	267
12.	Blockpersonal:									
	Blockält.-Schreib.	Lager					45	45		
	Blockpersonal	Lager		3				28o		
	Blockpersonal	BII/b	Schaumburg,Teuber,Meisner				21	168		
	Blockpersonal	BII/c	Grese,Omes,Kietmann				26	29		
	Lagerält.-Capo	Lager-BIIbc		3				11	92	333
15.	Büros:									
	Rapport.-Fhr.	Lager	Ruppert	1			3			
	Arbeitsdienst	Lager-BIIbc	[illegible]uiters		1			1o		
	Arbeitseinsatz	Lag.BIIbc	Perschel		1		5			
	Häftl.-Schreibst.	Lager.BIIb					37			
	Revier-Schreibst.	Lager					11			
	Schutzhäftlg. "	Lager	Kortmann		1		2			
	Polit.Abteilung	Lager-BIIb					4o	1		
	Läuferinnen-Dolm.	Lager-BIIb					*	25	98	36
										[illegible]
	Lagerwirtschaft:								703	2094
	Aufräumungskdo.:									
	Instandsetzung	Lager-BIIb						4o5		
	Rein.-Blockfst.	Lager-BIIb						12		417
6.	Kartoffelbunker	Birkenau	Dietrich		1			1oo		1oo
7.	Sicherheitskdo,:									
	Kaminkehrer	Lager						3		
	Luftschutz	Lager						1o		
	Kanalisation	Lager-BIIb						19o		2o3
	Abladekdo.-Holzhof	BIIb						1o9		
	Esskdo.f.Quarant.	BIIb						5o		159
										879
	Amtsgruppe C-Bauwesen:									
	Kriegswichtige Zwecke:									
Flo3.	Kdo .Baubüro	KGL.					1o		1o ✓	
	Amt W.5. Landwirtschaft:									
F21.	Kdo.Mokrus	Plawy	Mokrus		1	3		3o7		
24.	Kdo.Zippenpfennig	Babitz	Zippenpfennig		1	2		15o		457
		Übertrag:		18	6	5			713	343o

346 b

-2-

Kdo. Nr.	Arbeitskommando:	Arbeitsort:	Kdo.Fhr.:	Aufs.	Kdof.	GP.	Fach. arb.	Hilfs. arb.	Gesamt FA.	Gesamt HA.
	Übertrag:			18	6	5			713	343o
	ℌ- Dienststellen:									
	ℌ- Lazarett	Birkenau						83		83
	Plan.Tr.-Unterk.	Birkenau	Hornung			1		1oo		1oo
	Entwesungsk.II	B.II/g	Hoppmanns	1				1o25		1o25
	Rüstungsbetriebe:									
	Zerlegebetriebe	Bergepark						6		6
	Flak-Sonderbaultg.									
	Batt.Holzhagen	I.G.Farben						5o		
	Batt.Birkenau	"						5o		
	Batt.Chelmek	"						5o		
	Batt.Pcsiecow	"						1oo		
	Batt.Bobrek	"						5o		
	Batt.Barki	"						75		375
	Privat-Betriebe:									
	Pampenbau	Auschw.	Jos			2		1oo		1oo
	Bedingt tauglich:									
	Weberei	BA.III	Schulz, Schreiber	2			1o2	2348	1o2	2348
	Beschäftigte Häftlinge:			21	6	8			815	7467
	Nicht einsatz u. nicht arbeitsf.Hftl.									
1.	stationäre Kranke		1672							
2.	stationäre Kranke BII/b		256							
3.	stationäre Kranke BII/c-III		33							
4.	Blockschonungen		594							
5.	Arztmelder		45							
6.	Jugendl.u.14.Jahre		132							
7.	" " BII/b		4o							
8.	Inval. ü.6o Jahre		43							
9.	Quarant.(Krätze-Malaria)		583							
1o.	" (Zug.)		756							
11	" (Zug.-Warsch.)		849							
12	" (Warsch.Kinder)		37o							
13	" (Entl.)		97							5470
	Unbeschäftigte Häftlinge:									
1.	Zugänge		8							
2.	auf Transport		1254							
3.	Transportvorber.		688							
4.	Unbeschäftigte		9056							11oo6
	Durchgangs-Juden:									
1.	stationäre Kranke		937							
2.	Transportvorbereitungen		1627							
3.	Jugendliche		596							
4.	Zugänge		-							
5.	Verfügbare		8488							11648
			SA.:	21	6	8			815	35591

-3-

Kdo. Nr.	Arbeitskommando:Arbeitsort:Kdo.Fhr.:		Aufs.	Kdof.	GP.	Fach. arb.	Hilfs. arb.	Gesamt: FA.	HA.
Übertrag:			21	6	8			815	35591
	Dienstplan der Aufseherinnen:								
Lagerd.BII/c	Heise	1							
Läuferin:	Westfeld	1							
Strassenb.-Lagerd.	Zielonka, Kopold, Admiraal, Sacher, Eberth, Schulze, Pollak	7							
Mitter:	Miklas, Sollich, v.Esch	3							
Krank:	Görcke, Malik, Liehr, Preis, Klösters, Kyupers	6							
Ernte-Urlaub:	Kuk	1							
Sonderurlaub:	Tyssen	1							
Dienstfrei	Mittner, Meinel, Rösch, Lichai, Herzig, Fellmann, Reischl, Lupka, Schrottke, Witkowski, Zlotos, Brandl, Hasse, Hammerschick, Ihle, Schimmel, Lenk, Brunner, Bernart, ~~Schaumburg~~, Ullmann, Walter, Weigel, Pötzsch, Zimmermann, Pollak	25							
Kommandantur III	Bodem, Zajic, Thorrmann	3							
		Sa.:	2/69	6	8			815	35591

Gesamt-Lagerstärke = 36.406

Abteilung III/a.

SS- Obersturmführer.

CHAPTER 16
Lagerführerin

With a nod of approval from supervisors, Irma Grese had received a promotion to the second highest rank a woman could achieve in a camp. The former *SS-Helferin* now wielded more responsibility and prestige, moving into a larger, private room in the housing near the camp entrance. At twenty years old, Grese was also responsible for overseeing the entire camp of *C-Lager*, to include about seven interchangeable guards, the swelling population of prisoners in twenty-eight blocks encompassing prisoner lodging, a block for food, two or three blocks for latrines, two blocks each for storing - one for underwear and one for clothing – and had her own small office by the gate entrance. There was also a small guard shack beside the entrance for those soldiers monitoring the entry and exit.

It was the promotion to *Lagerführerin* when Irma Grese truly became The Hyena, where she must have realized usurped power existed beyond her means, and then flexed it uncontrollably. Her reputation quickly grew through the camp as someone who was to be avoided at any cost. One Auschwitz survivor says of Irma Grese and Josef Kramer, "they were of a different breed of people. They looked human, but these were not human beings. Humanity as we know it, even in the worst possible way, cannot behave that way." [171] Grese's attitude and behavior was unbelievable, a disbelief to the psyche, to the quiet, kind female prisoners who once lived in a careful, orderly sheltered world. Those prisoners hardened by the streets and tough lives were just as overcome with fear when they noted the swaggering blonde approaching.

Holocaust survivor Alice Cahana had lived with her loving, popular family in Budapest, Hungary (Sárvár) prior to being deported to Auschwitz. She would remember Irma Grese long after she and her sister were liberated. [172] "Irma Grese was the SS – the supervisor." Alice described Grese as "The most beautiful woman, like a statue … her blonde hair, beautifully coiffeured, and her beautiful shirt – blue shirt, starched and clean and crisp… and the way she walked…" Alice would learn to fear Grese, however. "(She) made us feel that we are less than animals. We are not human beings anymore. We don't have individuality … we don't have nothing left." [173]

The camps had a hierarchy of prisoner positions to assist Irma Grese and her fellow workers in keeping order: the system of *Kapos*. "This was a formalized process and status" Holocaust expert and historian Jill McCracken explains. [174] McCracken refers to the Sydney Jewish Museum and Emeritus Professor Konrad Kwiet, Resident Historian. "…an army of *Kapos* was a cost-saving measure" Professor Kwiet writes. "Only a small number of SS men was required to oversee an ever-increasing camp population. Also, it drove a wedge between inmates, turning groups against groups and victims against victims. The strategy of 'divide and rule' paid off." [175]

---

[171] Kaleska (1990, January 03)

[172] Alice had survived being gassed to death because the gas chamber system broke down while she and many others were locked inside. They were made to pile out and return to the camp. She would recall much later how amazed her fellow captives were that she returned to her hut, and how angry and embarrassed the camp staff became.

[173] Cahana, A. (1990, December 4). P. 17.

[174] Personal interview of Jill McCracken, May 26, 2024.

[175] May 20, 2021

Kapos supervised prisoners who were working. They also supervised the living quarters, and there was usually one per housing unit. *Kapos* included:

Lagerälteste (camp elder). A position of higher power for prisoners. They oversaw the other prisoner leaders and maintained order throughout the camp. Grese's chain of command would include this prisoner to run her errands, administrative work, and oversee certain work aspects.
Blockälteste (block elders) supervised the housing units. They ensured the block maintained standards.

Kapos could be as ruthless as the guards, some of which encouraged brutality to maintain order. A survivor, Vera Alexander, would testify at the Eichmann Trial how Irma Grese gave Vera a whip to use on prisoners. Vera, a *Kapo* over C-*Lager*, never used the whip. Some of the Kapos were kind. Others did the best job they could. Still others worked the system: *Kapos* realized the best way to keep the guards out of the blocks was to maintain a clean living area, keep illnesses at bay, and to refrain from drawing attention. Irma Grese's attention could be the worst. C-*Lager* prisoners and their prisoner bosses maintained hygiene as much as possible, resorting to punishment of offenders as necessary. Rumors of liberation and freedom had to be squelched immediately to prevent pandemonium. Discrimination was an issue between certain groups and had to be stopped. Women with certain skillsets – seamstresses, doctors, dancers, teachers – were placed in positions that would be most helpful to prisoner's survival. It was all arranged, in part, to keep Irma Grese and her comrades out of their world as much as possible.

Prisoners could be brutal to one another. The hierarchies created by the SS often contributed to the brutality; for example, women who worked in camp brothels were promised favors and early release. Holocaust survivor Nina Michailovna reported: "When we found out that a girl in our block was chosen (to work in the camp brothel), we caught her and threw a blanket on her and beat her up so badly that she could hardly move. It wasn't clear if she would recover. They just wanted to have a better life, and we punished them this way." [176] Irma Grese, like so many of the guards, was known to pit the prisoners against one another.

In autumn 1944, the Hungarian Jews were sent by the thousands for slave labor in various factories owned by the Reich. Certain businesses in the outside world flourished and prospered while the Hungarian Jews worked, some to death. Some factory work offered better conditions than work in the camps. Some offered worse. Prisoners learned which factories should be avoided.

It was in Auschwitz where the rumor of Irma Grese's promiscuity ran rampant. She is said to have bedded most of the higher - ranking men of the Nazi regime who were assigned to the camp, and this included Josef Kramer.

Josef Kramer (1906-1945) is one of the most notorious men in Holocaust history. Handsome and fastidious, he stood over six feet tall, wore his hair in a short brush cut, and had exceptionally large, powerful hands. Kramer had moved quickly up the ranks from guard to *Kommandant*. He had overseen the gassing operations of Auschwitz II – Birkenau from May to November in 1944, and then Bergen-Belsen from December 1944 to liberation in 1945. Kramer had worked a variety of jobs, unsuccessfully, until he became a

[176] Gaevert, T. & Hilbert, M. (2004).

concentration camp guard. He was a staunch leader and showed no mercy to prisoners, severely beating prisoners who hesitated to get into the transport truck to the gas chambers. Kramer was active in the selection process.

When Belsen was officially liberated, he was arrested amidst the mass graves, typhus running rampant, vermin attacking living people too sick to fight back, stacks of rotting corpses, and acres of excrement. Kramer remained unfazed while the British liberators would fall to the wayside to vomit. (Mala Tribich, Holocaust survivor, also recalls "British soldiers were fainting from the smell." [177])

There are no witnesses to Grese and Kramer exhibiting any physical attraction towards one another: no kissing, hand holding, or embracing. They may have been paramours, friends, or two coworkers with a shared sense of patriotism and loyalty to the Furor. [178] Both were good-looking people. Both had a reputation for callousness. Both found the prisoners physically disgusting from the poor diet, slave labor, and the dangerous, often deadly, typhus.

Once known as "camp fever," "jail fever," and "war fever," typhus claimed many lives of those unwashed and overcrowded individuals forced to live in squalor and filthy conditions. Holocaust survivors have told of squashing body lice constantly, but never being able to catch all the bugs that swarmed on their bodies, in their clothing, and in their meager bedding, until the tiny bugs became just another part of living conditions. Typhus ran rampant in the concentration camps as the tiny infected *Pediculus Humanus Corporis* (human body louse) – thousands at a time - moved from prisoners to their living area, laying eggs in hair and clothing. The itching was nonstop with each louse biting up to five times a day, and a female laying 200-300 eggs in her thirty days of life. The nits hatch about eight days from being laid, eggshells continuing to lay in the host area. The nits begin to feed on the host's blood immediately upon hatching. Lice were a never-ending source of pain and aggravation for prisoners in the Nazi camps, but typhus could be deadly.

Typhus symptoms begin to occur about two weeks after the infected lice spread the bacteria *Rickettsia Prowazekii*. Once a prisoner began running a fever and experiencing chills, with flu-like symptoms of coughing, body aches, vomiting, difficulty breathing, and exhaustion, they realized they were marked by certain death unless treated. Sometimes they received treatment with their fellow prisoners assisting. Staff regarded typhus as a nuisance. Those prisoners showing signs of infection were automatically sent "up the chimney" in camp parlance; and, in many cases, all of those living in the same building were gassed and burned in an attempt to quell the epidemic.

Typhus remained a threat after liberation as relapse in this disease occurs, and infection can occur without symptoms. Concentration camp living ravaged immune systems and aged people beyond their years. Brill-Zinsser is a relapse of typhus occurring months or years after the initial bout with milder symptoms but just as deadly due to the survivor's age or health.

Irma Grese would later admit she loathed to be near prisoners because of the filth and sickness. It was the reason she wore gloves when using her fists to strike and slap. Grese probably used her whip and truncheon in part to place distance between herself and her victim. She wanted to keep free from the tiny, six-legged, wingless disease vector that caused just another hell for those fighting to survive in Nazi concentration camps.

---

[177] Stubberfield (2020)

[178] Kramer also had a prisoner mistress, Lagerälteste Stanisława Starostek from Tarnów.

Irma Grese maintained her reputation for beauty and brutality in Auschwitz II – Birkenau. Grese's cruelty continually went beyond her general duties, beyond the scope of a woman's position in the camps per her training. At the Belsen trial, numerous witnesses would come forth to declare Grese took part in "selections" (selecting prisoners for the gas chambers). Witnesses and some historians place her assuming the role of making selections about fourteen months into her career at Birkenau. [179] Prisoners too old, sick, or weak were selected, or Grese might choose on a whim. She continually used the gas chambers as a punishment and as a threat.

Some historians, including Holocaust deniers and revisionists, will argue Grese never had the authority to send or threaten anyone to the gas chambers. She may have been present at selection, the dispute goes, but to conduct them would not have been allowed. Irma Grese would later say she had nothing to do with "selections" – she would never have determined what prisoners would be marked for death; her training and the rules prevented Grese from this position. These historians feel it is certain Grese could not have led a selection; she would not have been present when the trains arrived carrying prisoners.

However, there are numerous witnesses who have come forward testifying of witnessing Irma Grese taking part in selections. Holocaust survivor Edith Trieger was a teen when she was held at Auschwitz. She would live to testify:

> I saw many selections in Camp C at Auschwitz and Grese was invariably present. At the smaller ones I have seen Grese sort out the weaker women and send them off for removal to the gas chamber. I have also seen Grese beating women prisoners at the camp every day, sometimes with her hands, sometimes with a rubber stick and sometimes kicking them. [180]

For selections, Grese always accompanied a male, often SS Dr. Josef Mengele, whose formal duties included selections. Mengele would make his own specific selections: who would go to slave labor in Germany, who would go to the gas chambers, who would remain, or those he coveted for "experiments."

Grese may have been attracted to Mengele; he was quite the catch even before the Holocaust. He was considered handsome, with his thick brown hair, brown eyes, toothy smile, and smooth ways. Mengele held doctorates in anthropology and medicine. The six-foot tall, gap-toothed philosophy student loved art and music. He was exceedingly intelligent and a solemn researcher who wrote striking and intellectual published works. The highly decorated Mengele's uniform was tailored to a perfect fit. The inmates whispered his moniker, "The White Angel of Death." Mengele held all their lives in one leather-gloved hand.

In 1943, Josef Mengele was transferred to Auschwitz where he supervised the work of prisoner doctors in the prisoner hospital. Irma Grese had sent enough prisoners to this hospital. Any patient not recovering quickly enough went to the gas chambers. Medical experimentation was already being performed on prisoners at Auschwitz prior to his arrival, but his name is forever linked to the practice. These tests and experiments held no scientific value. He continued his studies on heredity and anthropology, fascinated with

[179] Brown, p. 48

[180] Deposition of Edith Trieger, paragraph 3, for the Belsen Trial

twins. (If he could learn how to create twins, Mengele reasoned, he could double the SS army.) Mengele would maim, slice, and murder in the name of medical science: He was observed removing a baby from a womb and tossing it into the ovens. He kept dozens of preserved human eyes pinned to a board on a wall for his "twin study." [181] Mengele regarded the prisoners as less than human, though he was observed to be kind to children before removing their body parts, entrails, or causing great suffering. Mengele would stand to watch prisoners unload from the train cars upon arrival; with the slightest move of a gloved finger, he would send people to death while whistling classical music. He was another man who would be linked as a perfect partner for Irma Grese.

Grese would later admit she played a miniscule role in selections but had no part in condemning prisoners. One of her "posts" at Auschwitz was the "selection parade," according to Grese's testimony during the Belsen trials; a whistle would sound across the camp and prisoners were to run into a large area and "fall into fives … it was my duty to see that they did so." Prisoners would later report how, if a prisoner slouched, did not run fast enough, or any other perceived infraction, Grese would fall upon them with her whip, a stick, or just shoot them dead. And the beatings were sometimes fatal. [182] "Dr. Mengele then came and made the selection." [183] Grese carried a "strength book" for jotting down notes and figures. This information was used to measure food rations. Irma Grese would explain:

> "As I was responsible for the camp, my duties were to know how many people were leaving and I had to count them, and I kept the figures in a strength book. After the selection took place the (prisoners) were sent into "B" Camp, and (Margot) Dreschel [184] telephoned and told me that they had gone to another camp in Germany for working purposes or for special treatment, which I thought was the gas chamber. I then put in my strength book either so many for transfer to Germany to another camp, or so many for S.B. (*Sonderbehandlung*). It was well known to the whole camp that S.B. meant the gas chamber." [185]

Grese failed to add what numerous camp survivors would later reveal: when she assisted Dr. Josef Mengele in selection, she utilized selection as a torture tactic on prisoners. Mengele might select a prisoner to live and Grese would ask him to deselect the prisoner. A sign to the selected they were doomed – or, sometimes, prisoners had no idea why they were selected: to live? To die? It was one of Grese's favourite mental abuses.

If prisoners attempted to escape this selection by running away to hide, it would often be Grese tracking them down, beating them into submission, then dragging them back into the line for the gas chamber. During a "selection" in October 1944, Auschwitz survivor and Block Leader Edith Trieger would witness Irma Grese wander the block as Dr. Mengele and a select few made selections. Edith knew Grese as "one of Mengele's principal accomplices" attacking women who attempted to escape the gas chamber. All

---

[181] They were the eyes of prisoners.

[182] Grese did not mention this detail in her Belsen testimony.

[183] "Selection" meant selecting prisoners to go to the gas chamber – it was a call to certain death.

[184] (1908-1945). A guard also recognized for her sadistic brutality. She would be executed when she attempted escape after the war.

[185] Bergen Trials Transcript

prisoners were made to strip. Some were selected to die. This group of nude women were placed in Edith's room "to await removal to the gas chamber…" Edith was ordered to block the door by spreading her arms. However, "(a few) selected persons" managed to escape the room by shoving past Edith. The group fled the barracks into the camp streets. "Grese saw this. One or two got away, but Grese caught the majority and beat them with her hands and kicked them until they were forced back into the room." [186]

Stanisława Rachwał (née Surówka), who was imprisoned in Auschwitz from 1942 to 1945, would later testify before the Main Commission for the Investigation of German Crimes in Poland, identifying Irma Grese as one of the most brutal guards. Stanisława witnessed children come off the incoming trains to be loaded immediately into a dump truck. The truck would drive to fiery pits that held the burning bodies of those murdered. The truck bed lifted, and the children tumbled into the fire pit, screaming until they died. [187]

Survivors recalled how Grese would also accompany Dr. Mengele to stand near the train stop at Auschwitz. Once the train stopped inside the camp and train car doors slid open, she undoubtably knew that Dr. Mengele would select what prisoners would live and who would join the line into the gas chamber. He kept a keen eye out for twins for his "studies" and anyone else he decided was interesting, such as dwarfs or midgets. Families were torn apart here; no one was told their true destination. By the time prisoners selected to live were shorn bald and outfitted, their loved ones had been murdered in gas chambers.

Survivor Klara Lebowitz would recall Irma Grese as usually in the company of Mengele. Klara would explain, "When Grese observed (a family) trying to stay together in selections…she would beat them until they were unconscious and leave them on the ground." [188]

Abraham Glinowiecki, a Polish Jew imprisoned and forced to labor at Auschwitz with his brother, observed Irma Grese as she ordered thousands of arriving Hungarians to the gas chambers. Some of the Hungarians seemed healthy; others appeared ill or lame. They ranged in age from infancy to elderly. Regardless of their health, abilities, or age, Abraham quietly observed the people unknowingly walk to their death. He was also aware of one of the blonde female camp leader's favorite tactics of appearing at inspections, select prisoners at random, and beat them down with a stick. The threat of the pistol strapped to her side was always present, and always in a well-polished holster and belt.

Alice Jakubovic (nee Roth) was a young Slovakian girl dreaming of being a teacher when she was taken from her home, along with the girls her age, and sent to Auschwitz. She was kept in Auschwitz I from March 26 to August, then transferred to B1B barrack 27 in Birkenau on August 6. She would remember asking Grese for mercy when a group of Hungarians arrived in the cattle cars on May 16. After stepping down from the cattle car, "two religious men in black caftans with beards with hats" approached Alice and asked for water. Alice went to Irma Grese to question her about water. "(Grese) said, 'don't bother with them because it could happen that they will take you also with them.'" Alice was forced to watch the group line up for the selection as they passed into Auschwitz. She recalled Grese as "… a beautiful lady – girl, a little bit crazy, but she wasn't so mean." Grese may have been standing and watching the Hungarians disembark. Alice did not

[186] McKale (2023). p. 36
[187] Testimony July 25, 1945
[188] Ibid. p. 37

mention this detail; in her retelling of the event she would say, "So we were standing, looking at them, and didn't say even anything." She does not expound on who "we" were; the walk from the Jewish men to Grese sounded as if Grese was nearby. [189] Alice would tell an interviewer, years later, that Grese "at the entrance, she wasn't cruel … there, no, there she wasn't (cruel)." [190]

Selections were not reserved for the trains or parades. A selection "team" would walk into barracks unannounced to choose candidates for the gas chamber. During one such selection, "in Camp A, Block 9, *Blockalteste* Ria and (SS Franz) Hoessler and Dr Enna, the prison doctor … (observed) two selected girls jumped out of the window. Grese approached them as they were lying on the ground and shot them twice," recalled a Holocaust survivor, Dora Szafran, imprisoned in Belsen at around twenty years of age. [191] (Her testimony would be countered by a statement that the windows in this block could not be opened. Dora stood by her testimonial.) Dr. Josef Mengele, resplendent in his perfect uniform and splendidly polished boots, would arrive at various times to assist in selections inside the camp.

Mengele was married, but – like most German superiors – procured mistresses. Supposedly, Mengele and Grese's trysts ended when Mengele discovered Grese was taking female lovers. There is no record of Grese being the lover of Mengele, and no living witnesses who state they observed Grese and Mengele together other than work. It may be a rumor. Rumors with men swirled around Irma Grese well past her death.

Speculations of Irma Grese's promiscuity in the camps were rampant, and is a large part of her legacy enough to mention in all her biographies. Grese may have been a sexual sadist. Or she was a young girl, away from home without the rules of chastity, social demands, and ladylike behavior. Possibly Grese was "husband hunting."

To have an SS officer or doctor as a husband, particularly one with the clout such as Kramer or Mengele, was a status symbol. With a husband Irma Grese would not have to work and would enjoy financial freedom. Grese would have the "name" and power: befriending high society SS wives, beautiful clothing, a lavish home. A high-powered Nazi wife may receive a title, such as Magda Goebbels' position as honorary president of The German Fashion Institute; or become Adolph Hitler's close ally like Emmy Göring, unofficially called the "First Lady of the Third Reich," treated like a movie star. [192] Catching a Nazi husband would be fulfilling the Furor's commands and wishes. Never mind these high-ranking SS men would have had to leave their wives and children to marry a mistress, but an uneducated, unworldly girl like Grese has dreams - either lying to herself or not considering harsh realities; it happens daily still.

Holocaust survivors would later discuss how they witnessed SS officers' sexual liaisons, to include prisoner relations. Prisoner Stanisława Rachwał (née Surówka) worked in the political department. She was privy to much of what occurred in inmate movement and accountability, selections, clandestine operations, the gassings, and the personal lives of the SS employed around her. She survived and would testify in court before the Main Commission for the Investigation of German Crimes in Poland:

[189] Jakubovic, A. (2002, August 27). Pp. 103-4
[190] Ibid. pp. 105-6
[191] Belsen Trial Transcripts, cross-examination of D. Szafran, September 25, 1945
[192] Wife of *Luftwaffe* chief Hermann Göring (1893-1973)

> The SS men and women at Auschwitz camp engaged in sexual relations. SS men bragged about it publicly, calling SS women *Huren* (whores) and speaking about them in a very disrespectful way. SS women acted flirtatiously towards SS men and male prisoners. Sexual intercourse between Germans was permitted and even secretly encouraged by the authorities on account of the desired increase in population. Engaging in such relations was made easier for Germans … for every one of them had a separate room, and the camp dignitaries had their own mansions in the town of Oświęcim. Sexual relations with prisoners were met with harsh punishment, transfer to the battle front, or degradation. Despite that, there were cases of SS men having intercourse with Jewish women in the camp. German women were promiscuous regardless of their rank and function. SS men and women alike were addicted to drinking. [193]

Until then, there was work. Irma Grese focused on proving herself to supervisors, becoming superior to her coworkers, including Luise Danz (1917 – 2009) and Margot Drechsel (1908 – 1945).

Drechsel was Grese's supervisor. Drechsel was far from attractive in anyone's eyes. Her buck teeth stuck out under a closed upper lip, and she was tall and thin, rangy, and vulgar. She wore her dark hair pinned behind the nape of her triangular face, wisps loose over her ears. At times Drechsel walked about with a bloodhound on a lead. She would sometimes dress as a doctor in a white coat and gloves, though she never held the rank. She had worked in an office prior to training at Ravensbrück. Drechsel moved somewhat quickly through the ranks between Auschwitz II – Birkenau, Auschwitz I, and Ravensbrück. Margot Drechsel was another woman who established herself with inherent cruelty. [194] "From the perspective of the SS, her only assets which made her exceptional in the whole female camp were education in the field of office work and being insusceptible to bribery" a witness would later explain. [195] Margot Drechsel was an associate of Mengele, forced prisoners to stand nude for hours at roll call, and assisted in selections with Mengele and Grese.

Grese's fellow *Lagerführerin* Luise Danz was another of the percentage of guards who were abusive in the camps. Danz had worked at several camps before landing in Auschwitz. She worked various details. One survivor, Halina Nelken, would later say of her, "Danz, tall, slender, and with a gaunt, boyish face was a specialist in punching jaws with her fist and at the same time bringing her knee up into a stomach. The woman she was mistreating fainted immediately." [196] Danz, sadistic and abusive, would employ her whip at any given time, taking pleasure in whipping and beating prisoners for little or no reason. [197]

---

[193] Witness testimony (July 25,1945). Interview by Judge Stanisław Żmuda (PhD). Commission for the Investigation of German Crimes in Poland.

[194] Dreschel attempted to escape when Nazi Germany surrendered, was recognized by survivors, and hanged by a Soviet court.

[195] Witness testimony of Stanisława Rachwał.

[196] Nelken (1996) pp. 216-17.

[197] Danz was arrested in June 1945, was tried and sentenced to life imprisonment but served 10 years. She was tried again in 1996, but charges were dropped due to her age.

By July 1944, Birkenau sector B-IIb was liquidated, with most of the 14,000 prisoners murdered in the gas chambers. Some biographers believe Grese was reportedly woefully incompetent for the job, so Luise Danz would be assigned to work with Grese. Auschwitz surviving prisoners disagree, recalling how B-IIb *Lagerführerin* Luise Danz, with nowhere else to supervise, ousted Grese from Camp-C. Prisoners learned quickly Grese's mood and quick temper determined her use of the whip, while Danz utilized the whip freely and randomly. Soon, cleanliness was no longer a goal, and camp violence increased. The rumors around the camps went across wires about how supervisors were unhappy with Danz. Grese replaced her only weeks later. Despite Grese's cruelty, there was a chance of measuring her behavior. Danz could never be gauged.

As the camp population increased, individual prisoner blocks built to hold 100 now held at least 1,000. Eventually, food became scarce; some starving prisoners were attacking those who carried the food out from the kitchen to the prisoner living quarters. The latrines began to overflow into the building so that prisoners were forced to relieve themselves anywhere there was a space. Bodies lay crammed together in the living quarters and the population of lice was more intense than ever. These prisoners, Irma Grese would later say, "behaved like animals." [198] She loathed to be near them because they were dirty and sickly. Still, Grese would be adding to the mass graves by wantonly killing many women daily.

The guards were powerless to change camp conditions, the state of the camp became uninhabitable, and there was no one available to blame but the prisoners. "Punishment" became wanton and more severe as time passed.

And again, the vicious cycle: the female staff were caught in an environment where they were helpless as both employees and as women. They could do nothing to better working conditions. They wielded little influence despite the decree of sexual equality. Affairs between staff continued as the norm. Numerous prisoners would later report the heavy use of drinking by SS staff when off duty, and alcohol procured from "organizing" was used to bribe staff and curry favors. Some of the guards stayed drunk or high while on duty, particularly those who worked at the trains and death squads. No records exist of prisoners who observed Grese under the influence.

If she wanted to escape by taking a few days leave in a real city, Irma Grese could travel to the nearby Polish town of Auschwitz [199] to shop and spend time with other Germans, perhaps meet someone outside of the camp walls. The remaining Poles now had to shop in their own designated stores of meager goods. (Higher quality items were available in "German only" shops.) Grese could purchase items unavailable at the camp. She would enjoy foods and goods unattainable to locals. New stores and restaurants were opening to cater to this "German only" new clientele. It is easy to visualize Irma Grese, proud in her uniform, striding through the town, perfect makeup, and lovely hair courtesy the prisoners at the Auschwitz salon for guards. She was no longer the farmer's girl, uneducated and unqualified, living in a tiny hamlet. Her pretty face and figure surely caught the attention of those around her, accented by the careful tailoring of her uniform, again courtesy of the prisoners. Irma Grese's good looks caught everyone's attention, even those who feared her.

[198] Irma Grese, testimony. Belsen Trials

[199] The town's name was originally Oświęcim; the Germans renamed it.

While prisoners and staff alike were taken by Irma Grese's thick blonde hair, bright blue eyes, and angelic face, they also recalled her enchantment in their suffering. Grese remained one of the guards who took personal pleasure in prisoner's misery. Recalls one survivor, "there was a beautiful woman called Grese who rode a bike. Thousands and thousands of (prisoners) were standing there on their knees in scorching heat, and she took delight in watching us."

Stanisława Rachwał testified that Irma Grese was "a light and very beautiful blonde with big, blue eyes ... shapely eyebrows ... long lashes, red lips ... lovely, small teeth and a beautiful neck. Pleasant, low-pitched voice, beautiful legs and dainty feet. She was a lesbian." According to Stanisława 's testimony, Grese was hostile toward male SS, telling Stanisława "I know what to expect from this element." Grese "had her favorites among the female prisoners, and liked young, pretty and mostly Polish girls." [200]

Another survivor reported "Grese used to be an actress, [201] she was a gorgeous, pretty young woman."

One survivor was witness to the indifference Grese showed in brutality: "one of the doors was closed in the back (of the bath barrack.) Grese came in through the other, she beat the unfortunate (prisoners) with a club, everybody tried to get away from her. (Another time) was the first time I saw a dead body in the camp, a woman was tread upon. Grese watched it indifferently, with a shrug of the shoulders." [*sic*]. Grese "put out the eyes of a girl because she talked with an acquaintance through the wires" another survivor would later recall. [202]

"She was the most beautiful woman I've ever seen" an unidentified Holocaust survivor recalls during one interview. "Her face had an angelic quality, and her blue eyes were the liveliest, the most clarity, innocent eyes imaginable." [203] Echoing the others, this survivor found it difficult to believe such an attractive woman was so brutal.

Polish Jew Hanka Rozenwayg was in her early twenties when she arrived at Auschwitz in the summer of 1943. She worked as part of a *Kommando* when a *Kapo* decided Hanka's work was not suitable. [204] The *Kapo* went directly to Grese, and Grese sought out Hanka; Grese was tugging on the lead of an attack dog. Grese commanded the dog to attack Hanka. It tore Hanka's clothing and skin, leaving scars that would still be visible when Hanka testified against Grese at the Belsen Trials, September 27, 1945.

Along with her whip, gun, and fists, Irma Grese employed one of at least 200,000 total dogs used in Nazi Germany during WWII. [205] Irma Grese's vicious dogs, that she reportedly starved, were used to intimidate, and attack prisoners. According to one biographer, the dogs used by Grese "were not only ferocious, but also rabid" which ensured death with one bite. [206] Irma Grese's use of "half-starved dogs" persist in accounts, and is a regular staple when discussing the Hyena of Auschwitz. It is another rumor.

Canine instructor and certified AKC Evaluator Linda Gregg has over forty years' experience in canine obedience, rehabilitation, and psychology, to include breed-specific

---

[200] Testimony July 25, 1945

[201] She was misinformed; Grese was never an actress, though she planned to pursue stardom after the war.

[202] Ibid

[203] TheUntoldPast

[204] In some documents, it was not a *Kapo* but Juana Bormann, "The Dog Lady."

[205] Lilly, R. J. & Puckett, M.B. (1997). P. 123.

[206] Jennings (2015). P. 40

issues, rescue, certifications, German style show, and over twenty years in *Schutzhund.* [207] She has trained across the United States. Gregg has also studied the history of Dachau concentration camp. Linda Gregg explains the "starving working dog" narrative is difficult to believe, and the "rabid working dog" near impossible:

> Starving a dog would only make it weaker, or unhealthy. Define 'half starved.' Missing a meal? Two meals? Starving a dog to increase its prey drive is a myth, just like 'feeding gunpowder and blood to increase viciousness' is a myth. And a dog is not going to attack a person just because it's hungry. Even if there's a piece of food in the person's hand, or on the ground, I just don't see it happening. [208]

To train a dog to protect (attack), the dog first must be strong tempered with a high drive, exceedingly intelligent with a desire to please. This is why German Shepherds make effective police dogs, Gregg rationalizes, "and they are psychologically intimidating." Gregg explains training a dog to attack is training a dog to protect, and it begins in puppyhood. "A handler cannot just 'make' a dog vicious. It takes commands, repetition, consistency, rewards, and a lot of time to train." There is very little chance Irma Grese's dogs, or any of the SS-trained dogs, were rabid. "A dog with rabies would be far too sick to work," Linda Gregg scoffs. "First, it would have neurological problems. It would have physical problems, such as foaming at the mouth. The dog would not survive. There's just no way a dog with rabies could be used for any sort of work." Irma Grese may have started the rumor herself "probably because it makes a good story," Linda Gregg guesses. "And creating fear: telling the (prisoners) the dog would eat people alive because its hungry." [209] Animal rescue groups note biochemical disfunction in starved animals, with organ failure, muscle weakness, low metabolism, loss of energy, and poor heart functioning. Thus, rescue agencies treating starving dogs must do so with utmost care at risk of further harm. The animal's body is shutting down to utilize muscle, body fat, and thyroid. Irma Grese's dogs, if they were starving or hungry, would not be able to perform work. This would include the look of intimidation, movement, and strong barks and growls– a dog will not be able or willing to work without a glossy coat, thick body, strong vocal cords, or developed muscles. Still, the myth of Irma Grese's use of "half-starved dogs" persist.

[207] German for "protection dog," includes protection skills, tracking, and obedience.
[208] Personal interviews with Linda Gregg, January 17, 2024.
[209] Personal interviews with Linda Gregg, January 18, 2024.

Kapos moving a body to the crematoria. The Kapos did the "hands on" work in the crematoriums; it was just one more layer of protection for the Germans to dodge blame of any accusations. It was also a step in staff keeping themselves clean and healthy. This location is unknown, but typical of the crematoriums like the ones where Irma Grese sent anyone who displeased her. This photo was posed for demonstration purposes.
(This and the following two images: Circa April 29-May10, 1945. Location Dachau. Photographer: unnamed Yugoslav prisoner. Photo courtesy the private collection of Ray Cook. Used with permission. These three images have been minimally altered for clarity.)

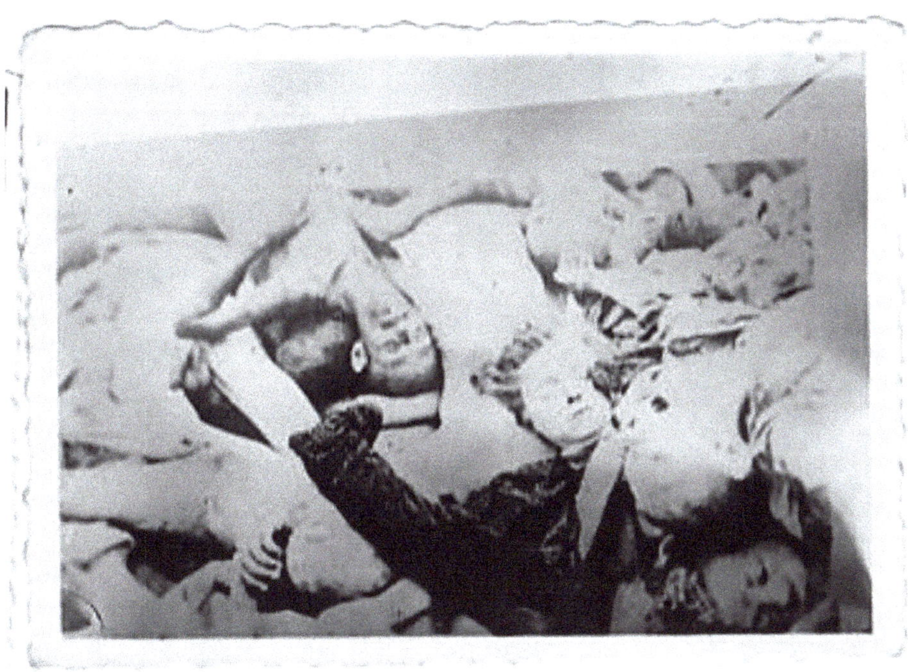

Pile of deceased. Irma Grese sent thousands of prisoners to the gas chambers. She also shot or beat them to death. Abuse did not stop when the prisoners died. Their bodies were robbed of gold teeth, hair, and bones were smashed and dumped into pits, over local crops, in a river, or on a road.

Preparing a body for the crematorium. This photo was posed for demonstration purposes. The man second from right appears to have a *Kapo* armband, according to one WWII historian.

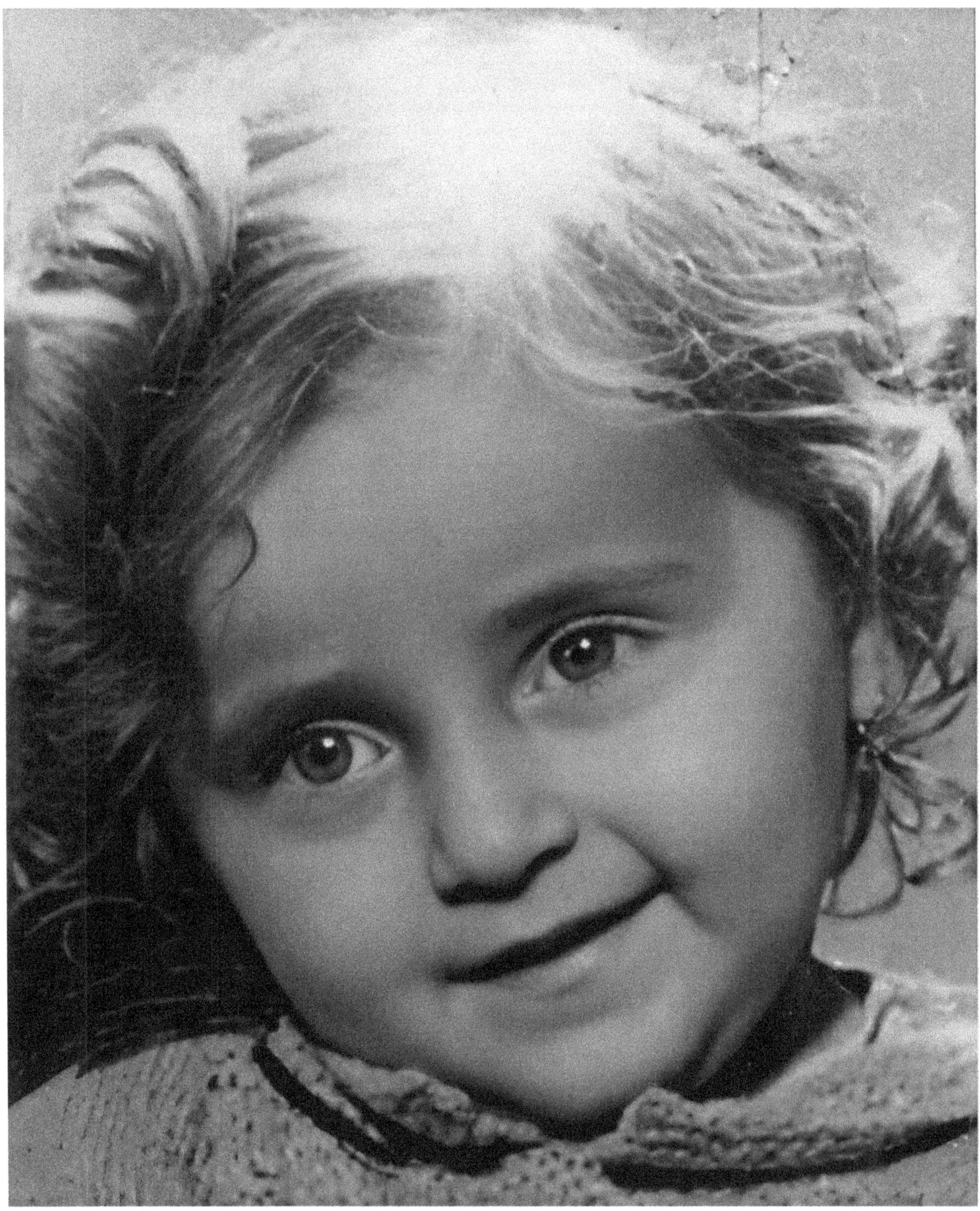

Zsuszanna Kovari, from Szatmarnementi, Romania was two years old when she was arrested and then murdered in the Auschwitz gas chambers on May 25, 1944. At the same time, Irma Grese was working as a *Lagerführerin* and assisting in selecting victims for death. (Circa: Unknown. Location: unknown, probably Szatmarnementi, Romania. Photographer: Unknown. Public Domain.)

CHAPTER 17
Life with the Hyena

By the autumn of 1943, Irma Grese was promoted *to Oberaufseherin* (Senior Overseer). "This was the second highest rank that SS female concentration camp personnel could obtain." [210] (The highest would be *Chef Oberaufseherin* – Chief Overseer. Less than five women, for the duration of the war, ever obtained this title.)

Gossip between existing prisoners and newly arriving prisoners would include how Irma Grese continued to dress in flawlessly clean and neat uniforms, with every hair in place. She would wear perfume. [211] Her jackboots and belt leather stayed polished; her clothing creased. When off duty she wore the best clothing procured from the suitcases of the prisoners, or she brought cloth to her seamstress. Prisoner Lilika Salzer was a seamstress before being arrested and taken to Auschwitz; she was housed in C-. Lilika secured better treatment for herself by designing and sewing clothing for Grese. She would ensure the clothing fit Grese perfectly. As part of her reward, Grese allowed Lilika to visit her sisters -escorted by Grese – who were twins. (Someone must have shielded these twins from Mengele.)

Several of Grese's seamstresses would report how Irma Grese would strip nude in front of them to walk about her room. She was either showing off her body or she did not consider the prisoners as humans; for Grese, it was akin to undressing in front of a pet dog or cat. One prisoner would later say she was unimpressed with Grese's figure, no matter how proud Grese was of her own physique.

In her memoirs, Holocaust survivor Rena Kornreich Glissen recalled the three years she and her sister Danka spent in Auschwitz. Irma Grese's psychological torture of Rena would cause this twenty-one-year-old prisoner to consider suicide on numerous occasions. Grese would taunt Rena how, after Germany won the war, all Jews would be sterilized and sent to Madagascar to be slaves. Rena would write she would have committed suicide because of Grese's verbal torture, but Danka's words and companionship kept her hope alive. [212] Grese knew exactly what mental abuses worked with individuals, and how best to cause distress.

Survivor Zdenka Ehrlich, a Czechoslovakian who had survived several camps, was about 22 years old when she was approached by The Hyena in Belsen. Zdenka was working in a field when she found a knife stamped with a swastika. The handle was quite heavy, but she hid the much-coveted tool in her clothing. "Until one day we were searched, and it was Irma Grese … who found it on me." Grese smashed the handle against Zdenka's head: "… I thought for sure she's going to crush my skull. And when she was finished with me, she threw it away and kicked me." [213] Zdenka made a bold move when, aching from the beating, she stepped out of the line of prisoners to retrieve the knife.

---

[210] Jewish Virtual Library (no date).

[211] Many biographers have Grese wearing perfume to taunt the prisoners to jealousy, a reminder they had no such luxuries. This author believes Grese also wore heavy perfume to mask the smell of the camps: the filth, the unwashed, the acrid smell of burning bodies. While psychological torture was certainly part of Irma Grese's repartee, the practical use of perfume should be considered. Although one liberating soldier would later report, "after being (at Belsen) for a couple of days, we was used to (the smell). It didn't affect us at all." [sic]. -Riches, F. A. (1987, September 19). Pp. 9-10.

[212] Kornreich-Gelissen (2015)

[213] Ehrlich, Z. (1985, August 8). P. 51.

Grese obtained a silver-plated pistol that stayed polished. The jewelry Grese wore, the perfumes, were only top quality. In a world of grey and black, bleakness and death, Irma Grese was light and perfection. She made sure of it.

There was an eccentric reason for Grese – and many high-ranking Nazi women of Germany – to appear well dressed, another juxtaposition of the Third Reich that seems senseless. In 1943, a group of prisoners set up a sewing shop to specifically create fancy dresses for the wives of Nazi soldiers. Despite Hitler's strict orders that no Jewish hands should touch clothing worn by Nazis, there was a waiting list of half a year for this dress shop's clothing. And it began in a high-ranking Nazi home with a Jewish prisoner.

A prisoner named Berta Berkovich Kohút, daughter of a tailor, had become the private nanny and seamstress of Hedwig Höss, wife of *Kommandant* Rudolf Höss. Prisoner Martha Fuchs joined Berta to create personalized dresses for Hedwig, and soon envious SS wives began asking Hedwig about her flawless dresses. A workshop was added to the camp administrative buildings and at least 40 women's lives were spared because of their talent at the helm of a sewing machine. Irma Grese was a customer of the mostly Jewish sewn garments. Nazi women of the higher echelon as far away as Berlin were placing orders; the work moved slow because the women in the sewing room were fastidious. They were rewarded with extra food, beds, small tokens of bribery – and escape from the gas chamber. For someone like Irma Grese, who insisted her clothing be perfect, the customized dresses were a necessity to women these seamstresses dared not look in the eyes.

Despite the treatment by the sadistic guards and the *kapos* who could not be trusted, there existed an underground resistance at Auschwitz. Some members were camp staff. These groups worked under Irma Grese's radar. One such group was composed of prisoners who risked their own lives to smuggle documents out of the camps. One of these resistance members was a plump Polish woman from Warsaw named Antonina Piątkowska. She entered Auschwitz in April 1942.

Prisoner clerk Monika Galica, also Polish, handled files and papers at the hospital in Block 28a. She was friends with Antonina Piątkowska. Monika noted how the hospital kept a ledger of all female prisoners who were deceased: typhus, gassed, shot, or injected with carbolic acid. This included pregnant women, and live babies who were thrown to rats. Antonina and Monika decided to make a list of Polish deceased women, so Monika copied the ledgers to pass off to Antonina, the long list of names in cramped handwriting. Antonia next began hiding the lists in various areas of the camp, right under Irma Grese's boots. The resistance planned to eventually smuggle out the lists.

Antonina ran a huge risk. Resistance members would be hung in the camp for all to see. There were prisoners who would run to tell officers just for an extra bite of food or scrap of clothing. Irma Grese certainly had her own snitches.

The lists were handed off and around to various underground resistance members and hidden through the camps until liberation, when Antonina retrieved the documents and handed over the lists to outside organizations. The documents would be published in the press; as a result, the Main Commission was alerted to investigate German Crimes.

Under the Hyena's nose

Auschwitz prisoner Antonina Piątkowska (prisoner #6805) was a covert resistant fighter. Working with others, she managed to smuggle lists of murdered Polish female prisoners. Antonina retrieved the documents after liberation to expose the truth about the Auschwitz atrocities. She would testify against Maria Mandl and Margo Dreschel. Irma Grese, while working at Auschwitz and Ravensbrück, never located these lists.

One of these preserved lists appears on the next page. (Circa 1942. Location: Auschwitz – Birkenau Memorial and Museum. Photographer: unknown. Courtesy Auschwitz – Birkenau Memorial and Museum. Used with permission.)

Polish Antonina Piątkowska was born in Warsaw. She was imprisoned in Auschwitz on April 27, 1942 (camp no. 6805). Antonina was evacuated to KL Ravensbrück where she was liberated. (Circa 1942. Location: Auschwitz. Photographer: unknown. Courtesy Auschwitz Memorial and Museum Archive. Used with permission.)

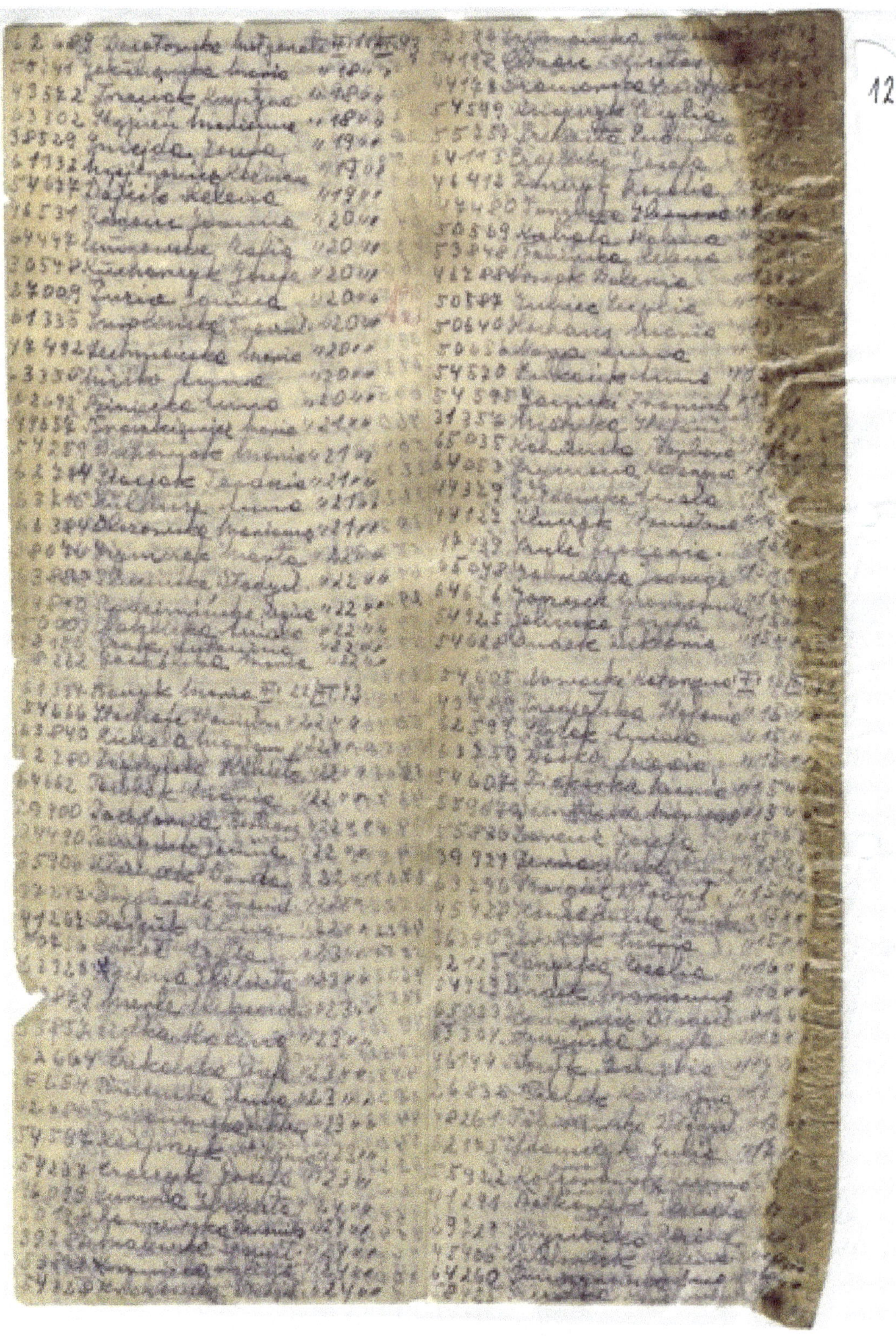

Many families finally discovered the true fate of loved ones through these lists. Antonina Piątkowska and her fellow resistance members exposed the truth about the atrocities at Auschwitz for the world to see. And it all happened on the watches of Irma Grese and those she worked with - Dr. Mengele, Luise Danz, Margot Drechsel, Josef Kramer, Marie Mandl, and the Nazi staff who believed they controlled the thousands of men and women in Auschwitz. [214] Irma Grese and her ilk had control of the life and death of prisoners; they held control over much of their emotions and thoughts. There were a few prisoners who did not allow control of their hope.

Hope remained alive in many prisoners. They picked up news of the war from what could be learned through the entangled prisoner grapevine. On January 30, 1943, Irma Grese was likely excited; she and her comrades were preparing to listen to live speeches from high-ranking Nazi Hermann Göring and Propaganda Minister Joseph Goebbels over the radio; it was the tenth anniversary of a Nazi event. Göring was slated to speak at 11:00 a.m. To the embarrassment of the Nazi party, the Royal Air Force dropped a bomb over Berlin just prior to Göring's presentation. Goebbels would also be interrupted by bombshells that day. The same occurred on April 20, 1943; for Hitler's 54th birthday, Berlin was racked by explosions. Grese and the SS would have been appalled. Prisoners no doubt quietly rejoiced.

Irma Grese would be employed at B IIc camp which contained 20,000 – 30,000 prisoners, the "family camp," when she was tested for syphilis at the Auschwitz *Lazarett* on January 22, 1944. It is unknown if this was a test for all employees or solely for the Hyena of Auschwitz.

Her diagnosis was Angina, "the most prevalent medical problem for which attention was sought." [215] Angina produced "chest pain that is caused by the tightening of the muscles around the heart, restricting blood flow – is particularly amplified by stress." Angina cases within the employees at the camp "were typically higher" than the population, "present in 7% of the records within (a) study sample" at a time when "the nation average …is around 2%." [216] This study suggests their working conditions placed guards under severe mental and physical conditions. At twenty years of age, Irma Grese was at risk for a stroke or heart attack.

May of 1944 saw the influx of the Hungarian transports: an estimated 434,000 Jews from Hungary were rounded up and sent to Auschwitz. People of all ages were herded off the train cars and told to wait in a grove of woods; they had no idea they would be dead in hours, the gas chamber taking their lives.

Jews had already been marked for death during the "extermination phase" with the March 1944 Nazi invasion of Hungary. Hungary had passed antisemitic legislation. (By October of the same year some 565,000 Hungarian Jews were murdered.) [217] During these transports, Irma Grese was working in C Camp at Auschwitz – Birkenau. She would have full knowledge of the mass deportation, of Hungary handing over Jews to the Nazis.

Grese supervised a *Strafkommando* during 1944. This "punishment company" oversaw female prisoners working in a quarry located outside of the camp. There was a small railway track that fit a heavy metal truck. Guards watched from behind strands of

---

[214] Antonina Piątkowska continued as a resistance member until she was evacuated to Ravensbrück; she was freed when it was liberated.

[215] *SS-Hygiene Institut Vol 11a/b (271) and Log, SS Lager-Lazarett* cited in Mears, C. (2020) p. 97

[216] Mears, C. p. 97

[217] Yad Vashem, The World Holocaust Remembrance Center.

razor wire as the prisoners loaded heavy rocks and sand onto the trucks, then push the filled truck up and downhill to unload. Grese's appearance, no matter how clean or perfectly attired, was enough to make these prisoners quiver with fear. The work was fast-paced, and if prisoners spilled the load or did not work fast enough it meant a severe beating or an attack by Grese's dogs.

D. Szafran would later testify at the Belsen trials what she witnessed:

Prosecution: Whilst you were at Auschwitz did you see any other persons beaten besides yourself?

Szafran: I saw it very often when I was working in *Kommando* 103, and we were carrying loads of earth and coal. I have seen Kramer beat a person so often that I cannot really say how many times … (Grese) had a pistol, but she was using a riding crop. The beatings were very severe. If they were not the cause of death, they were not called "severe" in the camp. [218]

[218] The Belsen Trails transcript

Irma's Accolades

Copies of proposed list for the awarding of the war service medal with and without swords for meritorious service from the *Kommandantur KonzentrationsLager* Auschwitz, and sub-camps.

In 1939, Adolph Hitler created the War Merit Cross *(Kriegsverdienstkreuz)*. It was awarded to military personnel and civilians.
WWII Historian and collector Dave Moore has studied and collected World War II memorabilia for over 20 years and is an expert on medals awarded to German soldiers. The retired U.S. Air Force pilot buys, sells, and trades items and set up an online site, WW2CollectorsWorld.com, for fellow enthusiasts. At any time, Moore's collection boasts at least 1,000 original items to include all original documents, weapons, clothing, and medals.
"The War Merit Cross with Swords recognized those military men whose acts of courage were above the call of duty, yet did not meet the criteria for the Iron Cross" Dave Moore explains. The recipient's actions could "either be in the form of bravery not under direct enemy fire or the planning / leading of combat operations." Award recipients could be females, males, general staff, soldiers, youth, adults, factory workers, and even non-Germans and Jews (they would be working special projects, still inside the camps).
The Cross "Without Swords" was awarded to civilians for "meritorious service in furtherance of the war effort." Dave Moore clarifies that "military personnel who qualified for the War Merit Cross in an administrative, medical or other service away from the front line received this award." as did civilians whose contributions were "important to the war effort." Civilians were also eligible despite their age or social class.
There were two classes of the awards. "When the Germans have a 1st Class & 2nd Class of the same award, you need to receive the 2nd Class award first and then receive the 1st Class after you effectively meet the same criteria. On rare occasions they will either skip the 2nd Class or present both the 2nd Class & 1st Class together." [219]

According to the following documents, Irma Grese was one of sixteen female employees, as an *Aufseherin*, to be nominated. She received the award, along with fellow recipients, on the tenth anniversary of Hitler's rise to power, circa January 30, 1943.

(The following two images courtesy of National Archives and Records Administration (NARA) and used with permission.)
(Photos of medals courtesy www.ww2collectorsworld.com)
Translation by Ann Marie Ackerman, J.D. www.annmarieackermann.com.

[219] Interview with Dave Moore of WW2Collectorsworld.com, February 23-5, 2024

(Opposite page)
TRANSLATION

Commander
Concentration Camp Auschwitz
[(fine print -- illegible)]

Nomination List No. __3__

for the

Bestowal ~~of the War Merit Cross~~

~~Class~~

~~With (Without) Swords~~

Dated this ____________ day of ___________, 19_____.

____
(Signature and rank of the [illegible])

To
____________________________ Through official channels
([illegible] Office)

2091 [illegible]

Kommandantur
Konzentrationslager Auschwitz
(Vorschlagende Einheit)

Vorschlagsliste Nr. 3.

für die

Verleihung ~~des Kriegsverdienstkreuzes~~ der Kriegsverdienstmedaille

~~Klasse~~

~~mit (ohne) Schwerter~~

, den 19

(Unterschrift und Dienstgrad des Einheitsführers)

An

a. d. D.

(Verleihende Dienststelle)

Page 2 & 3 of Nomination List No. __3__ (opposite page)

Source:
Nomination list of war service medal

Row 2: Surname
Row 3: First name
Row 4: Birth – location/date
Row 5: Rank
Row 6: Group
Row 7: Previously awarded decorations
Row 8: Brief justification and statement of the intermediate supervisor – In SS Service since: [for Irma Grese, 1-6-42]

[Note that "source" in the original is not a German word. Nor is "*Kriegsdienstmedaille*" the same word used to describe the military decoration on the official list "*Kriegsverdienstkreuz*"). And the German label is grammatically awkward. I suspect that the handwritten notation was made by an English speaker archiving or organizing the German documents and that he or she mislabeled the list. But because "*Kriegsverdienstkreuz*" was crossed out on the official cover sheet, I can't even tell what medal she was nominated for. There was a medal called the *Kriegsverdienst-Medaille* that was introduced in 1940. – *Translator*]

Translated by Ann Marie Ackerman, J.D. www.annmarieackermann.com.

Lfde. Nr.	Zuname	Vorname (Rufname)	Geburts- Ort	Geburts- Tag	Dienstgrad	Truppen
1	2	3	4		5	6
1	Danz	Luise	Waldorf	11.12.17	Aufseherin	Kdtr.K.
2	Ehlert	Hertha	Berlin	26.3.o5	"	"
3	Grese	Irma	Wrechen	7.1o.23	"	"
4	Lupka	Elisabeth	Klein-Dammen	27.1o.o2	"	"
5	Saretzki	Elisabeth	Gennin	28.11.2o	"	"
6	Gramattke	Lotte	Breslau	22.6.22	SS-Helferin	"
7	Lässig	Aniana	Wilstruff	24.3.25	"	"
8	Drews	Gisela	Leopoldshall	1o.5.2[illegible]	"	"
9	Schünzel	Charlotte	Braunschweig	8.7.19	"	"
1o	Schachtner	Hermine	Wettzell	19.6.26	"	"
11	Ernst	Gerda	Haynau	3o.8.23	"	"
12	Stieff	Therese	Hermsdorf	1o.9.23	"	"
13	Tietje	Erna	Altenhagen	21.1o.97	NS-Schwester	Stand
14	Derressauw	Paula	Gent	19.1o.24	DRK-Schwesternhelferin	"
15	Dilissen	Alda	KlieneBroegel	18.8.22	"	"
16	Hillaert	Alice	Wartebeke	8.5.2o	"	"

Bisher verliehene Auszeichnungen	Kurze Begründung und Stellungnahme der Zwischen-Vorgesetzten
7	8
-.-	Im ϟϟ-Dienst seit: 1.3.43
-.-	" 15.12.39
-.-	" 1.6.42
-.-	" 15.10.42
-.-	" 15.6.42
-.-	" 20.1.43
-.-	" 1.3.43
-.-	" 1.4.43
-.-	" 1.8.43
-.-	" 1.8.43
-.-	" 1.8.43
-.-	" 1.10.43
-.-	" 15.10.41
-.-	" 20.6.44
-.-	" 28.6.44
-.-	" 28.6.44

ϟϟ-Sturmbannführer

War Merit Cross (*Kriegsverdienstkreuz)* with swords – 2nd Class.
This is the original case it would have been issued to the recipient.

War Merit Cross (*Kriegsverdienstkreuz)* with swords – 1st Class.

War Merit Cross (*Kriegsverdienstkreuz)* without swords – 1st Class.
Both awards are in the original case that would have been issued to the recipient.

The War Service Cross-2nd Class Without Swords (*Kriegsverdienstkreuz II. Klasse ohne Schwerter*). Irma Grese was given such an award for her "splendid work." She received this particular award because she was not considered SS.

The author holding a medal identical to the medal Irma Grese was awarded. (Circa May 2024, Photograph by J. A. Yates, Property of J.A. Yates)

Maria Kruszel was interviewed by the Main Commissioner for State Security in November 1945. She would recall Kramer and Grese. "They never personally beat me," Maria explained, "… I often witnessed Kramer and Irma Grese beat prisoners." Grese usually carried a stick, and any "… lack of deference" by prisoners resulted in beatings. Prisoners were to stop work and acknowledged the two whenever Kramer and Grese walked by, Maria explained, but not all prisoners recognized the camp sadists. [220]

Occasionally Irma Grese's brutality had to be restrained by her superiors. Grese was becoming more out of control and sadistic in her work.

For the most part her supervisors regarded her as a true German, an exceptional girl, and a positive addition to the workforce. Irma Grese's name was submitted for an award, a medal for "meritorious war service" for her "splendid work." [221] Twelve female overseers (*SS-Aufseherinnen*) were awarded the War Service Cross-2nd Class without Swords (*Kriegsverdienstkreuz II. Klasse ohne Schwerter*). Irma Grese was nominated and awarded. [222] Female recipients included Dorothea Binz, Maria Mandl, and Johanna Langefeld. Margot Drechsel was nominated but not selected. Grese and her proud recipients were awarded their medals on the tenth anniversary of Hitler's takeover of Germany.

A prisoner named Maria Kruszel would later testify Irma Grese seemed to always carry a stick, and she and Kramer were known to beat prisoners for no reason. Prisoners who were working and observed Grese approaching admitted to instantly becoming fearful of Grese because her attack might come at any moment. If Irma Grese felt prisoners were disrespecting her, for any reason, the stick was used, and prisoners would be howling in pain. [223]

This included male prisoners. Grese would be transferred to the male camp, Auschwitz I, for two weeks in January 1945. She showed no mercy, and treated the males with the same sadistic fervor as she had with female prisoners. She was reportedly sexually abusing male prisoners as well.

On January 18-19, Irma Grese was ordered back to Ravensbrück, where her ruthless career began. She oversaw a transport of prisoners. The end of the war must have looked inevitable now, with the Russians gaining ground to the east, and the Allies obtaining victory to the west. Frantically, the Nazis were moving prisoners from camp to camp, documents were destroyed, and roads were littered with the bodies of prisoners who did not make the marches between transfers. Grese must have also felt the desperation as she was ordered to supervise another transport eight weeks later, this time from Ravensbrück to Bergen-Belsen. [224]

In June 1944, with a successful landing of D-Day, Allies began retaking most of Europe. To the East, the Soviet Union was driving back the Nazis. In desperation, the Nazis began evacuating the camps in eastern Europe, forcing thousands of prisoners by foot or cattle car to Germany: at least 85,000 to Belsen. [225] Many prisoners perished before arriving.

---

[220] Testimony of Maria Kruszel. (14 November 1945). Reported by Bellens, Alfons.
[221] Brown, p. 53
[222] The dates are unknown as there are no dates on the paperwork. See illustrations.
[223] Testimony on November 14, 1945, at The Main Commission for the Investigation of German Crimes in Poland
[224] Feig, K. (1981)
[225] Stubberfield (2020)

Irma's Medical Care

The existing medical records of Irma Grese. A sign-n sheet reveals she was seen by the medical department twice. (This image: Circa: 1944. Location: Auschwitz. Auschwitz medical appointments book. courtesy Auschwitz – Birkenau Memorial and Museum. Used with permission)

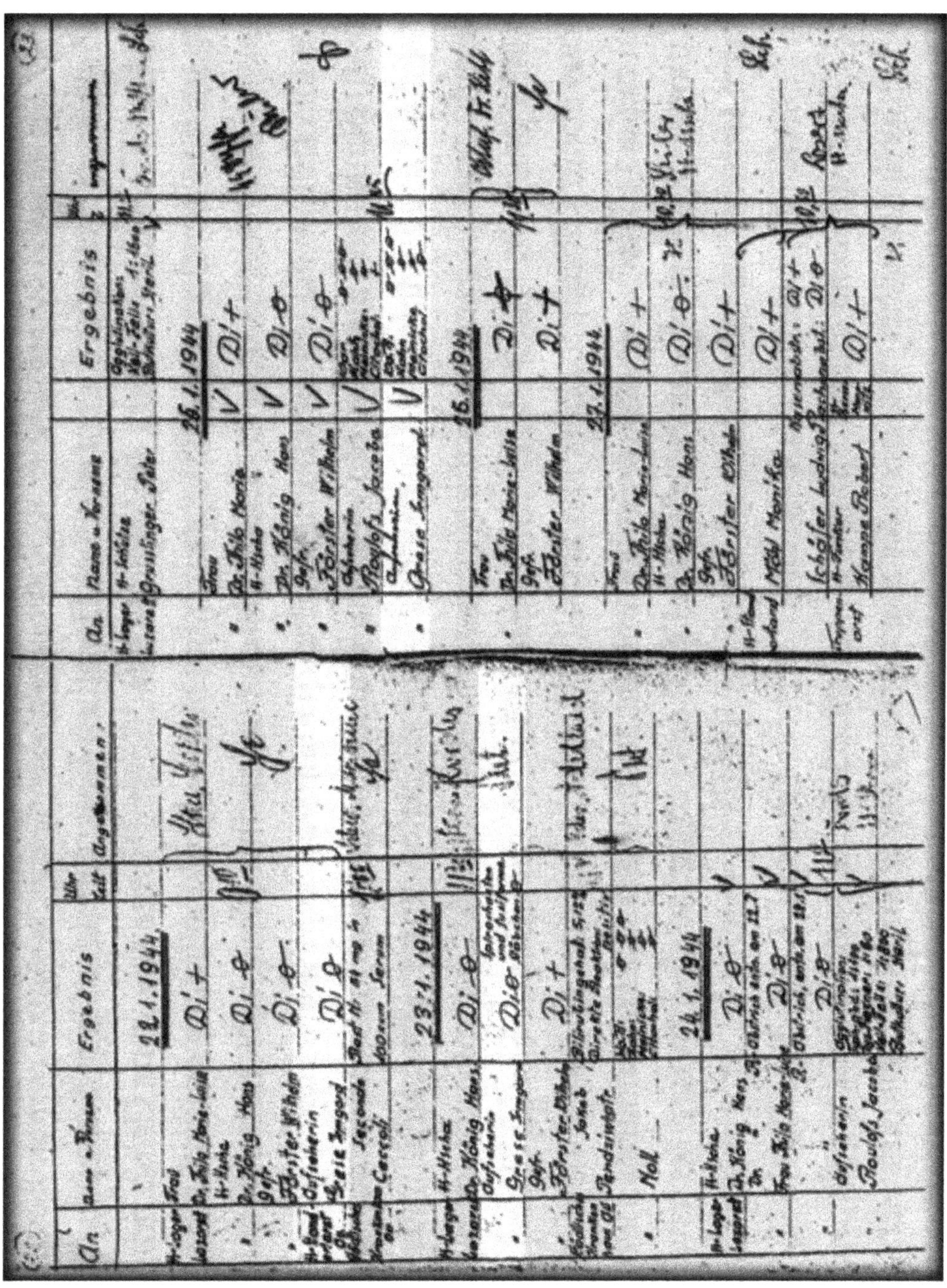

Next page:

A copy of a laboratory packing slip. English translation:

Hygiene-bacterial laboratory
of the Waffen SS Southeast

22nd of January 1944
Auschwitz, OS*, on 22nd Jan. 1944
~~1738/V/~~ 318- 23rd Jan.

These attachments were forwarded:

Material: throat culture, taken on 22nd Jan. 1944

to examine for diagnosis, Plaut-Vincent's angina

Last name, first name: Grese Irmgard

Rank, unit: warden

Clinical diagnosis: presumptive diagnosis of angina

Address of the source agency: SS-camp hospital Auschwitz

Comments: _____

[signature]
(stamp, signature)
SS-Obersturmführer (senior assault leader)

* OS may refer to Oberschlesien (Upper Silesia), the province in which Auschwitz was located, but some documents online say Oswiecim, the Polish name for Auschwitz.

Translation by Ann Marie Ackerman, J.D. www.annmarieackermann.com.

(Document courtesy Auschwitz – Birkenau Memorial and Museum, Oświęcim, Poland)

Hyg.-bakt. Unters.-Stelle der Waffen-SS, Südost

22. JAN. 1944

Auschwitz OS., am 22.1.44

1738 V 328 2 3. A

Anliegend wird übersandt:

Material: Rachen-Abstrich entnommen am 22.1.44

zu untersuchen auf Di, Plaut-Vincent 870/2.6c

Name, Vorname: Grese Irmgard

Dienstgrad, Einheit: Aufseherin

Klinische Diagnose: Angina, Verdacht auf Di

Anschrift der einsendenden Dienststelle: SS-Lager-Lazarett Auschwitz

Bemerkungen:

(Stempel, Unterschrift)

SS-Obersturmführer

Next page:

Copy of a Laboratory packing slip. English translation:

Hygiene-bacterial laboratory
of the Waffen SS Southeast

22nd of January 1944
Auschwitz, OS*, on 22nd Jan. 1944
S ~~318~~ 25th Jan.

These attachments were forwarded:

Material: Blood, taken on 22nd Jan. 1944

to examine for the Wassermann test [a test for syphilis]

Last name, first name: Grese Irmgard

Rank, unit: warden

Clinical diagnosis: angina

Address of the source agency: SS-camp hospital Auschwitz

Comments: _____

[signature]
(stamp, signature)
SS-Obersturmführer (senior assault leader)

Translation by Ann Marie Ackerman, J.D. www.annmarieackermann.com.

(Document courtesy Auschwitz – Birkenau Memorial and Museum, Oświęcim, Poland)

Hyg.-bakt. Unters.-Stelle der Waffen-SS, Südost

Auschwitz OS., am 22. 1. 44

22. JAN. 1944

33/3

S 318

25. 1.

Anliegend wird übersandt:

Material: Blut entnommen am 22. 1. 44

zu untersuchen auf WaR

Name, Vorname: Grese Irmgard

Dienstgrad, Einheit: Aufseherin

Klinische Diagnose: Angina

Anschrift der einsendenden Dienststelle: SS-Lager-Lazarett Auschwitz

Bemerkungen:

(Stempel, Unterschrift)

SS-Obersturmführer

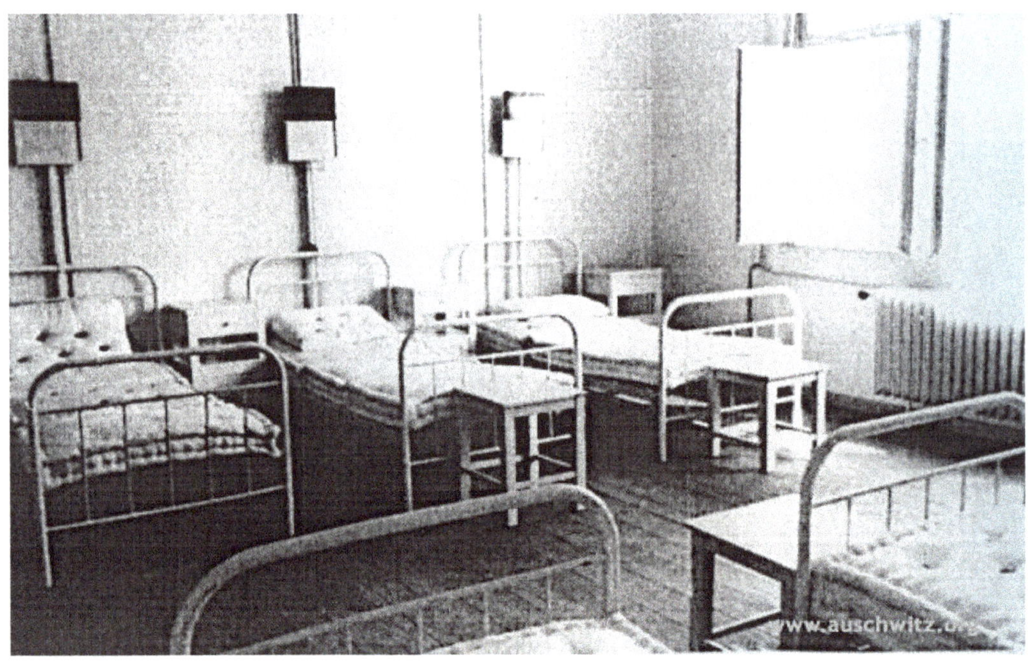

SS Staff Hospital in Auschwitz. Irma Grese would have gone here for testing. See image for "Auschwitz medical appointments book." SS nurses worked at the hospitals. (Circa: 1944. Location: Auschwitz. Photographer: unknown. Courtesy Auschwitz – Birkenau Memorial and Museum. Used with permission)

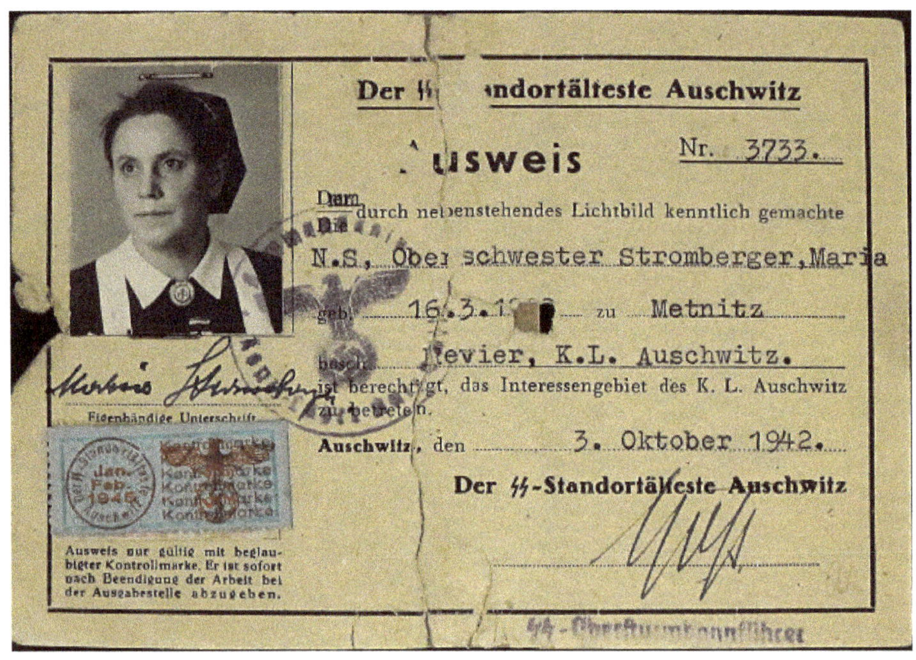

Der SS- ...ndortälteste Auschwitz

...usweis Nr. 3733.

Dem/Die durch nebenstehendes Lichtbild kenntlich gemachte

N.S. Oberschwester Stromberger, Maria

geb. 16.3.1... zu Metnitz

besch. ...evier, K.L. Auschwitz.

ist berechtigt, das Interessengebiet des K. L. Auschwitz zu betreten.

Auschwitz, den 3. Oktober 1942.

Der SS-Standortälteste Auschwitz

SS-Obersturmbannführer

Eigenhändige Unterschrift

Kontrollmarke

Ausweis nur gültig mit beglaubigter Kontrollmarke. Er ist sofort nach Beendigung der Arbeit bei der Ausgabestelle abzugeben.

The ID badge Irma Grese dreamed of wearing. This is a nurse's badge from Auschwitz. This ID was worn by Maria Stromberger (1898 – 1957). It is signed by Rudolph Höss, Grese's alleged lover. However, Maria was part of the underground resistance movement; Grese would have not taken part in this crusade. (Circa: 1942. Location: Auschwitz. Photographer: unknown. Public Domain)

CHAPTER 18
The Hyena Loose at Bergen-Belsen
March 1945 – April 15, 1945

Sometimes they called her "The Grey Mouse," [226] these ragged, famished prisoners of Belsen, who remembered her, as always, looking "perfect" in her shining boots, flawless hair and makeup, and perfectly tailored suit. When Grese arrived at Belsen she was assigned a labor service leader position. She also performed inspections of the living spaces, but it was only a formality; prisoners believed inspections were an excuse to punish and belittle them. Irma Grese was also remembered as a strutting, intimidating sight. Her show-off ways would have been a joke, survivor Hanna Levy-Haas recalls, if it had not been for Grese withholding rations for the slightest infringement, or imagined infringement, of rules:

> (Hut checks are) done by a young SS girl, the "gray mouse", who looks elegant and coquettish in her perfectly fitting uniform and pretty, shiny knee-length boots. Arrogant and noisy, she … gestures exaggeratedly, provocatively throws her body around sharply and utters theatrical, calculated, horrified cries whenever she sees badly washed dishes or a bed that has not been made carefully enough. She excels in slapping people in the face so as to produce a loud crack … without taking her glove off. [227]

A sudden slap of the gloved hand, a scream of anger, and then "the grey mouse" was on her way, those shiny boots crunching the gravel, a *kapo* following behind her, en route to the next dorm where she could intimidate more prisoners. It was a farce, a game, Hanna would remember later, for by now no Germans at the camp cared about cleanliness or sickness. A slow death of prisoners meant nothing. It was all just a sadistic ploy to humiliate prisoners.

Bergen-Belsen put into practice what was labeled "prisoner self-administration." Besides placing the Nazi party further away from culpability to the murders and abusive behaviors, it also saved on labor and funds. As a supervising guard, Irma Grese could direct day-to-day operations to the *Kapos* (*Kameradschaftpoliezi*): each subcamp had a camp leader (*Lagerältester*). These Camp Leaders supervised Barrack Leaders, (*blockältesters)* one for each block of prisoners. The Barrack Leaders lived in the block, but would usually have a separate room with perks: extra food, better clothing; they meted out punishment and rations. Many camp survivors later reported it was rare to see any SS.

Kapos walked precarious lines. They would have better living conditions than their fellow prisoners, but it came with a price. They were prisoners but were expected to behave like oppressors. They would never have the rank of the guards, but they had the guard's ear. These unofficial / official leaders could be as brutal and sadistic as their oppressors,

---

[226] Levy-Hass, H. (1982).

[227] Diary notes of Hanna Levy-Hass, September 1944 – April 1945

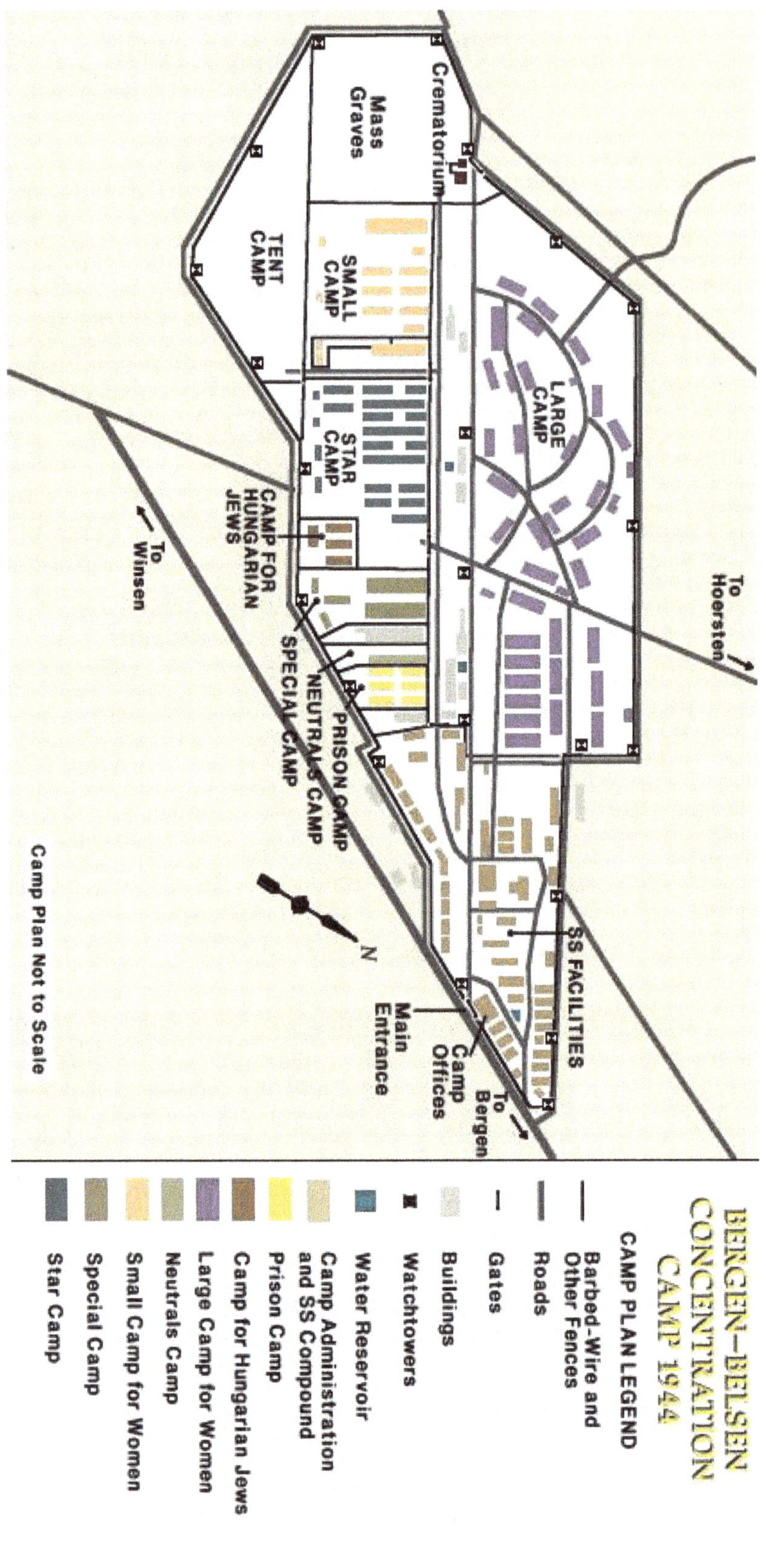

The Bergen-Belsen Concentration Camp as it appeared in 1944.
(Image courtesy The United States Holocaust Museum, Holocaust Encyclopedia)

and had their own prejudices. After the war some kapos went to court and were punished alongside their Nazi leaders.

Should Irma Grese decide to withhold rations from a certain block, she would order it through her Camp Leader, who would order the Barrack Leader to refuse food to the prisoners she supervised. Depending on their supervisor's humanity, the block of prisoners may or may not eat. Should the Barrack Leader rebel and sneak in a meal, the Camp Leader had a decision. Perhaps she wanted a coat; she could report to Grese about the infraction in hopes for a reward. She could let the infraction go unnoticed, understanding how many witnesses were in the block; if someone snitched on her foray it could mean anything from a beating to death to a return to the general population for the Camp Leader, the Barrack Leader, or both. Depending on how they treated the prisoners, returning to those they supervised might not be a positive experience. Irma Grese would make anything – even something like a stolen potato peel – become a life-or-death situation.

Discrimination was a considerable setback among the prisoners. Some of the women disliked Jews as much as their overseers. Most prisoners flocked together based on background, religion, or ethnicity to better communicate and endure. Survival at its most basic created animosity, a kill-or-be-killed acrimony as reported by Holocaust survivors. Some survivors report by working together they managed to subsist. Fights erupted over food particles, small spaces, bumping against one another, the wrong look, or a word. It played into the annihilation: *let them destroy one another,* the guards summarized. *Less work for us.*

A Holocaust survivor, Fela N., revealed her experiences during a post-war interview; she spoke of the roll calls ("*appell*") at Bergen-Belsen. These thousands of prisoners would be counted by SS guards, and one move could get them shot or sent to the gas chambers. "I remember (Grese) very well. She did terrible things … her face, you know, was so beautiful. Large blue eyes and beautiful golden hair. Beautifully dressed in such a trim SS costume and a stick in her hand and a large dog." Fela N. and her fellow prisoners were forced to wait for Irma Grese to arrive at roll call. The prisoners stood "four or five abreast" despite foul weather. "… we had to stand at attention till Irma Grese came. Then she would come. She had once prohibited us to have anything on our head (to protect them from the weather)." [228] When Grese observed a prisoner with a covering on her head, Grese allowed her guard dog to attack the girl, but did not allow enough leash for it to bite. She utilized the dog to scare prisoners. "She wanted to cause anguish and terror … (Grese would) kick and beat" anyone not obeying orders, using her whip. But when speaking with "the block senior (Grese would) show such a beautiful countenance, such a kind face." Grese's behaviors were such a contrast that "nobody could tell that just a moment ago she … was so bad… so merciless to people." [229]

The tips of Grese's shiny boots were often splattered with blood. Camp survivors would later report Grese's increasing enjoyment at torturing and killing prisoners, stomping, beating, shooting already fragile bodies slowly dying from mental and physical conditions. It was another function of the *appell* process: to torture, humiliate, weed out the sick and dying. Some rumors have Grese selecting victims who were, on her judgement, as attractive as herself. She sent thousands to the gas chamber and just as many dead bodies

[228] McKale, p. 42

[229] Ibid

into the death carts. She used a whip and a truncheon, [230] a trained attack dog, and the always-present pistol in her belt. Grese, witnesses would later recall, rode her bicycle through the concentration camp, pulling her pistol to shoot prisoners at random.

If Grese did not shoot prisoners, she would order them shot. Holocaust survivor Ilona Stein would later testify: [231]

> Sometime in August or September 1944, at (a) selection parade, one Hungarian woman who had been selected tried to escape from the line and join her daughter in another line which was for those not chosen.
> Grese noticed this and ordered one of the SS guards to shoot the woman, which he did. I did not hear the order but saw Grese speak to the guard, and (the prisoner) was shot at once. In the company of some nurses from the hospital I took the dead body to the mortuary. [232]

Irma Grese's beauty was always gossip in the camps and, later, in her last days.

"When I laid eyes on Irma Griese [*sic*], I felt sure that a woman of such beauty could not be cruel. For she was truly a blue-eyed, fair-haired Angel" [*sic*] writes Olga Lengyel, an Auschwitz survivor. She notes other prisoners would whisper, during roll call, of the blonde female officer, "how beautiful." But Olga remembers Grese well: "(she) inspired me to the most hatred I ever experienced." She noted Grese wore perfumes in her hair "sometimes she blended her own concoctions" of scents. Grese knew the effect she had, and would spend "hours grooming herself before her mirror and practiced the most seductive gestures … our 'angel' with the golden tresses." Grese had a favorite outfit, "a sky-blue pea-jacket that matched her eyes … a darker tie at the collar … her whip (sticking) jauntily from the leg of her boot." [233] No matter where she was stationed, Grese kept her dressmaker busy, still removing clothing from prisoner's luggage and tailoring them to fit. Grese continued to sport an admirable wardrobe.

Other survivors remembered Grese as spending hours in front of the mirror, ensuring every hair was in place, pulled back from her face behind her ears. Her bright blue eyes would scan her reflection, seeing that she was the epitome of perfect Nazi soldier – from insignias in place to her shining, knee-high black leather boots. With her prisoner tailor adjusting her uniforms, complimenting her figure, she would preen. A few prisoners recall Irma Grese when she began work as a camp guard, and how she had worn her hair in pigtails. Now, her hair was pulled back severely against her skull. She looked so much older.

All biographers note Irma as appearing flawless. Hair, makeup, perfume, uniform – all in order as she moved through the camps, down to how she carried the whip, usually stuck smartly in one boot. Perhaps she was aware of the psychological impact such an impression made upon the prisoners, in their rags, and the other officers in uniforms that were ill-fitting or not as clean, boots not as shining – if they wore boots. Her swagger and movement indicated power and self-confidence. Grese abused prisoners as she would have a lesser animal: using a whip, a kick. Everything about Grese, from appearance to physical

[230] Described as a "rubber tube" by prisoners testifying at the Bergen-Belsen Trials
[231] Ilona Stein would testify at the Bergen-Belsen Trials on September 26, 1945
[232] Belsen Trials Transcript, testimony of Ilona Stein, September 6, 1945.
[233] Lengyel (1948) electronic copy

moves, set her above standard. This alone created both fear and awe, two closely related emotions.

Irma Grese's workday would last eleven hours, in any weather. She visibly grew more confident in her role as a guard, learning how the system operated, when and how to use certain types of violence. Numerous Holocaust survivors would recount how a few of the female guard's behavior would change in the presence of male guards- some of the women increased the brutality and arrogance. Yet another motivation for Irma Grese to become cruel in her behavior – though her behavior had already been marked before her arrival to Birkenau and she was already fodder for promiscuity – in this cloistered environment, men noticed women on a new, skewed set of standards. "From the perpetrator's perspective," writes Koslov, "violence is also attractive and innovative" particularly to another sadist. While most of the guards in the camp were not sadists, and many of the guards disliked and stayed away from those brutal guards, sadists tend to gravitate towards one another. "(Violence) gain(s) prestige, to perform before an audience of colleagues, to realize oneself … an attractive option of behavior." [234]

Once assigned to Bergen-Belsen, Irma Grese rose quickly through the ranks. She would be promoted to *Oberaufseherin.*

Grese's days would now begin and end with staff meetings: As an *Oberaufseherin* she would advise the *Schutzhaftlagerführer* (who answered to the *Kommander*) and pass important messages to camp leaders, the staff mustering to hear their supervisor's instructions and updates before filing out for work. There would be reporting on food supplies, barrack's cleanliness, new regulations, new job descriptions for both inmates and staff, punishment, prisoner work, and any infractions. She would also inspect female guard's barracks for neatness and cleanliness and ensure the female guards followed the rules for staff. She could report infractions or follow up with the women. Grese's signature would appear on reports regarding prisoner punishments and evaluations. She was expected to work well with administration, guard personnel, and prisoners. Hers was a high-profile position; Grese was expected by all to be fair but firm, strict while abiding by rules and regulations. While some of her work was marked by these virtues, much of it was not. Irma Grese's career seemed to be marked by mayhem that went unchecked and she was said to love punishment and causing pain – "throughout her career, she was known as a sadist." [235]

Irma Grese was expected to make sound decisions using proper protocol with a professional demeanor. Prisoner testimony and records later revealed Grese fell short of the duties and expectations. By then, it did not matter.

"She must have been a very sadistic person" Holocaust survivor Masha Greenbaum would say of Irma Grese years later. She refers to "a terrible woman called Irma Grese … a beautiful young woman with long blonde hair … and when we saw her, we used to run, just run" out of fear. Masha witnessed Grese, numerous times, kick women to the floor, then kick them in the neck "with her boots, and she just killed people like this." Masha Greenbaum and the others gave Grese a wide berth because Grese would select prisoners at random to beat and torture. "At the end, (the British) hanged Irma Grese." [236]

[234] 2010, p.49
[235] Adele-Marie, p. 113
[236] Greenbaum, M. (1991)

Outside of the camps, Irma Grese probably did not confide how Auschwitz Officers would have "sport" with prisoners; meaning they would brutalize and abuse prisoners for no reason except the guards were bored or the day was slow. This "sport" did not break camp rules; it did not cross the boundary of unnecessary force. It could be ordering random prisoners to exercise, to stand for lengths of time, any ridiculous order that belittled and tortured prisoners. One of Grese's favorite "sports" (witnessed by prisoners) was to force prisoners to crawl on their hands and knees while Grese commanded they speed up the pace or face a potentially deathly beating. She would order the exhausted, ill prisoners to rapidly lay down and then stand; Grese commanded this performance for hours. And she went further than most of her fellow oppressors. Her favorite "sport" was to toss something into the security zone where prisoners were not allowed, then order a random prisoner to go fetch the item. Only male guards patrolled the security zone, and they had orders to shoot to kill anyone who stepped into the zone. The prisoner might not know the end was near if she stepped into the zone; some did not speak the same language so did not understand the guard's calls to halt, or the language on posted warning signs. Those who knew had a choice: the wrath of Irma Grese or being shot. Grese sent an average of thirty women a day on this suicide mission in Auschwitz, "until one SS guard refused to shoot a woman ordered out by Grese. He was charged with a violation of camp regulations, but when the SS inquiry discovered the circumstance, he was returned to duty and Irma was transferred from the detail." [237] Her behavior proved Irma Grese still did not follow the rules, enjoyed implementing psychological torture; "Irma Grese was not 'following orders' when she beat and murdered her victims. She was clearly freelancing - to the point that the SS themselves thought she was excessive." [238] The Hyena of Auschwitz was a predator.

Irma Grese had enough territory for a hyena to roam out of her supervisor's eyesight. Bergen-Belsen was haphazardly built, created of nine subcamps. Work to build the camp continued as the war continued; it was constantly under construction.

Gertrude Diament had survived both Auschwitz and Belsen. She was familiar with Irma Grese; like the prisoners around her she had learned who the sadistic guards were, who to avoid. Her deposition would be submitted as testimony against several *Aufseherinnen*.

Gertrude knew Grese, "when in charge of working parties beating women and girls with a stick. Her favorite habit was to beat them until they fell to the ground and then she kicked them as hard as she could with her heavy boots." [239] Gertrude helplessly watched blood flow from the prisoner's wounds. She never witnessed anyone dying from the beatings; she was aware of the rumors. At Auschwitz, Gertrude Diament watched Irma Grese make selections for the gas chambers.

Grese reportedly had many affairs while at the camps, and raped both male and female prisoners. In some texts it is listed as "having sex" with prisoners, but it is most

[237] Phillips, R. cited in Vronsky, P. (2007), p.389-90
[238] Vronsky, P., p. 397
[239] The Belsen Trials. Deposition of Gertrude Diament (late 9, Kolarova, Prešov, Czechoslovakia, sworn before Captain Alfred James Fox, General List, D.A.P.M. 86 Special Investigation Section, Corps of Military Police)

likely "sexual assault": Grese terrified prisoners, to include her prisoner "friends." In her book, "Five Chimneys," author and Auschwitz survivor Olga Lengyel writes how the chief camp directresses, to include Grese, would appear at the roll call where Olga and her fellow prisoners were forced to stand, five to a line, for hours. On Mondays, Wednesdays, and Fridays, there were "selections" at these *appells*. Grese was one of those who selected which prisoners to beat: the old, infirm, severely ill, and the more haggard of a starving, filthy lot. Lengyel recalls:

> The beautiful Irma Grese advanced toward the prisoners with a swinging gait, her hips in play... she was of medium height, elegantly attired, with her hair faultlessly dressed. The mortal terror which her mere presence inspired visibly pleased her. For this 22-year-old girl was completely without pity. (Certain prisoners) ... were Irma Grese's special targets. The blonde "Angel of Belsen," as she was later to be called by the press, made liberal use of her whip. She slashed wherever she wished... Our shrieks of pain and our spurts of blood made her smile. What faultless, pearly teeth she had! [240]

Roll call (held twice daily) continued to be a dangerous event for prisoners. It could last for hours in any weather condition. Whippings and beatings, sometimes even murder, if a prisoner stepped out of line or committed any infraction, remained a staple. Punishment could be at the guard's whim. Despite the women surviving a beating, they could be tossed into a truck with the dead, the truck rumbling off towards the gas chambers. Some women were burned alive.

Irma Grese also enjoyed tormenting prisoners with threats. Psychological torture was rampant in the camps, and Grese was a master at it. It is highly likely she used two infamous threats, two of the biggest arguments of the Holocaust era: human soap and human skin lampshades.

Two of the greatest stories to emerge from the Holocaust camp period are the "Soap Legend" and "Skin Lampshades." That Nazis were creating soap and tattooed skins lampshades from the dead bodies of the prisoners lasted long after the war and persists to this day.

The "Soap Legend" was, in 2006, proven to be partially accurate. That the soap was sold and used to and by the public and the prisoners is a recycled fallacy.

Historically, human body fat has been used in soap and candle making; there is a recorded incident where, in 1780, Paris' Holy Innocents' Cemetery was closed, and the bodies later exhumed. The bones were interred into the catacombs and the deposits of fat collected and made into much-needed candles and soaps. Much later, a rumor would be spread by the British and Belgian media during WWI that the Germans had a soap factory and were using their soldiers' dead bodies to create soap. The rumor made it all the way to the national press; after the war it was discovered the story was fictional. In WWII the rumor circled back, this time declaring the soap was made of the fat of camp prisoners and sold to an unsuspecting public and used by prisoners.

[240] Lengyel, O. (192007). P. 392.48) electronic copy

This "Soap Legend" arose due to several reasons: the shortage of fat, government – regulated soap production, poor quality of market-brand soap, and the production markings on the soap. The myth has been debunked numerous times since; but, during the concentration camp years, Nazi guards and soldiers would use the threat to frighten prisoners and civilians.

On October 13, 2006, the Auschwitz-Birkenau memorial and Museum would release an online statement:

> An inquiry by the Gdańsk Branch of the Commission for the Investigation of Crimes against the Polish Nation has concluded that soap was made from human fat and used for general cleaning purposes at the Anatomy Institute of the Gdańsk Medical Academy, under the direction of Professor Rudolf Spanner, during the Second World War. [241]

During interrogations, Spanner [242] explained he used the soap for "injection into joint ligaments." [243] It was utilized to clean medical equipment. Almond oil was added to mask the smell of the soap and kaolin to create abrasiveness for scrubbing.

Some sources state Irma Grese sold this soap when working the six months in the Lychen shop in the Uckermark district, Brandenburg. This is another falsehood. "Human fat was used to make soap, but experimentally. It was never industrialized" explains Holocaust expert and instructor Jill McCracken. "Sadly, the only upside is that these atrocities were limited in a scope, compared to the industry of death that was the Holocaust." [244]

Thus, Irma Grese would have never used soap made of human fat, and she would not have handed out or sold this soap to anyone, to include when she worked in Lychen. The practice was limited to the Anatomy Institute of the Gdańsk Medical Academy. There is no evidence supporting Grese was ever at the Gdańsk Medical Academy. She was most likely aware of the practice; according to some prisoners the threat was real.

Prisoners were taunted with stories: how "fat" prisoners were boiled down, and insubordinate prisoners would be threatened with being boiled alive for soap making. Auschwitz survivor Nina Kaleska described in a 1990 interview:

> So (the German guard will say) I'll see you tomorrow on the soap board. They would make all kinds of, I mean the Germans, the Nazis I should say, were very clever as to what they were doing. It sounds depraved. But at that time, it was a way of saying we know what's going to go on. [245]

Ilse Koch (1906 – 1967) was the wife of Kommandant Karl – Otto Koch at Buchenwald. She was accused during her 1947 trial of selecting certain inmates to be killed for their tattoos, then having items made from the tattooed skin, such as gloves, book covers, and

---

[241] Human Fat Was Used to Produce Soap…

[242] Professor Rudolf Spanner would be dismissed from the university in Cologne. He would work as a Schleswig-Holstein physician I,, and died in Cologne in 1960 (ibid).

[243] Ibid

[244] Personal interview with Jill McCracken, May 26, 2024

[245] Kuzmack, N. (1990, January 03)

lampshades. [246] The Nazi "human skin lampshade" inquiry began, and it was also attributed to Irma Grese. "The skins of three inmates that she had had made into lamp shades were found in her hut" one source reports. [247] Another source: "It was claimed that there were lamp shades, made out of the skins of three women prisoners, found in (Grese's) room at Birkenau." [248]

Holocaust expert and instructor Jill McCracken: "A forensic study done in 2023 genetically analyzed a number of artifacts, which confirmed such. It seems this was a product of gifting, Nazis giving such items to each other, rather than an industrial-sized practice."

"Objects made of human remains were only produced at the Buchenwald concentration camp and no other German camps," director of the Buchenwald Memorial foundation, Jens-Christian Wagner, announced at a conference in March 2024. [249] Gifts of human remains, to include Jewish skulls, were popular with Nazi members. A bedside lamp made of human skin would be confiscated by a prisoner of Buchenwald from an SS home in Buchenwald.

There is no testimony of Grese selecting inmates for death to obtain tattoos, no record of her collecting or keeping tattooed skin, or any period documentation of her possessing items created from human flesh in any existing record. Somehow through the telling and re-telling of the Ilse Koch "lampshade" story, Irma Grese's name has been inserted.

Frieda Salomon was about 21 years old in April of 1940, when she was imprisoned in Auschwitz. Years later she would explain in an interview:

> Irma Grese was a beautiful German woman, but she was the most sadistic person you ever saw. She used to come in, and she used to ask people with beautiful hands and beautiful skin, and they would - she would take them. We never knew what happened to those people, but then later on we read in the paper when we were freed - we read in the paper she made lamp shades of people's skin. [250]

Preserved tattooed skin had been found and confiscated in 1945 at Buchenwald, initially believed for constructing clothing or trinkets. The truth revealed SS doctor Erich Wagner was writing a thesis on the correlation of tattoos and criminal behavior. It is unknown how Dr. Wagner obtained the sheets of tattooed flesh for specimens. It is known Dr. Wagner was not creating anything but a study. There was a pathology department where the doctor was conducting his studies, and it had no connection to Koch [251] or Grese. Irma Grese is most likely innocent of owning or collecting human tattooed skin. Still, the myth, like the human soap story, persists to this day.

---

[246] It would later be determined in Nuremberg that the lampshade in question was made of goat skin.

[247] AICE (n.d.)

[248] Justice, J. (n.d.)

[249] Cited in Pflughoet, A. (2024)

[250] Salomon, F. (1983, April 13)

[251] Ilse Koch was probably innocent of owning any materials made of human flesh or collecting human tattooed skin, though she was not innocent of committing atrocities against prisoners. She would commit suicide while serving a life sentence. See also *Introduction* by Peter Vronsky.

Such mysticism floated through Nazism because the Nazis, in part, was created from mysticism and a slight air of secrecy and symbols. The lightning bolt ruins, the use of the swastika, all borrowed from the past but tarnished just enough. Nazis being perceived as such monsters and underworldly beings; it was easy to believe they were capable of anything as dastardly as human soap or items made of skin. Irma Grese's reputation as a sadist was associated. It added to the Irma Grese myth.

Though he scoffed at Himmler's mystics, Adolph Hitler had a penchant for wolves; he believed wolves to be somewhat mythical in power. Hitler named his war headquarters "Wolf's Lair" and called the SS "my pack of wolves." Irma Grese kept a wolfskin rug in her office. [252] One day, she was outraged that a camp doctor called her out in front of prisoner Olga Lengyel. Olga recalls this was one of the times she thought she was about to be murdered; Grese called Olga into Grece's office. Grese had Olga stand on this wolfskin rug, head bowed, answering questions, and then Grese threatened to shoot her. Instead, Grese beat her into unconsciousness and had Olga Lengyel's limp body tossed into a mud hole.

Grese must have bought into the mysticism as it was such a major segment of the Nazi system. The wolfskin rug was a Nazi symbol of power, of stealth and strength.

[252] Adolph Hitler loved German Shepard dogs because they were a Germanic "pure" breed and their resemblance to a wolf. One of his favorite songs reportedly was "Who's Afraid of the Big Bad Wolf;" however, this is conjecture.

Guard tower and fencing at Auschwitz I.

Female guards were not allowed to work security at the fence perimeters. Killing was considered a job for men. The areas between the fences, barren at the time, were forbidden zones; trespassing inmates would be shot without question. It was here Irma Grese would "have sport" with prisoners by making them run into the forbidden zones to retrieve items. This was one of the infractions she would receive. It is estimated she murdered 30 people a day in this "sport." (Circa August 23, 2008. Photograph by and courtesy of Jill Anne McCracken. Used with permission.)

CHAPTER 19
Sexual Sadist

Grese would brag about herself to prisoners, including Olga Lengyel, remarking on her own beauty. She was going to be a film star, she was convinced, after the war.

Auschwitz survivor and author Dr. Giselle Perl was a Hungarian Jew, a gynecologist before she was sent to the camps, selected by Mengele to care for the sick prisoners in the Auschwitz "clinic" that had few tools and no sterilization. Dr. Perl's entire family was murdered in the gas chambers. Dr. Perl would later write a book and cowrite a movie based on her life in the death camp. She clearly recalled Irma Grese whipping young girls purposely on their semi-developed breasts. She and the others lived in constant fear of Grese, for Grese would shoot prisoners on a whim. Grese was particularly frightening to Dr. Perl because of her good looks: she never had a hair out of place and her uniform was perfect as she beat prisoners to death, or close to death. Her good looks and charm were a dangerous mask.

Dr. Perl worked in the makeshift hospital, attempting to save prisoners from disease and infection with very little medical equipment. She was constantly forced to choose which woman to assist and which to leave dying. Irma Grese was not above going into the hospital to make selections for the gas chamber; anyone would do, no matter their prognosis.

One night, Grese contacted Dr. Perl that she was to meet her in the camp's hospital. She gave instructions to the former gynecologist and demanded the doctor to perform an abortion. In a cinematic version, Dr. Perl meets Grese in Grese's tent, a room Grese has decorated to look like a bordello with flowing curtains and big pillows. Grese manages to keep a pistol trained on Dr. Perl as she moves through the room to obtain tools. In real life, Grese met Dr. Perl in the "maternity ward" of the camp in the afternoon. "Will it hurt?" Grese had asked Doctor Perl on screen. "I can't stand pain ... a lot of pain. I'm afraid it will hurt." The irony was not lost on Dr. Perl, who had to carefully explain the pain levels to the woman she witnessed shoot, kill, maim, and disfigure women of all ages. [253] After the abortion, Grese flattered Dr. Perl's work as a doctor, saying Germany needed good doctors.

According to Dr. Perl's memoirs, the actual discussion did take place, and Grese could have had Perl sent to death at any time. Both were committing numerous, serious infractions: Perl was touching an SS woman and performing an abortion. Grese was having an abortion, speaking kindly to a prisoner, and allowing an intimate, personal exchange.

"The 'angel' with the pure face had many love affairs." [254] Gossip would have Grese bedding not only Doctors Kramer and Mengele, but also stealing around to have sexual liaisons with an unnamed SS Engineer. These clandestine meetings caused several pregnancies. Auschwitz survivor Olga Lengyel, as a former surgeon's assistant, assisted Dr. Giselle Perl when performing an abortion on Grese. Olga recalls Grese pulled a gun on the doctor, demanding the operation. At night, both Olga and Dr. Pearl arrived at Barrack 19, five o'clock, just as Irma Grese demanded:

---

[253] Sargent, J.

[254] Lengyel (1948) electronic copy

> "Irma Griese, the torturess [*sic*], was actually sweating from fear. She trembled and groaned and was unable to control herself. (Grese) could not endure the slightest pain without whining." After the procedure, Grese began speaking to the prisoners as if they were friends: "After the war, I intend to go into pictures. You will see my name in lights on the marquee. I know life and I've seen a great deal. My experiences will be useful in my artistic career." [255]

In Bergen – Belsen, Grese had a maid who was a prisoner. The maid confided in inmates, her old friends from home, "(Grese) had homosexual relationships with prisoners and then ordered the victims to the crematory." The maid also reported "(Grese) is a terrible sadist." [256] Reportedly, Irma Grese kept the prisoner sex slaves at her call. One Holocaust survivor writes how several prisoners were peeking through the walls in the wooden barracks where Grese lived and observing the Hyena beating a naked woman, cursing, and bringing down hard blows with her whip and fists. A handsome male prisoner, well known in the camp, appeared in the scene. Grese knew these two people were in love and she forced the man to witness her savagely beating the female. Later, she sent the man to his death and the woman to an Auschwitz brothel created for the soldiers.

Irma Grese's same-sex relationships were forbidden under paragraph 175a under the German constitution (sexual relations with an employee or subordinate), and the *Rassenschande* laws (sexual relations between Aryans and non-Aryans). Grese could have faced prison time.

It should be noted there is no documented evidence to her sexual liaisons with prisoners, same-sex or no, only hearsay. To portray Grese as a lesbian (or a bisexual) was to further tarnish her character. [257] "… homophobia influenced perceptions of women guards." [258] To create a sex fiend, more so. Like the abortion claim, it solidifies her cruelty, her loss of mortality and paints her as the opposite end of a good German woman. That Irma Grese was a lesbian or bisexual is, like many stories swirling around The Hyena, based on scant evidence (hearsay). However, several prisoners have reported Grese did have same-sex liaisons as well as heterosexual affairs. This is not to demean prisoners or question their integrity; it is noted here because, like so much information on Irma Grese, no formal documentation exists, and all aspects should be offered in this writing.

Much later, a prisoner who worked in the prison camp clinic would recall Grese would abuse large-breasted female prisoners, whipping their chests until their breasts became infected or the prisoner fainted from pain. Grese, according to a female prisoner, would become orgasmic when watching the painful surgeries performed on these female prisoner's sex organs.

Records from the medical clinic for SS reveal Grese visiting in January 1944 on the 22, 23, and 24th. Irma Grese was being tested for syphilis, a sexually transmitted disease. The syphilis test came back negative; she was diagnosed with tonsilitis. The secondary

[255] Ibid.

[256] Ibid.

[257] Recall the Nazis considered lesbians as "undesirables" and "deviants."

[258] Hájková, A. (2021) p. 3.

stage of syphilis can cause soreness in the throat, swollen lymph nodes, and problems with swallowing. The symptoms resemble tonsilitis. A bacterium causes both. Grese was most likely treated with antibiotics.

Although Grese is remembered as the lustful, sexually – charged SS woman in history, she was not the sole SS individual who was sexually promiscuous in the camps. Working in the camps was "a time of loneliness for many … In many cases, it is not surprising relationships flourished." One type of relationship was "quick dalliances in the lawless land of Auschwitz where the normal rules of female sexuality and morality no longer applied…" For some female staff, the camps "(were) a place of happiness and life." [259]

According to several prisoner testimonies, Grese did not limit her sadism to beating inmates. She enjoyed being present when the camp doctor treated the sexual organs of these abused females. Survivors shared how Grese obtained sexual energy from tying a pregnant woman's legs together as the prisoner gave birth, witnessing doctors as they were stitching up slashed breasts, removing or stitching parts of the vagina – all without anesthesia – Irma Grese would watch with excitement. Physicians worked with few instruments. A Holocaust survivor and witness to the medical experiments would report the groans, cries, and shrieks of the women caused Grese to "zone" – swaying, her eyes glassy from experiencing the woman's pain. Occasionally, Grese also kicked prisoners who cried or fought, the always-present black boots smashing into the women's malnourished and broken bodies.

[259] Mears (2020) Pp. 232-33

Karolina Wika (1920 – 1989) was sent to Birkenau towards the end of 1942. She was ill when Irma Grese took her to the camp hospital. Upon recovery, Karolina worked in the packing department called *Packetkammer*, searching incoming packages sent to the non-Jewish prisoners from the outside world. Karolina always credited Grese for saving her life, and never believed the accusations against Grese in court. (Date unknown. Location: Krakow. Photographer: unknown. Courtesy Magdalena Chomitkowska. Used with permission)

***Oberscharführer* Franz Wolfgang "Hatchi" Hatzinger (June 22, 1909 - April 23, 1945).** Irma Grese stayed on at Bergen – Belsen (leading to her arrest) because of this man. Grese would make clandestine visits with him during work hours, often having a prisoner acting as lookout. Hatzinger was married and almost fifteen years Grese's senior. Hatzinger would die from typhus before trial. (Circa: 1940s? Location: unknown. Photographer unknown. Source: bergenbelsen.co.uk. Public Domain.)

CHAPTER 20
The Pleasant Sadist

Irma Grese was not solely a physical sadist. A few prisoners found her caring and friendly, shockingly kind. Grese befriended a few, as close to a "friend" as a high-ranking officer in a Nazi death camp and a prisoner could be called "friends."

Holocaust survivor Hungarian Lilly Goldner was one of the prisoners transferred by train and by marches to and from the camps. In 2011, Lilly would detail her life, at about eighteen years old, during one of the "death marches" when Irma Grese was one of the 3-5 guards supervising the prisoners. Another female guard was "Stiglitz .... Was quite a better one." (Lilly did not remember the names of the other guards.) When the prisoners were ordered to sing as they walked, "Stiglitz was crying" at the sound. She observed stragglers being shot in the 4-6 day marches. She recalled the whip Grese kept tucked in a boot and "for nothing she would hit" the prisoners. "But somehow she liked me." The group had stopped in a town "to get (Grese?) some shoes." As Lilly went to "get shoes," she saw Grese was walking towards her. Lilly had purposely attempted to avoid the guards during the march, and now she tried to run from the cruelest of guards. Grese stopped Lilly, who froze with fear. "Come here," Grese waved her over. Lilly was consumed with fear but obediently went to Grese. "But she did not hit me. She took me to the shoes and told me to pick out some shoes. And that was not the average." [260]

Nina Kaleska was a prisoner Grese appeared to trust. Grese felt they favored one another in physicality. [261] Nina acted as lookout while Grese sexually abused female prisoners and was "rewarded with extra food and special attention." [262] Nina would later testify at the Bergen Belsen trial, "she (Grese) somehow liked me and occasionally gave me some extra piece of salami or piece of cheese." [263]

Nina Kaleska was about 14 years old when her family was sent on a transport to Auschwitz. She had managed to hold onto family photographs, which were promptly shredded when she was forced to strip and was shaved during processing. Her sister died in the camp, and Nina was taken in by older prisoners as her parents had gone straight to the gas chambers upon arrival. Nina resided in C Lager and recalls Irma Grese as "extremely beautiful, dressed as cleanly as possibly," her boot so shiny "you could see your face." But Grese frightened everyone as she constantly had a whip and an "enormous German Shepard dog ... she would sick [*sic*] on a poor inmate for no reason at all ... (and) just about demolish that person." Nina recalls Grese, despite her perfect looks, kept the entire block on edge. One evening, a *Kapo* came to tell Nina "Grese wants to see you." Immediately, everyone around Nina assumed Irma Grese would either murder or sexually assault the young girl. When Nina arrived at Grese's office, Grese was in civilian clothing, so pretty "like a vision out of this world" with her hair down, wearing makeup, and a yellow coat. Nina recalls vividly how Grese called her over, pinched her cheek, and remarked, "ah ha. They tell me you look a lot like I, and I wanted to be sure that was really true." Nina

---

[260] Goldner. L. (2011, March 9). Video, oral history.

[261] This conflicts with the rumor of Grese sending women who favored her directly to the gas chamber. However, Irma Grese was a woman of many conflicts.

[262] Adele-Marie, p.118

[263] Kaleska, N. (1990)

told Grese how beautiful Grese was, and how she did not feel there was a comparison. From then on, Nina became a guard for Grese whenever Grese had a female lover in her room. Nina polished Grese's boots and performed small tasks for her, "thank God, she never did abuse me." Grese seemed to genuinely like the young girl. Nina had observed Grese's many abuses, and she was not immune to the group tortures. Nina would later say of Grese, "she could be perfectly lovely. She was nice to me." But Nina also knew Grese would have killed her at a moment's notice. It was only after the war and long after the trials did Nina Kaleska learn the complete truth about Irma Grese; she read "The Belsen Trials." Nina was "in horror." [264]

Young Carola Stern Steinhardt was being held at Bergen-Belsen. She would go to each new group of people arriving via the transports, walking slowly through the group of women and girls. Craning her neck, Carola was carefully scanning the faces for her mother, or perhaps her sister. In the summer of 1944, she again was walking through new arrivals, scanning the freshly shaved heads, when she found her sister. They held onto one another. The sisters began sharing information through tears and embraces. Carola learned the rest of their family had been murdered. Carola then turned around to see Irma Grese, who she knew as The Beast, standing there, watching the sisters' exchange, and listening to them speak. Carola reports Grese was wiping tears from her own cheeks and told Carola she had "nothing to worry about," that the sisters would not be split up, and not to worry. "(Grese) stood there and cried. Something nobody had ever seen before." [265] However, the sisters were parted, forced to go to separate camps by the SS supervising their movement.

Poland-based historian Magdalena Chomitkowska has studied Irma Grese for years due to a family connection. Magdalena has two relatives who were interned in concentration camps. Stanislaw, her grandfather's brother, died in Stutthof, murdered after a month of incarceration. Karolina Wika (1920-1989) [266] was Magdalena's grandmother's cousin. Magdalena's childhood included listening to Karolina's stories of being a prisoner in Auschwitz – Birkenau.

Karolina's father was a doctor who did not support the Third Reich and those around him were aware of his staunch opposition. The day the Nazi soldiers came for the doctor, he was not home, so they arrested young Karolina. After imprisonment, Karolina was sent to Birkenau towards the end of 1942, housed in the B1b *Lager*. Her work crew was assigned to build a road, lifting heavy stones all day. "One day she saw their *Aufseherin* had been changed," Magdalena recalls Karolina's story. "The new girl (*Aufseherin*) was blonde, young, and very shy. Other inmates told my aunt that 'her surname is Grese.' Irma Grese was staring at Karolina all the time. My aunt didn't know why. My aunt's friend told her that Irma had a crush on my aunt." Karolina, aged 23 at the time, would become quite ill, but still forced to work. "Grese walked over to my aunt and asked if she was okay. My aunt told her that she was ill and would die here. Grese asked her if she had any family members in this camp. When she said, 'no,' Irma took her to the hospital for inmates and asked somebody who was a doctor to help my aunt." Karolina was diagnosed with bilateral pneumonia and treated. She would explain, years later, Irma Grese saved her life. Once recovered, Karolina began working in the packing department called *Packetkammer*, searching through incoming packages sent to the prisoners from the

[264] Kuzmack, L. G. (1990)
[265] Ringelheim, J. (1996, June 3).
[266] Maiden name unknown

outside world. Initially, Elizabeth Volkenrath supervised this detail, but Irma Grese oversaw this station for a short time. She had assisted a prisoner named Walentyna by finding her employment in the same department. Grese would wander over to ask Karolina, "do you have something for me?" Organizing any items of interest. Magdalena believes these items were given as gifts to other prisoners. Magdalena clearly recalls her aunt Karolina saying she "had never seen Irma with a dog, beating or killing anybody. She told me that (Grese) was hanged because they had to kill somebody and (Grese) was pretty, shy, and was a normal girl who didn't fit the rules." [267]

Years later, Karolina would recall Grese also favored a Polish girl who was employed as a *Blokova.* Irma did understand the Polish language, having worked with Polish prisoners until she was promoted to *Oberaufseherin* in *Lager C.* [268]

There is the story of another prisoner who survived the Holocaust because of Irma Grese. When Alice Tenenbaum speaks in public about her teenage years in Auschwitz – Birkenau, she recalls "this horrible creature they called the beautiful beast" saving Alice "16 times when Dr. Mengele sent me to the gas chamber. She would come and take me out. That's how I survived Auschwitz." Alice was fourteen years old at the time. Prisoners who knew Grese told Alice that Grese "had a sister around my age and I looked a little bit like her. The reason she saved me so many times was because I looked like her sister." [269]

For all of those who remembered Grese as a torturer, a murderer, and a sadistic sexual predator, one Holocaust survivor named Magda Hellinger recalls an Irma Grese who was not a "one dimensional monster" but ".... Also, a damaged young person who, underneath everything, was vulnerable and impressionable." Magda Hellinger was employed as a clerk for Grese when Grese was a *Lagerführerin* permanently based in *Lager* C. Besides also acting as a lookout while Grese's sexual assaulted prisoners, Magda assisted Grese in a small office near the camp's gate. "At least once a day she would seek me out to talk to" Hellinger recalls in a memoir. "It felt like she saw me as a big sister." Magda felt Grese was attempting to impress the older woman in a naïve way. Grese discussed her family history, how the BDM split her family. She shared details with the prisoner about her "career" and felt Professor Doctor Karl Gebhardt was a "saint." Grese said the Nazis had sold her on the camps as being wonderful career moves, "and that she couldn't have imagined they would be as bad as they were."

As they spoke more often, Grese explained she had done her best to look professional and stand out. At only 20 years of age, Grese was a *Lagerführerin.* It was unheard of for someone so young to advance so rapidly to the second highest rank available for a female. Perhaps this is why she had not made friends with her female coworkers. "I was the only person she could talk to," Magda Hellinger remembers, and was astonished, being Jewish and a prisoner. She recalls in her memoir as admonishing Grese for abusing prisoners, slashing open their breasts with a whip:

> "I dare you to strike me too," I said. "I know you like to see blood. *Ich bin beleidigt* (I'm offended)."
> I turned and walked away. Later, to my astonishment, Grese came to me and said, "*Vergib mir* (forgive me)."

[267] Interview, Magdalena, March 16-18, 2024
[268] "camp" C
[269] Camurati, A. (2024)

> From then on, she rarely showed her sadistic side if I was around, but sadly that side did come out many times. She wanted power and all the luxuries she could have with it, and that meant outshining all the other female SS in both looks and brutality. [270]

Magda sought out Grese out when she needed information on camp movement or inside information as a group of Russian boys were taken out of the camp. "Magda, don't you bother about that" Grese told her. Grese explained the boys were going to be given to "farmers who don't have any children" to work on the farms and "after a few years of Germanization" the boys would forget their heritage. [271] This often occurred with children in the camps.

The practice of taking camp children with Aryan features and giving them to German families was not a constant, but it occurred several times during Grese's camp career. Irma Grese was obviously aware of the practice. Pretty, Polish children up to one year old were moved to a short quarantine. A prisoner number was tattooed on their legs. Families could pick the child up from the camp; the children were also shipped to the families.

Magda learned to control Grese and other Nazi leaders by using their weaknesses. Grese's was vanity. The prisoner suggested Grese stay out of a heavy rain one day, a terribly hot day another and the Jewish female captive would perform Grese's duties. Magda was purposely keeping Grese out of certain areas with the excuses. Their relationship would change into something of a schoolgirl friendship at times, with Grese teasing Magda about having a boyfriend, a fellow prisoner; Grese would sing a silly, teasing little tune to the man. Magda would later write of Grese requesting Magda's opinion on Grese's boyfriend and asking Magda to go with her to the men's camp to visit *SS - Sturmmann* Fritz [272] Hartzinger. Hatzinger, once introduced to Magda by Grese, was kind to the prisoner himself, even requesting Magda's boyfriend, a jazz drummer, to drum a tune on the seat of the Nazi's trousers as Hatzinger bent over. Hatzinger expressed pleasure at the music while the two prisoners internally quaked in fear. Grese desperately seemed to want Magda to like Fritz. Yet, Magda Hellinger lived with the constant dread of being killed by any of her captors at any given time. She knew what Irma Grese was capable of, from throwing scalding soup onto an innocent prisoner to shooting or maiming, making selections for the gas chambers, and ordering Magda to harm fellow prisoners for infractions. Magda had precarious relationships with a few of the high-ranking Nazis in Auschwitz until liberation. [273]

One biographer would have Grese meeting Hatzinger "in the evenings" with Grese telling her beau "The female concentration camp was her empire [*sic*] and she would do as she pleased." Grese, according to this account, enjoyed telling Hatzinger of her "rank and power" at the camp. [274]

Iris Langer was a Jewish prisoner in Birkenau who would later recall Irma Grese's sexual advances towards her. When Grese flirted, Iris pointed out the yellow star sewn to her uniform, explaining to Grese that Iris was a Jew; any contact between Jews and

---

[270] Hellinger

[271] Hellinger & Lee (2021). P. 130.

[272] True name Franz

[273] See "The Nazis Knew My Name" Hellinger & Lee (2021) for a full account.

[274] Clark & Larson (2018) p. 45

Germans was strictly prohibited. Grese told Iris she was different, not like other Jews. Whether this saved Iris from sexual advances it is unknown; any sexual liaisons between the same sex were strictly taboo during this time and it is rare any of the parties would admit their involvement.

Olga Schnurmacher was a Hungarian Jew living in the Hajduhadhaz ghetto when she and hundreds of others were forced into cattle cars and taken to Auschwitz in early September 1944. Olga noted how Dr. Josef Mengele motioned the crowd to the left, straight to the gas chamber, or to the right, to be worked to death. Olga, an attractive young girl, was motioned to the right. Her head was shaved and the clothing she was issued did not fit, so she traded rations for a needle and thread, used her drink to polish her shoes, and incorporated rags to make a scarf for her head. Despite the other prisoner's warnings, Olga stood out for her appearance. And at an *Appell* (roll call), Irma Grese noticed Olga.

Grese demanded to know why a Jew could appear clean and her ragged dress fit. Olga explained how she had amended her clothing because she would rather have shining shoes than the drink. The prisoners around her held their breath. Olga was looking Grese in the eye and she was, according to camp rules, being insolent. She could have been murdered on the spot – the prisoners knew women who had been beaten or murdered for lesser infractions.

"You are clean enough to work for me. Starting tomorrow morning, you will report to my living quarters. You will polish my boots … tend to my garden … be my personal maidservant" Irma Grese told Olga. While Olga worked for Grese, she witnessed both kindness and cruelty. Grese secretly shared information on Olga's parents, who were killed in the gas chambers, and researched Olga's siblings. Grese found Olga's sister in the camp and allowed them to visit. Grese also asked Olga about her family, was curious about her siblings and their ages, and personal questions about their lives. In turn, Olga quizzed Grese about her life. Both women's kindness and questions violated so many regulations. Olga could have been murdered. Grese could have been severely punished for these infractions. Grese was still "evil but beautiful," however; Olga was present when Grese shot a teenaged female dead for stealing a potato, turned to Olga and ask calmly, "we don't steal now, do we?" Olga was too horrified to respond. Olga also remembered Grese watching Olga shower. "You have beautiful breasts" Olga said Grese told her. "You should never let a man touch them." Olga added Grese "always had a Czech girlfriend … who was also a beautiful blonde." [275] Olga believed Grese saved her life from the gas chambers. She remembered her as a woman who looked like the movie star Ingrid Bergman but who was dangerous and not to be crossed. Still, there was a kind side, a surprisingly soft side who asked about family, located then arranged a private visit with her beloved sister, and appeared to love her own sisters deeply.

Those who witnessed the kind side of Irma Grese would remark the Hyena of Auschwitz was most kind when she was discussing families. The Hyena must have pined for her sisters, perhaps for loving parents. She was quite close to Helene, her sister being the only known contact she had with family before the trial. It is unknown if anyone visited Irma while she was employed in the camps. Leni was the sole family member who would talk about her sister Irma to a media outlet.

---

[275] Schnurmache (2021)

"The famous ward who was cruel and kind and nice to children," Renata Laqueur describes Irma Grese in a 1995 interview. Renata remembers Grese as "A hefty blonde." She could not recall when she observed Grese, but she definitely remembers Grese's "… stiefel, her boots and the whip…" Renata did not expound on her "kind and nice to children" descriptor. [276]

While in Auschwitz during selections, when a prisoner committed some infraction, Irma Grese pulled her gun and shot the culprit through the head. Holocaust Survivor Vera Alexander was standing behind such an executed prisoner, whose brains splattered on Vera's shoulders as the prisoner fell dead. "The next day, after the selections, Irma came to see me. I refused to talk to her," Vera would later explain. "She asked, 'Are you angry with me?'" [277] Vera's response was "you nearly killed me yesterday." She recalled Grese's response as "One down; it doesn't matter." [278]

Again, multiple infractions countered with a need for approval, or for some sort of redemption.

There is the possibility Irma Grese's kindness was not about others, but all about Irma Grese: a mental health condition, self-need that was never fulfilled, the exploitation of others for her own selfish pleasure.

Lawrence Josephs, PhD (2015) discusses traumatic narcissism:

> It is a relationship in which a dominant person coercively pressures a dependent person to mirror that person's goodness and greatness. The subordinate is granted a place in the narcissist's entourage … if the subordinate submits to that coercive pressure. The subordinate is allowed an existence and an identity as a narcissistic extension … (it is) a relational system of subjugation. (p. 222)

Grese's friendliness to certain prisoners may only have been a ploy to force the prisoner to worship her, to thank her for the prisoner's very existence. Grese did have power over life and death of every prisoner in the camp. Grese was not sophisticated and did not realize Magda Hellinger was manipulating her. Grese knew she had power over Dr. Giselle Perl, Olga Lengye, Grese's maids and seamstresses, Olga Schnurmacher, and Vera Alexander. In her naïveté of the world, she was creating (pseudo) friendships (she had admitted she had no friends) yet as a narcissist was both unable to understand and incapable of developing "real" friendships. Regardless of the reason, these "friendships" were obviously not true nor realistic, and neither was the kindness.

"The traumatic narcissist exploits a vulnerable individual's dread of being made to feel worthless..." [279] The prisoner's self-esteem – or feelings of safety - have already been destroyed; what little they have gained by being Irma Grese's "friend" or employee is balancing precariously. Yet another example of Grese's mental torture: her "kindness" may not have been kindness as traditionally defined, but a bastardized version to manipulate

---

[276] Ringelheim, J. (1996). P. 66. It is possible Renata Laqueur was confusing blonde Maria Mandl with Grese. Mandl was stout and she did enjoy giving the children sweets and playing with them, and then taking their hand to walk them to the gas chamber to be murdered.

[277] Noks (2014)

[278] Belsen Trial Transcripts, Testimony of Vera Alexander.

[279] Josephs, Ibid.

and mentally break down psyches that have been broken or, in Grese's opinion, need to be "taken down a notch."

Three of the nine criteria for narcissistic personality disorder includes a willingness to exploit others (for selfish reasons), envy (to include expecting envy), and the need for admiration (true or imitation). There is no known cause of narcissistic personality disorder; it may be attributed to genetics or childhood experiences, environment, or developmental thinking. Because so little is known of Irma Grese's childhood it is impossible to properly conduct any psychological profile.

There were rare times when Irma Grese revealed a playful side to prisoners. Maria Mandl's biographer interviewed one Auschwitz survivor who shared a story of the group being allowed a walk outside of the camp as a reward. Grese supervised with her attack dog on a lead. One of the prisoners slipped and fell, and immediately the dog lunged. Grese had tied the lead around her wrist, so down went Irma Grese. The rest of the group automatically dropped to the ground in fear. "Everyone, including Grese, laughed" at the visual of guard and prisoners lying flat on the ground as the dog leapt about, barking, attached to Grese's wrist. [280]

Holocaust survivor Vera Alexander was just not impressed with The Hyena. If anything, she found Irma Grese laughable. "She didn't go to school," Vera would recall years later. "She was a farmer's daughter. I thought she was a small, silly country bumpkin. She became 'someone' just because she was wearing a uniform and had a whip in her hand." [281]

---

[280] Eischeid, p.160

[281] Rees, L. & Talge, C. (2005)

PART V

Trapping The Hyena

"Genocide and mass killing are tragedies for the perpetrator also."
- Ervin Staub

"She was such a bastard."
- **Auschwitz survivor Anita Lasker – Walifisch discussing Irma Grese**

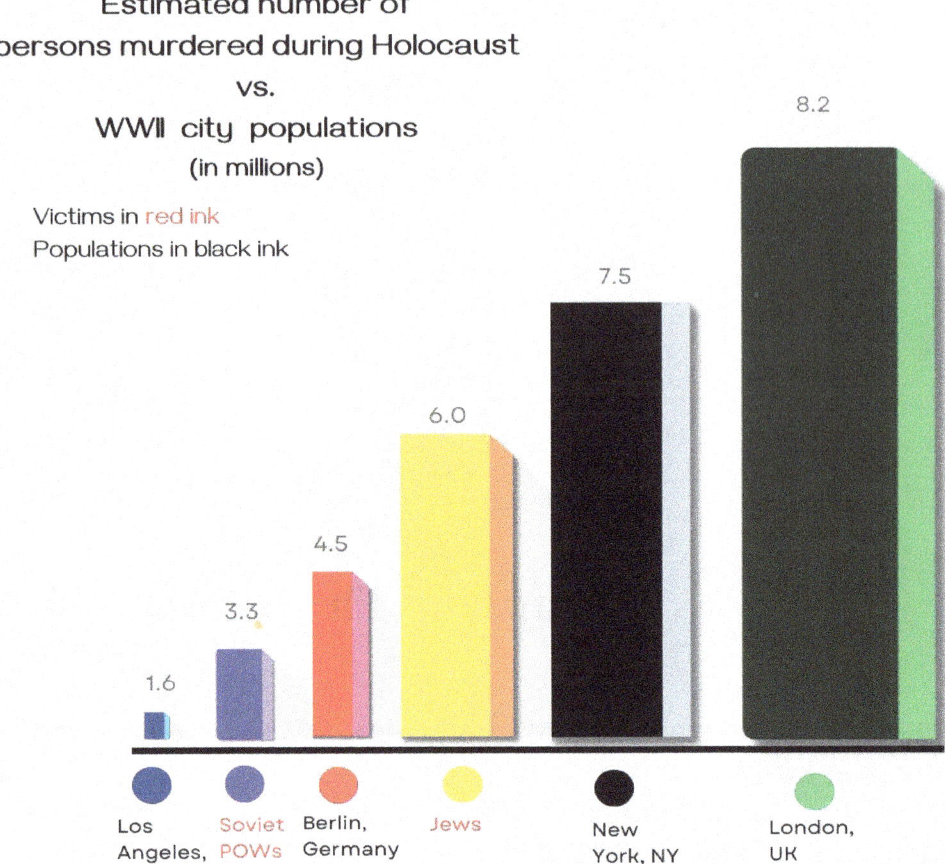

This chart compares the two largest numbers of populations annihilated during the Holocaust versus city populations during WWII. The numbers are estimates based on numerous resources (including census counts and WWII history records.) Not all exact city populations were available each year; the population numbers are based around 1942.

At the beginning of WWII, London was the largest city in the world with an estimated 8.2 million inhabitants. Around 1942, Berlin had a population of 4.5 million, and Los Angeles, California was home to 1.6 million people. New York City's population was around 7.5 million.

During the Holocaust, an estimated 6.0 million Jewish people were murdered. The second highest population murdered is Soviet Prisoners of War with 3.3 million lives lost.

Thus, if 1942's Los Angeles and Berlin were emptied of people, it would amount to about the number of Jewish people murdered in the Holocaust.

The combined number of Jews and Soviet POWs murdered is higher than the population of 1942's London, UK.

This does not count the other groups murdered during the Holocaust.

CHAPTER 21
The End Begins

Forty per cent of Berlin's population had fled by May 1945; 1.7 million people had grabbed what they could carry and left the shell of a city. [282] By now, more than a quarter of Berlin was uninhabitable or unusable. [283] Irma Grese's visits to a beautiful city teeming with fashion and style had stopped with about 68,000 tons of explosives being dropped into Nazi Germany's capital city by British and American aircraft. [284] The Red Army had also unleashed hell on Berlin. At least 363 times, the air raid horns had resonated across the city for inhabitants to race for shelter. [285] Many of the Nazi flags flying so proudly now lay in dust and rubble and people tried to put their life into some semblance of order, climbing out of the shelters to patch back their homes and shops. News reached Irma Grese and her comrades in piecemeal. The young woman who had once bragged of the "very clever" Nazis was now hoping Nazis could even survive. [286] She may have huddled around the radio and grabbed newspapers to stay advised.

The end of the war was inevitable and, by 1945, so was the Third Reich. There was to be no great empire of Aryans. There was no takeover of the world, no future total Nazi power. The destruction of Berlin meant the inevitable loss of the war for Germany. Secure in the Berlin air raid shelter *Führerbunker* Adolph Hitler formally married his longtime lover Eva Braun as the Soviet army loomed closer; the following day he put a gun to his head and shot himself on April 30, 1945. Braun sitting nearby, took cyanide. On May 1, German radio announced his death.

By now, Joseph and Magda Goebbels and their children had been hiding in the bunker with Hitler. They had watched the Reich crumbling. They observed Hitler, in fits of madness, attempt to save their beloved Germany from the allies. He was sending troops when there were none to send. His moods were shifting dramatically. Children had been recruited to fight and were being slaughtered. Cities were crumbing under explosions. Civilians were dying. Nazis were either fleeing or giving up, hands held high and hoping the opposition would show mercy. Joseph and Magda Goebbels, refusing to live in a world not led by the Nazi party, gave their children poison, the adults following suit. All five bodies would be carried out of the *Führerbunker.*

Irma Grese once bragged to a prisoner, "we are sure we will win the war. Nobody will believe any stories about the gas chambers because we have a complete register of the women's deaths. You see... we are clever." [287]

There was a turn in the air of something foreboding for the keepers, a flicker of hope for those held prisoner. Still in Auschwitz, survivor Alice Cahana remembered:

> The fabric of Auschwitz started to slowly break down. The order. The closer the allies got; more chaos came about. The food was not distributed

[282] Overy, R. (2014). P. 301, 304.

[283] RAF (2004).

[284] "Target Analysis" (1945). P. 154.

[285] Taylor, F. (2005). p. 216

[286] Hellinger & Lee (2021). P. 136

[287] Ibid

> anymore in time. The … the nervousness of the … the SS was just very felt. And the chaos was bigger and bigger. Mengele didn't come anymore. Irma Grese didn't come anymore. And they say that … selections … went on and on, and fast. [288]

Grese was transferred back to Ravensbrück on January 18, 1945, she would later testify at her trial. She supervised a march of prisoners. From Ravensbrück, she would transport prisoners back to Bergen-Belsen in March. Some prisoners were transported via "death marches," others were taken by trucks or train.

Ron WG Jones became a British prisoner of war (POW) in 1942 and eventually sent to Auschwitz E715, the POW camp. It was one of the better facilities at Auschwitz. [289] Ron and his fellow POWs would sneak food from their Red Cross parcels to the Jews, ensuring the kapos were not looking. The POWs were watching a group of barefoot Jewish women planting potatoes in a field of sewage. Ron and his friends were calling out a window to the women when someone said, "the woman in charge of them … that's Irma Grese!" The POWs would be witness to Grese whip the Jewish women with a leather whip, shouting at them "Treat them terrible. Terrible." Ron would later say. [290] "We never had a problem with the German (male) guards." [291] But Grese was memorable due to her brutality.

She was again about to be reassigned by *Kommandant* Kramer when Grese made a request: she asked to stay at Bergen-Belsen. With the war's end looming and German force's crippled attempt to stay alive, and Bergen-Belsen being close to the American front, it appeared a strange request. Irma Grese had her reasons.

Grese had stayed on at Belsen for personal reasons; *Oberscharführer* Franz Wolfgang Hatzinger was at Bergen – Belsen as the chief engineer of the Auschwitz 1 construction department. Irma Grese and Franz Wolfgang Hatzinger were lovers. Official records have him assigned to Auschwitz arriving March 31, 1940. A photo shows a studious looking man with close-cropped hair, bulbous nose, and thin lips. Hatzinger was married and almost twice her age, but Irma was smitten.

In 1987, Helene Grese would tell a journalist she was in Neustrelitz for a business trip in January 1945. Sister Lieschen was there by now, employed as a nurse. "Hatzi," as Irma dubbed Franz Wolfgang Hatzinger, "was already in Auschwitz making sure that Irma got out" Helene explains. She and Lieschen met Irma in Feldberg and "drove to (Kurt) Baron von Schröder's in Hullerbusch, where I worked. Irma stayed for one night and had to leave again in the morning. She talked a lot about 'Hatchi,' how she had met him in Auschwitz and how he was the one who kept her "out of everyone." [292]

If it is true Helene was working as a nanny for Kurt Baron von Schröder (1889-1966), she indeed had strong connections to the Nazi party. Schröder had close ties to Heinrich Himmler, Rudolph Höss, and Adolph Hitler. He was instrumental in Hitler's

---

[288] Cahana, A.

[289] Per the Geneva Convention of 1929, POWs were to be treated according to certain standards. Germany had signed, agreeing to the terms.

[290] Jones, R. (2012, July 9). Interview by D. Little. P. 16

[291] Ibid, p. 26.

[292] Wieble (1987, May 23)

becoming Chancellor in 1933. Dubbed "midwife of Naziism." Kurt Baron von Schröder held several powerful positions of business and government in the Third Reich.

While the sisters visited at Baron von Schröder's, Irma was insisting on returning to Belsen to meet Hatzinger, despite her parent's pleas of staying away. Helene would drive her back to the concentration camp. Irma insisted to her sister that she be with her boyfriend. Helene agreed with her sister's wishes. (It would be to no avail; on April 23, 1945, Grese's paramour *Oberscharführer* Franz Wolfgang Hatzinger died from typhus.) He was thirty-five years old.) [293]

Helene would later tell the court at Irma's trial she recalled seeing her sister in April 1945. (By then at least up to 6,000 [294] Ravensbrück prisoners had been murdered in the newly constructed gas chamber.) Helene had cut ties with their father, leaving home after her baptism. According to Helene, Irma told her sister that she had left Auschwitz and was working as a postal employee and sometime guard.

The next time Helene would see Irma was to testify at the Belsen trial. It would be Helene's attempt to save her sister from the gallows.

Whatever the story, Helene was either protecting her sister, possessed quite a poor memory, or was a liar.

In February 1945, prisoners dreadfully observed the construction of a new building in Ravensbrück: a gas chamber. The work went quickly. In less than four months this killing machine was ready to send additional acrid stench into the air.

The allies continued advancing from the west and the Russians were closing in from the east. The smaller concentration camps were evacuating. Those prisoners who were not murdered onsite or did not die along the death marches staggered through the gates surrounding Belsen.

Holocaust survivor Alice Cahana arrived at Belsen with her sister in a cattle car after they had attempted escape during a death march. Belsen, she recalled, "…was hell. Day and night. You couldn't escape the crying … the praying … the mercy… it was a chant. A chant of the dead." She and the other prisoners stepped or crawled over the dead. She recalled a *Kapo* who "went insane." There was "no way to re-enact Auschwitz," Alice would say, years later. "But there's no way to tell anything about Bergen-Belsen." [295]

Heinrich Himmler knew it was the end of his reign. British and Canadians advanced on Bergen Belsen, and Himmler agreed this camp would peacefully surrender to the allies. It was without the Furor's stamp of approval. Irma Grese and her ilk were probably just as broken over Himmler's decision. "We will win this war," Grese continued bragging to camp prisoners. "We are very clever." [296] It would be interesting to know how clever Grese felt now. On April 11, Himmler officially made the agreement. It did not stop the cruelty so many miles away at the actual camp.

Rumor began circulating that the allies would soon attack Belsen and liberate all prisoners. Personnel began abandoning their posts knowing the likely consequences of arrest on duty. Irma Grese's torture of prisoners was unaffected. "If anything, her cruelty, as well as the other Nazis, worsened." Two weeks before the liberation, an unnamed

[293] Clark & Larson, p. 48
[294] Ravensbrück concentration camp: History & overview…
[295] Cahana, A. Pp. 27-28
[296] Chindler, W. Pp. 69-70

survivor recalled Grese "marched into the kitchen for inspection, picked out a random prisoner and then whipped her mercilessly, without being provoked in any way."

Dr. Klein approached Josef Kramer to warn him how the British soldiers will have no qualms about executing all camp personnel for the camp conditions. Klein had been responsible for "experiments" on prisoners and for making selections. Klein donned a Red Cross armband. Caches of medicine and medical instruments were suddenly available. Kramer and his staff also wrapped white armbands around their biceps.

Heinrich Himmler's reign dissipated as the agreement was officially signed on April 13. It was close to 1:00 A.M. Nineteen square miles surrounding the camp was now declared neutral. The former chicken rancher and manure salesman, whose very presence struck both fear and awe, was now just a criminal. Those working at Bergen-Belsen watched as Hungarian and German troops took up watch posts around their personal kingdom where rules and laws melted away.

Survivor Agnes Sassoon was about eleven years old when she was a prisoner in Bergen-Belsen. Agnes spotted a potato on one of the hundreds of dead lying about. She took the potato to cook it in a small fire. She was roasting the potato when Irma Grese spied her; Grese "...kindly asked ..." Agnes to place her hand over the flames as punishment for stealing food. Agnes trusted Grese in part because of Grese's good looks. Grese stomped down on her hand until her fingers were smashed and bloody, scalded from the hot ash. "People later told me that this must have been the infamous Irma Grese." Agnes, at the time, did not know The Hyena of Auschwitz. [297] Agnes would recall, "A beautiful woman ... she looked like Irma Grese and with a beautiful strong shoe with nails and a beautiful face. Oh, they were beautiful. And she told me, 'Oh yeah, it's a nice potato. Warm your hand over it.' And I put my hand over it, and I looked at her. She smiled like she was good, and she started to put my hand down until they [sic] squashed the potato in the fire." It broke at least one bone in her hand. "So even now I have signs from my hand on it." Agnes managed to survive. She was placed in a hospital; she would guess she was about twelve and a half years old. "They found that woman who did push my hand with the potato. Always I thought it was Irma Grese, and I don't know, I don't know, but they told me (it was Grese)." Agnes was asked if she would go to the jail to identify the perpetrator, but she refused. "I said no. I would not do to anyone anything. She could do to me. She could do to other people ... if God will punish her, it's God's will." [298]

From the Belsen Trials transcript:

Grese's counsel: Do you remember telling us that you had seen Grese No 9, beating a girl in Belsen about a fortnight before the British troops arrived?

D. Szafran, witness: I remember it now, it was in the kitchen. Grese was not the kitchen *Kommandant*, she came in there with the *Lager Kommandant* on inspection. She beat the girl with a riding whip made of leather.

[297] Ibid

[298] Sassoon, A. (1985 October ?).

Grese's counsel: If I tell you that at Auschwitz Grese carried a stick and sometimes a whip, but at Belsen she never carried either, are you sure that you are not confused over this incident?

D. Szafran, witness: In Auschwitz she wore a pistol and in Belsen she went about with a riding whip. She was one of the few SS women who had a permit to carry arms. I cannot say whether she was wearing a pistol at the time of this incident. Perhaps it is possible that by that time members were not allowed to carry arms. [299]

Upon arrival to the camp, Anita Lasker – Walifisch had been pulled from selection to the gas chamber to play the cello in Maria Mandl's Women's Orchestra of Auschwitz. Now she was hearing the rumours of liberation as well. And she was acquainted with the Hyena of Auschwitz. Anita would recall much later,

> "When things were obviously going very badly for the Germans, (Grese) started talking to me. Unheard of! She said - that I'll never forget - she said, 'now we'll soon be home.' We! We are suddenly 'we'! The same group of species. 'We'll soon be home.' And I thought 'my God things must be going bad for you.' Acting like such a nice lady. She was such a bastard." [300]

[299] Edda Treforest, Belsen Trials transcript
[300] Stubberfield (2020)

Coworkers to codefendants.

Any of these women are often labeled as Irma Grese in the media. According to the Ravensbrück Memorial Photo Library the correct names are 1. Hildegard Kanbach, 2. Senior supervisor Irene Haschke, 3. Elisabeth Volkenrath, and 4. Herta Bothe.
This photograph was taken after the women had been arrested. They wear their *Aufseherin* uniforms. They are being walked to carry the thousands of dead bodies to the mass graves in Bergen - Belsen. Some of them complained they had no gloves, though they forced prisoners to do this work sans gloves for years.
(Card on the reverse of the original photograph reads: "Belsen Camp B.U. 4065. For story see caption sheet. S.S. Women are also made to work. These women are the equivalent of the men for brutality. (Circa: April 17, 1945. Location: Belsen camp. Photographer: Lt. Wilson or Sgt. Oakes. Stamped "Released IWM." Public Domain.)

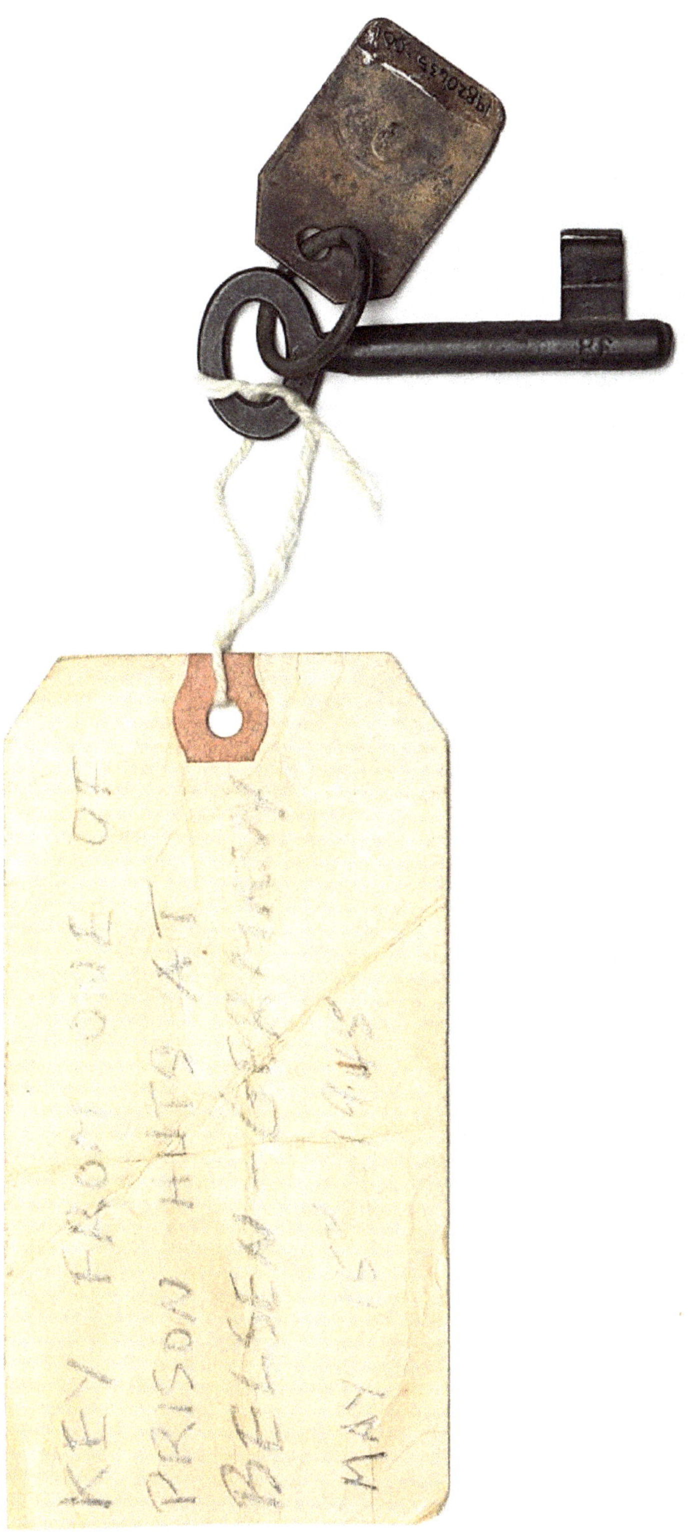

The key to Irma Grese's Belson camp "hut." It was confiscated from Grese during the Liberation. (Circa 1945. Location: Canadian War Museum. Photographer unknown. CWM 19820635-001 Canadian War Museum. Used with permission.)

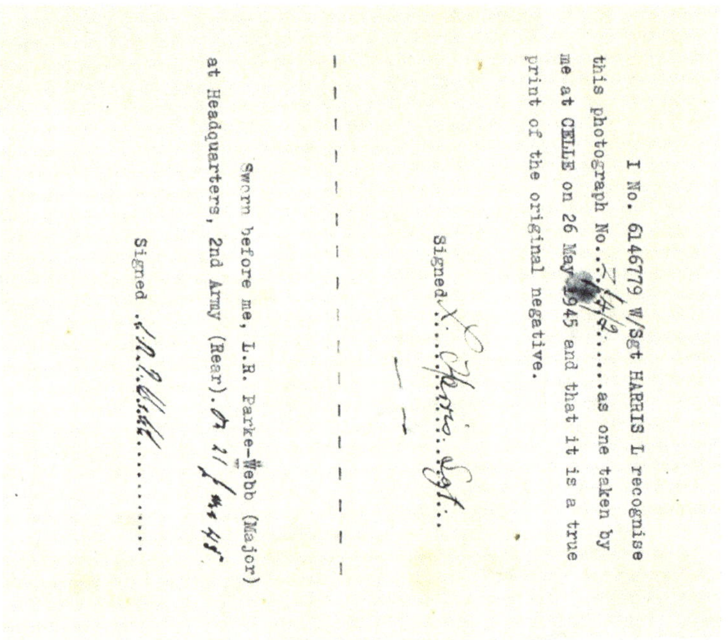

I No. 6146779 W/Sgt HARRIS I recognise this photograph No. 7/4/2...... as one taken by me at CELLE on 26 May 1945 and that it is a true print of the original negative.

Signed .... Sgt...

Sworn before me, L.R. Parke-Webb (Major) at Headquarters, 2nd Army (Rear).

Signed ....

Irma Grese (#2) and Hilde Gebhardt (#3) after they were arrested at the liberation of Bergen-Belsen. Lohbauer is identified as Grese in some photographs. Note Grese kept her black boots shined to a high gloss to the end.

While this is not a rare photo, it is the original print of the original negative and includes the border and photo information. It was labeled as I No. 6146779. (Taken at Celle Prison, May 26, 1945, photographer Sgt. L. Harris. Duchy copyright material in the National Archives is the property of His Majesty The King in Right of His Duchy of Lancaster and is reproduced by permission of the Chancellor and Council of the Duchy of Lancaster.)

CHAPTER 22
Liberation & Arrest

Irma Grese's final downfall was marked by a unit of the British SAS (Special Air Service [301]) jeeps reverberating and bucking through the forest. Silver birch and pine trees, fallen branches and loamy earth filtered through the air. And then the indescribable stench took over the soldiers, eventually settling into the nostrils, the eyes, the hair, and the cloth of their uniforms. It lasted several days of the journey.

SAS Lieutenant John Randall and his driver were leading the main force of the SAS on a reconnaissance expedition. Randall ordered the driver to stop and pull into some large, open gates leading to a road of sand. "It must be some sort of big, fancy estate," Lieutenant Randall told his driver. It took driving about a mile to approach a ten-foot high barbed wire fence and a secondary open gate. "A POW camp," Randall mused. "There might be some of our men here." It was April 15, 1945.

Canadians and British troops were advancing on Bergen-Belsen and, in an attempt to hide as much evidence as possible, the camp Nazis were keeping busy the prisoners who were able to move. The frenzy to bury and burn bodies was at height, as was the destruction of documents and other evidence. It was mid - 1945. Healthy prisoners whispered to the sick to *hold on. It won't be long now...*

Typhus was a fusty cloud over the camp; the German army declared the camp, as well as the area surrounding it, an exclusion zone. If Belsen was liberated and the prisoners were allowed to walk away, typhus would spread across the region to travel across country. Germany's Nazi hierarchy feared what it had created and now was desperate to contain it.

Any SS staff left behind were now preparing to flee. A percentage had already deserted. Irma Grese was staying for love. She was convinced she and "Hatchi" would be together. Most SS camp staff across the country disappeared into other lives, but a few stayed in the camp to "uphold order," including Josef Kramer and Irma Grese. Hungarian and German troops would be placed to guard Belsen's perimeter.

By now, scant few of the British army knew Belsen existed. Sachsenhausen, Dachau, and Buchenwald had garnered little ink in the press and only by the survivors. The British were reportedly far from familiar with the concentration camp system.

And finally, April 15, 1945, SAS Lieutenant John Randall and his driver were about to crack open hell.

Their jeep approached the second gate cautiously. Lieutenant Randall's pistol was in his hand and close to his thigh as the Nazi soldiers looked blankly past him. Despite the potential threat, and the stench which was now unbearable, Randall noted a flower garden and white stones bordering these gates. A strange detail, a sick backdrop to the thousands of living corpses that shuffled, crawled, and lay across a clearing and out of the doors of huts and filth. These wretches were also struggling through a potato field, claws scraping the dirt for substance. Some of the living were in better condition, but Randall had to

[301] "The SAS was a 'regiment' of the British Army, but typically operated in small groups. The SAS operated independently, but would be temporarily attached to larger units." – interview with WWII historian Dave Moore (Sept. 13, 2024).

swallow vomit when his eyes tracked the thousands of corpses, stacked in piles, arms, legs, and skulls sticking out of the piles as if still reaching for life or a last, futile escape.

Gunfire could be heard in the background. Nazis were frantically shooting prisoners in a last effort to cleanse Germany. Lieutenant Randall and several of his men, including the chaplain, watched a female prisoner who pathetically scratched for a rotten turnip just outside the barbed wire. A Nazi guard walked over to casually shoot her dead.

Irma Grese would be at Josef Kramer's side when Kramer, a wide smile across his course face, approached Lieutenant Randall and his small group of men, including SAS Reg Seekings and Major John Tonkin. "Alongside (Kramer) stood a blonde woman in the neat dark-blue uniform of a female camp guard; (Kramer) introduced her as Irma Grese, the warden in charge of female prisoners." Kramer asked if the soldiers would enjoy a camp tour, adding, "… he was not responsible for the condition of the inmates." [302] Kramer escorted them into a hut full of dead and dying. A few of Randall's men, who were already veterans of heavy combat, fell out to vomit and retch. They stumbled a few feet before they observed an SS guard beating a prisoner to death with a rifle. SAS Reg Seekings glanced to his superior for permission, strode to the guard, and punched his face so hard the guard did not rise from the dirt.

Major John Tonkin would order the detaining of Josef Kramer and Irma Grese. They were to be temporarily held in the guardroom. "We are now in charge," Tonkin was calm and authoritative as he addressed these two former leaders. "Not you." Tonkin explained any SS guard "who attempts to treat a prisoner with brutality will be punished." [303] Tonkin's addressing the leaders in a polite tone would be a demonstration of civility. He was aware the companies accompanying him would have easily opened fire on the perpetrators of this atrocity. Judging by Grese's later conversations with her sister, Leni, it was clear the former farmer's daughter – turned – Hyena was neither repentant nor anxious. Irma Grese felt she had done nothing wrong.

Additional British troops planned to reach Belsen on April 14, but heavy fighting prevented troop movement. Lieutenant John "Jack" J. Crosbie of the Royal Artillery assisted in the liberating of Belsen. Much later in March of 1964, Crosbie recalled he could still see, hear, and smell Belsen in his memory as he wheeled a jeep into the Belsen compound, and "battle-scarred veterans were sick on the spot" with "men … weeping openly" at the site. He recalled the "SS women" spitting "in our faces without the slightest provocation" and the attractiveness of Irma Grese, whose good looks hid her "vile character." Writing his story was the first time since liberation Lieutenant Crosbie could recount how he came to be part of the liberating troops:

> Our Commanding Officer … hurried each morning to Brigade Headquarters demanding another commitment for the Regiment. He was determined that we should not be left behind and he was not to be disappointed. On 12th April 1945, the German Military Commander at Bergen-Belsen … approached the Commander of the British 8th Corps and negotiated a truce

[302] Macintyre, B. (2016). P. 329.
[303] Ibid. p. 330.

to avoid serious fighting in the area of the Belsen Concentration Camp, which was at the time some 12 miles behind the German front line. [304]

Members of the British Royal Artillery 63rd Anti-Tank Regiment liberated Belsen on April 15, 1945. One of these liberators would recount how SS personnel met the line of troops at the main gate, standing in a ceremonial line. Josef Kramer was friendly, smiling, as if presenting his troops at a party. Behind him were at least 10,000 rotting corpses.

Prisoner Fania Fénelon came close to being one of those corpses. She was lying in a Belsen barrack full of sick or deceased female prisoners; weighing only sixty-five pounds, Fania was fighting typhus she believed would kill her. There was no air, no windows, and no water. Corpses lay rotting. The women around her were bathing in and drinking urine. Fania was a member of the Women's Orchestra of Auschwitz. She later recalls how, on April 15, she could feel herself drifting away from typhus and her fellow prisoners begging her not to die. "Above me, over my face, I felt a breath of air, a vague smell, a delicious scent," Fania recalls. *"Meine kleine Sangerin,"* a voice told Fania. *"Stirb nich."* [305] Irma Grese was standing over her. It was not a plea, Fania Fénelon explains, "that was an order, and a hard one to obey." Fania managed to focus on Grese's "glorious fair plaits which surrounded her head like a halo, her blue eyes and dazzling complexion." She managed to observe that Irma Grese was amused by Fania's precarious situation. *"Stirb nicht!"* Grese was shouting at the prisoner. *"Deine englischen Freunde sind da!"* ("Don't die! Your English friends are here!" [306]) The Hyena of Auschwitz was enjoying a last taunt of a prisoner.

Grese would later state she "never tried to gain favor with inmates, even when she knew Germany would lose the war." [307]

There were the sounds of machine guns, boots in the gravel, and then an English soldier was sobbing at Fania's side upon viewing these thousands of dead and dying women. The man explained he had arrived from Hanover when chasing German soldiers, and his company was stopped by German SS waving white flags of surrender. This tearful man and his company had no idea there was a concentration camp in Belsen.

Captain Derek Sington of the Intelligence Corps was commanding the number 14 Amplifier Unit and acting interpreter for Lieutenant Colonel Taylor. In his command was an armored vehicle bearing a white star emblazoned on the side, with loudspeakers atop the heavy tarp and interpreters standing by. Sington's truck was accompanied by several vehicles of the 63rd Anti-Tank Regiment, Royal Artillery.

Captain Sington would later write how three handsome, smiling, smartly dressed SS leaders met Sington at the Belsen gate, and one introduced himself as Commander Josef Kramer. There was small talk, and then Kramer stood on the running board of Sington's military vehicle as he directed the convoy into Belsen. Kramer suggested Captain Sington refrain from using the loudspeakers as it might cause a ruckus. "Just over the shoulders of Kramer and his comrades," Captain Sington would write later, "were 10,000 unburied dead

[304] (2019, May 2)
[305] "My little singer, don't die."
[306] Fénelon, F. (1977). P. 4
[307] Brown, D.P. "The Beautiful Beast." pp. 62-6. Cited in Morris, F. p. 67

piled in twisted heaps; [sic] mass graves containing 40,000 bodies and survivors perishing at the rate of 500 a day – all civilians dead or dying…" [308]

Prisoners began crawling and tottering out of buildings, streaming to the fences – walking, stumbling, some held one another. The screams and cries echoed across the liberators. Survivor Masha Greenbaum recalls seeing a young British soldier in a tank. The soldier looked out at the prisoners, barely alive, at the scraggly living carcasses dressed in rags. Tears coursed through the dirt on the soldier's face, running in never-ending rivulets as the prisoners began to kiss the ground at the tank, even kissing the tank itself, so happy to finally walk on free soil.

Captain Sington told Kramer "(you have) created a near approach to hell."

Kramer was offended. The camp's decline was only recent, he snapped. [309] Kramer explained curtly these prisoners were homosexuals, habitual offenders, and felons so they *must* be imprisoned. When asked, Kramer was vague about how the camp supervisors were feeding the prisoners.

The SS officials, Kramer included, were angry that the liberating soldiers had disrupted camp operations. Kramer became haughty and was caught in more lies about prisoner treatment. Several SS men had to be stopped from beating and killing prisoners in front of the liberating soldiers.

Video would be taken of the female camp guards. Most of them, walking with former comrades, shared an angry expression.

Setting up camp, Captain Sington noted another group of British soldiers who were now forcing the Nazis to carry and bury the dead prisoners. An SS officer attempted to run, escaping the group; he was shot dead.

Thus far, Captain Sington did not know "SS wardresses" existed until after a "few days" of being at the site. None of them had been arrested. He observed "several of them scrubbing and sweeping an empty store- room" to make it ready for prisoners. In his memoir he would note their uniforms, their "robust and some hefty" appearances, "most of them were on the young side." Sington noted one blonde who "wheeled a bicycle beside her," which caught his attention, "looking rather busy and active." This was the captain's first time seeing Irma Grese. [310]

Grese was lucky she had been detained and was not partaking in a gruesome and wretched mission. An estimated 500 prisoners were dropping dead each day. [311] The female guards were arranged in groups to assist in burying the dead. The 6'3" Herta Bothe, the former nurse, insisted she was unable to carry out this duty. She whined how her bad back prevented her from labor. Other captive guards raised a cry. They feared contacting typhus. Bad back or no, they were forced to remove the dead from the camp, slinging the skeletal bodies into the back of a truck. They had to sit on the piles of corpses in the three-ton trucks now growling across the compound. These trucks would stop at mass pits. The captives dragged, carried, or slung the rotting dead over their shoulders to drop them into the pits.

Liberating officers forcing these Nazis to bury the dead had to step away to gag. Covering their faces with cloth, the captured Nazis also retched. Some of the dead bodies

---

[308] Playfair, G. & Sington (1957). P.151.
[309] Ibid, p. 152
[310] Ibid. p. 154
[311] "The 11th Armored Division (Great Britian)." The Holocaust Encyclopedia.

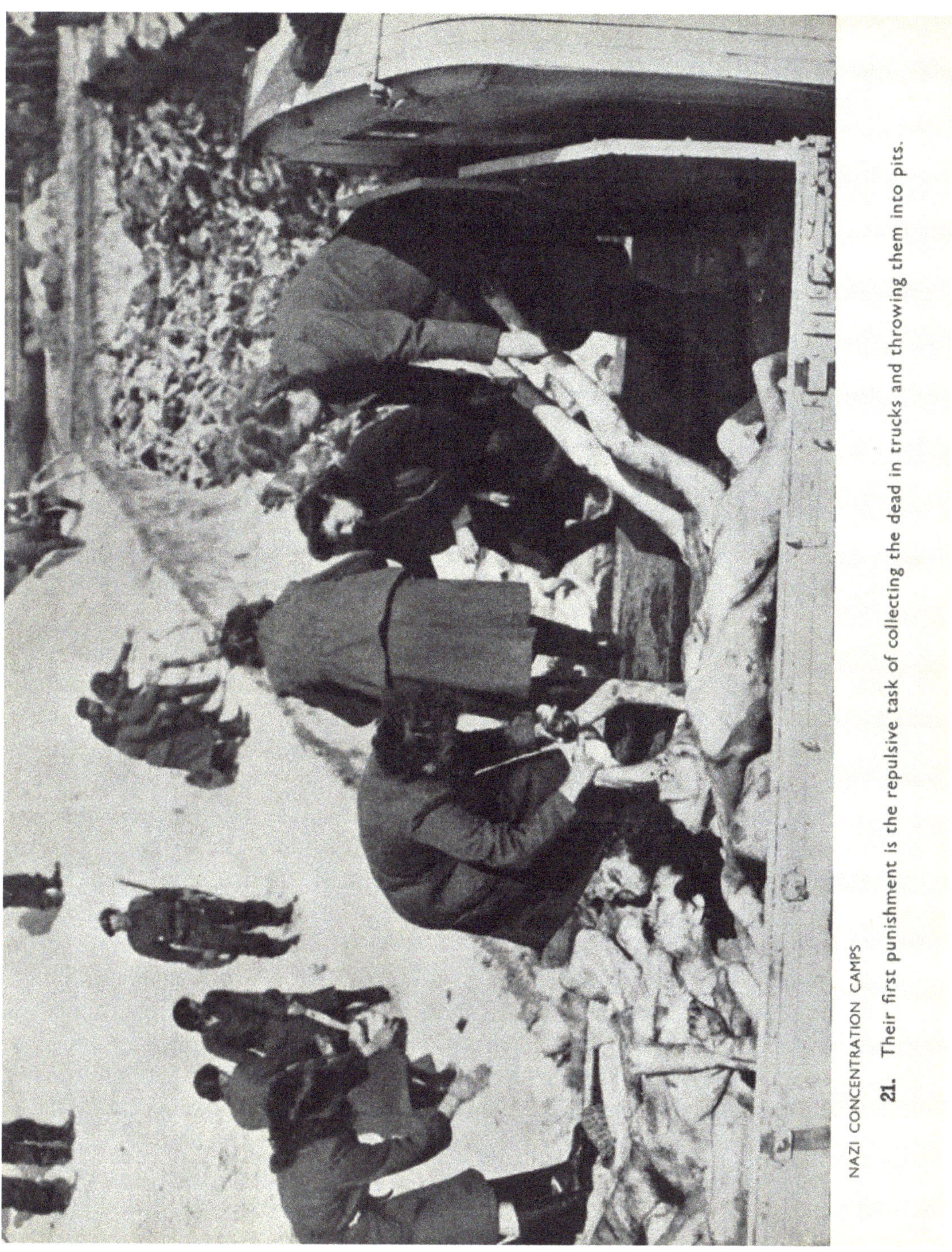

NAZI CONCENTRATION CAMPS

21. Their first punishment is the repulsive task of collecting the dead in trucks and throwing them into pits.

(Circa April 15, 1945. Location: Belsen camp. Photographer: unknown. One of 23 photographs of Nazi Concentration Camps, issued by the Ministry of information, 1945 (c). NAM. 1994-04-105-21. National Army Museum, "out of copyright" per NAM)

were so putrefied that skin sloughed off in hands and limbs broke away. The Nazis, who for years had forced the prisoners to carry the dead in this condition, complained they had no gloves. The dead were placed in the mass pits, then covered using a bulldozer.

Surviving prisoner Masha Greenbaum watched from a distance as the former keepers now carried the dead. "They complained bitterly," she recalls. "They screamed. They said it's against the Geneva Convention, that they are ranked, 'so I'm not supposed to do this work.'" Still, The British soldiers "made them give a decent burial to the bodies." [312]

Irma Grese could have been one of the 17 Nazi staff members who died of typhus after handling the dead, who passed within two months of the task. "Another committed suicide, and three others were shot and killed by British soldiers after trying to escape." [313] Grese instead was sitting in a makeshift jail, glaring at her captors.

It was easy to confuse the identity of Grese with her blonde, blue-eyed coworkers. There was so much activity in the camp. Decades later random *Aufseherinnen* are misidentified as Grese in photographs.

For example, as Intelligence Corps Captain Derrick Sington and his team continued to liberate the camp, he would recall noticing a young, beautiful blonde assisting with burying corpses. Later, he would identify the woman with the dour expression as Irma Grese.

A legal team arrived several days into liberation and posted photographs of the camp personnel. Testimony from prisoners was taken, with detailed accounts of torture, torment, and murder. Witnesses used the photographs to identify their abusers, though some knew them by name. Captain Derek Sington noted the "formidable array of testimony … accumulated against" Irma Grese. [314]

Irma Grese was officially arrested along with other female SS personnel. Grese's first mug shot was taken; she is standing in front of some windows holding a square board with the number "2" written on it. She wears the grey skirt and pointed-collared blouse of her uniform. Her hair is pulled back revealing a high forehead. Her eyes are shadowed. She appears older than her true age.

Edda Treforest, survivor of Auschwitz, would recall Grese working at Auschwitz. "They called her, something like a lion, or a tiger. She was a beautiful looking girl, but she really must have been demonized, as Satan, as a person. She did terrible things to everybody … so many were shot by her." When the camp was liberated, Treforest states screaming prisoners grabbed Grese, drug her into the latrine, and shoved her head "into a toilet." [315]

Survivor Paula Dash (née Garfinkel) had been held in Bergen-Belsen since being evacuated from hard labor in Bremen. She was about twenty five years old when liberation took place at Belsen. She remembered Irma Grese as "the Nazi woman." Fainting from typhus, her friends located Paula curled up in a ditch and wishing death. The following day they were liberated. There was a shout over the camp loudspeaker: "*ihr seid frei*!" Initially, she believed it was a trick. "We saw Kramer being driven away. We saw all the Nazi women being driven away and put in a prison. And we were outside taunting them." [316]

---

[312] Greenbaum, M. (1991)
[313] Shephard, B. (2007). Electronic copy, no page number.
[314] Ibid. p. 155
[315] Treforest, Edda interview
[316] Dash, P. (1992 June 1). Oral history

There are numerous accounts of when and how Grese was captured and arrested. Whatever the true account of Grese's detainment, the liberating soldiers continually worked around corpses of freshly dead and rotten bodies. It was noted that some of the living prisoners had resorted to cannibalism of the dead to survive. Flies, maggots, and vermin had taken over. Many of the living was merely existing, and hollow eyes followed their liberators as if the moving bodies were merely ghosts.

One of the liberating Regiment's soldiers, Frederick Riches, recalls the stench of Belsen, unable to describe it. Frederick Alexander Riches was an ambulance driver with the Royal Army Service Corps; until the day of liberating Belsen, Frederick had never heard of a "concentration camp." The Royal Army Service Corps and the Medical Corps banded together to liberate Belsen the day Frederick learned about "Belsen" and "concentration camp." Prior to entering, Frederick and his team had to be disinfected, covered in the white powder, and were instructed to go into certain huts and remove the prisoners. Frederick observed Kramer and Grese handing out turnips to the prisoners. It was not an altruistic act, but a desperate effort to show the SS was kind to their prisoners. And as soon as prisoners attempted to grab the food, Kramer and Grese "…was pushing some people away and letting someone else get (the turnips)." [317]

The liberating soldiers came upon three hundred nude female prisoners: "they looked like human skeletons…their skin was yellow…their eyes were sunken---" who greeted the soldiers. "How can these people treat 'em like that?" Riches recalls wondering of the SS supervisors. He explains how the regiment observed "Kramer, the chief there, and Irma Grese, that was his second in command and both of them were pushing people away" as the regiments drove through Belsen. He would later hear from fellow soldiers how, upon arrest, "Kramer was placed in a car and driven away" as was Grese. Grese and Kramer were detained in lock-up and the "infantry" fed "the same food as (the camp staff) had fed the (prisoners)" in this temporary lock-up. [318] Eight females and a larger group of former male German Belsen employees – including Kramer – were kept in an enclosure closely guarded by liberating officers.

As a subtle punishment, a member of the Royal Engineers offered only turnips for Irma Grese and her former coworkers to eat. The turnips were set at the end of the SS captive's enclosure, so the captives had to get their own food. Infantry would join in the punishment by first placing the turnips at the end of the enclosure, far from the group of captives. As the captives walked some distance to the turnips, the soldiers transferred the food to the far opposite end. Grese and her former coworkers were then forced to switch directions and take another lengthy walk. The practice would go on all day. Initially, the former torturers and sadists refused to eat the turnips. Some of them complained that, as prisoners of war, they were to receive decent meals. "You get what we give you," the captives were told, "same as you treated these other people (the prisoners)." [319] The male SS gathered around Kramer until their former leader was removed from Belsen, placed in a car and driven away.

Another account has Grese arrested with her vicious dog in tow, a liberating officer would report. This officer was wary of the dog – it was underfed, and dangerous. Just in

[317] Riches, F. A. (1987, September 19). P. 6
[318] Herr, J. (1987)
[319] Cited in Riches, F. A.; P. 6.

case, the officer would later say, "I had to save one bullet because (I) wasn't too keen on having Grese's Alsatian being around." [320]

A former military police lance corporal recalls setting up a camp after liberation. This camp was in the same quarters where Kramer had lived. The lance corporal recalls "an attractive young girl with a cruel mouth, blonde hair, and looking a picture of health – a typical kind of hiking girl – came forward" to request a pass. The girl spoke little English but said she wanted to visit a "sweetheart" convalescing in a nearby hospital. She was sent to the Military Government, who then telephoned the lance corporal explaining a "former detainee" had identified the girl as suspicious. The girl was located walking down a road. When she was returned to the lance corporal's offices, "she burst into tears." [321] The girl was identified as Irma Grese. She was held for a week in a small spare room. Grese would constantly ask when she would be set free. Each morning it was noted "her eyes were very red." She had an innocent countenance and was dubbed "Little Irma." On a day Grese was allowed outside for exercise, former female prisoners recognized her, and fought to grab her. Grese "was at that moment a different girl…she gaped at them with a cynical smile." [322] The lance corporal sat guarding Irma Grese until she was removed for transport to jail.

Harold Burgh was a World War II veteran and former warrant officer in the Royal Electrical and Mechanical Engineers of the British Army. Years later, Burgh gave presentations at Holocaust Remembrance events discussing his memories of Bergen-Belsen after liberation in 1945. His unit was there assisting. It was a helpless feeling, for they could distribute food, but food could threaten the survivor's lives – so few were so unused to eating that they became sick or even died. And so many were close to death. He would describe, while at Belsen, "seeing the two most evil faces I have ever seen or will ever be likely to see;" one was Irma Grese, the other Josef Kramer. [323]

Large wooden signs would be placed at the entrance and smaller signs around the camp: TYPHUS. It was a warning to all incoming troops. Trucks were instructed to drive slowly lest they stir up dust and the bacteria that rest in the soil.

Captain Eric Melrose Brown has been honored with the Distinguished Service Cross, the Air Force Cross, and a chest full of campaign medals. He holds the world record for most aircraft carrier landings, was one of two survivors of the *HMS Audacity* sinking. A lengthy list of degrees follows his name. Yet it was witnessing the liberation of Bergen-Belsen that most affected the war hero. Of the camp conditions, he recalls, "I was utterly, utterly appalled." He also states he interviewed and interrogated high-ranking German prisoners at the end of WWII, including Irma Grese. Of his entire career, "She was" Captain Brown would recall, "the worst person I ever met." [324]

Captain Brown, who spoke fluent German, has stated he interrogated Irma Grese after Bergen-Belsen's liberation. "I ask her four times (whether she had any regrets over her actions) when she suddenly leapt to her feet and with a salute called out at the top of her voice, 'Heil Hitler!' and sat down again. We never got another word out of her." [325]

Seventeen-year-old British soldier Walter Jokel reports he captured Grese, and decades later would vomit and cry over the thoughts of Belsen's liberation and Grese's

---

[320] Brown, p. 64
[321] North Shields Postman "delivered" blonde Irma Grese (1845, September 23). P.1.
[322] Ibid
[323] A case study of… (2014)
[324] Jones, L. (2014)
[325] British war veteran tells ITV…(2015)

behavior upon arrest. Interviewing Grese was the most shocking part of the horrific war for Jokel. Newspaper accounts would have Jokel finding a frightened, blonde woman hiding in a local barn, covered in hay, and wearing the remnants of a Nazi uniform. The woman was identified as Irma Grese, and it was the last time she appeared anxious. Walter Jokel would report he interrogated Grese, alone, for twelve days in a small wooden hut. Grese never showed remorse, never appeared sad or fearful. She laughed and postulated about the cruel ways she tortured prisoners. Her arrogance was unbelievable.

It is now reported that Jokel's testimony at the Belsen Trial helped convict Grese and he was a witness to her hanging.

When interrogated by British officers, Grese denied any participation in "selections" for the gas chambers. She would state that Mengele made the selections without her. She swore she had little knowledge of the gas chambers. "I know from the prisoners that there were gas chambers at Auschwitz and that prisoners were gassed there." She would admit that she knew what "selections" were for. She denied any ill treatment of prisoners. Selected prisoners, she said carefully, "had gone to another camp in Germany for working purposes or for special treatment, which I thought to be the gas chamber. It was well known to the whole camp that S.B. meant the gas chamber" she said regarding her "strength book" notations, where she tracked the number of prisoners selected or transported. Grese insisted "Jews were used as spies in this camp and had certain privileges." She bemoaned how "Jews" had "denounced" her for allegedly saving prisoners lives, earning her a disciplinary two-day lockdown in her room by her superior officers. [326]

The remaining camp staff were held in custody until April 17 when the legal teams arrived at Belsen, after the staff were all formally charged. They would be held three kilometers [327] away from Belsen at the Wehrmacht Panzer Training Academy. This was a large area containing barrack-type buildings where military men trained in working, driving, and using tanks for the armed forces. The female guards held in these barracks had been expecting, at any moment, to be removed from these cells and marched outside to be shot.

They undoubtedly heard about what occurred when Buchenwald was liberated on April 17. The infantry had broken the locks on the gates. The remaining SS were turned over to the prisoners. Prisoners with the fortification gouged out the eyes and tore the limbs off some of their former jailers until another liberating unit arrived and stopped the practice. The SS men were stripped first, making it easy to identify due to the double lightning bolt tattooed in the armpit or under testicles.

On April 19, 1945, Alexander Smith Allan arrived at Belsen. Alexander was an Officer with the 113th Light Anti-Aircraft Regiment, Royal Artillery, 368 Battery. His regiment had received orders to move to an unnamed destination under a flag of truce. They arrived at night. As the sun was rising, they were met with a horrid sight. "…there was just a carpet of bodies," Alexander would describe, years later. "It was a gruesome horrible sight." When the pits were filled with the dead, a layer of soil covered them "and then a notice was put up, the date, and number of bodies, or approximate number of bodies." Alexander and his regiment were covered in disinfectant, the white powder down their bare backs, and disinfected again before they could leave. Alexander would note two of the camp leaders were "under close arrest." He would remember Kramer as "a funny

[326] McKale, p. 41
[327] Close to 2 miles

man" and Irma Grese as "the rather fat buxom Germanic type of woman who was supposed to be rather sadistic towards the prisoners and so on." Of both Kramer and Grese: "I think they were quite arrogant. But the arrogance seemed to fade until such time they were transferred to Celle." Alexander's regiment stayed six weeks to assist. He admitted a life-long hatred of Germany as the result of experiencing the horror at Belsen. [328]

Two days after she was arrested in Belsen, *Daily Express* journalist Paul Holt was interviewing Irma Grese in her cell. The correspondent had become interested in the beautiful but cruel Nazi camp guard. Grese was leaning against the wall of a small cell and her chest heaving. Several of her former *Aufseherinnen* stood with her.

Also outside of this cell, a group of armed British officers merely stared at Grese and her coworkers; these young men were still affected by the camp conditions. A former French political prisoner accompanied the journalist. The survivor was clad in the prison's blue and white striped filthy clothing. He was screaming at Grese, "stand up straight! Don't lean against the wall! You aren't masters now! The British are masters in this camp! Why did you do these things?" [329]

She coolly ignored the shouts. Finally, unable to ignore him, she snarled, "We acted under orders!" Grese would tell Paul Holt how "it was our duty to exterminate anti-social elements to make the future of Germany tranquil." She said nothing of her whip, the gun, or her use of force. [330]

From here, Irma Grese's name began to circulate. "The Beautiful Beast of Belsen" was born into the public eye. [331]

Grese and her fellow Belsen guards were transferred from the Wehrmacht Tank Training Kaserne to Celle [332] on May 17, 1945. Grese was interrogated by the investigating officer from the Legal Department of His Britannic Majesty regarding her involvement and activity in the camps. She did not hide or try to cover what she did. She felt it was justified. She was accused of participating in war crimes; a royal warrant was issued. Grese, along with Josef Kramer, and 43 others employed at Belsen would be formally accused: murder and abuse of prisoners at Belsen and Auschwitz. She was one of the 19 females (there were 26 men) transported away from the Wehrmacht Panzer Training Academy to await trial.

Celle Prison (*Justizvollzugsanstalt Celle)* is an older architectural style prison with high walls and strong, square corner buildings. Located in Lower Saxony, Germany, its construction lasted from 1710 to 1724. The prison is still utilized at this writing, making it Germany's oldest functioning prison. The buildings are a creamy white and the roof brick-red. A Pantene tower stands over the entrance. Peter Clapman, Major in the British Army, would be serving as governor of Celle, Lunenburg from June 1 to December 12, 1945.

Irma Grese and her group arrived to sparse cells. She and her fellow inmates were fed soup and not much else. Gone were the cozy housing units and meals, the treats, alcohol, parties, and fine items stolen from the dead. They were inmates and would be treated as such per prison regulations, no special treatment, and no waivers. They were no longer the prisoner's keepers.

Major L.S.W. Cranfield was assigned to represent four of the defendants in court: Irma Grese, Ilse Lothe, Hilde Lohbauer, and Josef Klippel. All defendants would be

[328] Allan, Alexander Smith. (1991, March 4).
[329] Holt, P. (18 November, 1945, p. 4)
[330] Ibid
[331] Some reports state "Beautiful Beast" was a moniker given to Irma Grese by the press after her arrest.
[332] Also referred to as "Lüneburg prison" in some documents.

transferred to Lüneburg Prison for the trial. Grese's mug shot had been taken at Celle in August of 1945; it accompanied the file of paperwork to transfer her and her codefendants. She refuses to look into the camera for the photograph, instead glaring at something in the distance. By now, Irma Grese's soft features had hardened. Photos, to include her mugshot, revealed bags under her eyes and her mouth set in a grim line. Her eyes glare angrily. She appears much older than 21 years. She has changed her hairstyle for trial, wearing it pulled back severely and blonde "sausage curls" ringlets behind her ears. [333] Her blouse collar is sharp triangles against a dark vest.

Did she know it was the end, or did she hold on to a glimmer of hope?

[333] During one cross examination it was suggested Grese changed her appearance to confuse witnesses.

Scrapbook from Hell

Irma Grese in uniform at Celle being paraded before media with other arrestees. After arrest on April 15, 1945, Grese and her fellow Belsen guards were held briefly at the Wehrmacht Tank Training Kaserne. On May 17, 1945, they were transferred to Celle. (Circa April 1945. Location: Celle. Photographer unknown. Public domain)

Opposite page: Irma Grese and other female Belsen guards in photos from the Arthur George Standivan collection (Album 2), a collection of photographs taken during and after the liberation of Belsen. Irma Grese is wearing a checkered skirt. An unknown person wrote "Irma Grese * hanged" in the book and added "X" over her head in one photograph. (Circa April 1945. Location: Celle. Photographer unknown. 2024, https://ibccdigitalarchive.lincoln.ac.uk/omeka/collections/document/36413. Used with permission.)

Above: Irma Grese and her female comrades are identified in this photograph. Grese wears a checkered skirt. Notice she has folded down or exchanged her infamous boots.

The following image is a copy of the original, now tattered with time and use. Each copy gives a differing perspective.

CHAPTER 23
"Father and mother weren't there!"

Irma Grese and the other Belsen war criminals, as they would be dubbed in future internal memorandums, were to be held to a slightly differing set of rules than "regular" inmates once they arrived at Celle. Each defendant was to be housed in a single cell. Josef Kramer would not be allowed to speak with, or spend time around, Grese or any of his former comrades. Depending on the number of jailers available, a limited number of these defendants would be allowed outside of their cells at a time. Grese and the others understood their days of self-owned leisure and fun by the lake was no more. Exercise times would depend solely on court hours. "Some exercise daily is most important" noted a memorandum. Should the weather not permit outside time, arrangements were to be made. Grese and the female defendants were allowed to speak to one another but only during this exercise time with "reasonable precautions." Legal advisors would be the sole visitors allowed before and during the trial. These visits would be accompanied by "a selected member of the prison staff who will … see and hear all that takes place." No firearms were allowed inside the prison, and British troops will be placed as sentinels at the main entrance and specific sections outside of the institution. A Wardress (female jailer) was specifically assigned to the cadre as all the existing officers were male. There must be no chance for these defendants to escape or harm anyone while in custody and during trial.

The press was already scrambling for information on Irma Grese. An article appeared in the *Lüneburger Post* on September 14:

> (Interest in Irma Grese) is understandable, because it is all too obvious to ask why a pretty woman with even features could come into Kramer's company and act as the guardian of an abyss, the revelation of which horrified the whole world ... Many prisoners remember her from Auschwitz as the best-looking of the female guards. [334]

During Irma Grese's arrest and interrogations, her parents were desperately trying to escape. However, with the Russian army heading in, the family was overtaken. Dejected, the Greses turned back to their home.

Alfred Grese's children were scattered. Helene was still working as a nanny for Baron von Schröder in Hullerbusch. Otto had been fighting at war; the Americans eventually capturing him. Lieschen was continuing her nursing in Neustrelitz. More than ever nurses were in high demand to treat the wounded staggering in from a war-torn world: the soldiers, the refugees, the innocent people caught in the crossfire. There were no more idyllic sunny days at Wrechen.

According to Helene, her parents had joined the refugee treks. They passed trains stopped on tracks, dead citizens holding lifeless babies. Helene would eventually flee

[334] Cited in Müller, J. M. (2024) p. 24

with Baron von Schröder's family, hopping aboard bicycles and carriages to bypass the people on foot.

Alfred Grese and his wife arrived at their home to find almost everything looted. Their Nazi flag still hung behind the door, one of the few things left in their possession.

Helene would explain "we fled to North Mecklenburg, where the Americans were, and later to the Baron's relatives in Lübeck," but never explained who went – the Grese family? Helene accompanying the von Schröders? Nonetheless, in Lübeck the von Schröders began to treat her like a pariah. She did not understand until she read a newspaper, "something about Irma." Helene claims the family knew Irma from the January 1945 visit. She was appalled the family tried to stop her from going to help her beloved Irma when "(the von Schröders) were Nazis, too!"

It upset Helene to learn what had occurred at the camps and she questioned "what was supposed to have happened there." But there was a consoling thought about the concentration camps, Helene Grese later told her biographer. She was relieved "Father and mother weren't there!" [335]

[335] Wieble, P. (1987, May 23)

Part VI
Hyena on Trial

“The traditional victims of brutal violence and repression often see the world rather differently from those who are used to holding the whip.”

- **Noam Chomsky**

Irma Grese with codefendant Josef Kramer and unknown guard at Celle. Grese was one of the 19 females transported to Lüneburg Prison / Celle to await trial. Notice she now wears her glossy boots. Rumor at the camps was Grese and Kramer were lovers though it was never proven. (Circa August 8, 1945. Location: Celle. Photo by Sgt. Silverside & Lt. A. Turner. Courtesy Imperial War Museum. Used with permission.)

CHAPTER 24
"Each of us is numbered."

We arrived here on 13 September 1945
And we were immediately taken into solitary confinement.
We were locked up in twos and threes
And gawked at through the bars of the door.
The show trial will begin on 17 September,
the whole world is streaming in to see it.
Reporters from the whole world
Have been appointed to cover this sensation.
Numbers are produced for us.
Each of us is numbered
so that the newspaper
we can be better identified by our numbers.
In front of the iron prison gate
Three big cars drive up.
All three are meant for us
And well guarded by tanks.
We climb into the gigantic vehicles
And drive through the town like a baggage - train,
with a mighty rumble
around the street corner we go.
When we arrive at the court
the reporters welcome us.
They show their artistic deeds
with their cameras.
Now we are sitting in the waiting room,
the waiting is a torment for us.
One of us speaks to another:
"When does it start?" – "I don't know."
We are led into the big hall,
And are blinded by the lights.
Here sits, represented and appointed,
in short, the whole world.
The reporters stand ready to strike,
And make use of the short time,
snapping and clapping, flashing and crashing,
in an instant many pictures are taken.
Now for as long as five weeks,
we are supposed to sit in the dock.
As I can see in advance
We will end up with sore bums.
The prosecutors took their oath,
but believe me! They are just lying!!!
They often put forward such stupid things,

All we can do is laugh at them.
And no matter how much it annoys us
They are believed.
And before those guys realize it
They have committed perjury.
The Lunenburg people scream
That we are all criminals.
They read it in the newspaper
Which reported about us.
In alleyways otherwise so empty
Stand crowds of people pressed close together,
They point at us
When we get out of the car.
Children, old men, old women,
all eager to look at us.
How they treat us with scorn and contempt,
threatening us with clenched fists.
But never say die, whatever happens,
May will bloom for us once again.
Even if we have to do penance for years
We will once again
Love and kiss!!!

Poem written by Irma Grese after arriving at Lüneburg for the Belsen Trials, dated 13 September 1945 [336]

[336] Axis History Forum (translated from German)

Into the Defendant's Box

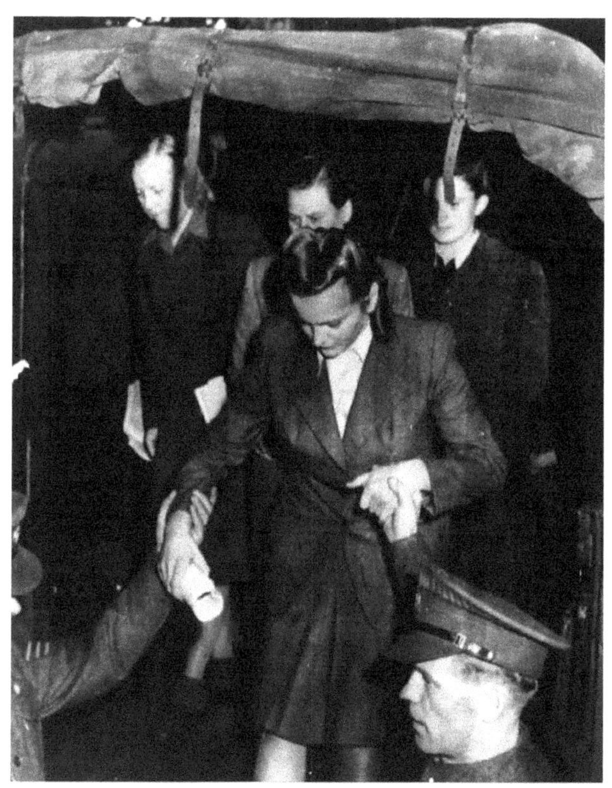

"Death Camp Leaders Meet Justice." Irma Grese, responsible for an untold number of murders, receives assistance to step out of the truck that carried the defendants to trial each day.
(Circa: 1945. Location: Lüneburg, Lower Saxony, Germany. Producer: United News Company; Producer: United States Office of War Information. Accessed at United States Holocaust Memorial Museum, courtesy of National Archives & Records Administration. Used with permission)

Grese walking to /from her seat, Belsen Trials. The press would constantly note her clothing, her hair, her beauty. One journalist would write of the papers she carried in her hand. She scribbled notes as the trial wore on, to include "*Kopf hoch!*" ("head high!"). Some sources list this photo as Grese departing after the death sentence was imposed. (Circa: 1945. Location: Lüneburg, Lower Saxony, Germany. Producer: United News Company; Producer: United States Office of War Information. Accessed at United States Holocaust Memorial Museum, courtesy of National Archives & Records Administration. Used with permission)

Irma Grese, #9 on the dock front row, observing trial proceedings. The other defendants surround her. She giggled at certain testimony and flirted with the press. This is a still taken from the newsreel "Belsen Death Camp Leaders Meet Justice." People from around the world were introduced to Irma Grese, "Kramer's chief assistant, 21 years old and a veteran of five years of atrocities." Grese would now begin to captivate journalists and the public with her good looks and cold demeanor. (Circa: 1945. Location: Lüneburg, Lower Saxony, Germany. Producer: United News Company; Producer: United States Office of War Information. Accessed at United States Holocaust Memorial Museum, courtesy of National Archives & Records Administration. Used with permission)

KEY TO NUMBERS AND NAMES OF ACCUSED.

1. Josef Kramer.
2. Fritz Klein.
3. Peter Weingartner.
4. George Kraft.

5. Heussler.
6. Juana Borman.
7. Elizabeth Volkenrath.
8. Herta Ehlert.

9. Irma Grese.
10. Ilse Lothe.
11. Hilda Lobauer.
12. Josef Klippel.

14. Oscar Schmedidzt.
16. Karl Flrazich.
17. Ladislaw Gura.
18. Fritz Mathes.

19. Otto Calesson.
20. Medislaw Burgraf.
21. Karl Egersdorf.
22. Anchor Pinchen.

23. Walter Otto.
25. Franz Stofel.
26. Heinrich Schreirer
27. Wilhelm Dor.

28. Eric Barsch.
29. Erich Zoddel.
30. Ignatz Schlomoviez.
31. Vladislav Ostrowski.

32. Antoni Aurdzieg.
33. Ilse Forster.
34. Ida Forster.
35. Klara Opitz.

36. Charlotte Klein.
37. Herta Bothe.
38. Frieda Walter.
39. Irene Haschke.

40. Gertrude Feist.
41. Gertrude Sauer.
42. Hilde Lisiewitz.
43. Johanne Roth.

44. Anna Hempel.
45. Hildegard Hahnel.
46. Helena Kopper.
47. Anton Polanski.
48. Stanislawa Staroska.

Defendants were numbered for the Belsen Trial. It was an attempt to create a fair trial. Copy of original Bergen – Belsen Trial “Key to number & name of accused” - Irma Grese assigned #9. (Circa: 1945. Location: Bundesarchiv. Courtesy the German Federal Archive / Bundesarchiv. Used with permission.)

- 4 - JAG No: 12

INDEX TO PROCEEDINGS (Contd.)

TWENTYFOURTH DAY - Saturday, 13th October, 1945 — Page

Prosecution request to show film of AUSCHWITZ CAMP 2

The Accused ELIZABETH VOLKENRATH (Contd.) 6

Witness : ERIKA SCHOPF 7

The Accused HERTA EHLERT 15

TWENTYFIFTH DAY - Monday, 15th October, 1945

Soviet film of AUSCHWITZ CAMP shown and a commentary in English given by Interpreter 2

The Accused : HERTA EHLERT 4

Witness : JUTTA MADLUNG 31

" INGA MADLUNG 32

TWENTYSIXTH DAY - Tuesday, 16th October, 1945

Application for additional Defending Officer . . . 2

Opening speech for GRESE, LOTHE, LOHBAUER and KLIPPEL 7

Witness : HELENE GRESE 17

The Accused : IRMA GRESE 20

TWENTYSEVENTH DAY - Wednesday, 17th October, 1945

The Accused : IRMA GRESE (Contd.) 2

Arguments in admissibility of affidavits 20

The Accused : ILSE LOTHE 29

TWENTYEIGHTH DAY - Thursday, 18th October, 1945

The Accused : HILDE LOHBAUER 2

Opening speech for KLIPPEL 16

The Accused : JOSEF KLIPPEL 18

Witness : PAUL KREUTZER 27

" EMMI SOCHTIG 30

" EMILE KLTSCHO 30

TWENTYNINTH DAY - Friday, 19th October, 1945

Witness : STEFAN HERMANN 2

Opening Speech for SCHMITZ 4

The Accused : OSCAR SCHMITZ 4

Opening speech for FRANCIOH 18

The Accused : KARL FRANCIOH 19

Copy of original Bergen – Belsen Trial "Proceedings" shows Helene and Irma Grese testifying on the 26th & 27th days of the trial. (Circa 1945. Courtesy the German Federal Archive / Bundesarchiv. Used with permission.)

CHAPTER 25
Trial

"The first batch of Nazi butchers … awaits the verdict of Allied justice!"[337] the commentator announces on the newsreel played across the globe; here, for the first time, strangers meet Irma Grese. She stands out from the other accused with her good looks, though a dour expression on her face hides her age. Whatever light once shone in her eyes, so often spoken of between prisoners and coworkers, has dissipated.

The video shows the female arrestees exiting down from a transport vehicle into the courthouse. Irma Grese holds out a hand so the soldiers can help her step to the ground safely.

The film could be considered a propaganda piece, though it did feature atrocities at the camps by focusing on the heaps of dead and revealing those deemed responsible. The film does not discern as to who was guilty or innocent; Grese and her codefendants were already guilty and equally responsible for the carnage prior to the trial. "Belsen's women (are) … as savage as the men." The narrator explains those on trial are responsible for "a thousand deaths apiece." Grese is called out as "Kramer's chief assistant … veteran of five years of atrocities." [338]

The Belsen Trial, where Irma Grese and her codefendants were to go before a court of law, was preparing to begin. It was the first trial of three, informally called "The Trial of Josef Kramer and 44 Others." This was the first global awareness of the atrocities committed in concentration camps. Cline (2014) explains:

> The Moscow Declaration of October 1943 mandated that war criminals be tried by the countries in which the crimes had been committed. Excluded from this, were those individuals whose crimes were not confined to one geographic area, such as those who staffed the concentration camps. These criminals were tried under the London Agreement on the Punishment of the Major War Criminals of the European Axis, established in August 1945. This created the basis for the International Military Tribunal. The Royal Warrant 'Regulations for the Trial of War Criminals' Army Order 81/45 June 14, 1945, set the guidelines for British military trials. (p. 92)

Allied occupational forces conducted the trials "(as) a military court, it was legally based on the *Regulations for the Trial of War Criminals made under Royal Warrant* of 14 June 1945." [339] Holocaust atrocities were not considered war crimes; the violation of human rights and treatment of Prisoners of War were legally crimes: morally and lawfully erroneous.

---

[337] *Belsen Death Camp Leaders Meet Justice (*1945)

[338] Ibid.

[339] Transcript of the Official Shorthand Notes of 'The Trial of Josef Kramer and Forty-Four Others'

There were six judges of the court including Major General Berney Ficklin presiding. British officers served as the prosecutors and advocates. The court staff included:

President Major-General H.M.P. Berney – Ficklin, C.B., M.C.
Members: Brigadier A. DeL. Casonove, Colonial G.J. Richards, Lieutenant - Colonel R.B. Morrish, and Lieutenant -Colonel R. McLay.
Judge Advocate C.L. Stirling, Esq.
Prosecution: Colonel T.M. Backhouse, Major H.G. Murton-Neale, Captain S.M. Stewart, and Lieutenant -Colonel L.J. Genn.

The case language was English, translated into German, and sometimes into third languages, which made for a longer trial than expected. Prosecutor Colonel T.M. Backhouse spoke no German, for example, so his questions and comments were translated to German. The responses in German had to be translated back into English.

Three main trials would be held to punish Nazi war criminals: the Krakow trial of Auschwitz staff (by the Polish government), the Ravensbrück, and Bergen-Belsen (both conducted by the British).[340]

A gymnasium in the British occupied zone Lüneburg, Lower Saxony, Germany was being renovated into a courtroom for the event. This large, grey brick building at Lindenstraße 30 boasted large windows; it would hold 500 people and include a cinema screen; for the first time, film evidence will be utilized in a court of law. The room still held the remnants of a gymnasium as it was stuffy, with little air transfer.

Soldiers guarded the front (public) entrance, which was marked by a large, square sign indicating this was the "Court Room." There was a double – door entryway for "press & military personnel only."

A wooden cage was built at a separate door where the accused would enter and exit the building. Despite this security, armed military officers would crowd against the cage should a revenge-seeker, or supporter, decide to take some type of action.

Walking into the courtroom was probably a bit overwhelming for first-time court watchers. The courtroom was akin to stepping into a box, with most of the court sitting on a dais.

Those supervising the trial were seated on the narrow side of the room. A few feet off the floor sat Court President Major General H.P.M. Ficklin. Alongside the President would be the Members of the Court at a long, rectangular desk. Deputy Judge Advocate C. L. Sterling was seated to the president's right. Sterling would turn to his right when eyeing the witness box.

To the President's left the prosecution team would huddle and converse over strategy. The prosecution would be presenting their case utilizing oral testimony and written affidavits (the latter questioned for fairness) of victims, citizens of ten different allied nations per The Royal Warrant. These victims were representatives of those millions who had no voice, who lay dead in the fields, the forests, the mass graves.

[340] There would be smaller trials, to include the famous Eichmann Trial (1961) and the most recent: 97-year-old Irmgard Furchner convicted in 2022 was found guilty of aiding and abetting over 10,500 murders as an 18-year-old civilian typist at Stutthof.

The court-watchers and attendees would walk across long, grey runners on the floor to take seats in the second-floor gallery built to hold about 400 people. Sitting in the gallery would afford them the best view of the defendants, who sat across the room on the first floor. However, large pillars supported the gallery and blocked some views. The attendees could check coats, use the restrooms, and stop at an information desk, all created for the trial. They could check luggage if needed. Telephone booths lined up for the reporters. Anyone coming in from out of town would be hard-pressed to find an available place to stay. This will be the trial hundreds of people will attend.

Directly across from the President are the defendants, sitting in a bleacher style dock, padded with straw to give them a view of the proceedings. This would make viewing the defendants difficult for court-watchers, particularly with the added security. The defense counsel took seats placed in front of their clients, on the same level as the members of the court. This includes British Major L.S.W. Cranfield, defense attorney for Irma Grese. All the defendants here have pled "not guilty."

And everywhere, on each desk, papers, pencils and pens scribbling, low voices consulting, heads together to discuss and debate. The court was an all-male, all white staff in military uniforms.

Each day of trial, the defendants were transferred from Celle, the closest town with a suitable jail. Helene Grese later told her biographer, confidently, that many people supported and admired her sister Irma, including jailers. Helene confided how a female jailer was inspecting Irma's cell one night, Irma gave an order to stop, and it was followed. The jailers were sneaking notes between Helene and Irma. And everyone, from the defense attorneys to those who guarded her in their shifts, loved Irma and did not see her as a criminal, Helene would insist.

The female defendants sitting in the defendant's bench near Grese, besides Elisabeth Volkenrath and Johanna Bormann, included:

Isle Lothe - was conscripted to work in a munitions plant by the Labor Exchange. She refused and was sent to Ravensbrück. She worked at Auschwitz I and Budin. She was made a *kapo* until that position was taken away. She would eventually regain *kapo* status and was punished three times for smuggling a letter out for a prisoner, burning prisoner beds for firewood, and organizing food and cigarettes.

Herta Ehlert was conscripted into the SS as a guard by the Labor Exchange. She worked at Ravensbrück, Majdanek, and Krakow, then to Auschwitz and Bergen-Belsen. Here she would become Deputy Wardress. She claimed she was demoted for being too nice to prisoners, but this would be proven a lie.

Irene Haschke was recruited by the SS. She trained and worked at Gross-Rosen and then Bergen-Belsen.

Gertrud Feist – was conscripted into the SS as a guard. She worked in a factory and then became an *Aufseherin* at the factory. She then worked at Bergen-Belsen.

Frieda Walter - was conscripted into the SS as a guard. She was ill for some time before she worked in Bergen-Belsen. She wore a headscarf during the trial.

Ida Forster - was conscripted into the SS as a guard and worked at Langenbielau for training, then to supervise factory workers, and finally worked at Bergen-Belsen.

Ilse Forster – Ida's sister was conscripted into the SS as a guard. She was posted at Langenbielau Camp, transferred to serve at Guben as a supervisor, then to Belsen.

Herta Bothe - was conscripted into the SS as a guard by the Labor Exchange. She worked at Ravensbrück, Stutthof, and then as an overseer at Bergen-Belsen. She was known as a sadist and for brutal treatment.
Helene Kop(p)er – she began as a prisoner of Cracow for possession of anti-German leaflets. She was transferred to Ravensbrück, then to Auschwitz and Bergen-Belsen, where she was camp police.
Klara Opitz - was conscripted into the SS as a guard by the Labor Exchange. She worked at Langenbielau for training. She worked in a factory and then became an *Aufseherin* at the factory, and worked at Bergen-Belsen.
Charlotte Klein - was conscripted into the SS as a guard. She was friends with Bothe and roomed with her and Gertrud Reinhold at Bergen-Belsen.
Hildegard Hahnel – did not arrive at Belsen until days before liberation.
Hilde Lisiewitz – she worked at Langenbielau and later in Belsen. She admitted to chasing and slapping prisoners.
Johanne Roth – she was arrested and sent to prison for living with a Polish person, then was moved around to various prisons. She would become a *Stubendienst*. She would deny harming prisoners, though accused of beating a woman to death.
Anna Hempel - was conscripted into the SS as a guard, trained at Ravensbrück, where she performed office work. Eventually she was moved to Bergen-Belsen. She was abusive to prisoners and known to punish her work crews to work faster.

"Pasty – faced girl, a great, flopping, fat middle aged woman" one journalist would describe the female defendants, "... faces showed marks of cruelty ... the callousness of animal stupidity." The journalist described other female defendants as "handsome in the way some Nazi young men are handsome..."[341]

The male defendants were kept separate from females, when possible, to include transport. One truck pulled over to a stop at the prison to wait for the females, while two identical trucks loomed nearby to transport the males. Each group would climb into the back of one of three 3-ton military trucks and settle in along with guards, bracing themselves when the vehicle shifted away from the curb. A flotilla of armored escort cars and military tanks would fall into place, military drivers and passengers armed, heads on a swivel and scanning for signs of conflict. A preselected route had been mapped carefully and was now closed to traffic. The trucks were large, heavy lorries, a thick canvas drop covering the back of the exit and flapping slightly as the truck picked up speed. Some of the city children called out to the defendants from sidewalks and roadsides, "Irma Grese! Irma Grese!" As if calling out to a famous singer or cinema star. One of Grese's co-defendant would testify this gave the young blonde "great delight" – Irma's plans were, after all, to become a famous actress after the war. [342]

These vehicles would rumble to a halt at the Lüneburg courthouse, the transport truck gears would grind and creak to back up close to the caged door, and the accused would step down from the trucks – briefly - onto the pavement and into the building. Armed male guards and female A.T.S. officers would remain vigilant. The trucks carrying males would drop off their prisoners and pull away with a shifting of gears; the third truck would

[341] Willis, C. (1945). P. 3A.
[342] Playfair, G. & Sington, D. (1957). P. 159.

pull into place to drop off the females. Some of the females needed a hand to step down off the truck – Irma Grese was one who needed assistance - guards or fellow female defendants obliged.

The defendants retire to a private room in between sessions, and they will walk a long corridor closed off to the public to enter the court room.

Helene Grese would claim she sometimes stood and watched the procession. She bragged, "(when the) guards saw me, they immediately told Irma: 'Your sister is standing over there.' They also asked if they could give me something or if I needed anything. But Irma didn't want any of that: 'No, everything should be correct!' She never tried to socialize with them either." [343] Again, an improbable claim from Helene, who was convinced her sister was respected by all.

As the defendants settled in, spectators waited their turn to walk into the courtroom. German spectators would be searched before they entered the courtroom. Female officers patted down female court watchers and inspected purses.

The trial began on September 17. Court President Major General H.P.M. Ficklin, a slender, smallish man with a craggy face stood outside to inspect the guard before proceedings. The guard went through drills, snapping rifles to shoulders and back again, their baggy uniform trousers, beret caps, and long-sleeved jackets military – sharp. With a last salute, Ficklin tucked a riding crop under one arm and strode smartly through the door reserved for military personnel.

The British military have been traveling to local towns and issuing admission tickets to the Belsen trials. It is important that Germans attend to witness the fairness of the trial, to see the court was just. The passes are white, shaped like business cards, and good for only a day. The user must show the pass with military or legal identification before admittance. Each card is numbered, signed, with an official stamp. As court watchers filter in, their passes and identifications are scrutinized. A dark slash across the pass indicates it has been used.

It is 10:00 a.m. Court is about to be in session. It is a major phase in world history.

---

[343] Wieble, P.

“The Trial of Josef Kramer and 44 Others”

“The Belsen Trials” were actually a series of trials. Allied occupational forces conducted all Belsen trials in Lüneburg, Lower Saxony, Germany.

Irma Grese was tried in the “trial of Josef Kramer and 44 others” where 45 former SS men and women, including 12 former Kapos, 16 female SS “helpers” and 16 male former SS.

The trials were held by a military court. The *Regulations for the Trial of War Criminals made under Royal Warrant* (June 14, 1945) was the legal basis. The charges would be related to international law. The defendants were charged with war crimes and crimes against citizens (of the Allied countries).

A British military tribunal conducted the second Belsen trial June 13-18, 1946. There were nine defendants, including three females.

The third Belsen trial was held in April 1948. The sole defendant, Ernst Julius Curt Meyer, would be found guilty of war crimes for non-fatal abuse and received life. He would be released in 1954 after a sentence reduction.

The world met Irma Grese through the first of the Belsen Trials, and the Hyena of Auschwitz became one of the most infamous women in crime history.

Above: The Town Gymnasium ten days before the trials started. Trucks delivered Irma Grese and her co-defendants each day for trial. (Circa 1945. Location: Lüneburg, Lower Saxony, Germany. Photo by Sgt. Wilkes No 5 Army Film and Photographic Unit. Image labeled as Public Domain.)

Overhead view of full courtroom for "The Trial of Josef Kramer and 44 Others" (also labeled "The Belsen Trials.") The press was allowed to take photographs a few minutes before the trial began. Irma Grese can be observed in the center of the defendant's box, front row, to the right of the woman in the light suit. She ensured the camera's caught her good looks. (Circa 1945. Location: Lüneburg, Lower Saxony, Germany. Photographer: unknown. Courtesy Mirrorpix. Used with permission.)

Irma Grese, #9, became both fodder and fascination with media. (Circa September 1945. Location: Lüneburg, Lower Saxony, Germany. Photographer: unknown. Image courtesy Mirrorpix. Used with permission.)

The town gymnasium at Lüneburg, Germany, which was converted to a court of justice for the purpose of conducting the Bergen – Belsen war crimes trials. (Circa 1945. Location: Lüneburg, Lower Saxony, Germany. Photographer: unknown. Mary Evans /Vanessa Wagstaff Collection. Used with permission.)

Above: formal photo of the Belsen Trial officials. (Circa 1945. Location: Lüneburg, Lower Saxony, Germany. Photographer: unknown. Credit: United States Holocaust Memorial Museum Collection, Gift of the Canadian War Museum. Used with permission.)

THE PROSECUTING COUNSEL AT LUNEBERG: (L. TO R.) COLONEL T. M. BACKHOUSE, MAJOR H. C. MORTON-BEALE, CAPTAIN S. M. STEWART, AND LT.-COLONEL L. CONN. COLONEL BACKHOUSE DETAILED ATROCITIES UNPARALLELED IN HISTORY.

Above: The prosecuting council at the Belsen trial in Lüneburg: (left to right): Colonel T. M. Backhouse, Major H. C. Morton – Beale, Captain S. M. Stewart, and Lt. Colone. Irma Grese was impudent and arrogant on the stand. She acted inappropriate in the dock, giggling at testimony, waving to people in the gallery, and hand signaling to her sister who watched the proceedings. (Circa 1945. Location: Lüneburg, Lower Saxony, Germany. Photographer: unknown. © Illustrated London News Ltd./Mary Evans. Used with permission.)

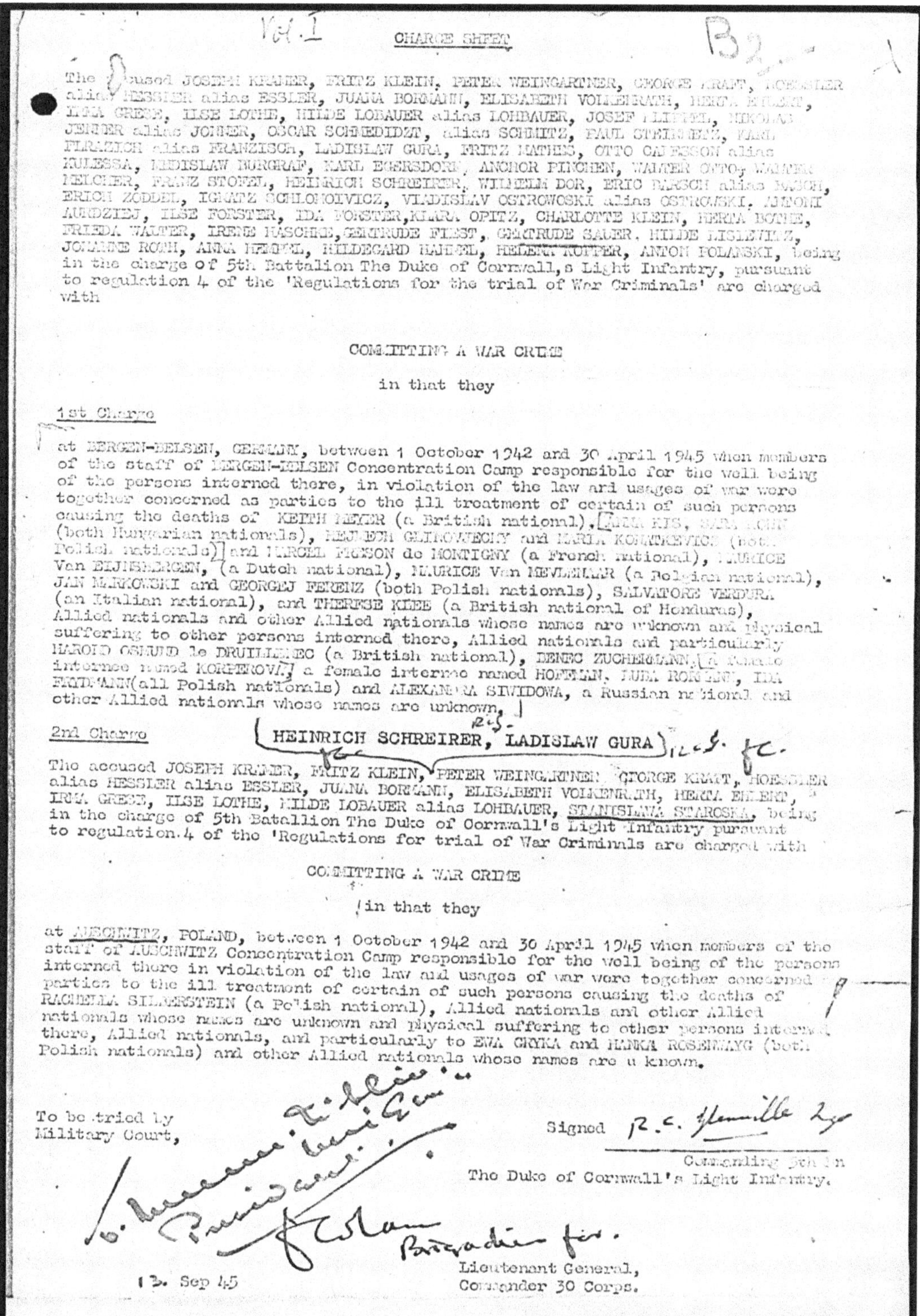

CHARGE SHEET

The accused JOSEPH KRAMER, FRITZ KLEIN, PETER WEINGARTNER, GEORGE KRAFT, HOESSLER alias HESSLER alias ESSLER, JUANA BORMANN, ELISABETH VOLKENRATH, HERTA EHLERT, IRMA GRESE, ILSE LOTHE, HILDE LOBAUER alias LOHBAUER, JOSEF KLIPPEL, NIKOLAS JENNER alias JONNER, OSCAR SCHMEDIDZT, alias SCHMITZ, PAUL STEINMETZ, KARL FRANZICH alias FRANZISCH, LADISLAW GURA, FRITZ MATHES, OTTO CALESSON alias KULESSA, MEDISLAW BURGRAF, KARL EGERSDORF, ANCHOR PINCHEN, WALTER OTTO, WALTER MELCHER, FRANZ STOFEL, HEINRICH SCHREIRER, WILHELM DOR, ERIC BARSCH alias BASCH, ERICH ZODDEL, IGNATZ SCHLOMOIVICZ, VLADISLAV OSTROWOSKI alias OSTROWSKI, ANTONI AURDZIEJ, ILSE FORSTER, IDA FORSTER, KLARA OPITZ, CHARLOTTE KLEIN, HERTA BOTHE, FRIEDA WALTER, IRENE HASCHKE, GERTRUDE FIEST, GERTRUDE SAUER, HILDE LISIEWITZ, JOHANNE ROTH, ANNA HEMPEL, HILDEGARD HAHNEL, HELENA KOPPER, ANTON POLANSKI, being in the charge of 5th Battalion The Duke of Cornwall,s Light Infantry, pursuant to regulation 4 of the 'Regulations for the trial of War Criminals' are charged with

COMMITTING A WAR CRIME

in that they

1st Charge

at BERGEN-BELSEN, GERMANY, between 1 October 1942 and 30 April 1945 when members of the staff of BERGEN-BELSEN Concentration Camp responsible for the well being of the persons interned there, in violation of the law and usages of war were together concerned as parties to the ill treatment of certain of such persons causing the deaths of KEITH MEYER (a British national), [ANNA KIS, SARA KOHN (both Hungarian nationals), HEJMECH GLINOVJECKY and MARIA KONATKEVICS (both Polish nationals)] and MARCEL FRESON de MONTIGNY (a French national), MAURICE Van EIJNSBERGEN, (a Dutch national), MAURICE Van MEVLENAAR (a Belgian national), JAN MARKOWSKI and GEORGEJ FERENZ (both Polish nationals), SALVATORE VERDURA (an Italian national), and THERESE KLEE (a British national of Honduras), Allied nationals and other Allied nationals whose names are unknown and physical suffering to other persons interned there, Allied nationals and particularly HAROLD OSMUND le DRUILLENEC (a British national), BENEC ZUCHERMANN, [a female internee named KORPEROVA] a female internee named HOFFMAN, LUBA ROR[illegible], IDA FRYDMANN(all Polish nationals) and ALEXANDRA SIWIDOWA, a Russian national and other Allied nationals whose names are unknown.

2nd Charge

HEINRICH SCHREIRER, LADISLAW GURA

The accused JOSEPH KRAMER, FRITZ KLEIN, PETER WEINGARTNER, GEORGE KRAFT, HOESSLER alias HESSLER alias ESSLER, JUANA BORMANN, ELISABETH VOLKENRATH, HERTA EHLERT, IRMA GRESE, ILSE LOTHE, HILDE LOBAUER alias LOHBAUER, STANISLAWA STAROSKA, being in the charge of 5th Batallion The Duke of Cornwall's Light Infantry pursuant to regulation.4 of the 'Regulations for trial of War Criminals are charged with

COMMITTING A WAR CRIME

in that they

at AUSCHWITZ, POLAND, between 1 October 1942 and 30 April 1945 when members of the staff of AUSCHWITZ Concentration Camp responsible for the well being of the persons interned there in violation of the law and usages of war were together concerned parties to the ill treatment of certain of such persons causing the deaths of RACHELLA SILBERSTEIN (a Polish national), Allied nationals and other Allied nationals whose names are unknown and physical suffering to other persons interned there, Allied nationals, and particularly to EWA GRYKA and HANKA ROSENWAYG (both Polish nationals) and other Allied nationals whose names are u known.

To be tried by Military Court,

Signed R. C. [illegible]

Commanding 5th Bn
The Duke of Cornwall's Light Infantry.

Lieutenant General,
Commander 30 Corps.

13 Sep 45

Copy of original Bergen – Belsen Trial "Charge Sheet" with a list of formal charges against Irma Grese. (Circa: 1945. Location: currently Bundesarchiv. Courtesy the German Federal Archive / Bundesarchiv. Used with permission.)

Next page:

A used pass for Irma Grese's liaison, allowing him to escort her to War Crimes Court in Luneberg (dated October 1st, 1945).

Issued to "Commander A. H. Cherry, B.N.L.O.[1] Bremen (ANCXF[2]) and party." Passes were valid for one day. This item is exceedingly rare and was auctioned for an undisclosed amount of money.
The black diagonal line across the pass indicates it was used.
This may have been the pass issued to the escorting officers who transported Grese to trial.

(Circa October 1945. Location: N/A. Photographer: unknown. Image courtesy B. Chatt, Vintage Productions vintageproductions.com. Used with permission).

Irma Grese, #9, was observed preening for the camera during court proceedings. She would ensure her hair looked perfect. (Circa September 1945. Location: Lüneburg, Lower Saxony, Germany. Photographer: unknown. Image Courtesy Mirrorplex. Used with permission.)

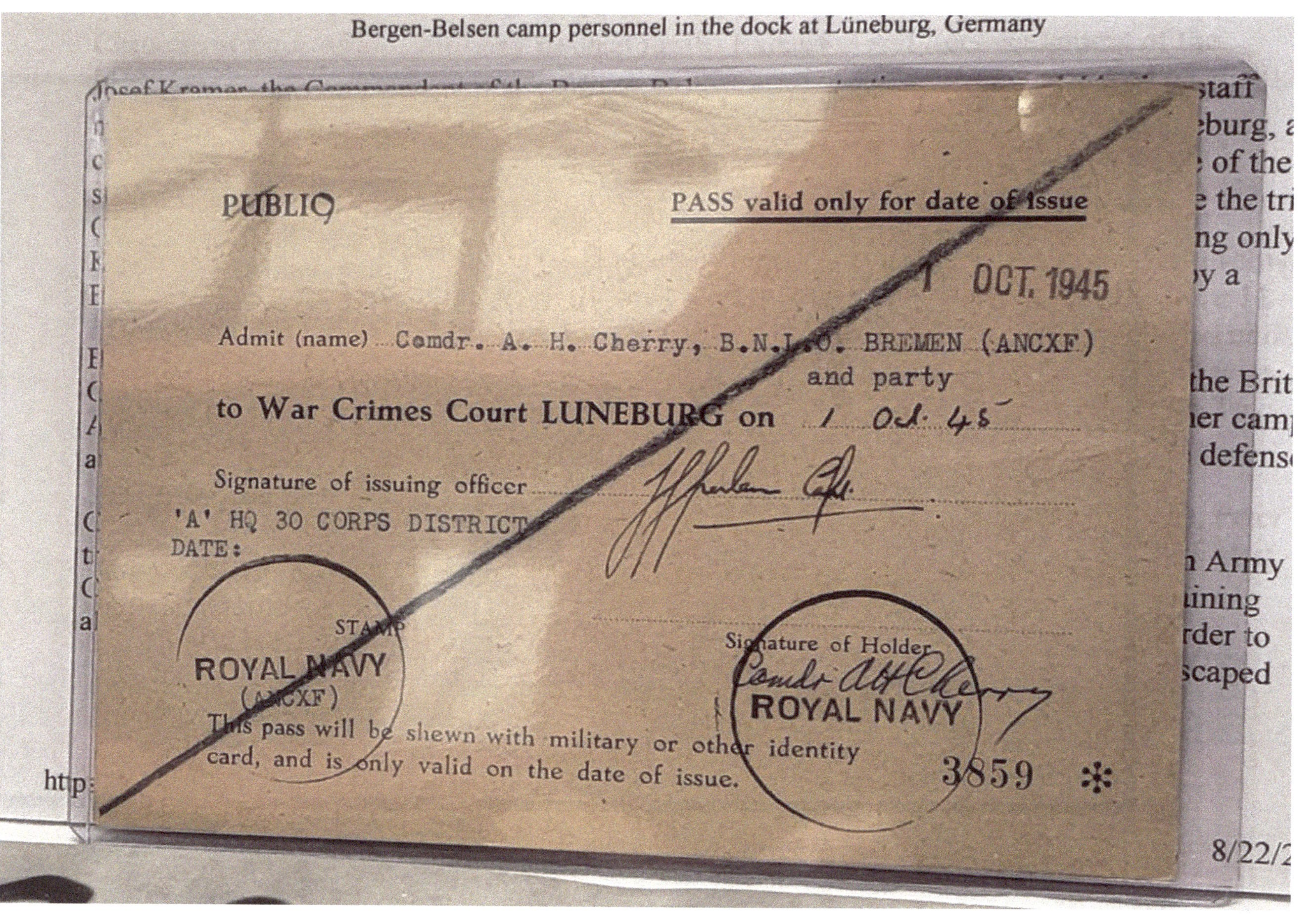
Bergen-Belsen camp personnel in the dock at Lüneburg, Germany

PUBLIC

PASS valid only for date of issue

1 OCT. 1945

Admit (name) Comdr. A. H. Cherry, B.N.L.O. BREMEN (ANCXF) and party

to War Crimes Court LUNEBURG on 1 Oct. 45

Signature of issuing officer J J Harlan Capt.

'A' HQ 30 CORPS DISTRICT

DATE:

STAMP

ROYAL NAVY (ANCXF)

Signature of Holder Comdr. A H Cherry

ROYAL NAVY

This pass will be shewn with military or other identity card, and is only valid on the date of issue.

3859

The Bergen – Belsen Trial partial "List of Exhibits" included #112 – Affidavit of Irma Grese, and #126 - Irma Grese's belt. (Courtesy the German Federal Archive / Bundesarchiv. Used with permission.)

LIST OF EXHIBITS (Contd.)

Exhibit No.		
101	-	Affidavit of Engel Sandor
102	-	Affidavit of Elizabeth Herbst
103	-	Affidavit of Regina Borenstein
104	-	Affidavit of Rozalja Szparaga, Szymkowiak Czeslawa, Maria Synowska
105	-	Affidavit of Arnost Basch
106	-	Affidavit of Sophia Rosenzweig
107	-	Affidavit of Ernst Poppner
108	-	Affidavit of Adam Moocks
109	-	Affidavit of Sevek Kobriner
110	-	Affidavit of Kopper
111	-	Affidavit of Herta Ehlert
112	-	Affidavit of Irma Grese
113	-	Affidavit of Hessler
114	-	Affidavit of Dr. Klein
115	-	Affidavit of H. Lohbauer
116	-	Affidavit of Volkenrath
117	-	Affidavit of Antoni Aurdziej
118	-	Further affidavit of Josef Kramer
119	-	Copy of original telegram to Kramer dated 6.5.44
120	-	Copy of original handing over document, Belsen Camp
121	-	Copy letter written by Kramer to Berlin dated 1st March, 1945
122	-	Strength return of Belsen for fortnight, 1st March, 1945
123	-	P.C. from Erika Schopf
124	-	Affidavit of film "Auschwitz", U.S.S.R. Producer
125	-	Commentary of Auschwitz film
126	-	Grese's belt
127	-	Further affidavit of Regina Bialek
128	-	Copy affidavit of Dr. Bimko
129	-	Affidavit of Esteria Guterman
130	-	Affidavit of Hammermasch
131	-	Affidavit of Sophia Litwinska
132	-	Affidavit of Hanka Rosenweig
133	-	Affidavit of Ilona Stein
134	-	Affidavit of Dora Szafran

CHAPTER 26
"The only pretty girl in the dock"

Now the defendants walk into the courthouse under a plethora of spotlights; the lights were removed from the Belsen camp and are used here. Reporters and court watchers who could secure a coveted seat have been sitting about an hour. At 10 a.m. the defendants filtered into their predetermined seat on long benches, each defendant with a white card bearing a black number pinned to their shirt front for identification. Irma Grese wore a "9." She would be seated in the center, on the first row of defendants, between number "8" Hertha Ehlert and "10" Ilse Lothe. The defendants were ordered at various times in the proceedings to remove the numbered cards and to exchange seats prior to a witness taking the stand. Removing this identification, they were told, would ensure a fair trial when witnesses were asked to identify any defendants.

Court President Major General H.P.M. Ficklin instructed the press there was 20 minutes to take unlimited photographs prior to court proceeding. As cameras clicked and flashbulbs popped, one of the women next to Grese appeared faint. Grese pushed her to sit. The defendants stared straight ahead as they were photographed. British Movietone (1945) was there to film the opening day of the trial. "No men or women," the narrator states, "have ever faced charges of such a loathsome nature." The number of prosecutors "was one third the size of the defense which has impressed the German people." [344] The narrator noted Irma Grese as "one of the most prominent" of the accused.

One journalist noted the female defendants "wore grey German prison uniform … their hair was carefully done. One wore a white scarf; another carried a bundle of papers. [345]At least three wore silk stockings … some women smirked and preened (for the cameras)." [346]

Intelligence Corps Captain Derrick Sington, whose team was one assigned to liberate Belsen, was to give testimony. He would later explain of those defendants, "the most alert and spirited – looking of the women… was Irma Grese." Sington believe Grese was "the only pretty girl in the dock … her hair was blonde, with fair ringlets resting on neat shoulders. Her eyes were clear blue under a high, broad forehead." He compared her to a "handsome young nurse" or "a secretary," or "the head perfect of a girl's school." [347]

One court watcher will compare her to an angry schoolgirl. Another person in the gallery whispers Irma Grese looked more like a circus ringmaster. And still another expresses Irma Grese's resemblance to a snobby, autocratic queen peering at her loathsome subjects.

But much of the press seemed in love. Here they found the most interesting of contrasts: evil and beautiful. And she was made more interesting by emphasizing her (false) youth. Long (2021) notes:

> (Irma Grese was) a young adult and a *Oberaufseherin* [sic], the highest-ranking office a woman employed in the concentration camp system could

[344] British Movietone. (1945). *Belsen Trials.*
[345] Irma Grese carried the papers.
[346] Hirst (1945) p.8
[347] Playfair, G. & Sington, D. p. 159

> hold. Applying the term "Head Girl" to Grese is interesting, as its application in the British youth education system denoting a leadership position held by a reputable adolescent girl clashes sharply with Grese's culpability and active participation through her employment in mass murder [348] … it was recorded that Grese's "iron calm" gave way to "tears and shouts" after the five-week trial period. [349] Even Grese's emotional outburst is described in similar terminology to that of a childish tantrum. Whether this youthful depiction was intentional or unconsciously done, it conceivably served to undercut the authority and power that Grese held as a *Oberaufseherin* in a public forum. Along with emphasizing Grese's 'desirable' hair color, she was also nicknamed the "blonde Queen," and the "Beastress of Belsen." [350] (pp. 50-1)

Irma Grese, the Hyena of Auschwitz, was forever labeled: the beautiful girl who committed atrocities as a high-ranking Nazi.

Today, a journalist will describe her as "Her face, which is actually well-formed, with its blond hair, has something pale and spongy about it, her lips are razor-sharp and her cold, water-blue eyes look gloomy and oppressed." [351]

The charges were read this first day, in English only, as the defendants stood to listen. Herta Ehlert swayed, white-faced, tears falling from her eyes. Irma Grese held Ehlert's arm to keep her from fainting.

Herta Ehlert had worked as a guard at several camps, beginning in 1939 at Ravensbrück. She was transferred for being too lenient with prisoners, too polite and nice to them, before training under Dorothea Binz. Ehlert worked under Irma Grese at Bergen – Belsen. Perhaps the training by Binz and supervision by Grese had changed her character, for Ehlert transformed from being lenient and polite to torturing and beating female inmates. Ehlert was described by a Holocaust survivor as "immensely obese, sly, vicious in character, and an absolute master in using the whip." [352] Now here she stood, paying for this cruelty. Would she be punished with a death sentence?

Ficklin next ordered the defendants to take their seats. They were surrounded by security: a line of soldiers placed under the first row of defendants, an officer at each end of the rows, with officers behind the group joined by an army doctor and nurse Norma Goldstein. Had any of the defendants asked, they would have learned their nurse was a fascinating woman.

---

[348] "Belsen Girl Blames all of SS"
[349] "Belsen Woman guard weeps, denies guilt"
[350] "Branded Victims see Beast of Belsen Swing," *Toronto Star*, 14 Dec. 1945; "Beast of Belsen, 9 Others to Die for Camp Deaths," *Toronto Daily Star*, 17 Nov. 1945.
[351] Cited in Müller, J. M. (2024). p. 30.
[352] Graf, M. (1989). P.113.

CHAPTER 27
The Nurse on the Back Row

Nurse Norma Goldstone Falk (1924 – 2023) would, only years later, be interviewed regarding her station during the Belsen trials. [353] Norma's training and career was typical until September 1945. It was the segue into a fascinating career and interesting life. "She was something else!" her son would later say with great pride. [354]

She was raised in a loving Jewish home with three sisters in a close-knit, warm family. They resided in Sheffield, England. It was a given that the Goldstone family welcomed anyone in to share a traditional Jewish meal or holiday, and Norma learned the arts of grace and giving from her parents. While pragmatic, she also loved the arts, music in particular. Norma loved to sing and would later travel with an international opera group after the war.

Norma was only fifteen years old, dreaming of being either an opera singer or a nurse, as WWII interrupted the calm lives of people across the globe. Against her father's advice Norma dreamed of becoming a nurse, something "nice Jewish girls don't do," her father insisted. She began her career employed in a small hospital tending to the poor coalminers of Yorkshire. From there, Norma volunteered as a nurse for the British Army. (She would complete her degree in nursing by the end of WWII, her son explains.) Near September of 1944, she had been employed at a Lüneburg hospital as the sole Jewish employee. Norma never felt discrimination as a Jew while working as a nurse, she would later say. She and her fellow nurses had not yet grasped the enormity of the war until rumors of the atrocities began. They would learn the Belsen Trials would be held at Lüneburg.

Norma was still unaware of the tragedies of the concentration camps when a matron would assign her to take the station at the courthouse a few days into the trial. The assigned nurse had left the position. "She went into the trial a few days late," Norma's son explains. "She wasn't even assigned the position (originally)." [355] Norma took the position with curiosity, without knowing what her job would entail, and she was not one to balk at a supervisor's command. She would later recall the "so appalling" defendants, to include Irma Grese.

The defendants would arrive in the morning to a private room in the courthouse to prepare for trial. Nurse Norma Falk's day began when an ambulance drove her to the courthouse; she would station herself in a first aid room for medical supplies. Norma spent the morning listening to their medical complaints: "a lot of them had headaches." Some complained of sore throats. There were complaints of stomachaches because their prison diets consisted of soup. Sometimes there were minor cuts. Aspirin and Band-Aids ("plasters") [356] were doled out. The irony would not be lost on Norma Falk: she was a Jewish woman giving pain relievers to the people who were so brutally cruel. The defendants spoke to few people, though it may have been a language barrier: they spoke

---

[353] The interview is an excellent insight into a personal observation on the Belsen Trials and working as a nurse during WWII. See USC Shoah Foundation. (2012, May 17).

[354] Personal interview with Rodney Falk (2024, May 06)

[355] Ibid.

[356] Grunwald- Spier (2018). Electronic copy no pg. number

Nurse Norma Goldstone Falk (1924 – 2023) was assigned as the nurse on duty during the Belsen Trials, doling out aspirin and listening to the medical complaints of Irma Grese and her codefendants. The irony was not lost on Norma that she was a Jewish woman nursing the most heinous Nazi killers in the Third Reich. (Circa 1940s. Photographer unknown. Photo courtesy Rodney Falk and used with permission.)

no English and Nurse Falk spoke no German. She did not have to speak German to understand they were an angry group, from the time they filed in, to the time they departed, in the large, grumbling truck. Should the trial schedule demand, a lunch was prepared at Celle and brought to the courthouse for the defendants to eat while on a break. Norma would continue to provide aid to the defendants at lunch.

Norma would later explain how Irma Grese appeared so "normal." The nurse would recall, "if you see her on the street, she would be a perfectly normal person. It is so hard to understand how she got into this position." [357]

Nurse Norma would later say "Irma Grese was one of the worst people in Belsen. She was twenty-one years old. She committed some of the most abdominal atrocities. And there was no remorse at all. And it was quite extraordinary." She remembered "(Irma Grese) always flicking her hair, always looking up at the gallery (and) smiling. I remember that very, very clearly." [358]

Norma would remember Grese decades later after Grese was dead. "She had this long blonde hair and tossed her hair the whole time. No sign of emotion." About the same age as Grese, Norma was mortified upon hearing of Grese's crimes, "… like bashing children against a wall…" [359] Listening to Grese on the stand, Norma Falk would shake her head, still disturbed by Grese's testimony. "I could not comprehend that a woman of twenty-one could shoot, could beat women who were half starved anyway. And laugh about it! It was a joke (to Grese)." It would affect Norma so deeply she did not want to speak to anyone at the end of the day. She was not allowed to discuss the trial proceedings, which was a blessing and a curse. There was no way to vent, but it was all too awful to think about constantly. As she prepared to sleep at night, she thought of the "nightmarish" day. And Irma Grese upset her "most of all." [360]

After the trial and upon returning to nursing work, Norma would discover her paternal grandparents, an aunt and uncle, along with everyone in their village, were taken into the nearby woods and shot to death during the Holocaust.

She admitted to having a strong bias against Germans after witnessing the trial and having her family members murdered, always wondering who around her was involved in the genocide and escaped persecution. She would eventually take up fencing to discover her coach was the former fencing coach for the Nazi party and had been hired by the British to teach. It made Norma angry towards the coach, and she mentally fought to keep the lessons business-like. She also found herself "getting a bit cross" at people who "grumble about everyday things … silly little things." The Holocaust taught her "nothing was as bad as what these (concentration camp prisoners) had been through." Norma could barely read through the Belsen Trials transcript when it was published as it was traumatizing. "I bought the book when it came out" son Rodney explains. "I think she read it cover to cover." [361]

Nurse Norma Goldstone Falk was playing tennis and staying active into her eighties. She had also enjoyed horseback riding. She was a philanthropist and relished life, but the Belsen Trial and Irma Grese stayed a dark cloud in her memory, always with her.

---

[357] Cited in Vida, B. (2016). P. 537.
[358] USC Shoah Foundation (2012)
[359] Grunwald-Spier. Electronic copy no pg. number
[360] USC Shoah Foundation
[361] Personal interview with Rodney Falk (2024, May 06)

Norma passed away just before she turned 99 years old. "She was very active up until the last few years of her life," her son recalls. "And I miss her. She was a great lady." [362]

She is remembered as a proper English lady with an impeccable home and style, active as a volunteer and loving her job as a mother and grandmother. However, she said in one interview, "the human race is very hard to comprehend." [363]

One of Grese's co-defendants will later recall Grese's behavior during court recess. Irma Grese would make requests that the co-defendant (most likely Elisabeth Volkenrath, a hairdresser prior to her days with the SS) comb and style Grese's hair just so for the next portion of the trial. It is important to Grese that she appears resplendent on the dock. And as the codefendant combed and arranged, Grese would constantly ask, "What will 'Hatchi' think of me?" Meaning Hatzinger. [364]

Irma Grese's sister Helene – and for a few days, their brother, Otto - attend the trials. Several press photos will catch them stepping outside of the renovated courthouse, walking on the sidewalk in front of the building. The press identifies her as "Leni," and she physically favors Irma. She wears her dark hair parted on the side, swept behind her ears under a fedora with a dark dress and jacket.

Otto wears a jacket a size too small, hair slicked back. His face is lean, his eyes troubled. His current situation was dire: he was in jail after being arrested during wartime.

Helene will be testifying. Irma Grese's loving sister rode her bicycle about 60 miles from Lübeck to attend the trial. The defense team pays for her accommodations and expenses, so she doesn't have to work during the trial dates. Helene stays at a local inn.

Beginning day two, translators are provided to defendants. This is when, laments various sources, the accused finally understand the serious charges levied against them. Many of them, including Irma Grese, found the entire trial a mockery.

Another moment in courtroom history was made on September 20, 1945, when a video labeled "Belsen Concentration Camp" flickered on the screen. The conditions of the camp and the thousands of dead are narrated as the camera pans over the dead, the near dead, the conditions of the camp. A female prisoner, a camp doctor, stood in front of a group of scrawny, hallow-eyed women prisoners and described the living conditions: the horrific food, the typhus and lack of medication, the hardscrabble living conditions. Survivors had resorted to cannibalism, she explained. The survivor detailed some of the medical experiments by the Nazi doctors. The camera captures the prisoner reactions to liberation: human skeletons stare blankly into the cameras, a woman grabs a liberating soldier's hand and cuddles it, unable to control emotions. The dead lay scattered near the living in stages of decay, eyes and mouths gaping open, some covered in bruises and open wounds. The camera watches as the SS are forced to load the thousands of dead, picking up the corpses and loading them onto a truck, then tossing them into open pits. The bodies tumbled in like filthy jointed dolls, falling together, until bulldozers were necessary to push in the last and cover the pits. The military officer driver is forced to cover his face due to the stench. Irma Grese does not appear in any of the video footage; she had already been

[362] Ibid.

[363] USC Shoah Foundation

[364] Playfair, G. & Sington, D. p. 160. Grese was still not aware that Hatzinger was dead.

arrested and taken away. The video lasts just under six minutes and twelve seconds, but it introduces the revulsion of only one of the Nazi camps to a new audience and sets the tone for the trial.

Irma Grese sits straight up as the film begins rolling. The images flicker off her expressionless blue eyes. The comrades around her watch passively, and Kramer scribbles notes on his pad of paper. Grese begins scribbling on her own paper, tears out the page, and has it handed off to the defense. An image of a bulldozer pushing a hill of emaciated corpses into a mass burial pit flashes onscreen; Grese blows her nose, adjusts her curls, and continues to watch impassively. The stick-like bodies, some missing ears, cheeks, internal organs, and body parts from desperate cannibalism by prisoners, mean nothing to her.

There are tears, throats clearing, muffled sobs throughout the building. These reactions are not from any of the defendants.

Next page: News article "How a Girl Became A Beast"
Irma Grese became the source of fascination and disgust for the media covering the Belsen trial. Long after the trial's end Grese remained a headline.
This is a review by J. Taggart about the book "The Offenders: Society and Atrocious Crime." The book argued against all executions. The book review was illustrated by photographs of Irma Grese, called the "Beastess of Belsen." (*Star* newspaper, 17 October 1957, p. 8)
From the Arthur George Standivan collection (Album 2). This article was pasted into the scrapbook. (Circa 1957, Germany-Bergen, Celle-Belsen. *IBCC Digital Archive*, accessed April 6, 2024. Used with permission.)

AGE 8—THE STAR THURSDAY, OCTOBER 17, 1957

SHOULD IRMA GRESE HAVE HANGED?

HOW A GIRL BECAME A BEAST

STAR BOOK REVIEWS by Joseph Taggart

LIKE a good many more opponents of capital punishment I have had to admit a few exceptions. Creatures who really had lost the right to live.

Two of them were Kramerthe Beast of Belsen and Irma Grese the Beastess.

And my view has been cofirmed by a book which otherwise makes a powerful case against ALL executions.

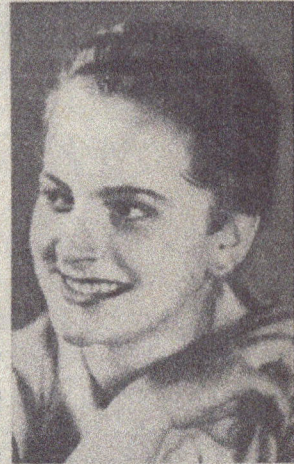

The authors of The Offenders: Society And Atrocious Crime (Secker and Warburg, 25s), Giles Playfair and Derrick Sington, have included Irma among their cases along with Heath and the Rosenbergs.

That doesn't help their argument. But we are given a spine-chilling picture of this inhuman girl, mainly written by Mr Sington, who led the way into that camp of horrors and was a prosecution witness at the trial of the Beasts.

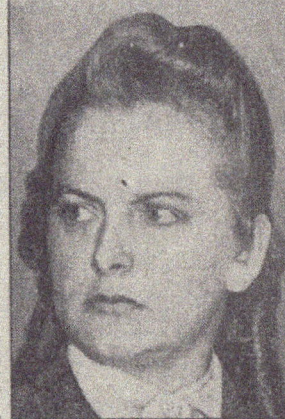

Monster

The two pictures on this page show what about three years as a concentration camp wardress did to Irma.

She was the pretty daughter of a respectable peasant family in Mecklenburg. With appalling ease and speed the Himmler machine turned her into a frozen-faced monster.

By day she plied a whip and enthusiastically marshalled squads of men, women and children for the gas chambers.

By night she joined with equal enjoyment in the customary orgies shared by the men and women guards.

Defiant

When arrested she never flinched or budged. Says this eyewitness:

"Irma Grese, apparently convinced that she had been the servant of 'a cause' did not cringe or attempt excuses or self-exoneration (as so many did); she made no effort to collaborate, but stuck firmly by the political creed she had been taught."

"It was our duty to exterminate anti-social elements, so that Germany's future should be assured" she flung at her accusers.

Throughout her seven-weeks trial, records Mr Sington, this de-humanised girl of only 21 broke down just once.

Not when some particularly horrible crime was being alleged against her, but when her sister spoke of their family and childhood.

The authors say that her execution was "useless and barbaric." I still think these were among the exceptions who could not be allowed to live.

Why angry?

THE Angry Young Men are still protesting that all they are angry about is being called angry.

In DECLARATION (Macgibbon & Kee, 18s) seven of them and a woman novelist, Doris Lessing, set out what they think is wrong with things and what they would do about it.

Some of them talk a lot of sense about our mixed up world. But they certainly don't seem so terribly furious when you think of such by-gone prophets of the wrath to come as Bernard Shaw and D. H. Lawrence.

John Osborne, who earned this group its resented label, hits the hardest. He includes royalty among his targets.

Briefly recommended:

A BIT OFF THE MAP (Secker & Warburg, 13s 6d) by Angus Wilson. Short stories which give sharp pictures of the present-day social scene.

FORGOTTEN ISLANDS OF THE SOUTH SEAS (Allen & Unwin, 18s) by Bengt Danielsson. Still roaming around the side-turnings of Polynesia, the Kon-Tiki man makes another entrancing book about his adventures.

A VICTORIAN CANVAS (Bles, 25s) Nevile Wallis has packed into one absorbing volume the best of W. P. Frith's rambling three-decker memoirs which the artist first published 70 years ago.

The two looks of Irma Grese

Irma Grese as a smiling young girl (above). And, left, after the Nazis had finished with her.

...and alarming discovery.

For it was evident that the V2 could be launched vertically from practically any clear patch of ground—even from a forest clearing difficult to detect.

This was not at all what Britain's rocket boffins had originally expected.

The Air Ministry had been looking for (among other things) "some sort of tube located in a disused mine out of which a rocket could be squirted."

UNDETECTED

In fact Germany's rocket launchings, when they came, were so successfully dispersed and hidden that they defeated Allied photographic reconnaissance.

BUT there was little else that escaped the probing eye of the camera as picked pilots flew deep into enemy territory to photograph factories, ports, ships, airfields, cities.

There was a dramatic moment when, after months of searching photographs, a WAAF Constance Babington Smith, first spotted a flying bomb—the V1—on its launching ramp and realised what it was.

Miss Babington Smith was one of Britain's most skilful "interpreters" of air photographs. Now she has told the achievements of photographic intelligence in a fascinating book published yesterday, EVIDENCE IN CAMERA (Chatto and Windus, 18s.).

Alan Fairclough, using a long-focus lens, says: "Let's have a real close-up!" He has been reading EVIDENCE IN CAMERA by Constance Babington Smith.

CAUGHT!

The battle against the V-weapons is only part of her story. Equally enthralling is her account of:

HOW the battleship Bismarck was caught.

WHY—despite photographic intelligence—the 1944 German offensive in the Ardennes took the Allies by surprise.

HOW Germany was photographed **BEFORE** the war.

Constance Babington Smith doesn't say so—but there is a case for claiming that the long-range camera, fitted in Spitfires and Mosquitos, was the decisive weapon of the war.

DUDS

Fortunately for this country, the Germans were duds at "interpreting" air photographs whereas our experts were the finest in the world.

I recommend this book without qualification. And I suggest to the publishers that it should be followed by a full collection of the air pictures which provided the EVIDENCE IN CAMERA.

The twenty-three pages of pictures in this book are not enough!

CHAPTER 28
Hyena on trial

Dora Szafran walks into the courtroom and, as she strides to the witness stand to testify, she takes a hard look at Irma Grese. Grese stares back at Dora. When she leaves the stand, she again glares at Grese, who breaks the gaze to look about the court, shake her hair back, and ignore her accuser. It is September 25, 1945, and today will be the first day Irma Grese shall be named as a tormenter in the Belsen trials.

The prosecution has gathered survivors whose negative experiences with Irma Grese (and her co-defendants) may be recalled in clear, concise testimony. The elderly, children, and the very traumatized will not be questioned; the prosecution knows some of their recollections leave doubt due to age and disposition. Given this criteria, Dora Szafran is an excellent witness.

Former Belsen prisoner Dora Szafran will attest she witnessed Grese shoot the two girls who jumped out of a window to escape selection. She will also testify to Grese's arrogance, her carrying a pistol, and how Grese would beat prisoners for wearing what Grese considered the incorrect stockings or shoes.

Twenty-one-year-old Hungarian Ilona Stein survived the Holocaust. She will be taking the stand to testify against her captors. She easily identifies Josef Kramer and Irma Grese. "Three attractive girls in the court, obviously from Belsen, jumped up delightedly as Miss Stein walked across and identified Kramer and Irma Grese by name" a journalist would later report in the Maple *Leaf* newspaper. [365]

Ilona testifies how roll call (*Appelle*) was brutal and, at times, deadly. She remembers people dropping dead as they stood, and their bodies being left in place. Ilona discusses selections. "Grese nearly always took part in the selections… if (prisoners) could not come to roll call they were sent away to the crematorium." She also testifies how the only water allowed prisoners "was that lying on the roads" and it was only to be had by "influence and was considered a real treat." [366] Prisoners would slurp the filthy water as they lay on the ground.

As Ilona describes Irma Grese using a whip to beat defenseless prisoners, Helene Grese sits in the gallery with bowed head sobbing into her hands. Helene will be a regular fixture in the gallery, attending daily, staying from the opening of the courtroom doors to court adjourning. Helene was allowed to visit her sister on one day. There is no official record of what was said or discussed.

Patently, Helene is not the sole spectator in the gallery who knows Irma Grese personally. A newspaper article in the *Daily Mirror* notes at the end of the day's trial on September 24, Grese was leaving the dock with the others when she "looked up to the gallery, smiled and waved to a Czech girl who was a prisoner at Belsen." The unnamed girl smiled down. The woman was not identified except she was now employed by "the Americans in Germany." [367]

They had all just witnessed the testimony of Zofia Litwinska, a Polish officer's wife who, for reasons unknown, had accidently been caught in a gas chamber of naked victims

[365] Describes "Leg Inspections" of Women (1945, 27 September)
[366] Belsen Trial: Witness Accuses Irma Grese (1945). P. 1
[367] Irma of Belsen Smiled and Waved (1945, September 25) no pg. number.

and rescued just before she was killed. Zofia told of the naked women who screamed until they died from the fumes, the strong supporting the weak, and how she could not see anything due to the tears in her eyes.

On Wednesday, September 26, Helen Hammermasch testifies. "I did not personally see (Irma Grese) do anything," Helen explains. "I heard she beat up people." [368]

Abraham Glinowiecki survived three years in Auschwitz; his brother died from a beating a few days prior to liberation. He had observed Irma Grese daily due to his work detail. He recognizes Grese as the camp leader at Camp C. Abraham witnessed Grese making selections when a large group of Hungarians arrived at the camp. He would see her walking in and out of huts for inspections, and always carrying a stick and a pistol. Abraham wears an American army uniform when he takes the stand to testify on September 26. As the questions began regarding his brother, emotion overtakes him, and the man cannot continue. Abraham is examined by the medical officer on duty, and is deemed unable to endure, so his testimony will continue the next day. The court adjourns.

September 27 and Abraham Glinowiecki appears again on the stand. He identifies several of the defendants, and then he identifies Irma Grese, who stands on the court's command and listens to his testimony. Abraham testifies again that Grese oversaw C-camp and had sent many prisoners to the gas chambers. He states he had personally witnessed Grese beating prisoners and carrying a gun. One news journalist will describe Abraham's voice as "husky" when the survivor details witnessing Grese selecting "thousands and thousands of people" for the gas chambers of Auschwitz, with "the eyes of the whole court trained upon her." The testimony lasts "three minutes" during which time Grese's face begins to "flush." [369] This was considered a rare sign of emotional response from Grese.

"Irma Grese breaks down at last" the headline read in the September 28, 1945, edition of the *Daily Mirror*. The unnamed journalist noted how "stony-faced" Grese "broke down and wept" [370] when she investigated the gallery and saw her brother (Otto) now sitting and observing the trial. Otto was wounded twice on the Eastern front before taken captive by the Americans; he has been allowed to attend the trial. Otto's photo would later be taken with Helene as they stood outside of the courtroom. (He is allowed to visit Irma during lunchtime.)

It is on this date defendant Helene Kopper [371] begins screaming hysterically and must be taken out of the courtroom. A military policeman observed Kopper spitting on the floor during the trial; he nudged her to stop and Kopper began screaming abuse. It takes about ten minutes before the court can continue.

---

368 Belsen Trial Transcripts (1945).

369 "She flushed in court…" (1945). P. 1

370 In some publications he is identified as Alfred, also her brother.

371 Kopper arrived at Belsen on December 27, 1944. She would testify in court she was an "assistant" to a *Blockälteste*, playing down her role. She was known to be tough, not at all lenient as she will claim.

Q. How did she behave to the internees? A. She behaved very badly indeed. She was beating the prisoners for things like improperly not a scarf, or boot laces improperly made up.

Q. What did she beat them with? A. Mainly with her hands.

Q. The next woman you recognised was No.9 (Grese). What can you tell the court about her? A. From Auschwitz I can say very little about her, but in Belsen she was work leader, arbeitsdeinstfuhrer.

Q. How did she behave? A. In the same way, very badly. On one occasion our kommando was coming back from work and one of the girls lost a piece of rag from the pocket. As a punishment for this the accusedmade the whole kommando run up and down, kneeling and rising, and it lasted about half an hour.

Q. The next person whom you recognised was No.10 (Ilse Lothe) What do you say about her? A. I cannot say anything about her. I know only that she had some special function in the camp, but I do not know anything about her.

Q. In which camp? A. In Belsen.

Q. Now No.11 (Hilde Lobauer). A. I know her from Auschwitz and from Belsen, but I do not know anything particular about her, because I was outside the camp and she was in the camp.

Q. No.16 was the next one (Karl Flrazich). A. He came to the same cookhouse that I worked in in order to learn the job because he intended to obtain a job in another cookhouse. He was a short time there and during that time he was beating the personnel in the cookhouse terribly, so we were trembling when he came.

Q. Now No.34 (Ida Forster). A. I do not know anything special about her; she was an aufseherin.

Q. Do you know her name? A. I know her only by sight.

Q. Where was she aufseherin? A. It was in Belsen. She led the kommandos for work.

The original transcript from the eleventh day of the Belsen trials, Friday, September 28, 1945. Colonel Backhouse questions Holocaust survivor Lidia Sunschein. Lidia explains she and her family arrived at Auschwitz on July 22, 1944, a Monday night. Her entire family was promptly sent to the gas chambers. Lidia knew Irma Grese from both Auschwitz and Belsen. She describes Grese's behavior towards prisoners as part of her testimony. Lidia Sunschein is just one of the survivors who testified against Grese. (Circa 1945. Location: archival. The Belsen Trial Transcripts. Public Domain.)

Both Josef Kramer and Irma Grese scribble notes during the trial. Grese writes notes to herself. *Kopf hoch!* She would write to remind herself to hold her "head high!" [372]

On September 29, Helene Klein testifies about the "sport" the SS guards enjoyed. Grese had prisoners line up in rows of five and, upon Grese's command, were made to exercise drills on command: stand up, sit down, stand up, sit down … nonstop, for hours. Helene Klein also observed Irma Grese with a whip and pistol at various times.

Some witnesses, survivors of the camps, wrote depositions against the defendants. Some legal factions considered depositions unfair. It was unusual for judicial consent. Given the situation, depositions were allowed in this trial. Several depositions, read on October 3, confirm Irma Grese beat and kicked prisoners until the victims fainted or managed to survive.

On the sixteenth day of trial, October 4, 1945, another such deposition (Belsen Trial exhibit 53) was written and signed by Klara Lebowitz, who had been transferred from Auschwitz to Belsen in January 1945. Klara stated she had observed the *Appelle*, with Irma Grese in charge, and how it could last from hours into an all-day event. She confirmed female prisoners were to stand for hours during count without food or water. Anyone who wavered was beaten to the ground with a rubber truncheon. Some were made to kneel holding heavy stones over their heads per Grese's orders. Some of the victims were beaten so badly they were taken to the clinic.

On the same date, survivor Edith Trieger, also transferred to Belsen from Auschwitz, testifies against her former captors. Her testimony includes what she observed in the camp and Irma Grese. Edith had watched as a Hungarian woman stood outside of her block watching arrivals from the train. Grese rode up on a bicycle, ordered the Hungarian woman back into the block, and without hesitation shot the woman dead. Grese had not given the woman time to follow the order. Grese calmly rode her bicycle away out of sight. Edith had also watched helplessly as Grese beat women with her hands and the truncheon, unprovoked, kicking them, and sending some to the gas chamber.

Luba Triszinska was a nurse to babies in a Belsen camp unit. She had also been a member of an *Arbeitskommando* at Auschwitz, with a group on foot who followed Irma Grese on her bicycle. Grese brought along a large dog. They went into the woods to pick herbs. Anyone who could not keep up the pace was sent to the gas chamber on Grese's orders.

More former prisoners take the stand to tell of atrocities committed by Irma Grese. Hedda Gomba, Auschwitz survivor, testifies. She would later be interviewed for the Shoah Foundation's Visual History Archive (VHA). She would state in the VHA interview, "I remember only (Grese). Because she was an attractively beautiful beast."

Another survivor, Cecilia Einhorn, also testifies at the Belsen trial; she will also discuss Grese on VHA, "such a beautiful girl, a German, who loved to go around and shoot people, you know, the (prisoners) all over." Cecilia never personally encountered Grese, admitting, like all the other prisoners, "we were afraid of her! No, thank God! I did not have direct contact with her. (Grese) killed our people... for her, take something and go around wherever she saw a girl, maybe two, and she was just going around and killing … killing women... killing young women!" [373]

---

[372] Lustgarten, E. (1968). P.102.

[373] Cited in Vida (2016), pp. 535-6.

And on and on they testify of the barbarisms they suffered at the hands of people who beat, kicked, starved, mutilated, and left them for dead; keepers who treated them less than animals, who forced human beings to live in filth, squalid conditions of disease and waste. The torturers included Irma Grese.

There are two constant themes when witnesses are describing Irma Grese. One was that she was particularly brutal, so much more brutal than other female guards and many of the males. "She was the worst of the SS women," one deposition read. [374] The second theme was Grese's physical attractiveness, and how it clashed, in the survivor's opinions, with Grese's brutality. This was never the case with any other defendant, male or female.

As part of courtroom proceedings on October 5, Prosecutor Col. T. M. Backhouse reads affidavits that Grese had been writing for the last month, with objections from the defense. Grese's affidavits explain how her father had beaten her for being part of the concentration camp system, and how all the SS were guilty. Knowing about the gas chambers and mass killings, Grese had written, "I have hidden mothers and children during selection in order that they might not be chosen. I once was denounced by Jews who were used as spies... and given special privileges. I was put under arrest in my room for two days." Her confessions conflicted: in one affidavit she explains she never beat anyone; in another, she admits to physically hitting prisoners. Head bowed, biting her lips, Grese listens to the confessions as Backhouse reads them aloud to the court. "The ill-treatment of prisoners … has been on my conscience…" [375]

On the same day, a witness testifies and recalls Grese's "sport" in having prisoners unknowingly walk into a restricted area and shot to death. Grese enjoyed selecting prisoners who did not speak German so they would not understand the warning shouts. Grese would force an interpreter to tell these women to cross the barrier, and when they seemingly ignored the SS guard's shouted warnings it amused Grese how they were shot down. Grese, says the witness, laughed when the dead were carried away by prisoners.

Former SS guard Peter Weingartner testifies on October 10, 1945, the twenty-first day of the trial. Weingartner is attempting to save his own life and claims to strike a prisoner only once. Grese loses her angry countenance and claps her hand over her mouth to suppress laughter.

More laughter from Grese, along with Lothe and Ehlert, erupts when Rosina Kramer, Josef's wife, responds to a question on the stand. Rosina Kramer testifies her husband was an emotional wreck when he came home from his shift. He would pace the floor crying about the treatment of prisoners at Auschwitz. The three women giggle together, shoulders hunched and leaning into each other like tittering schoolgirls.

It is one of the few days Rosina Kramer can attend the trial. Because of their three children, and living in Wathlingen, she is unable to be there for Josef. Rosina is leaving court on October 10 when a woman on the street rushes up to slap Mrs. Kramer on the face. The woman was a witness for the prosecutor, lingering with other witnesses in a courtyard. "Your husband killed my husband and children in Auschwitz!" One of the witnesses shouted at Rosina as police rushed to her side. "You still have your children!" [376] Rosina is escorted away as the shout echoed in the ears of other witnesses.

---

[374] The Belsen Trials. Deposition of Gitla Dunkleman.
[375] " Hájková by Nazi woman" (1945). Pp. 1-2.
[376] Kramer's wife slapped (10-10-1945.)

The court glimpses into the harsh reality of camp survival on October 15. Former *Aufseherin* Herta Ehlert testifies she allowed female prisoners to beat another prisoner for snitching. Helena Kopper, a prisoner who was spying on her fellow captives for the SS, had reported three other female prisoners were holding jewelry. The charge was false. Ehlert turned Kopper over to the other females. The women attacked Kopper. It brought a chuckle from the courtroom; Major General H.P. M. Berney chastised those laughing observers.

A Soviet documentary is next, revealing the conditions of Auschwitz Jews upon liberation by the Red Army. There is no laughter now. The defendants watch the film intently – all except Irma Grese, who turns to whisper to Herta Ehlert. Grese appears to have no interest in the black and white images of horror.

Officials ensure the Belsen prisoners are treated fairly and justly, but without any privileges. A "Diet Sheet" for October 1 to 7, 1945, reports the meals and grams allotted to each prisoner for every day. For Monday's supper, Irma Grese and her comrades are served "potato soup 1400g., margarine 10g., and bread at 200g." 1610 calories to last until Tuesday morning, where "bread and coffee 300g" will be served. On average, each Belsen prisoner consumes 6,670 calories daily. [377] (In 1944, as the German war economy was crashing, Bergen-Belsen prisoners were lucky to receive 700 calories daily.) Each prisoner's weight is carefully monitored. On October 14, Irma Grese is weighed in and the report indicates she has gained 1.2kg. On October 21, she gains .5 The starchy diet of mostly potatoes and bread, and the lack of exercise, has added a few pounds at 67.5kg (about 149lbs) in mid-October. [378]

On October 16, 1945, Major Cranfield presents an opening speech for his clients in which he declares, "Brigadier Glyn Hughes said there was no shame or privacy in Belsen. With all due respect, a large number of the camp inmates have never known privacy before." [379] It would not be the last time Major Cranfield would apply what appears now as victim blaming/shaming. Given the job of defense it may be one of few possible tactics. It is a difficult line he walks, defending the accused while respecting the survivors and their loved ones.

[377] P. Clapham Collection, United States Holocaust Memorial Museum. Accession Number: 1994.A.0022.

[378] Weight check sheet, 14 October – 21 October 1945.

[379] Belsen Trial Transcripts, cited in *Institutional repository oops* (n.d.) p. 55

hear again of her many cruelties at Belsen.

No. 8, Ehlert, was an S.S. guard. She joined the S.S. on the 15th November, 1940. She claims to have been a conscript. You will hear that after a career in various concentration camps she eventually arrived in Belsen, after a spell first of all in Auschwitz. She was the second in command of the women, and like so many others she considers that the conditions there were a shame and disgrace, but, of course, were caused by everybody other than herself.

The next, Irma Grese, was the Commandant of working parties, and for a time was in command of the womens punishment quarter at Auschwitz. She has been described by some of the people as the worst woman in the camp, and there is not one type of cruelty which took place in that camp for which she has not been known as being responsible. She regularly took part in the selections for the gas chamber, made up punishments of her own, and when she came to Belsen she carried on in precisely the same way. She too specialised in setting dogs on people. She has made three statements which vary interestingly. I will not go into the details of them now, but you will see how gradually the light comes to her when her memory returns, and she gives some very interesting accounts of her own antecedents.

The next one is Gura, who was a block fuhrer there. You will hear evidence of at least two murders by him there.

The next is Schreirer, who was in charge of block 230, a block fuhrer. There again you will hear evidence of his regular cruelty.

These are the S.S. members who were in Auschwitz. The remaining three persons charged in respect of Auschwitz are Ilse Lothe, No. 10, Lobauer, No. 11, and Storoska, No. 48. These three were themselves prisoners. You will hear that they were referred to as Capos, which is a universal term applied to prisoners placed in authority, or as block altesters, or lager attesters. Lobauer was in charge of the womens working parties there, and you will hear that she was just as cruel in her treatment as any of the S.S. women and encouraged S.S. women to turn dogs on internees. Lobauer, No. 11, was the lager capos, that is to say, the leading woman prisoner in the camp. She took an active part in the selection of victims for the gas chamber and in many other cruelties. Lastly, No. 47, who was first of all a block altester for one of the blocks and later lager altester, and took an equal part in the cruelties. These are the persons concerned with Auschwitz.

With regard to the others at Belsen, I can take a group fairly quickly together. I do not propose to go into any detail about them beyond saying that these persons were all S.S. men in charge of or working in kitchens.

No. 12, Klippel, No. 16 Flrazich, No. 18 Mathes, No. 22 Pinchon, No. 28 Barsch, No. 33 Ilse Forster, No. 34 Ida Forster, No. 39 Haschke, No. 42 Lisiewitz, No. 44 Hempel. They all worked in the kitchens, and you will hear again how each and every one of those people behaved to the internees. If you ever had any doubt as to whether there was evidence of

38.

Page 38 of the Belsen Trial transcripts. Coronel Backhouse, acting as Council for the Prosecution, discussing the defendants tells the court that Grese was "… the worst of the women guards." Note his handwritten notations. (Circa 1945. Location: archives. Public domain.)

Helene ("Leni") - Artist's rendering of Irma's sister, who supported her. Seeing her family members at trial was the only time Irma Grese cried in public. (Circa: 2024. Artwork: fiverr.com/nobestudio, copyright J. A. Yates)

Otto Grese. Artist's rendering of Irma's brother, who as a POW was allowed to leave jail and attend Irma's trial. (Circa: 2024. Artwork: fiverr.com/nobestudio. copyright J. A. Yates)

Q Anything else ? A And that sometimes she had been detailed to guard duties.

Q Now so far as you are aware, as your sister any experience with firearms ? A No.

Q In this case it is alleged that your sister killed by shooting with a pistol prisoners on four occasions. I want you to tell the Court what you think of that.

COLONEL BACKHOUSE: I do not want to interrupt my friend, and I want to give every latitude I can, but where are we getting ? This girl says she has only seen her sister twice since she was a child. First she is asked if her sister has any experience of firearms, and now she is asked what she thinks about the Prosecution's evidence. Really I think it is going too far.

THE PRESIDENT: I think you are right; I quite agree. She cannot say that.

MAJOR CRANFIELD: If you please. (To the witness): In this case your sister is accused of savagely striking prisoners under her charge so that they were left in a bleeding condition. What do you think of that ?

COLONEL BACKHOUSE: Again I object. This girl cannot give expressions of opinion on the Prosecution's case.

THE PRESIDENT: I do not think you can ask those questions as to what the witness thinks of the Prosecution's case. So far as I see it those are not statements of fact at all.

MAJOR CRANFIELD: In my submission this girl is the sister of the accused and knows her better than anybody else present. The accused is accused as a very young girl of acts of very great savagery and cruelty, and I think this witness can say, as her sister, whether she thinks her sister is a person likely to do that or not. I do not say it goes for very much.

COLONEL BACKHOUSE: She has seen her sister twice in the last seven years. If she likes to give evidence as to facts which happened seven years ago, or to say her sister was a good girl at home, which is always very popular in Courts, I do not mind.

THE PRESIDENT: I do not think she can express opinion on evidence which has been produced by the Prosecution.

MAJOR CRANFIELD: From your knowledge of your sister, do you think her a person likely to beat the prisoners under her charge ? A No.

Q Have you any reason for saying that ? A I know it from our school days when, as it sometimes happens, girls were quarreling and fighting. My sister in such a case had never the courage to fight, but on the contrary she ran away.

Q Is there anything else you would like to say about the charges against your sister.

COLONEL BACKHOUSE: Well, really ----

THE PRESIDENT: I do not think she can criticise the charges against her sister.

MAJOR CRANFIELD: Very well.

(There was no cross-examination by the remaining Defending Officers.)

18.

From the Belsen Trial transcript: Helene Grese's partial testimony on October 16, 1945. Helene Grese was the sole Grese family member who testified for her sister, Irma. Helene attended the entire trial. She sobbed when Irma received the death penalty. (Circa 1945. Location: archival. The Belsen Trial Transcripts. Public Domain.)

CHAPTER 29
"An elephant out of a fly!"

It is still October 16 when Helene Grese steps into the witness box to testify on her sister's behalf. She is one of the few family members who will testify for any defendant. Helene, often called "Leni" by the press, is twenty years old, dressed in a handsome suit with skirt. Major Cranfield will be questioning her.

As Helene readies herself, Irma Grese, the Hyena of Auschwitz, shocks many when she breaks down and begins crying. She uses a handkerchief, and her tears spill over reddened cheeks as her sister begins answering questions.

Helene is asked for her opinion on the allegations of her sister using a gun, and then for her opinion on her sister beating prisoners. Both questions are overruled. The questions are now redirected; does Helene believe her sister is capable of physical abuse?

Helene explains Irma ran from schoolyard altercations between little girls. When asked for her thoughts on the charges against her sister, the question is struck; Helene cannot comment on the legal charges.

Helene shares how Irma's childhood was an unhappy one, with torments from fellow students at school and an abusive father at home. She explains where and when Irma had been employed prior to the Nazi camps, and when Helene last visited Irma. She describes the 1943 family reunion: Irma had written she was coming home on leave; Helene worked to make it a happy family get-together by gathering all the siblings around for a one-day celebration – "siblings" meaning Irma's full blood sisters and brothers. Their discussion about Irma's work in the camps, Helene insists, was always very limited.

She is asked, "From your knowledge of your sister, do you think her a person likely to beat the prisoners under her charge?"

"No," Helene says with conviction.

Colonel Backhouse cross-examines Helene. Helene remembers Irma did come home in uniform but was dressed in civilian clothing when she was home. She testifies to her knowledge of Irma and their father quarreling over Irma joining the SS, but she did not know if their father gave Irma "a thrashing" or why he forbids her to return to the home.

Major Cranfield then re-examines Helene. "When did you last see your father?"

"April 1945," Helene responds.

"Where is he now?"

"I do not know."

"Is he alive?" She is asked.

"I do not know." [380]

And with that, Helene steps off the stand.

Trial nurse Norma Falk leaves her seat beside the military police to accompany each female defendant when they walk to the stand to testify, "in case they fainted or something." She would escort the defendant back to her seat when the testimony ended. Two hours after Helene steps off the stand, the nurse accompanies Irma Grese to testify. The "dreadful wardress" Nurse Falk would later call her. [381]

---

[380] Belsen Trial transcript, testimony of Helene Grese, October 16, 1945

[381] Grunwald-Spier. Electronic copy no pg. number

Grese, eyes clear and demeanour calm, steps up on the dais in front of the microphone to testify. The *Toronto Star* would report "Blonde Irma Grese … looked more like a society fashion model than an accused murderer and torturer." [382] This article further elaborates on her appearance, specifically her attire, writing: "She stepped smartly to the stand, a striking figure in a well-tailored gray suit, pale blue blouse, and sheer silk stockings." [383]

She is sworn in to be examined by the prosecution, Colonel Backhouse. In her lap are copies of the affidavits against her, written in German.

She becomes angrier the longer she is questioned.

Irma Grese is keenly aware her life is on the line and does her best to save herself. Despite testimony after testimony, some from her own former coworkers, she makes denials or redirects the questions and comments. Like many of her counterparts, Grese claims she was forced into employment at the camp. As McGuiness (2021) notes, "They portrayed themselves as ignorant helpers - easily done in patriarchal post-war West Germany. Records show that some new recruits did leave Ravensbrück as soon as they realized what the job involved. They were allowed to go and did not suffer negative consequences."

Irma Grese, on the stand, relays a short account of her life, blaming the Labor Exchange for blocking her nursing career. The Labor Exchange was the reason she went to work in the camps. She answers to only what is asked and does not pontificate. She adds when and what camps she was employed, then her duties at the concentration camps.

She states the only "stick" she carried was "a walking stick" and admits to having a special whip made – "a very light whip," she calls the weapon. Grese denies carrying a truncheon. She only carried a gun for self-protection later in her work, but it was "never loaded." Grese makes multiple denials on the stand about the accusations of random and wanton shooting of prisoners.

Once prisoners arrived, Grese was reminded, the arriving prisoners were not told what would occur; those selected to live were rushed thorough showers, sprayed with disinfectant, their bodies brutally shorn, and placed in castoff clothing that never fit – sometimes, filthy, or blood-soaked clothes. Even this she played down. "They went into the washhouse, washed, had their hair cut…" she explains the process as if it were voluntary. [384]

At one point in her testimony, the court can hear just how skewed Irma Grese's logic had become when she explains her custom-made whip was used only when she was forced to punish prisoners. When the prison became so overcrowded "… a great deal was stolen and prisoners did not obey my orders, even though they were quite light orders. Every day there were complaints of things stolen from the kitchen." Grese placed two

[382] "Blond Irma, Dressed up on Belsen Stand."

[383] Iblid.

[384] Belsen Trial Transcripts, testimony of Irma Grese, October 16, 1945

there in this weaving factory they made all sorts of things and I had the idea to have made a whip out of cellophane.

Q What colour was it ? A It was translucentlike white glass.

Q Did it look like a riding whip ? A It was so long, and it had a swinging effect. (The witness demonstrates).

Q A type of switch you would use for a horse ? A Yes.

Q Then most of these prisoners who said they saw you carrying a riding whip were not far wrong, were they ? A No, they were not wrong.

Q They were cross-examined, and it was suggested they were talking awful nonsense, but it was right, was it not ? A My idea about a riding whip is quite different.

Q When did you have this whip made ? A From May to December, 1944.

Q That is when you were in lager "C" ? A Yes.

Q Did the other aufseherin have these whips made too ? A No.

Q It was just your bright idea ? A Yes.

Q Of course, in lager "C" you used to carry a walking stick too, did you not ? A Yes.

Q And you beat people sometimes with the whip and sometimes with the stick ? A Yes.

Q Were you allowed to beat people ? A No.

Q So it was not a question of having orders from your superiors to do it; you did this against orders, did you ? A Yes.

Q Pretty well everybody in the camp did it, did they not ? A I do not know.

Q Was it just you who was vicious ? A It has nothing to do with being vicious.

Q Were you the only person who beat the prisoners against the regulations ? A I do not know.

Q Did you go about with your eyes shut ? A On the contrary, I had my eyes always open.

Q Did you never see anyone else beat prisoners ? A Yes.

Q Then why keep saying "I do not know" when you are asked if they did ? A Maybe they got perhaps an order to beat; I cannot say; I cannot know.

Q That was not what you were asked. You knew quite well what you were asked. I asked you whether you saw anyone else beating prisoners in Auschwitz and you said, "I do not know". A No, you asked me whether the others were beating in spite of contrary orders, in spite of being prohibited to beat. My answer was, therefore, I do not know because I do not know whether maybe they got an order for that particular purpose.

Q Did you sometimes get orders to beat ? A No.

8.

Belsen Trial transcript page. The typed transcripts were taken from trial shorthand. Irma Grese's partial testimony during her second day on the stand on October 17, 1945. Colonel Backhouse conducts this re-examination. Here she details the whip she used to beat prisoners. (Circa 1945. Location: archival. The Belsen Trial Transcripts. Public Domain.)

guards in the kitchen; if thieves are caught, she ordered these guards to give the thief "a good thrashing." In the living quarters, any prisoner making boots or coats from blankets was ordered to turn these items in; it was considered theft and destruction of property. No one turned in these items, so she had to use her whip "on those occasions." [385] Her replies are carefully constructed: punishments were meted out for infractions only. If the prisoners were struck, it was never with force.

Grese also states she had never struck a prisoner to where they fell to the ground or hit them so badly, they needed medical care; she never caused a prisoner to bleed. She did tell the truth to one question:

> Backhouse: what was the condition of the prisoners at Belsen?
>
> Irma Grese: the condition of the prisoners were [sic] so bad that one had almost a horror of them. [386]

Irma Grese describes the roll calls, the *appell,* distancing herself from the selection process. She explains making prisoners kneel was only a way to keep them still so count procedure would go quickly.

No, she never had a dog. She was asked repeatedly if she had ever shot anyone, including a Hungarian woman who had stood outside of her block watching arrivals from the train. Grese finally loses her reserve to shout, "I never shot a prisoner! I never shot anyone!" [387]

Irma Grese changes the "making sport" incidents – where she forced women into the prohibited zones only to be shot – into a long-winded story about prisoners throwing packages of meat. She makes herself the kind hero of the story.

She leaves the stand on the first day, transported back to prison as every evening. The meal is the same: soup. Grese reportedly slept 45 minutes that night. She would return the next day just as defensive.

Irma Grese again takes the stand on October 17, 1945. Colonel Backhouse conducts the re-examination.

Grese tells more lies and half-truths as the trial wears on. Again, her logic – or lack thereof – reveals a manipulative mind. Most of her answers, in the beginning, are "no," "yes," and "I don't know" or "I cannot remember."

Colonel Backhouse asks a question in which Grese snaps "I was not interested in that."

Backhouse, not about to be intimidated, responds, "Well interest yourself now" and asks another question. [388]

The survivors who had written affidavits telling of her cruelty, Backhouse asks, "Are they all wrong?"

"Yes, all wrong," Irma Grese retorts. "These people exaggerated; they made an elephant out of a small fly." [389]

---

[385] Ibid
[386] Ibid
[387] "Belsen Woman Guard Weeps, Denies Guilt…"
[388] Belsen Trial Transcripts, testimony of Irma Grese, October 17, 1945
[389] Belsen Trial Transcripts, cited in Adele-Marie, p.122

Colonel Backhouse reminds her, "they say that you were the worse SS woman in the camp."

Grese shoots back, "Yes, they say so."

"You did get rather rapid promotion for a young girl, did you not?" He demands.

"No. During my service of two years."

Some of the accused were defiant on the stand. Others were muddled in their ignorance. Irma Grese was arrogant and coolly answered the questions thrown at her from the prosecution, who had tired of her "I do not know" responses:

> Backhouse: Did you go around with your eyes shut?
>
> Grese: On the contrary, I had my eyes always open.
>
> Backhouse: Did you ever see other prisoners beaten?
>
> Grese: Yes.
>
> Backhouse: Then why keep saying "I don't know" when you are asked if they did?
>
> Grese: Maybe they got perhaps an order to beat; I cannot say, I cannot know.
>
> Backhouse: That is not what you were asked. You knew quite well what you were asked. I asked whether you saw anyone else beating prisoners in Auschwitz and you said, "I do not know."
>
> Grese: No, you asked me if the other were beating in spite of contrary orders, in spite of being prohibited to beat. My answer was; therefore, I do not know because I do not know whether maybe they got an order for that particular purpose.[390]

"At times she was so furious that she beat against the microphone" one court journalist will report. [391]

The trial is only halfway through, and at closing Grese would be considered the most arrogant, the most sarcastic, of all the defendants. She refused to bend to Backhouse's accusations or anger. Her questioning lasted for hours due in part to her impudence. Backhouse asked a follow-up question to a question from the previous day on the stand, and Grese told him smartly she had already answered him:

> Backhouse: I know you told us yesterday. You see I am suggesting you did not tell us the truth yesterday.
>
> Grese: I have sworn to tell the truth and that is what I have been doing.

[390] The Belsen Trials, testimony of Irma Grese, October 17, 1945

[391] Schultz (1945). P. 8

Backhouse reminded Grese's "favorite habit," according to a Holocaust survivor, was to kick prisoners.

Grese: (perhaps it was the prisoner's) favorite habit to lie.

Nurse Norma Falk sits next to Grese when Grese is on the stand, as with all female defendants. She will later tell in an interview how she was "horrified by it all…" And recounted Grese's belligerence on the witness stand. [392]

She came from a small dairy farm, the prosecution asks, so how was she so quickly promoted to the highest office a woman could hold in the camp? Was it because she was so cruel? Irma Grese snarls, "that is nothing to do with the dairy."

The prosecution wonders if she was cruel to prisoners because of the schoolyard bullying. Was it payback?

Irma Grese: "yes, it might have been that I was frightened when I was a child, but I grew up in the meantime." [393]

The prosecutor asked Grese if there was "a big difference" between the gas chamber or being beaten to death and "she shrugged." [394]

"I always believed that the prisoners liked me. But now I see that they were all against me," Irma Grese will tell the court. [395] She adds that "no" prisoners were ever "hostile" towards her. [396]

[392] USC Shoah Foundation

[393] The Belsen Trials, testimony of Irma Grese, October 17, 1945

[394] Schultz

[395] *Zitiert nach* (10 August1945). *Irma Grese gesteht – "Sie widerruft frühere Aussage, in: Neues Oldenburger Tageblatt.*" cited in *Institutional repository oops* (n.d.) p. 62

[396] Phillips, R. (1949) cited in *Institutional repository oops* (n.d.) p. 56

The Hyena Caged

Lüneburg prison and court building as it appeared in 2016. Irma Grese and her codefendants were held in this prison during trial. (Circa 2016. Location: Lüneburg. Photo by Joanna Czopowicz. Courtesy of: Joanna Czopowicz. Used with permission.)

Grese

23 Uhr nicht geschlafen
24 " geschlafen
1 " geschlafen
2 " geschlafen
3 " geschlafen
4 " geschlafen
5 " nicht geschlafen

Lüneburg, den [illegible]

[illegible]

Hopper

11^oo geschlafen
12^oo geschlafen
1^oo nicht geschlafen
2^oo geschlafen
3^oo nicht geschlafen
4^oo geschlafen
5^oo nicht geschlafen

[illegible]

Lüneburg, den 27.10.45

Starostka

11^oo geschlafen
12^oo nicht geschlafen
1^oo geschlafen
2^oo geschlafen
3^oo geschlafen
4^oo geschlafen
5^oo geschlafen

[illegible]

Lüneburg, den 27.10.45

Activity check card for Irma Grese

Opposite page: Activity checks

Hourly checks were conducted for the safety of the defendants held in prison during trial. Irma Grese's card (top) reveals:

20:00 -- not asleep
24:00 -- asleep
o1:00 -- asleep
02:00 -- asleep
03:00 asleep
04:00 asleep
05:00 not asleep

(Circa: 1945. Location: Archival, Image courtesy United States Holocaust Memorial Museum Collection, Gift of the Canadian War Museum. Used with permission)

Irma Grese's cell in Celle prison probably resembled this cell. Records have been destroyed, so there is no sure way to identify her true cell number.

German: *"Justizvollzugsanstalt Celle, Zelle 17",*
English: "Judicial Penal Institution of Celle, cell 17".
(Circa: 1945? Location: Celle. Photographer: unknown. Public Domain.)

All translations by Ann Marie Ackerman, J.D. www.annmarieackermann.com.

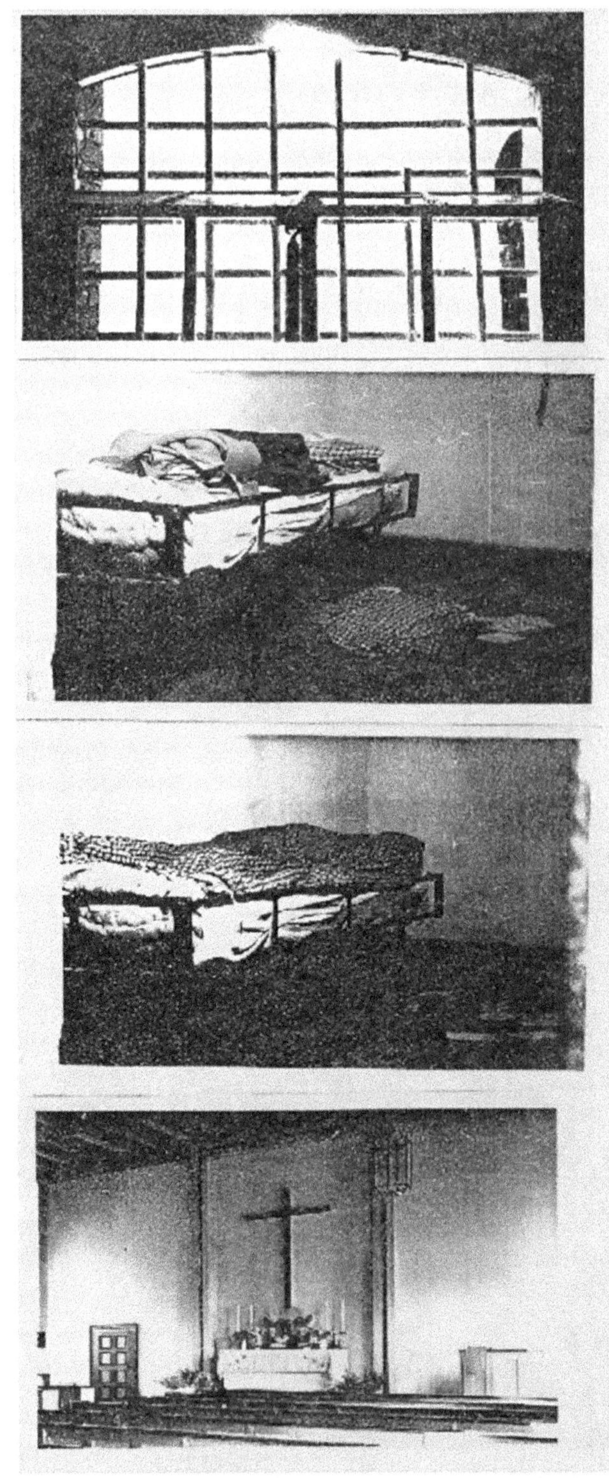

Irma Grese and her co-defendants were held at Celle Prison during the Belsen Trial. These are copies of photos showing a prisoner's cell and the chapel. Gone were the nice houses and apartments with fine household necessities procured from the dead. (Circa 1945. Location: Celle Prison. Credit: United States Holocaust Memorial Museum Collection, Gift of the Canadian War Museum. Used with permission.

AUSTRALIAN AIR BILL

LENI GRESE, SISTER OF IRMA GRESE, who was executed recently for her part in the Belsen camp atrocities, is shown here presenting her credentials in an attempt to pay a birthday visit on Irma while she was in prison. The request, however, was refused.

Helene Grese was a constant while Irma Grese was incarcerated and during trial. New Zealand's *Waikato Times,* December 17, 1945, p. 5: Helene Grese attempting to visit her sister for a birthday. The British guards did not allow Helene access. The image was printed after Irma Grese's death. (Circa 1945, Location: Celle Prison, Lüneburg prison, or Hamelin Prison. Photographer: unknown. Courtesy Stuff.co.nz. Used with permission)

Diet - sheet for prisoners of the B e l s e n - T r i a l.

For the period between 24 Sep 45 - 30 Sep 45.

	Breakfast.		Dinner.		Supper	
MONDAY	Flour-soup(flour) Bred Sugar	80 gr. 60 " 60 "	Rye - gruel Potatoes Margarine Bread	80 gr. 1200 " 20 " 100 "	Potato Marger. Bread	1200 g 10 " 200"
TUESDAY	Bread Coffee	200 gr.	Carrotts Potatoes Meat Bread	600 gr. 1200 " 3.- kg. 100 gr.	Cheese Butter Coffee	200gr 20"
W[illegible]NESDAY	Bread Coffee	200 gr.	Barley - gruel Potatoes Margarine Bread	80 gr. 1200 " 20 " 100 "	Quaker-oats Milk Bread	100 g 1 lt 200 g
THURSDAY	Bread Coffee	200 gr.	Potatoes Meat Bread	1200 gr. 3.- kg 100 gr.	Potatoes Marger.	1200 g 10 "
FRIDAY	Bread Coffee	200 gr.	White-cabbage Potatoes Margerine Bread	400 gr. 1200 " 20 " 100 "	Cheese Butter Coffee Bread	100 gr 20 " 200 "
SATURDAY	Bread Coffee	150 gr.	Peas Potatoes Margerine Bread	100 gr. 1200 " 20 " 100 "	Marmel. Butter Bread Coffee	100 gr 40 gr 200 "
SUNDAY	Bread Coffee	200 gr.	Green beans Potatoes Meat Bread	600 gr. 1200 " 5.-kg. 100 gr.	Sausage Bread Coffee	60 gr 300 "

W.e.f. today 24 Sep. above is increased!—
Total bread daily 600 gr.
Potatoes — 200 gr. more daily.

[illegible signature]

Diet record for September 24 -30, 1945. It was important the defendants receive the proper amount of nutrition, so the prison and court were not accused of torture or abuse. (Circa 1945. Location: archival. Courtesy United States Holocaust Memorial Museum Collection, Gift of the Canadian War Museum. Used with permission)

Wiegeliste

der weiblichen Untersuchungsgefangenen und Zeugen des Belsen - Prozesses.

Nr.	Name.	Gewicht b. Einliefer.	14.10.45	21.10.45
6.	Bormann	44 kg	46 kg	46,5 kg
7.	Volkenrath	61 "	63,4 "	65 "
8.	Ehlert	77 "	77 "	79,5 "
9.	Grese	66 "	67,2 "	67,5 "
10.	Lothe	66,5 "	69,6 "	68,5 "
11.	Lohbauer	66 "	67,4 "	68 "
33.	Förster, Ilse	51 "	53,1 "	54 "
34.	Förster, Ida	49 "	47,4 "	50 "
3.	Opitz	63 "	64,2 "	65 "
36.	Klein,	67 "	69,3 "	69 "
37.	Bothe	64,5 "	68,1 "	67,7 "
38.	Walter	54 "	56,6 "	55,5 "
39.	Haschke	55 "	56,7 "	57,5 "
40.	Fiest	64 "	66,2 "	66 "
41.	Sauer	58,5 "	60,6 "	61,5 "
42.	Lisiewicz	62 "	64,2 "	65 "
43.	Roth	67 "	69,1 "	70 "
44.	Hempel	73 "	73,3 "	72,5 "
45.	Hähnel	64 "	66 "	67 "
46.	Kopper	81 "	81,7 "	80,3 "
48.	Starostka	62 "	63,7 "	64.2 "
	X			
	Koblischek	69 "	70 "	69,2 "
	Linke	53,5 "	55,5 "	54,5 "
	Reinhold	61,5 "	63 "	62,5 "
	Steinbusch	53,5 "	56 "	55 "
	Kambach	57 "	58,7 "	57 "
	Neumann	60 "	60,3 "	59,2 "

Belsen trial defendants were carefully monitored for their safety and health. Above is a record of inmate weights on October 14 & October 21, 1945. Irma Grese is listed as #9. Hangman Pierrepoint would need this information for his work, but also had the condemned to individually weigh before execution. (Circa: 1945. Location: archival. Image courtesy United States Holocaust Memorial Museum Collection, Gift of the Canadian War Museum. Used with permission)

CHAPTER 30
"Blonde and smartly dressed."

The Daily Herald (1945) tells its readers of Irma Grese on the stand: "She has been tempestuous. She has been calm. She has been everything but 21, which is her age." [397] It is one of many articles describing Irma Grese during the 54 days of trial, "more than 100 representatives of the news media reported at length on the tial's progress." [398] Some press members seem enamored by Grese's beauty and shocked by her deeds, though repulsed and intrigued by her history. That such a normal – even beautiful – woman could commit such atrocious acts was both appalling and a mystery, and it made great headlines. Like other memorable SS staff, such as Josef "The Beast of Belsen" Kramer, Grese was given a headline-grabbing alias: "The Beautiful Beast." [399] Monikers given by the press, akin to serial killers who made headlines during Grese's lifetime: Germany's Peter Kurten ("The Vampire of Dusseldorf") and Johann Eichhorn. ("The Beast of Aubing")

According to the press, Irma Grese wielded as much power at Belsen as Joseph Kramer, which is untrue. She was never equal in power to any man in her career. One historian calls Grese "the most notorious of the female war criminals … after the *Kommandant* of Bergen – Belsen, Josef Kramer, Irma Grese was the most notorious defendant in the Belsen trial." [400]

As if there could be a competition of evil deeds, or a list of "most evil," Grese would be compared to other "foul women" long after she was gone. During the trial she is compared to the other female defendants – and some of the males – and determined to be the "worst" or "as bad."

Court began in session at 10 a.m. and ended at 5 p.m. Each day of the trial, Grese brings a comb and spends time on her appearance. If there is a break and the defendants stay in their seats, she runs the comb through her hair. Some journalists guess she is preening for the boyfriend / defendant she had met in Belsen, the man that had kept her in Belsen where she was arrested. [401] While she may be preening for the cameras, recall she had also told her "Friends" that she always tried to look her best – perhaps she is still vying for that elusive movie role. Grese's hair is also a topic in numerous articles, the color, and the style. She is now wearing it differently than she wore it at work in the camps, however.

There may be a sinister reason Irma Grese is wearing her hair pulled behind her ears with the curls. (While employed in the camp Grese had kept her hair pinned up.) A witness against Grese had been asked to identify her. The witness was unsure if the woman sitting in the defendant's chair was truly Grese due to the hairstyle. The witness explained Grese wore her blonde hair *pinned up*. The prosecutor had prepared and presented photos taken of Grese in the camp. The witness easily identified Grese through these photographs. Irma Grese later admitted she had changed her hair style before the trial.

---

[397] Fagence, p.3

[398] Knoch, H. (2010). P. 37

[399] She was also labeled "The Beastess of Belsen," "The Queen of Belsen," "The Blonde Beastess," and "The Blonde Monster."

[400] Bulow, 2004

[401] This would have been Fritz Hartzinger, but recall Hartzinger had died from Typhus by the time of the Belsen Trial.

The press notes other details. Irma Grese had once told her "Friend," Holocaust survivor Magda Hellinger, how she dressed smartly and professionally to stand out. Court is no exception. While the other defendants wear their former uniforms, Grese is wearing various clothes and shoes, thanks to Helene who is delivering her civilian clothing.

Grese's dress is detailed in the press. While the male defendants are described only by their manner and expressions, Grese is described as "… wearing a smart skirt and a powder blue blouse." [402] Another newspaper notes the "… iron calm of blonde, smartly dressed Irma Grese." [403] Her demeanor also fascinates reporters as she sits impassively, observing the trial, and listening to witnesses recount her atrocities. When discussing her demeanor, her "good looks" usually come into play. From the *New York Times*, "the 21-year-old blonde … managed to maintain the defiant contemptuous look that marred her undeniable good looks." [404] The following *NYT* articles again uses "blonde" and "smartly dressed" to describe Irma Grese. [405] As one witness sits on the stand describing the horrors of Belsen, Grese "titivated her blonde curls" a reporter from *The Daily Herald* notes. [406] London's *Daily Worker* reports how "the little blonde … glared unwaveringly at all." [407] "Seated together are the female of the species with Irma Grese 'the blonde beastess' [*sic*] No. 9 in the centre," one newspaper writer explains the scene, and then adds, "This chief woman S.S. guard at Belsen has just had her hair permed." [408]

During the trial, the court travels to what was left of the Belsen camp to understand the geography. Not much is left – due to the rampant outbreak of typhus and other diseases, the liberators had burned most of it to the ground. Several newspaper writers noted Irma Grese is dressed nicely for the journey, to include a "beautiful pair of silk stockings (and) a neat pair of leather shoes … not many women would have refused them." [409]

An unnamed press writer adds, "It defies belief that such a pretty girl could be so cruel when she walked through the camp with her whip in her hand. She was surrounded by a cloud of choice perfume." [410]

An unidentified journalist declares Irma Grese possesses "an angel's face and snake eyes." [411]

And even the court refers to Grese's appearance. Major Cranfield would go so far to suggest those who testified against Irma Grese did so out of jealousy because Grese was pretty:

> "I think that in the case of Grese it should not be overlooked that she is a young girl, and she is better looking than the other female accused - probably better looking than the other wardresses in these camps. She was in authority over these young women who have come here as prosecution witnesses, and it is now that the positions are reversed, I think it is not

---

[402] Leicester- Mercury, 1945
[403] "Belsen Woman Guard Weeps, Denies…"
[404] Ibid
[405] Cited in McKale, p.44
[406] *Beast Dozes, Blonde Irma Titivates, Herta Smiles Now)1945). P. 1*
[407] *Kramer Beams, Takes Notes.* (1945). P. 4
[408] *"British Victim Accuses The Beast."* (1945). P.1.
[409] Allan, M. (1945). P. 1
[410] TheUntoldPast
[411] Ibid

> surprising to see the spite and the vindictiveness with which they picked her out from among the others and make their accusations against her." [412]

A letter would appear in the October 29, 1945, issue of The *Palestine Post*. It read in part:

> We, your victims, do not want you to die. We would much rather that you live, as we had to, with billows of filthy black smoke from the chimneys of the crematoria constantly before your eyes. We want to see you dragging heavy stones barefoot and in rags …beaten, cruelly and mercilessly as you, cruel and without mercy, beat us. We want you to go so hungry that you cannot sleep at night, as we could not. We want to see your blonde hair shaved off, as you made us shave our heads.[413]

The author, Auschwitz survivor Isabella Rubinstein (now Batsheva Dagan), had wanted to testify at Grese's trial, but was not allowed a travel certificate. At the request of the Editor of the *Post*, she penned the letter to Grese, and it was published. [414]

Ilse Lothe, defendant number 10, takes the stand after Grese. She admits that all the female supervisors beat prisoners. She claims she had refused to work in an ammunitions plant so was sent to a concentration camp to work; Lothe was a former prisoner. She trained at Ravensbrück and then worked at Oswiecim in 1943. Someone caught her smuggling a letter for another prisoner and she was placed in a "Stalin swing" – draped over a pole with wrists bound to ankles while beaten by "SS men." [415] Despite she and Grese both stating they had never worked together; she was charged with accompanying Grese when Grese allowed an attack dog to attack prisoners.

Coronel Backhouse, acting as Council for the Prosecution, tells the court that Grese was "… the worst of the women guards." [416]

Defense attorney Major L.S.W. Cranfield discounts the comment. He calls Grese "a scapegoat of Belsen…Corporal punishment (was) acceptable in a prison (even when) inflicted on women." Cranfield tells the judges Irma Grese's behavior as an officer "seemed 'reasonable conduct in the circumstances.'" He charges the witnesses as liars. "I do not think it is unnatural or surprising that those young Jewesses should be vindictive … or to seek to avenge themselves…" [417]

Major Cranfield reminds the court of Irma Grese's childhood: she had grown up poor, motherless, and uneducated. Irma wanted to be a nurse, but she was forced to work in the camp. She was susceptible to Nazism. Don't blame Irma Grese; blame the Nazis for these atrocities. Grese was only following orders. And Grese herself would take the same defense when, on October 5, 1945, her statements are read in court.

Reportedly written while in custody, Grese had "thought it over" and "wished to confess." She blamed (Henrich) Himmler "for all that has happened … but I suppose I have as much guilt as all the others above me." She did everything within her power to help, but

---

[412] Transcript, Bergen Belsen Trial, October 16, 1945
[413] Shefler (2012)
[414] Years later, Dagan would be embarrassed she ever wrote the letter
[415] Schultz
[416] "SS Killed 4,000,000…
[417] McKale, p. 45

"conditions were very bad" at Belsen and she was powerless. She admits to observing crimes at Belsen and Auschwitz, and now agrees that "doing nothing to protest or stop them" made all the SS guilty.

"I consider the crimes to be murder."

Her second statement, also read to the court, explains she has "again reflected" and admits to beating prisoners "with other than my hand" but clarifies "this was at Auschwitz when for a week at least several of the SS women had short whips before the whips were taken away as an unauthorized." Grese gives these statements to clear her conscience. [418]

It is as close to an admission of guilt as Irma Grese would ever make.

Following two pages:
Trial transcript of Irma Grese's original deposition given during the Belsen Trials.
Grese continues to shirk responsibilities and victim-blame. Grese also places blame on other camp employees, and names Margot Dreschel and Taube. (Margot Dreschel was not tried at the Belsen Trials. She was tried in a Soviet court, condemned, and executed in 1945.)
SS Unterscharfuhrer Adolph Taube was Commandant at Camp Hindenburg, a sub-camp of Auschwitz. Prior to this post he was employed at Birkenau. (Taube was not tried at the Belsen Trials; his fate is unknown.)
(Circa: 1945. Location: archival. Duchy copyright material in the National Archives is the property of His Majesty The King in Right of His Duchy of Lancaster and is reproduced by permission of the Chancellor and Council of the Duchy of Lancaster.)

[418] Irma Grese condemns SS horror (1945) p.6

Exhibit "~~9~~ 11c"

IN THE MATTER OF WAR CRIMES

AT BELSEN AND AUSCHWITZ

DEPOSITION of IRMA GRESE (Female) SS KOMMANDOFUHRERIN at Auschwitz and Belsen, late of WRECHEN, near FELDBERG, sworn before Lieutenant-Colonel Leopold John Genn, Royal Artillery, Commanding No 1 War Crimes Investigation Team.

1. I have said in a previous Statement that I have never beaten or ill treated prisoners. I have thought it over and I now wish to confess that I have done so and to tell the truth.

2. My duties at Belsen included taking "Appel" or roll-call twice a week. My rank was KOMMANDOFUHRERIN. I was employed as AUFSEHERIN. In this capacity it was my duty to supervise tidiness and general cleanliness in the Camp. My duties were in the Womens' Camp only. I never struck prisoners during the 3½ weeks I was at BELSEN.

3. While at AUSCHWITZ I struck female prisoners on the face with my hand for using dixies as latrine buckets. Though I never struck prisoners in BELSEN and I never saw anyone else do so, I remember seeing RAPPORTFUHRERIN DRESCHEL strike prisoners at AUSCHWITZ. She did this with her hand. I only saw it from a distance but they were struck only on the head. I myself did not strike prisoners often but quite frequently when they did something I didn't like.

4. On the whole I consider that I treated prisoners well. I did not think that any of them were hostile to me when I was working in the Camp. I now find that they all appear to be hostile to me. I think that is because they are hostile to all SS because they cannot forget the number of people among them who were gassed at AUSCHWITZ. I myself think they are perfectly right to feel hostile towards us.

5. I have been shown Photograph B.U. 3746 showing a woman with bad scars on her face which I believe to have been caused by beating with a stick. I have never seen such a thing happen at BELSEN but I have definitely seen UNTERSCHARFUHRER TAUBE beat people in this way at AUSCHWITZ. He did it with a stick.

6. I have again reflected and I wish to add that I have in fact beaten prisoners other than with my hand as already described. This was at AUSCHWITZ when for at least a week several of us SS Women had short whips made in the Camp Workshops with one of which I several times struck prisoners before these whips were taken away from us as unauthorised. *Arms were never carried or possessed by any S.S. women.* *[initials]*

7. I also now admit that I punished prisoners by making them kneel on the ground for periods of a quarter of an hour at a time. I did not at the same time make them hold their hands above their heads but I saw this being done when I have made my report to another part of the Camp at AUSCHWITZ. I do not know the names of the people in AUSCHWITZ responsible for inflicting this punishment.

8. I remember saying in the first statement I made to an English Officer that "Himmler is responsible for all that has happened, but I suppose I have as much guilt as all the others above me" I meant by this that simply by being in the SS and seeing the crimes committed on orders from those in authority and doing nothing to protest or stop them being committed makes anybody in the SS as guilty as anybody else. The crimes I refer to are the gassing of persons at AUSCHWITZ and the killing of thousands at BELSEN by starvation and untended disease. I consider the crime to be murder.

Irma Grese.

-1-

9. I know about the Gas Chamber at AUSCHWITZ becuase prisoners who worked in it told us about it. I only saw it myself from a distance but I have no doubt that many were gassed there.

10. I recognise a number of people on photographs I have been shown of SS Guards who were at BELSEN. No 3 on Photograph 1 was a Clerk at AUSCHWITZ. I do not know his duties at BELSEN. No 4 on Photograph 3 was an Electrician at BELSEN and AUSCHWITZ. No 1 on Photograph 5 was a Cook at AUSCHWITZ and in the Food Store at BELSEN. No 2 on Photograph 5 worked with No 4 on Photograph 3 as an Electrician both at AUSCHWITZ and BELSEN. No 4 on Photograph 7 was a cook at BELSEN. No 5 on Photograph 9 is Doctor KLEIN. No 3 on Photograph 9 was a waiter in the Officers Mess at BELSEN. No 1 on Photograph 9 was only at BELSEN a few days. He came from MITTELBAU. I do not know how he was employed. Nos 1 and 3 on Photograph 12 were employed at both AUSCHWITZ and BELSEN in the Guardroom checking prisoners in and out. On Photograph 22 No 6 was in charge of all SS Women Guards. No 5 was No 6's Second in Command. No 3 was a Telephonist. No 1 was in charge of the Bread Store. On Photograph 19 No 6 was in the Kitchen for a little while, No 5 and No 4 were AUFSEHERIN, No 3 looked after the Pigs, No 2 was a Telephonist. On Photograph 25 No 5 was in charge of the wood cutting and chopping, No 4 supervised outside working parties. On Photograph 35 No 1 was a Telephonist, No 2 was sick whi~~l~~e I was there, No 3 worked in the Kitchen. On Photograph 37 No 2 was in the Kitchen, No 3 was also in the Kitchen.

11. I never saw any of the beforementioned SS ill treating prisoners in any way. I have now confessed to all the ill treatment of prisoners of which I was guilty because it has been on my conscience. I have nothing else to admit.

S W O R N BY THE SAID DEPONENT IRMA GRESE AT CELLE, THIS 14th DAY OF JUNE, 1945, BEFORE ME

I. Grese. Irma

[signature] Lt-Col, R.A.

I HEREBY CERTIFY that, the said Deponent not understanding English, this Affidavit was translated in my presence to the said Deponent before swearing and I am satisfied that its contents were fully understood by the said Deponent.

DATED this 14th day of June 1945

[signature] Lt-Col RA

I HEREBY CERTIFY that I have accurately translated this Affidavit to the said Deponent

DATED this 14th day of June 1945

P. Colbergh. Cpl

CHAPTER 31
"A Strange Woman"

In 1987, Helene Grese told a journalist she was able to communicate with Irma at any time during the trial. This is highly unlikely.

Helene said a guard continued to smuggle the sister's letters, which the two women immediately destroyed after reading.

They used "sign language" during court proceedings. "Much too boring, much too uninteresting…" Irma would convey to Helene regarding the trial.

According to Helene, Irma's defense attorney allowed Helene in chambers any time the sisters wanted to visit. "What do you think, will they even judge us? And if so, what will it be, a year or two?" Irma asked Helene at the beginning of the trial. She was anticipating her sentence would not last over three years.

While Irma was housed in Celle, she placed a chair on a table and leaned out a window while Helene stood under the window. They conversed, then wished one another "good night."

And when she was sentenced to death, Irma told several people "Hatzi" (Hatzinger) would be waiting for her in heaven. [419]

When Helene came to Irma crying because Helene was spat at by survivors on the street, Irma scoffed at the tears. She saw no reason Helene should cry when it was Irma who was on trial!

And the trial continued as the sisters waited, Helene the always present support.

Nurse Norma Falk takes breaks along with the court. She enjoys coffees in a "duty room" and visits with members of the court. Not much is discussed here. Occasionally, a defendant comes to ask Norma for aspirin, or complains of an ailment, and she will have to go fetch supplies. She continues to be affected by the testimony, and will later admit how she sought escape, sometimes in the form of riding the horses left behind by the German army. "As a Jewish girl I felt it was important to learn what had gone on (in the camps)." The court proceedings were "terrifying" but at times "interesting." Of Irma Grese, Norma would remember taking a photo of her (along with a photo of Kramer and another camp leader). "She was about five-four, about as tall as I was, with the long, blonde hair. Quite a nice-looking girl. She was quite slim, quite a nice figure, actually. Quite a nice-looking face. When you see her in the photograph sometimes, she looks quite sort of severe sometimes, but sitting in the court, I couldn't believe she had done all this. She looked sullen." If Grese smiled, "it was up at the press gallery. (Her speaking voice) was just normal, nothing exceptional." If Grese or any of the defendants needed anything medical, they would point to indicate the ailment "to their head, if they had a headache." Norma and Grese interacted little, but due to Grese's youth and beauty it "was so hard to comprehend" Grese's crimes. [420]

Infamous criminals have always drawn a crowd, some who become completely enamored with the defendant. Irma Grese has developed such a fan, of sorts, in the gallery of courtroom watchers. A girl named Annelise has become somewhat enamored with Irma.

---

[419] Wieble, P.

[420] USC Shoah Foundation

Throughout the trial, the young woman sits in the gallery and keeps her eyes on Grese. Annelise travels from Hitzacker, a picturesque little town bordering the river Elbe in the Lower Saxony district. When possible, the woman travels almost a mile to attend the trial and secretly cheer for Grese. She befriends Helene Grese and sends Irma letters through Helene. Irma calls her "Anneli." Annelise would later play a strange but important role in Grese's last days.

One author will later question the fairness of the trial. Captain Derek Sington of the Intelligence Corp, who had assisted in the liberation of Belsen, is aware of the atrocities committed at Auschwitz. Sington, at the time of his writing, also believes Grese has been thoroughly brainwashed by the Nazi regime. "In normal conditions" in a trial, Sington reflects, "(the court would) ask for a report on her background, her family life and her circumstances … carefully examined for her mental condition; her past life would be exhaustively investigated." Sington believed such an investigation is imperative in Grese's case. "But defeated Germany in 1945 was hardly a theatre in which to expect crime to be treated objectively or in a spirit of healing." Years later is too late to delve into the reasons why Grese committed her crimes, Sington believes; the psychological investigation should have taken place during trial. [421]

Irma Grese will have a few defenders, including the men and women who worked beside her, who now sit in the same lines of benches. Her attorney never calls the prisoners who Grese counted as "friends" – the ones she assisted or kept from the gas chamber. Perhaps it is too huge a risk. Despite Grese's "kindness" so many of them acted out of fear. Her attorney may consider these witnesses unreliable. Thus is the nature of a trial: the best witnesses for either side, and the professionals who will side with your story.

Josef Kramer, now on the stand, assures the court he never observed Irma Grese handle a dog while employed at Birkenau, and this included when she was off duty. She never used her gun; she never shot any prisoners. She never mistreated any of them. She was a serious officer and valued for her work. What of the evidence given about Grese beating prisoners? Kramer explained any beatings were done without his approval or knowledge. Kramer explains he is also an innocent man, doing his duty, just as Irma Grese was a good officer who did her duty. He sits on the witness stand and answers questions carefully, giving his word that anyone speaking against Grese is lying.

Franz Hoessler testifies former prisoners have lied about Grese and himself throughout the trial. Hoessler is quizzed about Dora Szafran, who has told the court about a selection in Camp A, Block 9, when two selected girls jumped out of a window and Grese shot and killed them. Dora Szafran, Hoessler says, is lying. The windows in Camp A, Block 9 could not be opened, and Irma Grese was incompetent in loading or firing a pistol. She was a reliable officer, Irma Grese, who only worked in the post office and helped with roll call at night as an Overseer. She never used a dog.

Hermann Muller, former *Unterscharftihrer* [422] was overseeing the Belsen food stores. He testifies he never witnessed Grese with a stick or a whip.

Elizabeth Volkenrath remembers Irma Grese as a subordinate at Belsen and Auschwitz. No, she responds to a question, Grese never had a dog assigned to her.

They attempt to save one another. They attempt to save themselves.

---

[421] Playfair, G. & Singeton, D. p. 164-5

[422] A noncommission officer in the SS.

November 8, 1945, Day 46. Major Cranfield 's speech for his closing arguments, and three quarters of it is about Irma Grese. Cranfield explains that Grese forced prisoners to kneel for hours during roll call only for the ease of counting. He questions the validity of some testimony, including the dates of some events. He waves Grese's leather belt at the court, marking it exhibit # 126. It is a light and thin belt, Cranfield declares, so how could anyone be seriously harmed by lashings from this belt?

Cranfield casts doubt against testimonies. Eleven witnesses had recognized Irma Grese in court, but only six made allegations against the Hyena of Auschwitz. Gertrude Diamant's testimony about Grese's making selections was "vague." Testimony that roll calls lasted six to eight hours a day were "nonsense." Edith Trieger had testified Grese shot a Hungarian woman; the woman was instead an Allied National. Enough witnesses had corroborated Grese did not have a dog. As to the other testimony:

> Grese's evidence that she was in charge of the punishment *Kommando* for two days only, and in charge of the *Strassenbaukommando*, which was a type of punishment *Kommando*, for two weeks. The allegation ... was that she was in charge of the punishment *Kommando* in Auschwitz from 1942 to 1944, but (on the stand) she said that the accused was in charge of the punishment company working outside the camp for seven months. Was it probable that Grese would be in charge, the only Overseer, of a *Kommando* 800 strong, with an S.S. man, Herschel, to assist her? If 30 prisoners were killed each day, should there not have been some corroboration of this story? [423]

Allegations of Irma Grese shooting anyone were never corroborated and they were all made by affidavit "except one ... produced as an afterthought in re-examination." [424] The camp was utter chaos, with thousands of prisoners, disease, poor communications, little food, and horrible sanitation. Order had to be kept, or the camp would cease to function. Irma Grese was so young. There was no way she could be held responsible for camp conditions.

On November 13, Colonel Backhouse spends an entire day on the prosecution's closing argument, addressing each of the defendants. Most of his presentation is spent on Irma Grese. "A strange woman" Backhouse calls her, "who deals very openly with all the accusations against her." [425]

Now the trial has come to the "Summing up" portion, days fifty-one to fifty – three, on a Wednesday, Thursday, and Friday, November 14-16, 1945. Judge Advocate Mr. C. L. Stirling looks quite British in his traditional wig and flowing robe. He addresses the court on specific points, to include the witnesses ("unfortunate people who have had to undergo these terrible experiences" [426]) Of Irma Grese, Judge Advocate Stirling states:

> "She is quite a young woman. You have heard about her antecedents, and you have seen her sister. She is very young, and it is extraordinary you may

[423] Belsen Trial Transcripts. *Major Cranfield's Closing Address on Behalf o f Klippel, Grese, Lobauer and Lothe.*
[424] Ibid.
[425] Belsen Trial Transcripts, cited in *Institutional repository oops* (n.d.), 6.4; p. 65
[426] Belsen Trial Transcript, Summary, November 14, 1945

> think, that a girl of this age should have been given the responsibilities which she was given. This woman seems to have had more than her share of publicity. She seems to me to have been tried many times by unofficial courts all over the place, and found guilty by all sorts of people." [427]

Judge Advocate Stirling then details some of Grese's abuses: kicking, beating, abusive roll calls, and – finally – participating in selections. He reminds the court that not all the defendants are accused of participating in selections. He details how gassings were carried out, quoting a survivor.

Stirling makes no other lengthy comment about any female defendant in the dock.

On Day 53 of the Belsen Trails, November 16, 1945, Irma Grese spends the night weeping in her cell. Witnesses will state she cried nonstop.

The Belsen Trial is coming to its final day. Originally, it was predicted the trial would last three weeks at longest. Instead, it took about two months.

Long after Day 54, November 17, 1945, the fate of Irma Grese and her defendants will be argued for decades. This trial is the first where Holocaust perpetrators in occupied Western Germany are being held legally accountable for their actions. The defendants are only a trickle of Holocaust perpetrators who will be punished. Selected testimony is hearsay - much of the charges rely on eyewitness testimony. One debate arises: the survivors had lived under constant stress and physical sickness – how could their memory be trusted? Yet the male and female defendants who sit in this heavily guarded box are on the record for the collective murder and torture of thousands of innocent people. They destroyed generations of families with a nod. They acted on orders, but they also acted on their own free will in cruelty and mayhem. They could have easily refused orders and walked off the job, but by doing so walked into a war - torn world where nothing – food, shelter, safety – was guaranteed. None of these people were monsters, but they were people who acted as monsters. Were they scapegoats or guilty as charged?

[427] Cited in Playfair, G. & Sington, D. (1957) p. 178

Helena Grese (with hat), sister of Irma Grese, is assisted from the courtroom at Luneburg after hearing the death sentence passed on her sister at the conclusion of the Belsen Trail.
Irma Grese's brother Otto is with Helena. The unidentified female may be Annalise; Irma's champion who had a solution to escape the gallows. (Circa November 17, 1945. Photographer unknown. Location: archive. Courtesy Imperial War Museum. Used with permission.)

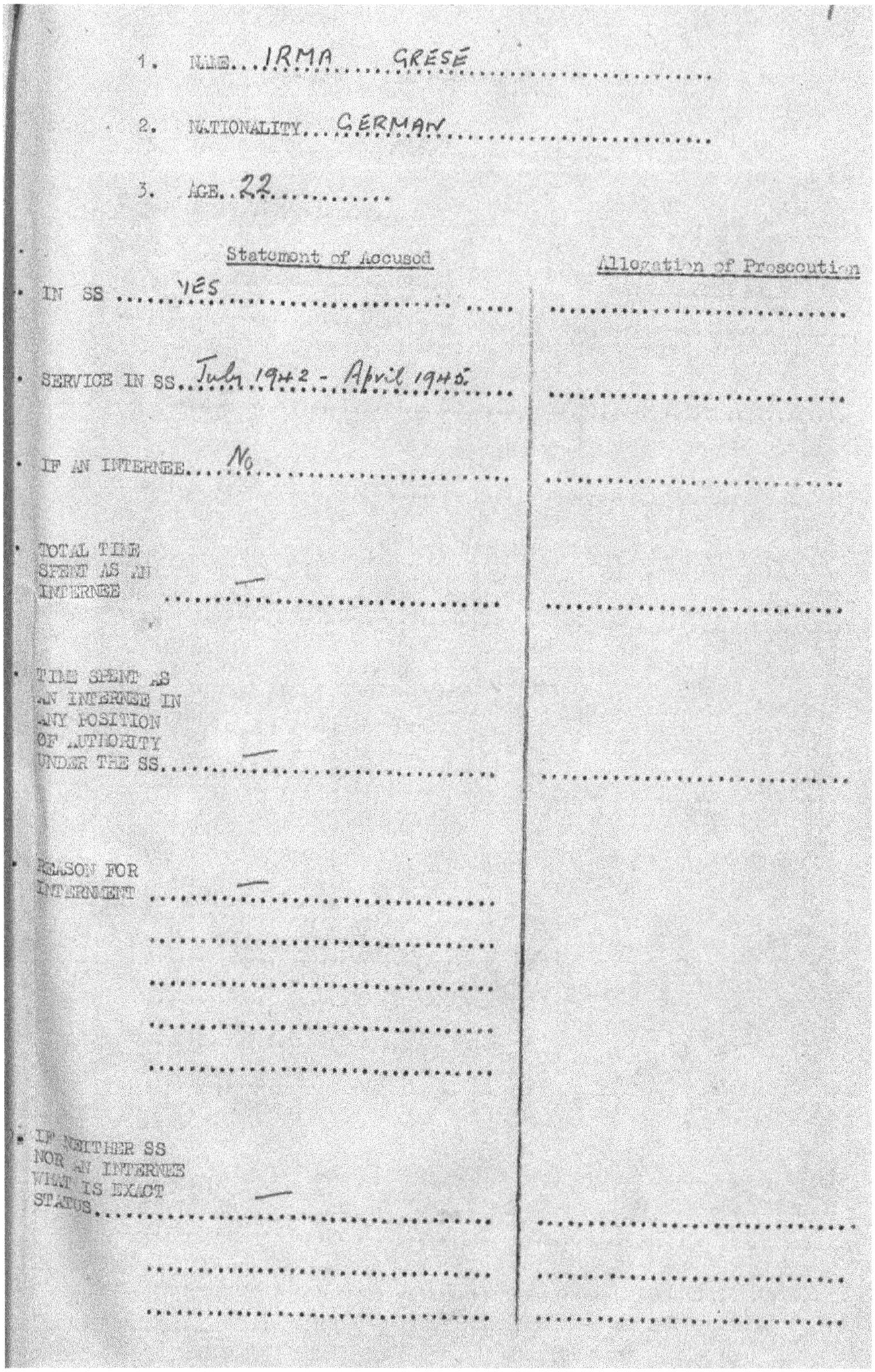

1. NAME... IRMA GRESE

2. NATIONALITY... GERMAN

3. AGE... 22

	Statement of Accused	Allegation of Prosecution
IN SS	YES	
SERVICE IN SS	July 1942 - April 1945	
IF AN INTERNEE	No	
TOTAL TIME SPENT AS AN INTERNEE	—	
TIME SPENT AS AN INTERNEE IN ANY POSITION OF AUTHORITY UNDER THE SS	—	
REASON FOR INTERNMENT	—	
IF NEITHER SS NOR AN INTERNEE WHAT IS EXACT STATUS	—	

Report on standard form relating to "previous character" of accused Irma Grese dated Nov 16, 1945. It was a tool to assist in determining sentencing. (Circa: April 1945. Location: archives. Source: KEW; Ref # 1723)

MILITARY GOVERNMENT - GERMANY

MILITARY COURT - WAR CRIMINALS

DEATH WARRANT

TO: The Director or Officer in charge of ZUCHTHAUS, HAMELN.

WHEREAS one IRMA GRESE was on the seventeenth day of November One thousand nine hundred and forty five convicted by a Military Court at LUNEBERG of a war crime and sentenced by such Court to the penalty of death by judicial hanging and

WHEREAS in accordance with Army Order number 81 of 1945, such sentence has come before me for confirmation and after due consideration and in exercise of the powers conferred upon me, I have confirmed the sentence of death by judicial hanging so imposed.

NOW THEREFORE I hereby order you to execute such sentence within twenty four hours of receipt of this warrant by judicial hanging and for so doing this shall be sufficient warrant.

Upon execution of said sentence the return below will be completed and forwarded to this Headquarters (A(PS.4)).

B. L. Montgomery.

7 December 1945.
HQ BAOR.

Field Marshal, Commander-in-Chief.
Confirming Authority.

RETURN OF WARRANT

The above sentence imposed on IRMA GRESE,

was put into execution at Hameln Zuchthaus
(Location)

on 13 Dec 1945. (Date)

1003. (Hour)

[signature] Capt.
(Signature and Appointment of Prison Official)
Governor, U.N. Wing, Hameln Zuchthaus.

[signature] Maj. Witness
(Countersignature and rank identifying witness)

The death warrant for Irma Grese. She was one of several defendants who attempted to appeal. All appeals were denied. Special gallows were built down the hall from her cell. (Circa: December 13, 1945. Location: archives. Source: KEW Reference #1656)

Form L-P 8

MILITARY GOVERNMENT - GERMANY

ORDER FOR TRANSFER OF PRISONER
GEFANGENENÜBERWACHUNGSBEFEHL

Date 11. Dezember 1945.
Datum

It is hereby ordered that G r e s e, Irma
Es wird hiermit angeordnet, dass (Name)

Prisoner number ...., a prisoner now confined in the
Gefangenennummer *zur Zeit in Haft im/in*

Landger. Gefgn. Lüneburg, be transferred to
(Institution – *Gefängnis*) *nach*

Zuchthaus H a m e l n, *überwiesen wird.*
(Institution – *Gefängnis*)

there to be dealt with under the terms of the original commitment
um dort mit ihm/ihr gemäß dem ursprünglichen Strafvollzugsbefehl zu verfahren. Die Ueber-

which shall accompany the prisoner at the time of transfer
mittlung des Strafvollzugsbefehls hat gleichzeitig mit der Ueberweisung des Strafgefan-

and serve as authorisation to hold the prisoner in accordance with the terms thereof.
genen zu erfolgen. Sie dient als Ermächtigung ihn/sie gemäß den darin enthaltenen Verfügungen in Haft zu halten.

The following records will accompany the prisoner:
Die folgenden Urkunden müssen gleichzeitig mit dem Strafgefangenen übermittelt werden.

Gerichtsbeschluß liegt an.

Am 11.12.45. 12⁰⁰ Uhr Abg. Zuchth. Hameln

Signed .... Capt.
Unterschrift (Title – *Amtstitel*)
S.O.III. Prison 914 Mil. Gov.

DISTRIBUTION:

1 copy to accompany prisoner to Receiving Institution.
1 copy to Releasing Institution.
1 copy to MG Det File.

Irma Grese lost her appeal and was transferred from Celle to Hamelin Prison to await execution. This is the official paperwork for the transfer. A copy would have been with her paperwork as she traveled. Each Belsen defendant found Guilty and transferred to Hamelin Prison had a transfer order. Irma Grese's order is dated December 11, 1945. (Circa: April 1945. Location: archives. Source: Courtesy United States Holocaust Memorial Museum Collection, Gift of the Canadian War Museum. Used with permission

CHAPTER 32
Defendant to Prisoner

It is Day 54 of the Belsen Trails, November 17, 1945. Irma Grese is one of three females brought into the courtroom, guarded by female military officers. Her name and number are read aloud, and she steps forward.

President Major General Berney – Ficklin quietly reads, "The sentence of this court is that you suffer death by being hanged." [428]

Irmgard Ilese Ida Grese, AKA Irma Grese, AKA "The Hyena of Auschwitz" is found guilty of crimes at Auschwitz and Bergen-Belsen and is one of eleven defendants sentenced to hang. She is one of three women sentenced to death; eight of the male defendants will also receive the death sentence. Nineteen receive varying sentences in prison.

The women who sat beside Grese during trial are sentenced: number "8" Hertha Ehlert receives 15 years imprisonment. Number "10" Ilse Lothe is found "not guilty."

Those condemned to die are told they have the right to appeal. All but one of the defendants plans on it.

After pronouncing sentencing, Colonel Backhouse snugs his black hat on his head, turns, and walks out of the courtroom without emotion.

Grese is reported to have blushed, but otherwise none of the women react. As the women are led out of the courtroom, cries echo off the hallway; Irma Grese is suspected. Helene, still sitting in the gallery, sobs.

Nurse Norma Falk recalls Irma Grese being sentenced to death, how Grese and the others "walked very quietly with their heads down, not looking at anything. No emotion." This was how the defendants normally walk in and out of the court room; now sentenced, "it was very quiet. I remember that quite clearly." However, "I think they knew … they knew the outcome of (the trial)." She turned to her left to watch the defendants walk out, watching Irma Grese's expression along with her codefendants. "No screaming, no hysterics, nothing." Norma was pleased with the sentence, though felt all the defendants should have received a death sentence. "They were all part of this. They knew they were guilty." [429]

Irma Grese's attorney, Major Cranfield, packs up papers and pens. He walks to visit his client in the back room, where the defendants had always waited for the trial, where the nurse had visited, where Grese had her codefendant brush and style her golden hair to perfection. Cranfield discovers Grese crying. According to Helene, Cranfield cries along with his client.

And just as they had every day at the end of the trial, the accused are led to the cage outside of the building. They are assisted into the trucks. The trucks make way down the streets and back to the prison, rumbling into the Celle courtyard to drop off the prisoners for the last time.

---

[428] Ibid, p.180

[429] USC Shoah Foundation. (2012, May 17).

Irma Grese is placed in her cell and the door locks behind her. The British soldiers guarding her ensures the door is locked and the prisoner secured. "Jut-Jaw" they have been calling her, due to her dour expression and how she clenches her teeth and pointing her chin at the courtroom. [430] "Jut-Jaw" has finally received what was coming to her, they agree.

[430] Scanlon (2011) p.14

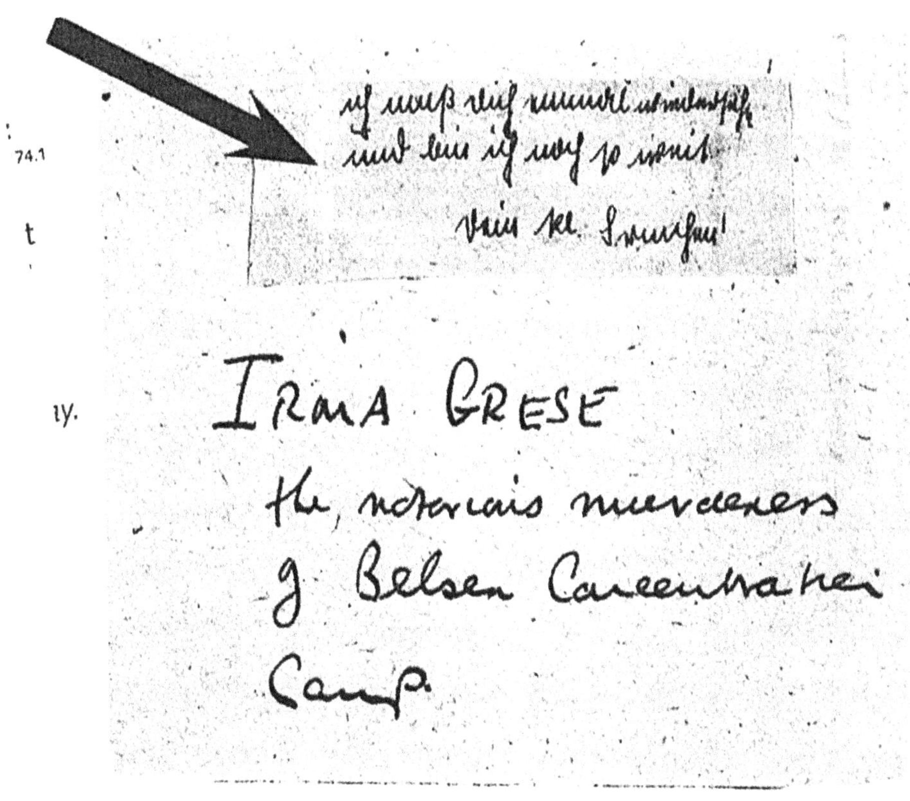

IRMA GRESE
the notorious murderess of Belsen Concentration Camp

Letter from Irma Grese (arrow). It is missing the upper section, which may be where the recipient's name was written. Grese wrote:

> --- I have to see you again one day and I'm still so far away. Your little Irmchen."

It is pasted onto a card which reads "IRMA GRESE the notorious murderess of the Belsen Concentration Camp." The date mailed and date received are unknown. [431] This letter was written during her incarceration.
(Circa: 1945. Location: archives. Source: Courtesy United States Holocaust Memorial Museum Collection, Gift of the Canadian War Museum. Used with permission)

[431] "Letter from Irma Grese." (n.d.) Peter Clapham Collection.

How did Irma Greese

DON'T WA

—get like this?

by **PAUL HOLT**

IRMA GREESE, whom some newspapers call the Blonde Beastess of Belsen, faces her judges today.

The evidence is given. Only the verdict now, after 59 days of trial at Luneburg, has still to come. Eight months she has been now in captivity; eight months in which to wonder and to inquire into these democratic processes of the law which she had never heard about before.

When she was a little girl Irma Greese cried when she saw that her brother had cut his lip. But within ten years of those tears she was using whip and gun and gas with skill and despatch on the hapless inmates of Belsen concentration camp.

Now what made Irma get like this?

There is a reason. There is a reason for all human actions.

I saw Irma Greese first in April of this year. It was two days after a British anti-tank unit of the 11th Armoured Division had overrun Belsen.

She was standing still in a cell, breathing heavily. She was leaning against a wall with half a dozen other women S.S. guards. In front of her a young Frenchman, wearing the dingy blue and white striped pyjamas of a political prisoner, was shouting.

"Stand up!" he screamed. "Stand up straight! Don't lean against the wall! You are not masters now. The British are masters in this camp!" He was hysterical with anger released.

Outside the door of the tiny cell four or five British officers, revolvers in their hands, were staring. They did not believe what they had seen outside, the mounds of waxy corpses, the shuffling sleepwalkers with clusters of flies at their eyes.

Still less could they believe what they now saw—six young German women, neat and passionless, listening to a Frenchman screaming that they had done all this.

The thought frightened the officers as battle had never done. Their nostrils flared wide with disgust, and they pushed at each other to get away and out of sight of these neat young women standing against the cell wall.

Sullen looks

IRMA GREESE and her girl friends did not understand this at all. She thought, they all thought, that they would be taken outside at once to be shot.

Irma was standing, I remember, next to a slim young mulatto girl wearing black riding breeches, with a thong slung to her left wrist. They both looked sullen, but composed. Their eyes were set.

Now, first, should we see what brought Irma Greese here? The process:—

She was born in the village of Neu - Strelitz in Mecklenburg, third of a family of five of a solemn, church - going farm labourer, Alfred Greese.

The last birthday she spent at home was when she was seventeen. They had a big supper and the family sang old German songs. That was in October 1940.

Vincent Evans, Express man at Luneburg for the trial, wrote me an interesting letter this week. He was giving his impressions of the evidence and information he had gathered from Irma's relatives who had come from Mecklenburg.

That October night in 1940 little Irma, still a girl, sang and danced country dances, hugged her family and was gay. Six months later she had been discharged from her job as a probationer nurse (nobody seems to know why) and she had been drafted under Nazi labour laws to be a trainee guard at a concentration camp at Auschwitz, in Eastern Germany.

Fun to swagger

THIS was the worst of all the camps, inmates have told me. Irma was given her grey uniform, her cocky kepi; she carried a revolver in holster. It was fun to swagger.

It always had been. When she was 12 she was already a Hitler

"She saw without horror the full practices of death."

Madchen, which is roughly like being a junior school prefect, I imagine.

She was a bossy little girl, liking her tunic and her medal and her little authority. She bossed the lazy and the absent-minded little girls. The first time she struck some woe-filled stubborn infant, she was (may I guess?) a little frightened, and the woman in her wanted to wipe away tears. But she was applauded for the deed.

Angry father

TO be a trainee at a concentration camp was no more to her than a promotion to a kind of approved school, a Nazi Borstal.

Imagine the shock to the girl when she went home for the first time in her grey uniform.

Her father was so angry to hear her news that he thrashed her and drove her out from home.

How easy now to see her swinging violently into the new environment.

She learned about Haushofer, a mad Munich recluse, who made Hitler believe that the science of Geo-Politics made Europe, the Mediterranean Basin and all of Africa the true German sphere of dominance.

She learned about Rosenberg, an elderly comic, who kidded Hitler that racial purity is the basis of morality in people and nations.

She learned about motherhood the Nazi way. She learned to despise marriage, to respect the unmarried mother who bears a child for a soldier of Adolf Hitler.

She learned to believe that Jews, gipsies, burglars, black marketeers and murderers are all the same. They are, according to her given creed, all "anti-social," and must be worked until they are not strong enough to work any more. And then they must be exterminated.

She learned the Nazi system for convicts. They must be available for all State duties. To her there became no difference whether 20 Belsen inmates were wanted to hoe sugar-beet or wanted for some Munich professor's guinea-pig experiments. She lined up one working squad and another for the gas chamber without thinking much about the difference.

Punishment camp

IT became a matter of routine. At Auschwitz, which was a "punishment work camp," she saw without horror the full practices of death by hounds, the selection o ftattooed prisoners for the gas chamber so that their skins could be used for artistic lampshades.

Her colleagues in the mess were old convicts who had become trusties and then guards. One of the guards at Auschwitz was that nine-day wonder, the Dusseldorf Murderer, who made front pages in the 'thirties when he slew 31 women before he was caught and given a life sentence.

When she was transferred to Belsen, which was known technically as a "convalescent camp" for those prisoners who were too weak to work any longer, she naturally thought her prisoners were poor trash.

To ease the boredom of the long hours—for Belsen was a hut encampment set ten miles deep in pinewoods beyond the little town of Celle—she and her companions amused themselves tying corpses to new women prisoners on the first night of their arrival. At dawn they would burn on a pyre the cold corpse and the demented prisoner together.

Then she grew afraid. More and more prisoners packed in from the east. Not enough food to go round, not enough guards. The whip and revolver began to be used for her protection.

At the crest of cruelty, buoyed up only by the belief that power is the sole arbiter of human conduct, Irma stood in Belsen camp one morning, alone, in a cell, surrounded by the baying, maddened inmates outside, and by half a dozen sickened British officers staring at her.

"Why did you do these things?" screamed the Frenchman.

Irma's mouth began to move. "We acted under orders. It was our duty to exterminate anti-social elements so that the future of Germany shall be tranquil," she chanted automatically.

She did not think she had done wrong and seemed to acknowledge freely the right of the new power to destroy her. Throughout this long trial she has chewed gum and stared insolently around her. When Otto, her brother—who cut his lip at a game one day, which made her cry—and Lieschen, her sister, came to see her in a Luneburg cell it was they who cried, she who was collected.

The girl whose record for cruelty probably exceeds that of any woman in history will not be surprised if she is sentenced to die. She has expected it.

WILLIAM

Rush t

WOULD - BE migrants are pouring into the four Dominion High Commissioners' offices in London at the rate of 1,100 a day. All receive the same answer: "We want you but there is no transport."

Not until troop movements cease is there any hope of the position easing. Meanwhile, every week, there is an increase in the number of people wanting to build fresh lives for themselves in the Dominions, to give their children a larger chance in life in a more untrammelled atmosphere.

Six months ago Australia House had a thousand people calling to inquire about passages every week. Today there are three times as many inquiries; next week the number will be larger still.

South Africa has 1,200 inquiries a week; Canada 1,500; New Zealand 900. All will have more next week.

THE migrants are of all ages. Half of them are young people, many newly married, some with small families. Twenty per cent are young single men, most of them from the Services; 1? per cent are young single girls; 15 per cent are older people, many of them with large families.

BY THE WAY *by Beachcomber*

Opposite page:
Daily Express journalist Paul Holt interviewed Irma Grese two days after her arrest. Holt would also interview Auschwitz survivors. A fellow *Daily Express* journalist, Vincent Evans, would observe the Belsen Trial. Evans would scribble notes and observations, interviewing Grese's family members and anyone who knew her. He sent the trial notes to Paul Holt. Holt wrote the article "How did Irma Grese get like this?" from their combined work. The article was published on page 4 the day the Belsen Trial defendants received the verdicts. Irma Grese would receive a death sentence.
Both writers gained a keen interest in the "Hyena of Auschwitz." They began what was probably the first in-depth investigation of Irma's life at the time. (Circa November 18, 1945. Location: archives. Image courtesy of *Daily Express*. Used with permission.)

Below:
The media assisted in documenting evidence to convict Irma Grese and her fellow camp employees in numerous courts. It was the first "inside look" for much of the world. This is a photograph obtained during WWII, taken by a committee of former Yugoslav prisoners for their records. It is one of the images widely distributed to American soldiers. Grese walked past scenes like this the last days of her employment. She stood amid at least 10,000 reported corpses when arrested. (Circa April 29-May10, 1945. Location Dachau. Photographer: unnamed Yugoslav prisoner. Photo courtesy the private collection of Ray Cook. Used with permission. This image has been minimally altered for clarity.)

CHAPTER 33
"Kisses from Irmkins"

Little is known about how Irma Grese busied herself behind bars in Celle, in Luneberg, and in Hamelin prison. Few records exist and they tell little details. She had requested and received a blanket, according to an in-house prison receipt. She and the War Crime Belsen prisoners were checked by prison officers on the hour, and the only notes these officers wrote were "sleeping" and "not sleeping" along with the date, time, and officer signature. These brief notations give little insight into the Hyena of Belsen, now turned prisoner.

Luneberg was a modern institution. People walked across linoleum floors, a luxury product in these times. Flush toilets and running water increased prisoner luxuries, along with comfortable mattresses and clean blankets. Irma Grese and her fellow inmates would have a breakfast that usually included bread and a coffee substitute. Her lunch might be a meaty stew. Grese might nibble on soup and bread, or perhaps bread, sausage, and cheeses. Prisoners received tea with meals.

Irma Grese would write letters [432] to her family from the small desk in her plain, tiny cell. She made a somber request to Helene: she wanted to commit suicide; she would rather take her own life than be hung like a "witch." Helene, who continued to believe in Irma's innocence, was all too happy to assist. Helene had a plan.

Helene spoke with Annalise, who somehow had a connection through her father. In a letter dated November 29, 1945, Grese would write Helene of her plans from inside prison:

Leni! My dear little sister!

You have made me very happy with the good news from home. I am quite another person. Now we must cross our fingers that I can stay alive. I am not letting my courage sink, and I hope that a little change will come into view.

Leni! It is true that my Anneli has left something good for me? This was my only wish, to get something like that so as not to be hanged like a witch! Now I am quite at ease, for now I know that I can avoid the terrible manner of death by making an easy end to myself. Leni, please send best wishes to my Anneli and many, many thanks for her sports event, [433] which has come to me as if on demand!

---

[432] All letters here are written verbatim (translated from German) with original grammar errors.

[433] Note the code word for the poison is "sports event" as in "sporting," the code word the concentration camp guards used for tormenting captives in the prison camps, sometimes "sporting" the prisoners to death.

If I should no longer be in a position to thank Annelies, you will have to look after it, for she is my savior --! (You know what I mean, don't you). Just imagine, Leni! Anneli likes me so much, she is putting her own life on the line just to free me from the fear of death. She is quite simply rescuing me from the terrible fate that is facing me. I can't find words of thanks, for it is the greatest happiness granted to me in the last days of my life! That happiness is a sports event from my dear friend Anneli!

Don't have any bad thoughts, for I am still a little hopeful!! -- If it really must be, and I am to do, don't you be sad, for I am dying for my country! You have to be as proud of that as I am! And I can still hope and not let myself be robbed of hope! -- If I have other thoughts I will write to Anneli too, since she deserves it!

kisses from

Irmkins

Regards to Anneli [434]

It is possible Grese was manipulating her sister by praising the accolades of Anneli(se), given Grese's past behavior. Grese has concluded she will die for her crimes yet allows miniscule hope to surface. She mentions in passing how she is dying for her country, but only briefly is she patriotic.

Sometime before Irma Grese's transfer to prison, Irma and Helene decided to forego Irma's suicide plan. One of them felt that their sister Lieschen would be blamed for smuggling in the drug as she was a nurse with access, and neither wanted her in trouble. Irma must have been willing to sacrifice her "savior" and "dear friend Anneli" who was willing to "put … her own life on the line" but not Lieschen.

As Irma Grese penned her sister, the Chief of the Legal Division of the Control Commission for Germany was typing out a memo, the result of several meetings regarding the additional security measures during the "Executions at Hamelin." The memo requested:

1. Certain roads near the prison be shut down to traffic.
2. Military guards for external prison security, to include the main gate and outside the walls. "I do not anticipate that this external protection will be required on all concessions," the memo read, but it was necessary the days up to and during the execution date.

[434] KOnsl (2012)

3. Penal Inspectors from the Legal Division "be on hand." Captain Peter Clapman was recommended. C.S.M. O'Neil would assist Major Clapman. A chaplain's presence was also going to be arranged.
4. The graves and coffins should be prepared prior to the execution date, and were to be prepared per a separate memorandum. Information on the graves, coffins, and burial plans "will be kept with the graves register as a confidential document." [435]

Plans for the execution of Irma Grese and her comrades were in place.

Letters were moving back and forth between Irma Grese's cell and her family. [436] She received a letter from her sister, Lieschen, dated December 5, 1945. By now, Anneli had embedded herself into the Grese family, who had just returned home from the trial. Lieschen writes:

My dear beloved sister!

We went home sadly today. Now we are sitting here in a cozy kitchen - living room with our mother in Lunenburg and are writing you a few lines. Leni is still shopping and Anneli is sitting next to me. We were in such a happy mood today, just because Anneli came and then we wanted to pass on the happy mood to you. Now everything failed. We arrived here and find out everything we didn't expect. Little dear, our dear, should we give up all hope now? I now know your answer; But do we want to fool ourselves forever? We can only look at things from the worldly side. You know my attitude and know that it gives me support; there's no question of knocking it over! Should it really be you who should sacrifice an idea for them? Decades will pass again, nature will demand a change again and a new time will blossom. The people who have really achieved something or worked on a work always live 100 years later. The sacrifices from 1923 to now will never be in vain! Your spirit will take root and spring up like ivy spreading! But why am I writing all this to you? You know my thoughts and I could much rather hide them. But we want to consciously experience this time and I ask you, my dear Irmachen, to write to me again with this in mind; Write down what you feel. I know that your thoughts are noble, so pure that they can be presented as an example to our children's children. We definitely don't want to fall into delusions of grandeur;

[435] Memorandum "Subject: Executions at Hamelin" dated December 1, 1945, P. Clapham collection.

[436] All letters to and from Irma Grese in this chapter are written as a direct translation from German to English, verbatim with grammar and spelling flaws in the originals.

Simply put, the way we grew up is how we now want to behave. We can now simply make an impression. You can act as a German woman; Even if you now stand very carefully, somewhat reserved but still elevated above everything. Showing yourself as a rebel now is not right. The whole world's attention was on you; don't appear indifferent to the outside world; Well, stay composed, but hostile attitudes can no longer be of any use to you in the last, most difficult time. My thoughts no longer stray from you and I take advantage of every visiting hour to really take in your face. The faith and hope for a possible good turn of events remain awake in me, always you will never have died, you will stand so brightly before us forever and you will be alive in us forever that that I am so grateful to fate, that I was able to come here and receive the most beautiful gift of my life, your presence is everything to me! It is indescribable how much a person can be sustained by hope and faith, and it must remain that way for the duration of our short time period we want and have to keep our heads up. It can't be any other way when we see your beaming face in front of us. It should stay that way forever.

So, my beloved little sister, I have now written down for you my thoughts that are currently swirling around in my brain. These are the first hopes that I buried today, but will pick up again tomorrow.

Please don't compare me to Alfred [437] at this moment. I think about all of these things quite soberly and in in favor of writing to ourselves what we feel. There will be too many disappointments today. I hope that Anneli will write something cheerful to you to balance things out again. Soon you will receive lines from me in a different sense again. I'm not able to write you anything else at the moment. You understand me and are writing to me again today with this in mind; Yes? I ask you very kindly. I'll leave the sheet on and please send my letter back to me, OK?

What longing means, what waiting means, can only be felt and known by people who know a dear member in their midst in an unreasonable distance! Accept many warm greetings and kisses from your eternally waiting for a good ending.

---

437 Lieschen, Irma, and Helene's older brother

Lieschen! [438]

Drawing from this letter it appears Lieschen feels Irma is innocent, and a "good German" as defined by Nazi code. The sisters continued to believe in a floundering ideology.

Irma Grese replied to Lieschen. Her first letter is dated December 8, 1945. [439] She assures her sister that she has not lost her pride:

Lieschen! My brave little sister!

I am extremely happy to describe you as brave, because weak, pitiful people make no impression on me. Lieschen, just as you have put your thoughts here in this letter, I have to tell you that they agree with mine. You have not made my heart difficult by doing this, no, you have instilled in me great peace and contentment! Everything you hope for from me in these hours will come true! I think you, my Lieschen, know me best and know what thoughts my little heart is occupied with. Not with fear and anxiety, nor with trembling and hesitation. No. First of all, with a great hope and with a stubborn pride it is firmly attached! I don't think anyone can break it now, no matter what weapon they use! Read carefully the lines that I addressed to Dad. I think they tell you what you wanted from me.

Although my hours are numbered, I am firmly convinced that I will still not die! That I will remain in your midst just as before! Lieschen! And this makes me even more courageous! Because I am therefore certain that I will not leave behind any siblings of little faith or weak-mindedness! You too should have the same conviction and know that I follow my destiny with a calm, sure step and iron nerves. I will never lose my honor because it means:

loyalty! Let me tell you that I have always loved you very much, because you are my beloved little sister!

---

[438] *Institutional repository oops* (n.d.) p. 136-7 140 (*Dokument* 9)

[439] Ibid p. 139-140 (*Dokument* 11)

Eternal greetings

Your I r m c h e n!

Grese had two weeks to file an appeal, and she did so; she was one of eight of the Belsen trial to appeal her sentence, and the sole female. Appeals were filed and referred to Field Marshall Montgomery. Most of those appealing did so based on an unfair trial. They also declared they had acted "under orders" of superiors and that their actions were based on their youth. Grese's legal representative asked the court to consider how much of the information during the trial was based on hearsay, and how Irma Grese had come of age during the Nazi ruling – she was immersed in the lies and propaganda; in short, she was brainwashed.

Once again, the defendants went before the court. Would Irma Grese's sentence be overturned? Would her youth, good looks, and filing for an "unfair trial" be enough to secure her a new trial?

Clemency was denied for all who appealed. Field Marshal Montgomery signed Irma Grese's death warrant on Friday, December 7. She was to be hanged on December 13. Her hopes were cut short, and she would not live much longer. Court reporters noted Grese made no move or eye contact with anyone, nor did she flinch; "once outside the courtroom *Fraulein* Grese, who had swaggered at the camp with a pistol strapped to her waist and a whip in her hand, broke into violent sobs." [440]

It was announced on the following day; Irma Grese and eleven others were transferred from Lüneburg to Hamelin, in Wesfalia.

Now sure of her fate, Grese penned a letter to her estranged parents. It is dated December 8, 1945:

Dear Dad, dear Mum,

In the last hours of my life I want to let you read my thoughts as a last greeting. I believe and hope that you, my dear Daddy, know your dear daughter very well and will keep me in your memory for all time. For that reason I have a last great request for you: cast off all your sorrows, your grief that have plagued you in these weeks. You must not say - If only. No, that is wrong. This is how you must think:

[440] "Kramer and Irma Grese will…"

My dear daughter Irma is and was a young, brave girl, with a pure German soul inherited from her dear Dad! My German courage and my brave mood gives me the strength to live and, if it must be, to die! If fate has determined to tear me from this earthly life so young, then let one thing be certain: that I, as your daughter as you know me, as a brave German woman and reproached by the Germans, will go into the unknown with a clear conscience and above all proudly! I refuse to let any trace of fear or despair enter my heart. Peace and a great strength have replaced them, and these two I will cling to, and they will be my true companions until my last breath. It was never my intention to exalt myself in any way. But they will not have the triumph of seeing me demean myself by even a finger's breath. And whatever they all think, if anybody asks, tell them, my dear Dad: Irma, yes, that was my daughter and always will be! You need not be ashamed of me. For I am doing my duty loyalty for my Fatherland! Just as I and others did our duty, so we go to meet our fate!

I do not count, because I was far too small. But those who do count will live on, and hopefully we'll repay like with like! Even if it takes a certain period of time, there will come a time not to leave injustice unraised.

Dad, hold your head high, even if it is hard. But I believe that both you and my dear Mum will be as strong as your dear daughter Irma.

Tell my dear friends, aunts and uncles, that I send them all my greetings; let them remember me as I was.

Mum and my brothers and sisters, take my last farewell, and think always that thought I die physically, I will always be with you.

My life is in the hands of the judges, but not my honor!

Your dear daughter

Irma [441]

---

[441] K0nsl

Irma Grese has written a letter as a proud German girl, a Nazi supporter who has given her life for the cause she knows has died. She sees herself as going down in flames of glory along with the swastika and the eagle. She is aware of her father's disproval of the Nazi regime. Her "mum" has been deceased for years (unless she was referring to her stepmother as "mum" for reasons of formality); It may be another jab at her father [442] to remind him about her choice of Nazism against his wishes – to insure it would stay with him forever. And by noting "with a pure German soul inherited from her dear Dad!" She lays blame on her father's psyche; to blame her father removes the blame from herself and punishes her father forever.

As Irma Grese wrote her letter, another document was completed: an *Order of Transfer of Prisoner* with her name typed crookedly in a blank space. On December 11, the official paperwork to transfer her and the condemned to Hamelin was completed, a transfer for each being typed and signed. Grese's time on earth was being measured in days.

Irma Grese hastily penned a letter to her brothers and sisters while awaiting transfer. Again, and still, she assures them she is a brave woman sacrificing herself for a greater cause, and to remember her as a loving sister and proud German. The letter is dated December 11, 1945:

My faithful, dearly beloved brothers and sisters!

For the last time I may send you my thoughts! The hour has arrived, there are only minutes left for me to stay close to you in bodily form. Everything eventually comes to an end, and myself as well. I cannot write to aunts and uncles, there is no time - please be so kind and do what I now fail to, write. I don't feel like having to go to meet death, it is more like I was sent to somebody who is waiting for me with great longing. No sign of fear of death makes itself felt in my excited heart!

Lieschen and Leni, for all your great sacrifices that you gladly made for me, I thank you for the last time. If I may entrust you with my last request, it would be to ask of you stay proud Germans exactly as before, never to show inconsistency or despair in your heart, but defiance, and prove unrelenting love to our beloved fatherland. There has always been my principles and take them with me to the

[442] See "Becoming the Hyena – Narcissistic Injuries"

death. I know not every person is alike. But you are my beloved brothers and sisters, thus with this holy belief I want to bear my fate, which is too harsh, in pride and defiance. - I ask of you to inform dad, Alfred, Otto, mom, about everything, and they should not hold it against me that they have so little in writing. - Tomorrow, if it should be granted to see to see you from the car, I want to bid you a final farewell in full lifesize, with a smile on my face and with the sign of placing the right hand to the left breast, it will not mean "here," but "Heil." To Anneli, my faithful one, I will once again pull tight the right side of my jacket, and you will be gone from my eyes for a short time, your spirit accompanies me and I will then visit you every night, and if it thus, to preserve you from all the evil. -!

The night hurries on and soon the morning will come, yes that is how it is going to be. I don't want to burden your hearts, in my written lines to you. I put the last kind goodbye to you, my beloved ones. You should always think of me. You should give faithful love to the fatherland. Even in the worst of trouble, I am loyal to my fatherland to the death. With this dedication, leaving you and this unjust world, your beloved sister.

Irma Grese!!!

P.S. When you get my belongings, and thus the ring, pick one out for Ms. Luhr, I am giving it to her as an eternal token. Anneli is to have my signet ring with the monogram J. G. As a loyal token. [443]

"Ms. Luhr," explains historian Magdalena Chomitkowska, "was like a mother to Irma Grese. She was a friend of Grese's family. And if you look at (official) documents, Irma spelled her name JRMA. She does not write 'Irma.'" [444] Thus, the ring was personalized with Irma Grese's initials.

[443] See Resource list for citation information for letters.

[444] Personal interview, May 12, 2024

Professional translator and historian Ann Marie Ackerman explains, "The German *J* can be pronounced like an *I*, but that spelling would be unusual … the *Sütterlin Schrift,* is the handwriting (Grese) would have learned in school." [445]

Lieschen was able to travel from Neustrelitz in time to unite with Helene. Josef Kramer's wife joined the Grese sisters, and the three women waited anxiously to watch Irma Grese, Josef Kramer, and fellow codefendants being loaded into transportation trucks at Celle. The condemned were taking their last ride, transporting away to Hamelin Prison. Helene shouted something at Irma's jailers and the police were called. She almost missed waving goodbye to Irma.

Irma Grese tucked a rolled blanket under her left arm as she followed her fellow condemned females Elisabeth Volkenrath and Juana Bormann to the rear of the transport truck. She carried a packaged item in her left hand, striding past the soldiers who watched the women load up. All three of the former female guards wore their uniforms. Their hair was unkempt. Grese's blonde sausage curls, still in place, hung down her back.

Helene, Lieschen, and Rosina Kramer watched their loved ones being driven away to death row. Helene would become enraged, she later said, because one of the escorting tanks came close to running her over.

Peter Clapman, Major in the British Army, previous Governor [446] of Lüneburg, was now appointed Governor of Hamelin as of December 13, 1945. Clapman would oversee Grese's treatment during her stay.

Grese and the others were each placed in single cells in Hamelin, small, simple rooms in a row facing a corridor. The doors had been replaced on the cells, adjustments made to accommodate death row and to prevent suicides. They allowed patrolling jailers a quick look inside to ensure their prisoners were safe.

Hamlin Prison inmates who wanted a shave or haircut could submit a request; prison barber trustees served this request based on a sign-up list. Some requests could not be granted due to German regulations not allowing a prisoner's appearance to be altered. Irma Grese did not have an outside professional change her hairstyle. It is likely Elisabeth Volkenrath continued to style Grese's hair, putting her hairstylist skills to use for the last time.

Inmate visitors had a wire mesh between themselves and the inmate. Visitors had to be approved for the safety and security of the institution, no matter the inmate's status – death row inmates, for example – and security had been upgraded for the war criminals. Approvals to visit were closely scrutinized; there remained sympathizers and foes who wanted to either assist, or punish, the war criminals.

Contact with the SS prisoners was tightly controlled. Private First-Class Peter Lumley was permitted to enter the prison to deliver the meals to the condemned. A memorandum with this information had to be typed and officially signed to allow Private Lumley access. British officers continued to act as warders for security detail.

Sentences would be carried out in five days. And still Irma's physical appearance was the talk of newspaper articles. "A British official" is quoted as reporting on Irma

---

[445] Personal interview, May 12, 2024

[446] The title is "Warden" in the United States.

Grese's appearance: "Her hair, once carefully brushed back, has been rumpled and untidy for the past week." [447]

Hamelin prison inmates were allowed to receive and write one letter a month. The prison's Governor could permit a "special letter" by request. No known records of letters bearing Grese's name exist. She had written letters of hope, and then a letter of resignation, from Celle. Had she given up by the time the doors of Hamelin closed behind her? Or had her letters, like so many Nazi documents, been destroyed?

Every day a dark-haired woman would come to the wall outside of Hamelin prison to shout at the building. A voice inside death row shouts in return. Helene Grese had arrived shortly after Irma was imprisoned and now walks the perimeter outskirts of the fifteen-foot-high wall shouting until her sister called down. Now that she knew her sister's cell location, they communicated thus, their voices traveling past the soldiers stationed on the wall surrounding the execution courtyard. The lights in the prison cells and corridors, save for a few security lights in the corridor and staff areas, blink off at 7:00p.m.

Nearly every prison in history receives its share of complaints from inmate's family and friends who believed their incarcerated loved one is being traumatized or abused. During the internment of the Nazi war criminals, Governor Peter Clapham and staff of Hamlin Prison received letters and calls regarding the treatment of the inmates on a regular basis. The complaints were either based on what the inmate told the loved one, or how the loved one believed the prison should be operated. One family member of the war criminals complained in a letter about the cell windows being too high and covered with bars, and how visitation was "no contact." Hamlin prison's British Governor responded with a formal letter, arguing the "high windows" was "...obviously a frivolous complaint ... it is customary in most countries in the world to build prisons for security and windows are normally built high to increase the difficulty of tampering with the bars." Regarding the "no contact" visitation: "... the removal of the (wire netting between visitor and prisoner) prevent(s) the passing of prohibited articles." The Governor also noted "previous experiences in this prison (removing the barrier)" prevents "more punishment for the prisoners and legal sanctions against visitors." [448] The war criminals had never received special treatment; the rules and regulations would not be altered for any of them.

The British Army's Royal Engineers were busy building the gallows in Hamelin. It was constructed to hang two prisoners at the same time. The men would be executed in pairs to expedite the process. Women would be hanged singularly (as they were likely to become hysterical, per one rumor). A lever would be pulled to release the large trap door where the prisoner stood. It was wide enough for two bodies to fall to their demise, the rope snapping vertebrae and promising instant death. Prisoners in their cells could hear down the long corridor from their cells: the gallows cranking, the drop of the hatch, the body falling. It was a well-built machine, constructed per the instructions of the executioner: Albert "the hanging man" Pierrepoint.

Albert Pierrepoint was a second-generation hangman whose father and uncle had inspired him from a young age to go into the business. Yet, Alfred was not a gristly person or out for retribution. Soft spoken and reserved, he believed once a person was put to death, they had paid their dues. "Execution is sacred to me" he wrote in his 1977 memoir. [449] He

[447] "Eleven Belsen 'beasts' hanged" (1945)

[448] Memo from British Governor, Hamlin Prison, Subject: complaints, dated April 14, 1947, from P. Clapham collection.

[449] Executioner: Pierrepoint. P. 187

never wanted to know the person's criminal history. Irma Grese was one of 200 people he put to death for war crimes. Pierrepoint hated publicity and avoided the press. Still, he received unwanted and strange accolades.

Albert Pierrepoint would make the Official Guinness Records as the longest serving executioner, executing between 435 – 600 people in 25 years. He was so meticulous in his work – measuring the condemned person's height and weight to rope length and drop length – each person died immediately upon the drop without a beheading.

In British prison, warders and medical staff would have been responsible for weighing and measuring the condemned prior to execution. For the Belsen case, Albert Pierrepoint and RSM O'Neil were assigned to the task.

The three condemned females were moved to ground floor cells in the old, castle-like prison. The men remained in cells above. Light in their cells filtered between the bars of the high windows; fresh air and light no longer bathed them.

Last Steps

Gerichtsgefängnis CELLE

Nominal Roll of SS-Women transferred
from Prison CELLE to Prison LÜNEBURG

1. BORMANN Johanna
2. VOLKENRATH Elisabeth
3. EHLERT Herta
4. LOTH Ilse
5. LOBAUER Hildegard
6. FÖRSTER Ilse
7. FÖRSTER Ida
8. OPITZ Klara
9. KLEIN Charlotte
10. BOTHE Herta
11. WALTER Frieda
12. HASCHKE Irene
13. FIEST Gertrud
14. SAUER Gertrud
15. LIESEWITZ Hilde
16. ROTH Johanna
17. HEMPEL Anna
18. HÄHNEL Hildegard
19. KOPPER Helena
20. GRESE Irma
21. STAROSTKA Stanislawa
22. KAMBACH Hildegard
23. NAUMANN Gertrud
24. REINHOLD Gertrud
25. STEINBUSCH Ilse

Certified that I have received today the bodies, kits, documents of the above named prisoners.

.... Signature

........SQ.......... Rank

.... Unit

....15 . 09 . 45.... Date

Security was closely documented around the Belsen inmates. A roll call of inmates had to be conducted before any movement. This is the roll call for the Celle to Lüneburg transfer on November 15, 1945. The penciled marks were made as each inmate was identified. (Circa November 1945. Location: archives. Courtesy United States Holocaust Memorial Museum Collection, Gift of the Canadian War Museum. Used with permission.)

Irma Grese (holding rolled blanket) between Elisabeth Volkenrath and Juana Bormann leaving Celle to travel to death row at Hamelin prison. This was Grese's last time in public. (Circa 1945. Location: Celle Prison. Photographer: unknown. Credit: United States Holocaust Memorial Museum Collection, Gift of the Canadian War Museum. Used with permission.)

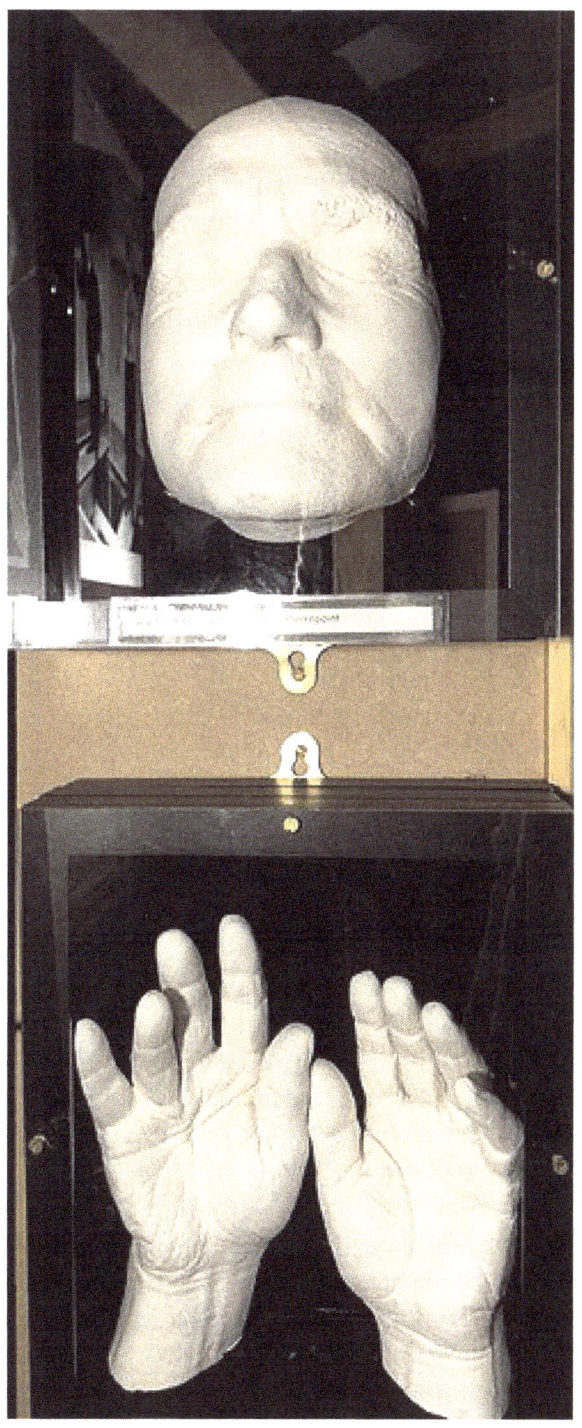

Above: The mask and hand casts of Albert Pierrepoint, one of Britain's official executioners. Items owned by Pierrepoint have high value and are sought by collectors. In 2019, a notebook, watch chain, cigar holder, and other personal items sold for over $24,000 USD (Bolden Auctions)

(Circa: 2018. Location: Wandsworth Prison Museum. Photographer: "SchroCat." Credit: "SchroCat" who kindly allows photographs of their exhibits. Used with permission.)

Date	Name	AGE	HEIGHT	WEIGHT	DROP
DEC 13 1945	ELIZABETH VOLKENRATH	23	5-3	151	7-5
DEC. 13 1945	IRMA GRESA	21	5-5¼	150	7-4
DEC 13 1945	JUANA BORMANN	42	5-1¼	101	5-8
DEC. 13 1945	JOSEF KRAMER	39	6-2	205	6-0
DEC 13 1945	DOCTOR FRITZ KLEIN	57	5-7	147	7-7
DEC. 13 1945	KARL FRANZICH	32	5-6½	151	7-5
DEC. 13 1945	PETAR WEINGATHER	32	5-6¼	148	7-6
DEC. 13 1945	ANSAGER PINCHEN	32	5-6½	144	7-9
DEC. 13 1945	FRENZ HOESZLER	39	5-7½	155	7-3
DEC. 13 1545	FRANZ STARFL	30	5-8¼	165	6-10
DEC. 13 1945	WILHELM DORR	24	6-2	176	6-5
DEC. 13 1945	SANDROCK	42	5-10	145	7-8
DEC. 13 1945	SCHEINBERGER	37	5-5½	141	7-10

Partial notes made for Albert Pierrepoint verifying age, height, and weight to determine the "drop length" for hanging the Belsen condemned. When weighed, Irma Grese was defiant and angry. Albert "the hanging man" Pierrepoint would later note her beauty. (Circa December 1945. Location: archives? Source unknown. Public domain.)

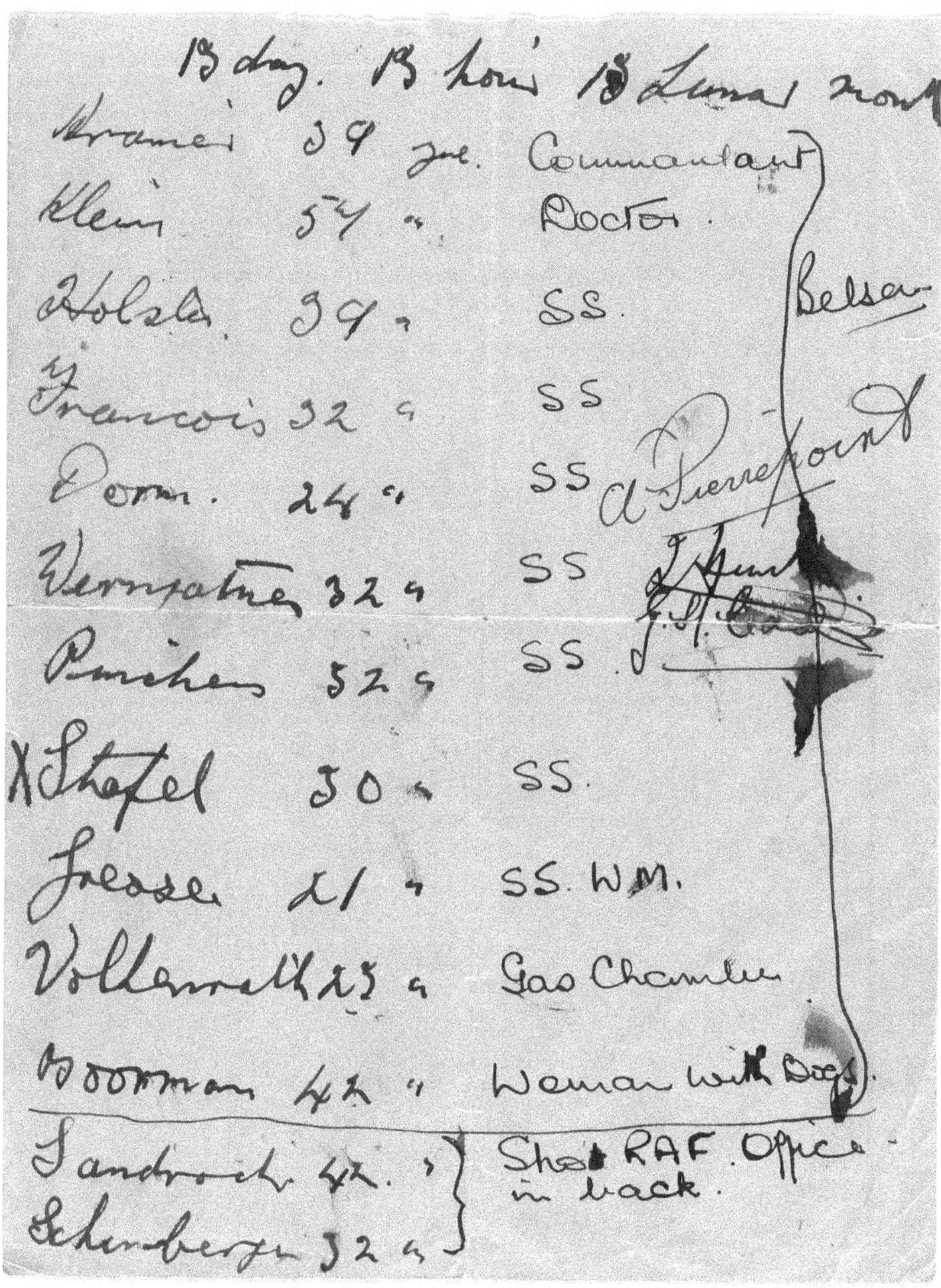

13 day. 13 hour 13 Lunar month

Kramer	39	yrs.	Commandant
Klein	57	"	Doctor.
Hössler	39	"	SS.
Francioh	32	"	SS
Dörr.	24	"	SS
Weingartner	32	"	SS
Pinchen	32	"	SS.
X Stofel	30	"	SS.
Gresse	21	"	SS. W.M.
Volkenrath	25	"	Gas Chamber
Boorman	42	"	Woman with Dogs.
Sandrock	42.	"	Shot RAF. Officer in back.
Schonberger	32	"	

Belsen

A Pierrepoint

Notes made by Albert Pierrepoint listing the ages of the condemned. Irma Grese is noted at 21. Pierrepoint signed the note and had gifted it. (Circa: December 1945. Location: archives. Courtesy Imperial War Museum. Used with permission.)

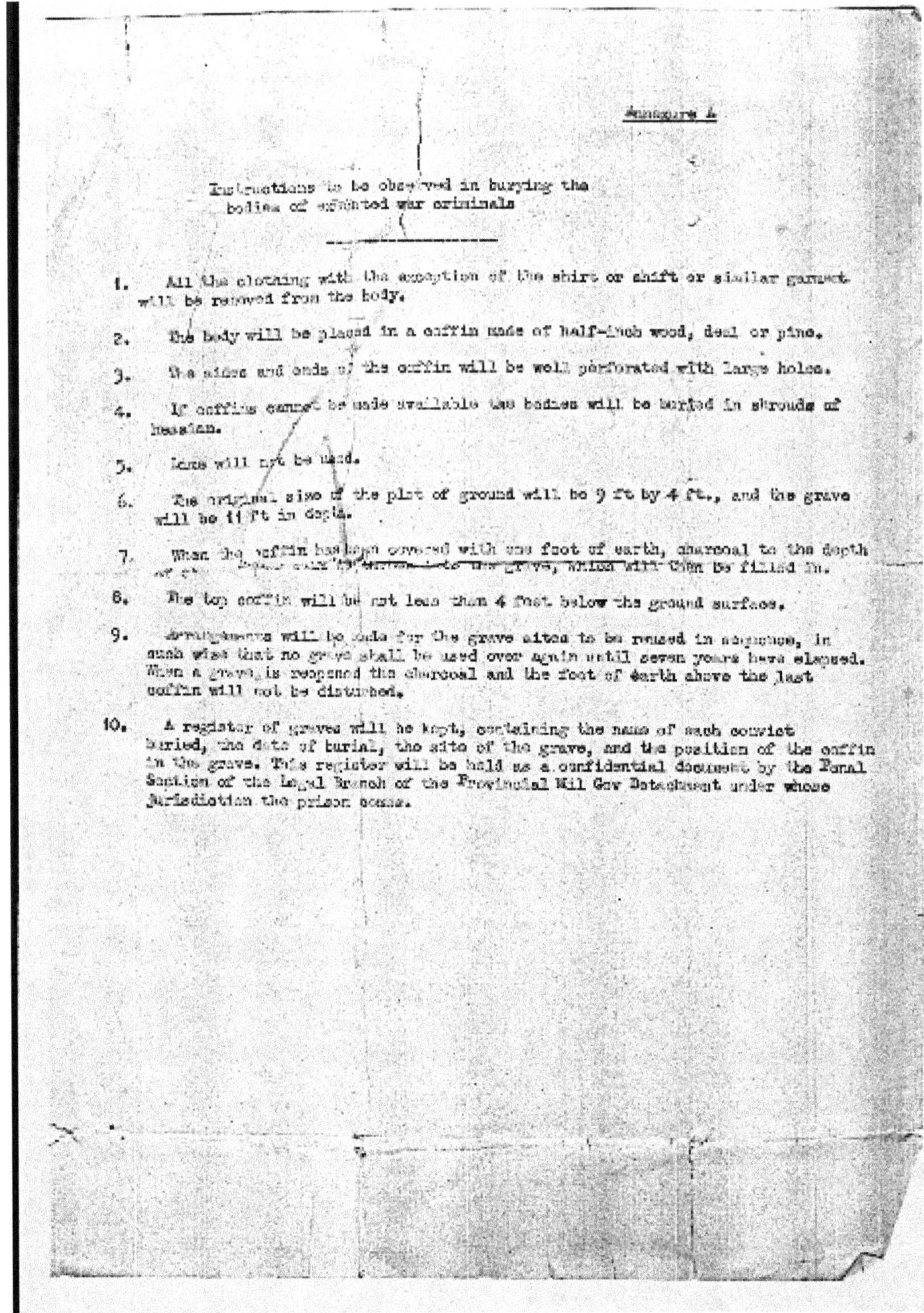

Annexure A

Instructions to be observed in burying the bodies of executed war criminals

1. All the clothing with the exception of the shirt or shift or similar garment will be removed from the body.

2. The body will be placed in a coffin made of half-inch wood, deal or pine.

3. The sides and ends of the coffin will be well perforated with large holes.

4. If coffins cannot be made available the bodies will be buried in shrouds of hessian.

5. Lime will not be used.

6. The original size of the plot of ground will be 9 ft by 4 ft., and the grave will be 11 ft in depth.

7. When the coffin has been covered with one foot of earth, charcoal to the depth of [illegible] will be thrown into the grave, which will then be filled in.

8. The top coffin will be not less than 4 feet below the ground surface.

9. Arrangements will be made for the grave sites to be reused in sequence, in such wise that no grave shall be used over again until seven years have elapsed. When a grave is reopened the charcoal and the foot of earth above the last coffin will not be disturbed.

10. A register of graves will be kept, containing the name of each convict buried, the date of burial, the site of the grave, and the position of the coffin in the grave. This register will be held as a confidential document by the Penal Section of the Legal Branch of the Provincial Mil Gov Detachment under whose jurisdiction the prison comes.

The official memo including instructions to bury Irma Grese and those who were hanged with her. Her coffin was placed in a mass grave. (Circa 1945. Location: archives. Courtesy United States Holocaust Memorial Museum Collection, Gift of the Canadian War Museum. Used with permission.)

CHAPTER 34
"Schnell!"

Albert Pierrepoint's autobiography describes, for the first time, meeting Irma Grese; he would never speak of her in any interview prior to writing his memoirs. It was December 12, 1945. As O'Neil weighed each of the condemned and noted their height, Pierrepoint noted each in his ledger in his neat, careful handwriting. When the male prisoner's statistics were completed:

> Our SM O'Neil ordered "bring out Irma Grese." She walked out of her cell and came towards us laughing. She seemed as bonny a girl as one could ever wish to meet. She answered O'Neil 's questions, but when he asked her age she paused and smiled [sic]. I found that we were both smiling with her as if we realized the conventional embarrassment of a woman revealing her age. Eventually she said "twenty-one," which we knew to be correct. [450] O'Neil asked her to step on the scales. "S*chnell!"* she said - the German for "quick."

In his meticulous handwriting, Pierrepoint listed Grese at 5 feet 5 1/4 inches tall and weight at 150 pounds. His mathematics gave her a drop of seven feet 4 inches. [451]

The surviving Holocaust prisoners were given passes to view the executions, but none are listed as attending. Witnessing the execution would be the British officer in charge of the executions, Brigadier Paton-Walsh, and the deputy governor of Strangways Prison, a Miss Wilson. According to Helene's memoirs, Irma had requested a priest to be with her. The executions for those condemned to death at the Belsen trials, along with one unrelated case, was set for December 13, 1945.

On December 12-13, 1945, Grese spent the night before her death singing German songs with fellow former guards Elisabeth Volkenrath and Juana Bormann. She also penned a two page "Last Greeting" letter in her flowing script. She speaks of how she and her fellow inmates were tortured at Celle and now in Hamelin, but being proud Germans, they withstood it all. And from the grave, she promises, they will be heard.

The next day was cold, snow in the air, the norm for mid-December. Grese ate a last "special meal of sausage, rolls, and real coffee" [452] rather than the coffee and bread offered during the trial.

Irma Grese was the second person to be executed. Albert Pierrepoint first spoke of Grese's walk to the gallows in his memoirs: [453]

> We climbed the stairs to the cells where the condemned were waiting. A German officer at the door leading to the corridor flung open the door and we filed past the row of faces and into the execution chamber. The officers stood at attention. Brigadier Paton-Walsh stood with his wristwatch raised.

---

[450] Grese lied; she was 22 at that moment.
[451] Cited in capitalpunishmentUK.org
[452] Cosner (1998) p. 63
[453] Prior to his memoir, Pierrepoint refused to speak of Grese's execution, even when offered large amounts of money.

> He gave me the signal, and a sigh of released breath was audible in the chamber, I walked into the corridor. "Irma Grese," I called. The German guards quickly closed all grilles on twelve of the inspection holes and opened one door. Irma Grese stepped out. The cell was far too small for me to go inside, and I had to pinion her in the corridor. "Follow me," I said in English, and O'Neil [*sic*] repeated the order in German. At 9.34 a.m. she walked into the execution chamber... [454]

Defiant to the end, Grese stared at each person who stood around her before she took the seven steps to the scaffold, shoes hollow on the fresh wooden steps. She utilized her final morsel of power when she commanded the executioner to expedite the process.

A Grese biographer notes one of those present was a designated chaplain, who extended a cross to Grese. Adele-Marie notes Grese "plant(ed) her lips on the cross" as a last religious rite." This is also mentioned in another work by D.P. Brown (who also adds Pierrepoint murmuring "forgive me" when placing the white hood and noose over Grese's head. [455]) The priest, nor the cross, nor any request for forgiveness are mentioned in Pierrepoint's nor any other memoir. [456]

The noose and white hood [457] were placed over the infamous blonde hair and pretty face. She dropped at 10:03 a.m. according to her death warrant. [458]

Pierrepoint wrote that Grese was first to die. She was considered the toughest female defendant; someone determined Grese was younger and was more likely to panic so it best she be taken first. Field Marshall Montgomery discharged a press release later, stating Grese was second to die; this is confirmed by the death certificates of the condemned females: Elizabeth Volkenrath at 9:34 a.m., Grese at 10:03 a.m., and Juana Bormann at 10:38 a.m. (Bormann's last words in German: "I have my feelings." [459])

These three women were members of at least 3,000 females who were employed in the concentration camps, 77 of whom were brought to trial. They were of the very few convicted. Many who were convicted received early release from prison or pardoned. [460] Most of the female guards who escaped before liberation were never pursued. Heinke (2008) "estimates that criminal proceedings were initiated against just 10% of female guards, with many never actually coming to trial because of the death of the accused or the 'absence of proof...'" [461] The vast majority of female guards, abusive or no, returned to normal lives, the world of Nazi Germany left behind.

---

[454] Pierrepoint, A. (1974) p. 150
[455] P. 93
[456] P.124
[457] Some photographs and media depict Grese's head covered with a dark hood. Pierrepoint only used white hoods. Images with "Irma Grese at the gallows," or "Irma Grese" in a white executioners hood, are false. Grese did not wear a dark hood. No photographs were taken of her in prison or at the gallows.
[458] Montgomery, B. L.
[459] Rough translation into English: "I have feelings, too."
[460] McGuinness, 2021
[461] Cited in Clark (2012) electronic copy no page number.

The Hyena's Demise

Irma Grese's unmarked gravesite as it appeared in 2016. Grave markers had to be removed as Neo-Nazis began gathering here for celebratorily events. The remains of Irma Grese and her codefendants were initially interned behind the walls of the prison yard not far from the gallows. (Circa 2016. Location: undisclosed. Photographer: Joanna Czopowicz. Courtesy: Joanna Czopowicz Used with permission.)

An die Angehörigen abgegebene Gegenstände der nachstehend aufgeführten Gefangenen:

G r e s e, Irma

1 Sparkassenbuch (Kreissparkasse Bielitz) RM 4 3o1.57

Bargeld: RM 439.66 (Vierhundertneununddreißig 66/1oo Reichsmark

1 Armbanduhr mit Lederarmband

6 Ringe, gelb Metall (1 Stein lose des einen Ringes)

1 Rucksack: Inhalt	1 Regenmantel	Strümpfe
	1 Staubmantel	
	1 Reithose	
	Leibwäsche	
1 Aktentasche:	1 Mutterspritze	2 St.Schlafanzug
	Teill. Gegenstände	1 Büstenhalter
	1 Tuch	1 Kleid
	1 Paar lange Stiefel	

K r a m e r, Josef

RM. 8o.oo Reichsmark Achtzig.

1 Hemd (von Frau an das Gefgs. gegeben)

V o l k e n r a t h,

RM 4o.- Reichsmark: Vierzig. 1 Ring u. 1 Armreif u.Beutel Flickzeug

D ö r r, Wilhelm

1 Brieftasche mit Bildern pp.

1 Paar Hosenträger.

Verw. Inspekter.

The official formal list of effects left by the condemned. The items would be turned over to the families. Irma Grese had many items to turn over to her sisters, more than any of the women at the trial. (Circa: 1945. Location: archival. Courtesy United States Holocaust Memorial Museum Collection, Gift of the Canadian War Museum. Used with permission.)

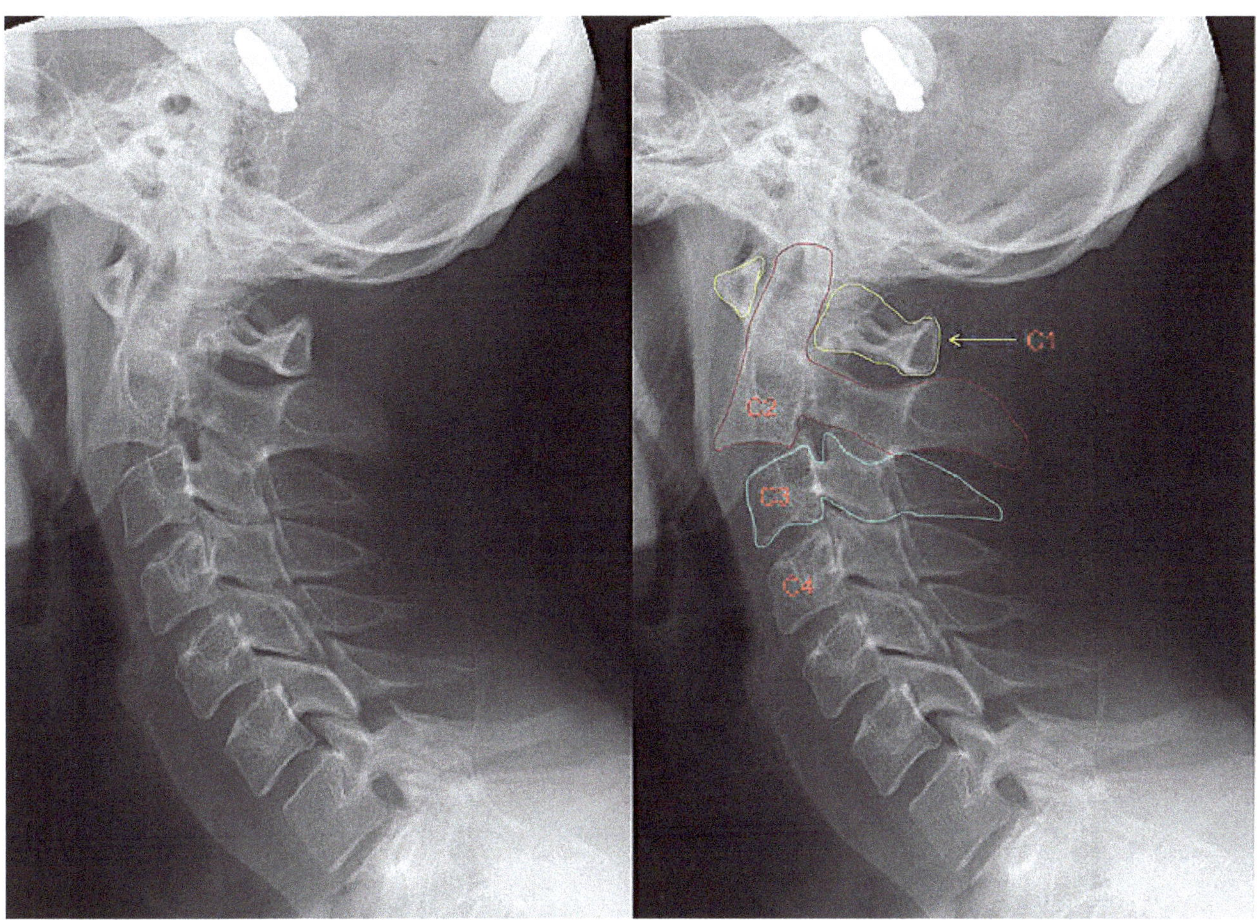

X-ray of the cervical spine with a hangman's fracture. Left without annotation, right with location of the bones. The C2 (red outline) is moved forward with respect to C3 (green outline).
Irma Grese's cervical spine would have resembled the above after her body was dropped in the gallows. "Long-drop" or "measured drop" hanging, used by Pierrepoint, calculated height and weight to determine rope length and slack. The inmate's neck was snapped but was not decapitated. The delivered energy to snap the neck was about a 1,000 foot-pounds force, with death occurring in about 0.632 seconds [462] by the closing of the airway, and jugular veins, and carotid arteries along with the snapping of the neckbones. This type of execution was considered humane for its time. (Circa March 29, 2009. Photo by Lucien Monfils. GNU Free Documentation License. CC BY ND 4.0.)

462 Capital Punishment UK, n.d.

Hameln, den
28. April 1949.
Aufgrund der Geburtsurkunde
Nr. 21-1923 Standesamts Göhren F wird
berichtigend vermerkt:
Die Vornamen der
Verstorbenen lauten richtig:
Irma Ilse Ida.
Sie war evangelischer Religion
und wohnte in
Belsen Kreis Celle
(Lager). Sie war
geboren am 7. Oktober 1923 in
Wrechen Kreis
Neubrandenburg
(Standesamt Göhren
Nr. 21-1923)
Die Eltern sind:
Alfred Anton Albert
Grese und Bertha
Wilhelmine Auguste Grese geborene
Winkler, beide
wohnhaft in Wrechen.
~~Der Standesbeamte~~
Bei F muß eingefügt
werden: "und aufgrund
standesamtlicher Ermittlung." Vorstehend
2 Schriftworte gestrichen.
Der Standesbeamte
Hecker

C

Nr. 725.

Hameln, den 30. August 1946

Die Irma Grese

wohnhaft in unbekanntem Orte

ist am 13. Dezember 1945, Stunde unbekannt um Uhr Minuten

in Hameln, Münsterwall 2 verstorben.

~~D. Verstorbene war geboren~~ am Weitere Angaben fehlen.

in

~~(Standesamt~~ Nr.

~~Vater:~~

~~Mutter:~~

~~D. Verstorbene war nicht verheiratet~~

Eingetragen auf ~~mündliche~~ - schriftliche - Anzeige von Military Government 123 Detachment Hameln vom 27. Dezember 1946

~~D. Anzeigende~~ Ref. 123/PS/33/31.

~~Vorgelesen, genehmigt und unterschrieben~~

Der Standesbeamte
Hecker

Todesursache: ~~Tod durch Erstlicken~~.
ärztliche Todesbescheinigung lag nicht vor.

Eheschließung der ~~Verstorbenen~~ Eltern der Verstorbenen am 14. 10. 1921 in Göhren

(Standesamt Göhren Nr. 8-1921

Opposite page: Irma Grese's obituary. The handwritten notation (in German):

Hameln, den
28. April 1949.
Aufgrund der Ge-
burtsurkunde
Nr. 21-1923 Standes-
amts Göhren **F** wird
berichtigend ver-
merkt:
Die Vornamen der
Verstorbenen lau-
ten richtig:
Irma Ilse Ida.
Sie war evangeli-
scher Religion
und wohnte in
Belsen Kreis Celle
(Lager). Sie was geboren am 7. Ok-
tober 1923 in Wrechen Kreis
Neubrandenburg
(Standesamt Göhren
Nr. 21-1923)
Die Eltern sind:
Alfred Amon Albert
Grese und Bertha
Wilhelmine Au-
guste Grese geborene
Winkler, beide
wohnhaft in Wrechen.

~~Der Standesbeamte~~
Bei **F** muß eingefügt
werden: "und aufgrund
Standesamtlicher Er-
mittlung." Vorstehend
2. Schriftswort ge-
strichen.

Der Standesbeamte
[signature, Heur or Heuer]

Translation into English:

*Hameln, 28 April 1849. On the basis of the birth certificate No. 21-1923 of the registrar's office of Göhren **F**, a correction is noted: The first names of the deceased are actually Irma Ilse Ida. Her confession was Protestant and she lived in Belsen in the county of Celle (camp). She was born on 7 October 1923 in Wrechen in the county of Neubrandenburg (registrar's office of Göhren, No. 21-*

1923). The parents are: Alfred Amon Albert Grese and Bertha Wilhelmine Auguste Grese, nee Winkler, both residents of Wrechen.

~~*The clerk of the registrar's office*~~ *At **F**, "and on the basis of the registrar's office's inquiries" must be inserted. The previous two words [meaning "the clerk of the registrar's office"] are struck out.*

The clerk of the registrar's office
[signature, Heur or Heuer]

Translation by Ann Marie Ackerman, J.D. www.annmarieackermann.com. (Circa August 30,1946. Location: unknown. Courtesy Magdalena Chomitkowska. Public Domain.)

Chapter 35
In the Hyena's Wake

Immediately after she was pronounced dead, Grese's body was prepared for burial per official instructions order for "burying the bodies of (unknown) war criminals." Her remains were stripped save for an undergarment, the body was placed in a coffin made of "half-inch wood" or a shroud (depending on what was available), with the sides and one end be drilled with large holes. The coffins had been preassembled, having arrived at the prison dismantled until ready to use. The top, bottom, and sides were removed from storage and assembled with screws, the job made easy and quick by perforations.

Grese's coffin would be stacked with two others in the grave, each covered in a layer of charcoal once in place in a mass grave nine feet by four feet, with a depth of eleven feet. "The top coffin (should be) less than four feet below ground surface." The graves were in Hamelin prison and not far from the gallows. The graves were not to be disturbed until "at least seven years," and the last grave (first to be buried in the stack) "the charcoal and the foot of earth … will not be disturbed." [463]

Irma Grese's belongings were given to two of her siblings, Helene and Lieschen. Grese had left behind 439.65 in Reichsmarks and 4,391.57 Reichsmarks in the bank. [464] Also listed were the two combs she took to court to carefully style her hair, a wallet and backpack, six rings, her birth certificate, underwear, and various clothing items to include "a pair of high boots" [465] (the infamous boots that caused such terror in the camps). On the official military form for Grese, the following was turned over to her family:

1. Savings bank book
2. Wristwatch with leather strap
3. Six gold metal rings including 1 stone loose in one of the rings.
4. One briefcase carrying items, including: 1 mother funnel, 1 pair of long boots, 1 dress, 1 bra, 1 suit, 1 body wash, socks.
5. A backpack carrying: 1 raincoat, 1 dustcoat, 1 notebook.

The "mother funnel" is probably a birth control method. It was a syringe vaginally placed that injected liquids into the cervix. "It was not a birth *certificate*,' explains one source. "It was birth *control*. The (author's) translation was incorrect." [466]

A photograph on page five of the December 17, 1945, issue of New Zealand's *Waikato Times*: a smartly dressed woman in dark suit and matching fedora showing credentials to uniformed soldiers at a gate. It is Helene Grese, and she is attempting to visit her sister for her birthday in Celle prison. She may have been trying to celebrate her own birthday, December 2, with Irma, or a late birthday of Irma's (October or November 7). The British guards did not allow Helene access. For whatever reason the photo was printed after Irma Grese's death.

---

[463] P. Clapham collection
[464] The Reichsmark would be replaced by the Deutschmark in 1948.
[465] Brown, p.116
[466] This historian asked to remain anonymous. Interview, March 20, 2024

Josef Kramer's wife Rosina wrote to the prison requesting a copy of her husband's birth certificate. She was destitute and now relying on public assistance for aid. The Nazi wife who once entertained guests with the finest of food and drink at her admirable home had children to raise and she desperately needed funds.

Trial nurse Norma Falk had returned to work, "relieved to go back to nursing." Decades later, she would say "to this day I still can't believe what I heard" during the Belsen trial. As a nurse and a humanitarian, she had been "terribly moved" at the sight of survivors, "wondering, how could they smile? How could they speak, after all this?" [467]

A small article appeared on page five of the April 16, 1946, copy of the *Wanganui Chronicle* newspaper of New Zealand. The unnamed journalist noted female German students had started an underground movement to support Irma Grese. "The girls wear red caps in imitation of the British military police uniform," and tell people how "Saint Irma" was "tortured into making a false confession." For a while, it was a movement to "make a saint of Irma Grese." [468] Again, a fan club of sorts created for an infamous criminal, supporting a high-profile convicted killer. Perhaps she was guilty of all she had been charged with, perhaps not, many admirers did not care. Grese was good-looking and popular. There were no red-capped teens canonizing Volkenrath or Bormann.

British troops were guarding what was left of Belsen when two women approached them on August 25, 1946. One woman was Rosina Kramer, wife of Josef Kramer. His loyal Rosina continued living in poverty. She had visited Belsen prior, and someone threw a knife at her.

The second woman approaching the troops was identified as Helene Grese. After the trial and executions, Rosina had contacted Helene Grese, now a nurse in Germany's Russian zone.

Helene indicated Rosina as they approached the British officers. "This is Frau Kramer and we've come for Irma Grese's jewels" Helene told the guards. Rather than allow them access, the guard escorted the women to the commander; the commander had the women arrested.

Frau Kramer now explained to the commander that she believed Irma had buried a box of "jewels" in a garden just before arrest. The commander allowed the women to examine this garden area. With a guard surveilling carefully, the two women combed and dug through the soil. After a three-hour search of this garden, nothing was discovered. [469]

And what of Irma Grese's two mentor trainers in the concentration camps?

Maria Mandl fled to her childhood home, but her father refused to hide her. She was arrested in August of 1945 hiding at the home of a family member. Her interrogators would note Mandl's high intelligence and dedication to the Nazi "cause." She was tried and found guilty in the Auschwitz trial and hanged in January 1948.

Dorothea Binz had fled Ravensbrück but was captured in Hamburg in May 1945. She was tried and found guilty in the Ravensbrück trial. She was hanged in May 1947, at Hamelin Prison by Albert Pierrepoint, the same man who conducted the executions at the Belsen trial.

Hamelin was scheduled to close in 1955, and the graves of those executed from the Belsen trial were exhumed in March 1954, to be released to Germany. The remains were

---

[467] USC Shoah Foundation

[468] Move to Make Saint of Irma Grese.

[469] Beast of Belsen's Widow Arrested (1946, August 26). P. 2

identified in part using dental forensics, and some of the clothing still clung to the bones. The remains of Irma Grese, like the others, were placed in small boxes and transported to Germany to be interred on German soil at Am Wehl Cemetery in Hanover, Germany. White crosses, one for each body, were placed to mark the graves. In an article dated March 15, 1954, *Time* magazine reported the mixed emotions. "'Relatives wanted to visit the graves, and we couldn't have all those strangers stomping through our jail,' an official apologized. 'At last,' crowed Hannover's Allgemeine Zeitung, 'they have found worthy resting places.'" An anonymous German stated "... 80% of (those buried) were innocent." [470]

"Neo Nazi groups would visit and hold rallies" so the crosses were removed [471] in the 1980s. All that is left of Irma Grese "the Hyena of Belsen" is a grassy patch of earth.

Albert Grese's arm had been seriously injured during wartime after he contracted blood poisoning. His stepdaughter had written to Helene they desperately needed alcohol and animal fat to save the arm. Albert's arm would eventually heal. As Germany and surrounding countries began restoration, Irma's name dropped from Albert's vocabulary. All that was important now was rebuilding the land and the cities the war had destroyed.

Lieschen would complain about the world's sadness over the mass graves at the Nazi camps. But no one, in her eyes, acknowledged the mass graves of civilians taken in the war, or the "dead soldiers" [472] buried in mass graves in Neustrelitz. [473] She felt it unfair.

According to records, Lieschen Helene Karoline Muller would die September 12, 2016, at the age of 89 in Bayreuth, Regierungsbezirk Oberfranken, BY, Germany. Little is known about her life except she was married and had children.

Helene Grese would die a few months shy of her ninetieth birthday in 2016 in Bayreuth, Regierungsbezirk Oberfranken, BY, Germany. It is unknown when and where her siblings, father, and stepmother died.

Albert Pierrepoint died on July 10, 1992. His life mask and hand casts are on display at the Wandsworth Prison Museum. An execution box, filled with equipment for an executioner, and an example of a British hangman's equipment are displayed nearby. His 1974 autobiography continues to be popular reading.

Holocaust expert, educator and historian Jill McCracken has toured multiple memorials and concentration camps for her studies. She now writes of her experience touring Auschwitz:

> I felt small. Sad and small. The gates, the fences...barracks...piles of clothing, glasses, prosthetics, canes, toys, hair... The decrepit remains of the crematoria, with reality incompatible with everything I knew, ... So many lives lost, for what? It was surreal. Auschwitz-Birkenau is huge, a site of pure hatred, distain, apathy. It just goes on and on ... execution sites, tiny cells, Nazi guard posts... Walking hallowed ground. Reverence in your heart, knowing that those who survived worked and agonized over

---

470 "Germany: Decent Burial." No page number.

471 TheUntoldPast

472 Wieble, P. (1987)

473 These mass graves were not of soldiers, but of civilians who had committed suicide at the end of the war due to fear of Russians caused by previous Nazi propaganda, and as the Red Army retaliated attacks from civilians by killing, looting, and raping. 681 suicides were reported in Neustrelitz alone (SPON magazine). Communist East Germany refused to report these as suicides.

> "helping" the Nazis to run the place. To refuse was folly, so you try to stay alive; these moral dilemmas spin through your mind …[474]

Celle prison still stands as Germany's oldest (functioning) prison. It is a high security institution holding male offenders serving 14 years to life sentences. In May 1984, two inmates constructed a working shotgun from scrap wood, curtain tape, match heads, lead, and iron bedposts, charged by two AA batteries. They used it to escape after taking a jailer hostage. The inmates were caught the next day; it was the second escape for one of these inmates, using the exact same ruse at Celle eleven years prior.

Hamelin Prison's last inmates would be moved out in 1978. A section of the prison was destroyed in 1981. At this writing, a fine hotel now stands where the prison once held Irma Grese and her doomed comrades. Most of its guests would never guess, since its 1992-3 renovation, the hotel was once a place where one of the most infamously cruel females in the Third Reich shouted through a window down to her sister in their last conversations.

To this day, most inhabitants of Wrechen are not interested in discussing Irma Grese. Numerous attempts by this author went unanswered. The people of Wrechen "are tired of lies and don't want to have anything to do with (the case)" says "C" who asked not to be identified. [475]

Though the Third Reich is gone, Neo-Nazi movement continues. Following the same doctrine as the original Nazis, the groups have evolved from the "skinhead" movement to the suit-and-tie organization, creating alliances with business, politics, and organizing both nationally and internationally. The movement includes groups such as the American Nazi Party, Greece's Golden Dawn, and the Third Path in Germany. The hate - filled rhetoric is often titled "white pride" to disguise agendas. Most of these organizations are dedicated to Adolph Hitler, celebrating the former Fuhrer's birthday, and reading the literature associated with his philosophy and rhetoric. Although the new neo-Nazis claim they are not affiliating themselves with the Nazi regime, and instead associate themselves with pride and laws, the underlying base of the groups embrace discrimination. The message trickles downward into the homes of people searching for identity, a cause, power.

A preliminary report from the Center for the Study of Hate & Extremism at California State University in San Bernadino reports 16 major U.S. cities have reported a 44% rise in reported hate crimes. Victims differ according to region, with local news impacting the attacks. For example, with a U. S. president blaming COVID on China, hate crimes against the Asian community rose 77%. When the high – profile case of the 2020 murder of black male George Floyd led the news, there was a reported spike in hate crimes against blacks. New York and Los Angeles reported the highest number of hate crimes, with "antisemitic incidents … the most commonly reported hate crime in New York City." [476]

These new leaders of the "white pride" movement, the suit-and-tie white males in business, politics, and nonprofit organizations, utilize the same implements as their predecessors:

- Loyalty to a Cause

[474] Personal interview with Jill McCracken, May 26, 2024
[475] Interview with "C" March 13, 2024
[476] Cited in Tillman, R. (2022)

- Disbursement of power
- Careful Creation of Leadership
- The filtering of staff
- Desensitization [477]

Their carefully crafted rhetoric is filtered down to those who are more prone to commit hate crimes: the lonely, disenfranchised people seeking recognition and purpose, usually with a mental impairment. Those in power claim hate is never a part of their purpose. These leaders host professional meetings while sending the message to the smaller "street level" groups, such as Order of the Black Sun and Aryan Freedom Network, two groups who protested outside the Florida Disney World Theme Park in September 2023. [478] While it is no longer legal or politically correct to demand discrimination or death against a selected group, prejudice and intolerance occurs still in corporations, government, and the private sector across the globe.

Would Irma Grese have been interested in today's Nazi movement?

[477] See chapter 24

[478] Both groups stood outside the park shouting at patrons. They were protesting against the GLBT community and Jews. The members screamed slogans and waved signs at the adults and children entering "The Happiest Place On Earth."

Hamlin prison as it appeared in 2016. It is now Hotel Stadt Hameln. (Circa 2016. Location: Hamlin, Germany. Photographer: Joanna Czopowicz. Credit: Joanna Czopowicz. Used with permission.)

Chapter 36
Irma Grese Was Innocent!

Irma Grese has her supporters, and they remain stalwart in their convictions to this day. Indeed, several books, articles, and websites decry her innocence of being nothing more than a young woman forced to work at a concentration camp by the Nazi government, treating "inmates" as they deserved. The rest is fabricated by jealous or angry inmates and staff who demanded some type of justice from a warped system. The same themes are found in all positive opinions of Grese:

- Irma Grese was forced into service by a German government that was compelled to place women in precarious positions due to the continuation of the war.
- Grese was only an *SS Aufseherin*, and never a supervisor of any true rank. She would not have the power to make selections or order anyone to death.
- The majority of the persons incarcerated at the concentration camps were criminals mixed with those in protective custody.
- A German employment agency cut her check; she was not paid by the SS.
- Grese had every right to carry a whip or stick to protect herself as prisoners vastly outnumbered her.
- Grese used the whip and truncheon sparingly to punish those who broke camp rules, which could easily create chaos within the orderly operation.
- Irma Grese was young, easily influenced, and had no supervisory or prison work experience.
- Grese was "brainwashed" by the SS and thus cannot be held guilty for her actions.
- Grese only enforced laws to uphold safety and security.
- Her father, Alfred Anton Albert Grese, was against her joining the Naz party; he even beat her for coming home in a uniform.
- At Auschwitz, "Most of her work was rather benign, such as sorting through parcels and overseeing construction projects. However, from May until December 1944, [sic] Grese was appointed senior *Aufseherin* for Compound C which turned out to be the eventual cause of her undoing." [479]
- Prisoners perpetrated their own issues. They would steal food, sabotage toilets to overflow, prisoners urinated and defecated on themselves and across the compound and were filthy by choice.
- Accusations (of beatings and murders) against Grese were never proven.

---

[479] Bellinger, J. (unk)

- "She had sympathy among the prisoners, she liked young, pretty girls, especially Poles." [480]
- Sexual acts by Grese were never proven, only testimony was given.
- Prisoners who were beaten or whipped deserved such, as prisoners around the globe, to keep them in order.
- Roll calls that lasted hours are typical of any institution with a vast number of offenders.
- Grese never owned any dog, including attack or guard dogs. She was never observed with a dog.
- Grese was probably aware there were gas chambers, but never observed one and did not have the authority to work at or near gas chambers. "Irma's sending people to the gas chamber is a big lie! Only doctors could do such those things. It's a historic fact." [481]
- Typhus was the result of inmates not cleaning themselves, their living quarters, and overcrowding. All these causes were beyond staff control.
- "Most of Miss Grese's time at Belsen was taken up with preparing funerals for SS staff members who were also dropping like flies in the camp due to the typhus epidemic."[482]
- The German government owned the camps and their rules could not be amended; to break any camp rules resulted in harsh punishment. Grese would not have broken rules for fear of this punishment.
- No records exist of people ordered to death by Grese. "We have no names of people Irmgard killed, but we (have) names of the people she helped."
- Holocaust survivor and author Fania Fenelon recalled in her book, "Playing for Time," how Irma Grese gave her a kind nickname, "Little Singer," and begged her not to die as the camp was being liberated. "*Stirb nicht*!"[483]
- Grese herself was happy the camps were being liberated.

During trial:

- Irma Grese's last letter from prison indicates she may have been abused by staff.
- The witnesses who testified were dishonest due to vengeance or out of jealousy.
- The trial took place only because the public demanded swift justice. "Though the Allied Control Council had yet to provide a uniform basis for prosecuting war criminals, outraged British citizens demanded justice." [484]
- Affidavits were not reliable.
- Grese was not properly defended.
- Grese was not properly accused.
- The prosecution did not prove "reasonable doubt" nor were they able to place Grese in any position and could not prove the accusations.
- The witnesses' statements could not be proven; many statements were just hearsay.

---

[480] Personal interview by email with Magdalena Chomitkowska (5 March 2024). Chomitkowska cites Stanisława Rachwałowa.
[481] Personal interview by email with Magdalena Chomitkowska (4 March 2024)
[482] Bellinger, J.
[483] Fenelon. (1997). pp. 2-3.
[484] Lerner, B. (10 September 2020)

- The witnesses were criminals, and their word could not be trusted.
- Irma Grese was illegally hanged after being found guilty in a Kangaroo court.
- "Neither her youth nor the truth saved her life from being terminated by some stuffy old English Judge faithfully fulfilling the orders and expectations of his own government." [485]
- The defendants at the "Belsen Trials" were German, but tried by an English court of law under English rulings.
- English hangman Albert Pierrepoint himself admired Irma Grese for her good looks, pluck, and charm.
- Pierrepoint felt guilt for hanging Grese, calling her "brave." [486]
- Authors have made erroneous claims in their works on Grese; therefore, no prior documents can be trusted. "(Author) made a mistake. She didn't have a birth certificate, only a birth control appliance." [487]
- Grese upheld her values and beliefs to the very end; she never wavered in her claims of innocence.

One writer, who has studied Irma Grese and her employment in the camps, wrote to the author:

> Was Irma Grese the sadistic murderess that history is trying to sell us, or was she the Joan of Arc of the Third Reich? If we analyze her case on the current legal basis, her conviction would not have been achieved due to the lack of tangible evidence. Unfortunately, we are talking about something that happened over half a century ago and where the human rights of the accused were not respected. In fact, his defense attorney's work is commendable, managing to spot discrepancies in his accusers' testimony. Several testimonies given against her at the trial were not taken into account because they were clearly exaggerated, inconsistent and contradictory. Other witnesses, including Sarah Langbein, Rachel Oro, Lei Flei and Lena Kapinski, admitted lying and recanted their initial testimony. [488]

In a secret document prepared by Dr. Tadeusz Cyprian (1898–1979) on October 15, 1945. The bespectacled, mustached Dr. Cyprian was a reputable, outstanding lawyer He attended the Belsen Trial and made notes further utilized by the United Nations War Crimes Commission. Of the trial witnesses, Dr. Cyprian noted "Some witnesses were extremely intelligent, but many were not, and they were of no great value to the court." This tainted the evidence: intelligent people "avoided being interrogated," translations were either misinterpreted or bias, and some of the interpreters were not "always intelligent." [489] Much was lost in translation, which rendered the testimony either partially or even completely false. This argument was applied to the Court: the tribunal would have better served the purpose if the officers and lawyers were German – speaking.

---

[485] Bellinger, J.
[486] Ibid.
[487] Personal interview with by email with Magdalena Chomitkowska (12 March 2024)

[488] Personal interview with by email with Magdalena Chomitkowska (3 May 2024)
[489] The Belsen Trial Transcript (1945) Section 1. Pp. 1-2.

Dr. Cyprian also wrote the 44 accused fell into three categories that should have been tried separately: the "main criminals" (including Irma Grese), the "minor criminals" (SS guards) and the "*kapos*."

It would be advisable to separate the atrocities at Belsen from Auschwitz, the doctor continued. Auschwitz was a large camp; it was independent of Belsen. The trial was further hampered by being held under British law and procedure. Testimony was obstructed by some lack of evidence – there were very few photographs of the camp prior to liberation and the buildings were burned down. The film that was used was of poor quality. This effected the defense team. "The Belsen trial will go down in history…" Dr. Tadeusz Cyprian surmised. "… a terrible example of human degradation …" [490]

[490] Ibid. p. 5.

PART VII
Becoming the Hyena

"Look at the psychology of the people who worked at these concentration camps. It's very interesting where they came from." [491]

- Anita Lasker – Walifisch, Auschwitz Survivor who personally encountered Irma Grese

"There comes a point when a man must refuse to answer to his leader if he is also to answer to his conscience."

- Lord Hartley Shawcross, Chief Prosecutor, Nuremburg Trials, 1946

[491] Stubberfield (2020)

"(Children will join) the Hitler Youth, where we have them for another four years... they are smoothed out there for another six, seven months ... and whatever class consciousness or social status might still be left... the Wehrmacht will take care of that." (Adolph Hitler, 1938)
Note the boys wearing the Hitler Youth uniforms. Several carry wreaths.

(Circa 1940s. Location: unknown. Photographer: unknown. Photos courtesy the private collection of Ray Cook. Used with permission. Lower photo has been minimally altered for clarity to remain true to the original photographs. This is the first time these images from the Cook collection have been made public.)

CHAPTER 37
"Smoothed out"

Long after the trial packed up and those involved departed, and years after Albert Pierrepoint and the other well-known names were gone, the questions regarding Irma Grese linger in text, in various debates, and, currently, in social media. Was Irma Grese truly the "Hyena" portrayed by the media, the courts, the witnesses? Did the Nazi regime create Irma Grese? Was it possible Grese was "brainwashed" into being cruel and sadistic? Did the press paint a truthful picture of Irma Grese? Was she a German patsy who took the brunt of Nazi transgressions in a British court?

Nazism did play an obvious part in shaping Irma Grese's character, but it cannot be held fully responsible. Nazi leadership was not comprised of mad men or mentally ill individuals; it was a carefully planned system that operated psychologically and sociologically. It worked long after Hitler died, after the red, black, and white flags were torn down and burned, and after those who once proudly wore the uniform denied any wrongdoing. It is easier to blame Nazi indoctrination and "brainwashing" by the Nazi regime than to delve into Irma Grese's sociological and psychological history. "Brainwashing" works in part because there is a fragment missing in the victim's psyche. For the victim to feel emotional security, they seek something nontangible; an essential part of the victim requires fulfillment, fulfillment that cannot be obtained in "normal" ways. [492] As observed in any cult, before one can be "brainwashed," the victim must want or need what the "brainwasher" is offering. This is the largest factor in the effectiveness of this psychological technique. Brainwashing does not occur in a vacuum.

Irma Grese was that pupil Adolph Hitler envisioned in a speech:

> These boys and girls enter our organizations at 10 years of age, and often for the first time get a little fresh air; after four years of the Young Folk they then go on to the Hitler Youth, where we have them for another four years... and even if they are not complete National Socialists, they go to Labor Service and are smoothed out there for another six, seven months ... and whatever class consciousness or social status might still be left... the Wehrmacht [German armed forces] will take care of that. (1938)

Hitler knew these youths needed the organizations as much as the organizations needed the boys and girls. The sense of belonging, friendship, teamwork, self-respect, protection, good health, and love are the basics of what most children crave: emotional security. Young Irma Grese and her fellow BDM members found their needs met and once wrapped in emotional security, they stayed despite the cost of losing family, friends, and their former life.

After the Labor Service, Irma Grese wanted the job of camp guard as much as the camps wanted Grese. Now the job gave Irma Grese the basics of what most adults crave: job security, money, esteem, possessions, friends, teamwork, self-respect, love, and a bright future. She stayed on, even as a dark part of her soul arose. The darkness was part of the job; for those few brutal guards like Grese, it was also a part of their psyche. Besides

[492] "Normal" would include work, environment, recreational, family/friends.

those basics of what many adults crave, Nazism ensured the dark desires of these people were met. Dark desires that, like esteem and a secured future, meant emotional security.

But if being entrenched in Nazi doctrine and so mesmerized with this "new world leadership" was all it took to become a sadistic camp guard, the camps would have been teeming with such sentinels. Only a miniscule number of German females became guards, and a much smaller number of female guards reached Grese's level of cruelty. Fulfilling dark desires would have been easy in a war-torn country, where "true" Germans were favored and celebrated, without working in a concentration camp.

The Nazi system was a perfect hierarchy. Irma Grese (and her comrades) believed they could never be held personally responsible; and they denied responsibility - some to their death – they blamed the system, their superiors, excused themselves as "only following orders." This was part of the contrivance and one reason why the system worked. But it was also an excellent and plausible excuse, more so than the truth: discrimination, purification of the German race, blaming others for misfortunes, mass murder. Grese and others claimed they were merely obeying supervisors, their government, and Hitler, all in the name of Germany. There was no "one" to blame. To deny responsibility was to remove oneself from the equation - no guilt, no self-blame (a major defense in the trials). Irma Grese never revealed her feelings in court, that she considered Jews as filthy vermin to be destroyed, which was indeed a mantra.

The Nazi Trials went beyond "trial of the century" level and Irma Grese was the infamous female defendant. She was hailed as the "most evil" of German female criminals who committed multiple murders. However, there were known female German serial killers operating "and apprehended" preceding Irma Grese. Anna Maria Zwanziger and Sophie Ursinus were poisoners operating in the 1800s. Elisabeth Wiese had been an "angel maker" killing unwanted children for money in 1902-1903. Grese overshadowed these killers in history in part because prior to WWII, nothing like the Holocaust had taken place in Germany and occupied territories. [493]

The press kept Grese alive in the public's eye and helped build her reputation. Irma Grese was the first female defendant to catch the British public's attention, to be a "media sensation," due to the press response. She was attractive *and* brutal. She was not the feminine norm, eschewing societal rules of feminine etiquette. The public met her "in person," to look her over and imagine her in the roles of torturer and murderer. The British press found Grese as culpable as her codefendant Josef "The Beast" Kramer and linked their names accordingly, heightening her role in the atrocities.

Irma Grese's trial was conducted by British military, and she was tried under British rule. Thus, it was the British press following the story most carefully, and it was Irma Grese who often became the headline. British journalists' coverage "tactics and style" writes Croskery, "in line with both government and popular sentiment ... emphasized the necessity of replacing Nazi ideology with British virtues and democracy." (p. 3). [494] Grese was not judged by what she *did*, some legal professionals argue, but rather, who she *was*: a symbol of the evil Nazi. Her apparent lack of empathy and appearing devoid of emotion were all heavily reported. When Grese laughed twice during the trial, the press reported it

[493] Decades later, survivors continue to be intensely affected. Studies have identified strong associations between the mental health of children and their Holocaust surviving parent's PTSD. For an interesting study, see Dashorst, P. et. al. (2019) "Intergenerational consequences of the Holocaust on offspring mental health: a systematic review of associated factors and mechanisms." *National Library of Medicine.*

[494] 2011

in detail, noting how she placed her hands and bent forward to suppress guffaws. "She became a good candidate for the press's particularly gendered representation of female Nazi defendants at the Belsen trial... (and) presented Grese's amusement in a way that exemplified childish antics (demonstrating) how Grese was portrayed as an immature and juvenile…" [495] Much ink was dedicated to Irma Grese's expressions, clothing, hairstyle, and likened these to past transgressions. Because she was never formally interviewed by medical authorities, assumptions were made of her personality based on what was immediately observed. Her feelings and thoughts were a mystery; her expressions and responses were not.

While highlighting her "juvenile" behaviors, the press was simultaneously portraying Grese as monstrous, a singular Germanic killing machine. She was tried and found guilty in the press before the final verdict of the court. In the media and in court there was little mercy shown, no investigation into additional motivations. (such as mental illness) The defense did argue she was an abused child who fell into the Nazi indoctrination, and the prosecution asked her if she became the bully because she was bullied; this was the extend of applying any psychological cause to Grese's crimes.

If mental health experts had analyzed Irma Grese, it would have taken time for her to be honest in any interview. In her only known interview by the press, she spouted simple, controlled rhetoric. There would have been little time between arrest and trial to obtain a true report. Like all the defendants, she was fighting for her life and knew it. Assuming she would have been truthful, and able to properly express herself, the investigation into her motives would have been fascinating. The court was not interested in science, but in determining just how culpable the arrestees were and proving their guilt. Irma Grese was guilty of torture and murder of hapless prisoners. She was observed violating rules of the Nazi regime; witnesses testified as to her horrific behavior. Many gave a first-hand account of being victimized. Whatever reason(s) caused her to purposely terrify innocent people; she was indeed a vicious, sadistic killer.

Irma Grese and those few vicious female guards were also weak, uneducated women (often incapable of serious introspection) who chose immoral over moral – the easiest choice – to maintain emotional security. Many of these women who were living on this rudimentary level were labeled "monsters."

Irma Grese was not a monster; monsters exist in the imagination. She was a flawed woman who deserved her punishment, but whose case could have contributed to criminology by being carefully studied. While the Nazi Regime did play a role, it cannot be entirely blamed for brutal behavior; the Regime only brought out the darkness that preexisted in Grese and others and allowed it to exist. The media's job is to tell the news but mostly to sell copy. In a court of law, it is the defense's job to assist the accused and the prosecutor's task to prove guilt; law is not built on emotion. The innocent lives damaged by it all will leave generations forever brokenhearted, and the world changed for eternity.

[495] Croskery, p. 28-9

Irma Grese's last letter

Next two pages: Irma Grese's letter she left in her cell, written the night of December 12/13, 1945. It was hours before she walked towards the gallows. (Circa December 12-13, 1945. Location: archives. Credit: United States Holocaust Memorial Museum Collection, Gift of the Canadian War Museum. Used with permission.)

German – to - English translation of Irma Grese's last letter

Last Greeting!

1) I admit now without any regrets that we laughed about all the things we suffered in these past seven months - about all the cruelty and malice we have seen.
2) It does not matter if nobody of you believes how they kicked us - we have never lost our nerves. We remained German and got never tired of it.
3) CELLE, LÜNEBURG - that are the places of horror. I can't find words for it.
4) If they have tortured us in Hamelin or not - nobody's eye has seen it. Our hours are counted already and we will go to the last way as strong as ever.

When on the blue sky clouds pass and the birds sing in the air. When roses are blooming again we will send 1000 greetings from our deep grave.

Irma Grese

Send a copy to Hannelohre

At the top of page 1, Grese wrote “"*Letzter Gruss*!" or “last greeting." It's a phrase often used as a condolence at a funeral – *translator's note.*

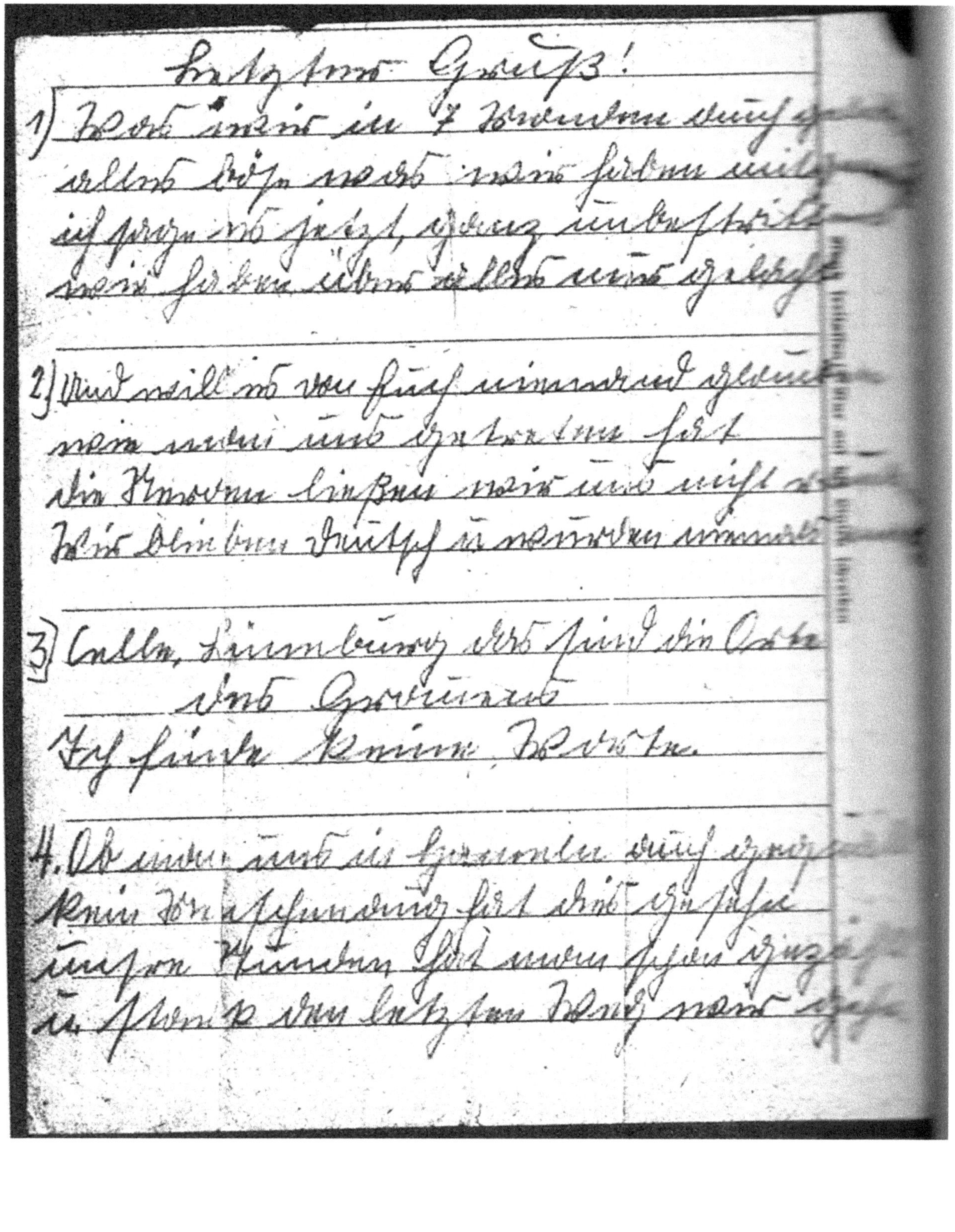
Letzter Gruß!

1) [illegible]

2) [illegible]

3) Celle, Lüneburg das sind die Orte
des Grauens
Ich finde keine Worte.

4. [illegible]

Rand freilassen! Nur auf die Linien schreiben!

CHAPTER 38
Nature or Nurture?

"The area of perpetrator history is well developed. The field has been generally split into two distinct camps of causation; those who believe genocide was carried out by individuals specifically motivated by Nazi ideology or personal abnormalities, and those who argue it was carried out by ordinary people." [496]

Some Holocaust survivors and historians believed Irma Grese was just an immature girl, flotsam, a lost soul. Others summarized Grese enjoyed the power and nice things status brought her. Regardless, Grese was not "made" a killer by the Nazi party.

The Nazis did not create killers any more than Charles Manson's "family" [497] created killers. Like a potter using a potter's wheel, both enigmas took what they had, molded it, carefully shaped it, and created what may become a killer. If their creation balked at taking part in murder, it fell to the wayside to become something else less heinous. Some concentration camp female guards became secretaries; most Manson followers living with the group had no interest in severe violence.

The Nazi hierarchy was created in a way that natural "bullies" would thrive. Hermann Goering (1893 – 1946) loved "power" toys - soldiers, uniforms, and war games - from an early age, he was known as an arrogant military man and would become one of the most powerful men under Hitler's command. Heinrich Himmler (1900 – 1945), the main architect of the Holocaust, was a socially awkward, sickly youth who failed in the military. Himmler found his power in creating killing machines (interestingly, he only *ordered* murder, and from a distance). Joseph Goebbels (1897 – 1945), Nazi minister of propaganda, was a sickly youth with a deformed foot, rumored to be of Jewish ancestry, and a failed author. He became a "best seller" with lies and propaganda as his best work. Underdogs seeking power and control found it in the Nazi party.

To understand criminal behavior, we utilize what we know about the criminal and what is understood about the crime. Next, we compare theories to explain why the crime occurred.

There is never *one* theory that can fully explain crime causation. Irma Grese did not take up a gun and shoot people specifically because, in her reptilian brain, there was a perceived threat. She did not whip innocent people to death solely because she suffered from a sexual sadistic disorder. There were enough narcissistic injuries throughout Grese's relatively short life to cause her distress, but these stressors alone did not create Irma Grese.

Irma Grese's kindness to prisoners has been discussed in this text, so she appears as an enigma, but closer scrutiny reveals she was neither generous nor considerate to prisoners. There were some signs of kindness towards prisoners, but it was behavior

[496] Cline, S.M. (2014) p.8

[497] Charles Manson (1934 – 2017) is believed to be responsible for numerous deaths when his "followers," AKA "family," murdered several people in 1969. He was sentenced to death in 1971.

controlled by Grese. Psychological abuse was part of Irma Grese's repertoire (as will be discussed in following chapters). While treating some prisoners kindly, she still held the prisoner's life in her hand via gun and whip, and each prisoner was constantly reminded of this fact. Grese usually bribed these prisoner "friends" with better living conditions and harboring them (and their loved ones) from death. Bribery is a means to control. Many of her bribes, in the guise of favors, never came to fruition. She promised a coat to a prisoner doctor who performed one abortion on Grese, yet never awarded the coat. She shed tears over the sisterly love between two new prisoners and promised they would stay together, but the sisters were separated. She reminded her prisoner "friends" of their place in the hierarchy by shooting other prisoners in view of these "friends." Grese may have saved some lives by taking them out of selection, but she still owned these people. Although dedicated to the Nazi ideology, Irma Grese constantly broke rules and regulations of the camp, and strayed from being a "good Nazi woman" by "helping" prisoners. Still, she remained dedicated to the ideology of *superiority*, something these prisoners never forgot. [498] The kindness Irma Grese showed any prisoner was psychological abuse.

There are some theories that should be heavily scrutinized, if not altogether dismissed.

"Her carefully made-up appearance and natural good looks became reasons for which (the prisoners) hated her even more" supposes one biographer, suggesting prisoners were only jealous of Grese's good looks. This writer also alludes to Irma Grese being made a scapegoat because of esthetics and blames the media's sensational interest in Grese for her harsh sentence when "more than a few (SS) women engaged in similarly sadistic behavior." [499] Simply stated, she was condemned to die because she was pretty.

One biographer of Irma Grese suggests Grese is a ESTJ type, referring to the Myers-Briggs personality test created by Isabel Myers and Catherine Briggs (based on their work with Jung's theory of personality). Using ESTJ, the biographer labels Grese as "humble, realistic, and efficient … straight-thinking and systematic … with good compassion and empathy for others." [500] This theory should be discarded as the psychological test is a question-answer inventory utilized to determine the quiz-taker's personality, and there is no record of Grese undergoing any type of testing.

An overused explanation for her destructive behavior is that Irma Grese was one of those "ordinary people," a bully - type sustained by Nazi leaders, secretly a kind girl, who fearfully acted under orders and railroaded to the gallows. She ordered no one to die because selection was not her job, nor did she possess that power. She could not have carried a gun because it was not allowed. Prisoners were simply confused, angry, jealous, mentally ill, seeking revenge, or simply lying. The latter is victim blaming/shaming.

Irma Grese did not limit her weapons to boots and whip. Survivor Zdenka Ehrlich, a Czechoslovakian who had survived several camps, was about 22 years old when she was approached by The Hyena in Belsen. Zdenka was working in a field when she found a knife stamped with a swastika. The handle was quite heavy, but she hid the much-coveted tool in her clothing. "Until one day we were searched, and it was Irma Grese … who found it on me." Grese smashed the handle against Zdenka's head: "… I thought for sure she's

[498] One possible exception may be new guard Irma Grese's behavior when initially meeting Magda Hellinger, a Jewish prisoner. See discussion in "Spectrum of Murder."

[499] Jennings pp. 36-7

[500] Tristan (2022). P. 19

going to crush my skull. And when she was finished with me, she threw it away and kicked me." [501] Zdenka made a bold move when, aching from the beating, she stepped out of the line of prisoners to retrieve the knife. Consider her responses in an interview:

> CXW: Did you get the impression that the bad guards were (being abusive) simply because they were ordered to, or did you ever get the impression that some of them were actually sadistic?
>
> ZE: All of them were sadistic. It was quite clear that this was almost a hysteria on their part as any other hysteria. They went that far that they had to go further, there was no way back for them. They had to be more and more cruel. I think they were lost people, anyway. [502]

In the following chapters three theories are discussed to additionally explain how Irma Grese became the "Hyena of Auschwitz."

Opposite page: "Synopsis of the Case" from the Bergen – Belsen official trial transcript. Irma Grese would be one of the defendants sentenced to die. (Circa: 1945. Location: archives. Courtesy the German Federal Archive / Bundesarchiv. Used with permission.)

---

[501] Ehrlich, Z. (1985, August 8). P. 51.
[502] Ibid. Pp. 57-8.

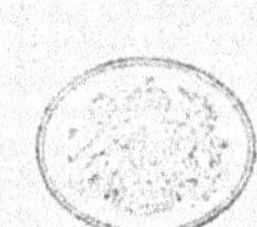

JAG NO: 12

[Bergen - Belsen and Auschwitz Concentration Camps Case]

Vol I

SYNOPSIS OF CASE

1. There were two charges :

The first charge against each of the 45 accused alleged that when members of the staff of BERGEN -BELSEN Concentration Camp, the accused were together concerned as parties to the ill-treatment causing the death and physical suffering of Allied national internees.

The second charge against eleven of the accused made the same basic allegation in relation to AUSCHWITZ Concentration Camp.

2. Particulars of the findings and sentences are summarised at Appendix II of the Minute of Preconfirmation Advice. Briefly :

Eleven of the accused were sentenced to death on conviction and subsequently executed.

Fourteen of the accused were acquitted.

No finding was made in respect of accused No.17 owing to his absence, through illness, from part of the trial.

The nineteen remaining accused were sentenced on conviction to various terms of imprisonment. ZODDEL (No.19) was sentenced to death on conviction for another crime and executed. All the other accused sentenced to imprisonment have been released having purged their sentences, except KULESSA (No.19), and OSTROWSKI (No.31).

KULESSA and OSTROWSKI, who were accused of the first charge only, were each sentenced on conviction to 15 years imprisonment. Their earliest release dates are :

KULESSA 7. 5. 55

OSTROWSKI . . .24. 6. 55

22.1.54

Signed: K. E. Smyth
Compiler of Case Record JAG NO:12.

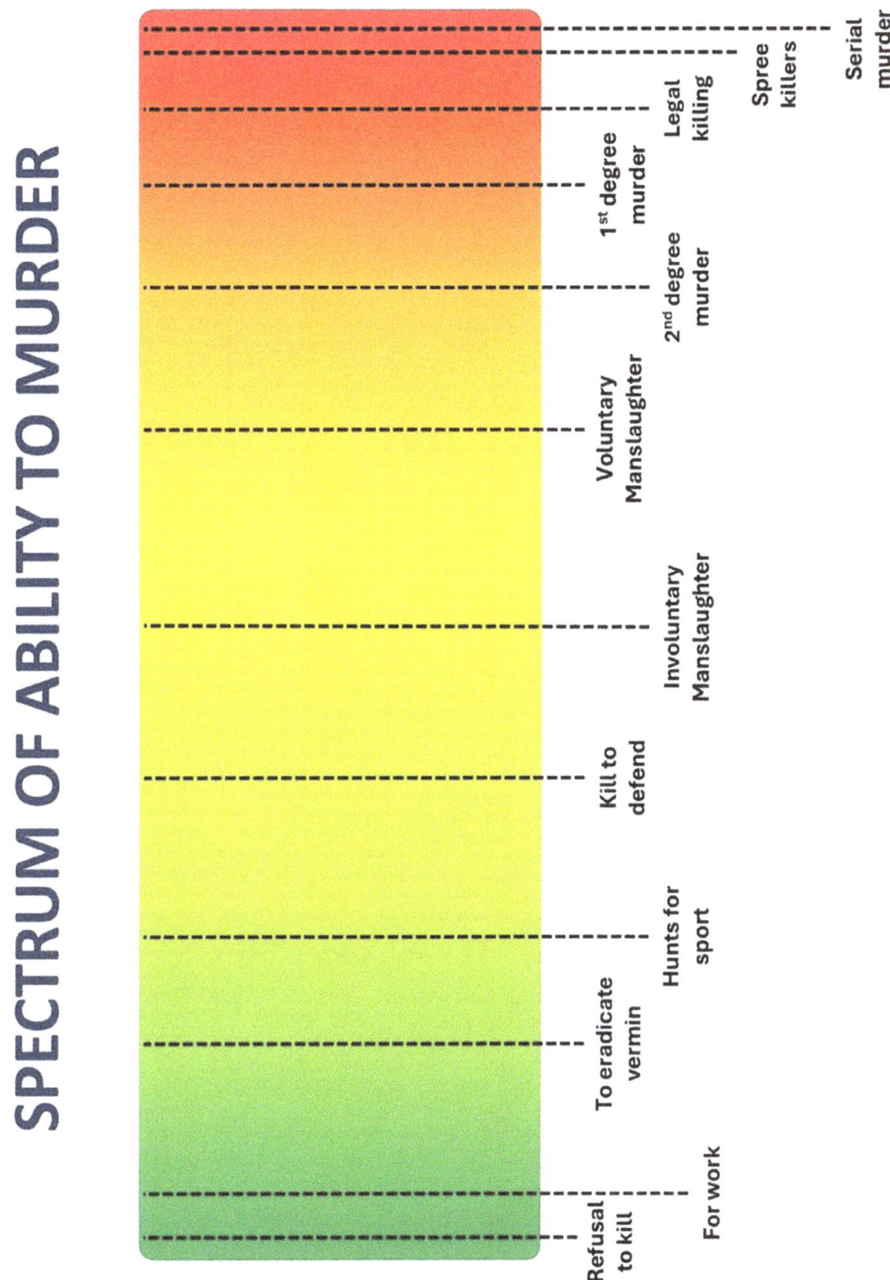

"The Natural Ability to Murder Spectrum" depicts how humankind is capable of murder from Green (i.e. refusal to kill) to Red (i.e. Serial killers). Given what little is known, the child Irma Grese was on the lower end (green) of the murder spectrum; she quickly rose to the higher end of the spectrum. Above are examples of categories of killing and does not encompass all. (Circa: 2022. Location: author's collection. Image by Judith A. Yates. Must obtain written permission to use.)

CHAPTER 39
The Natural Ability to Murder – A Spectrum

"There's a predisposition; there's a predilection to the kind of evil. They must have been chosen for the very fundamental and the mental qualities that these people possessed to be able to perform and do what these people did." [503]

- **Nina Kaleska, Auschwitz survivor, on Irma Grese and Josef Kramer**

The natural ability to murder is on a wide spectrum. Some people could smash an insect without a thought; others could kill a human being with the same disinterest. For "Natural Ability to Murder," encompasses all murder, from insects to human beings.

Criminologist and Investigative Historian Peter Vronsky, PhD explains "natural evolutionary prerogatives" are the "unifying underlying impulse driving serial killers." [504]

The ability to be a serial killer existed in all human beings until humans became civilized – the brain began biological advancement, winnowing down serial killers to only a small percentage of humankind. I suggest the ability to murder exists in all human beings because of evolution. Due to biological differences the ability varies; a small percent of the population is more likely to enjoy murder while a minor group refuses to kill, even to save themselves. In between are the largest group: those who must have variables in place before they can take a life. *Every* person, however, is capable of murder.

The ability to take a life exists in all DNA, the survival mode within humans from conception to death. It exists in the reptilian brain. "Kill or be killed," "Survival of the fittest" assisted primates 65 million years ago, since evolutionary history can be traced. Select members of humankind survived as "the fittest" because they were larger, faster, had protection (a pack/tribe or a weapon), or were stronger than their opponent. Along with learning to survive came instinct/intuition, cunning, and the physicality to assault or withstand attack.

Women have better instinct than males simply because history demanded it; few of our ancestral females were bigger, stronger, faster than males; they did not have the physique. The female of humankind was forced to learn to survive using instinct. In the modern world this is dubbed "women's intuition" or "mother's instinct" – though not all women possess the latter because not all women are maternal. The female became chiefly the caretaker because of physiological and psychological makeup. Men became the breadwinners- the hunters, due to brute strength, physicality, and reliance on that strength and hunter's instinct.[505] However, both males and females historically learned to kill or be killed, to kill for survival (food, as one example), and to kill in times of war.

Men rely on strength and brutality. Females rely on wits and psychology. As an example, coping mechanisms for partner infidelity. Men punch (physical) and women key cars (emotional). Men distract themselves with work or sports (something controllable);

---

503 Kuzmack (1990, January 03)

504 Vronsky, p. 35

505 Historically, matriarchal societies have existed; this author is discussing the majority of civilization.

women will brood over vengeance and pain (psychological warfare).[506] Consider the lyrics of a song where the female singer seeks revenge on her male partner:

> I dug my key into the side of his pretty
> little souped up 4-wheel drive
> Carved my name into his leather seats
> Took a Louisville slugger to both headlights
> Slashed a hole in all four tires
> Maybe next time he'll think before he cheats [507]

The ability to kill continues to rest in our subconscious, existing in the rudimentary brain, and flowing through chromosomes in DNA. It is as natural as walking, talking, eating, and drinking. A human can take a life in the name of survival (defense from predator attack) and protection (to save a life); humans kill in the name of war (military service), employment (slaughterhouses), mass murder (spree killing at random) or serial killing (intentionally murdering numerous victims). Humans are the only species who murder for revenge, spree kill, or serial kill.

Psychologist, professor and author David Buss conducted a survey to utilize in his book "The Murderer Next Door: Why the Mind is Designed to Kill (2006)." Buss discovered 91% of males and 84% of females surveyed have "thought about killing someone" and declared pre-determined, specific methods and selected hypothetical victims. Buss explains everyone has considered committing murder, and it is related to impulses triggered by history and science.

Author and neuroscientist Douglas Fields: "we all have the capacity for violence because in certain situations it's necessary for our survival. You don't need to be taught defensive aggression, because it's a life-saving behavior that's unfortunately sometimes required." Fields explains the response is quick, and it sometimes misfires. It is responding to the threat, not the environment, so that the "modern world presses on the defense mechanism circuitry in ways that can lead to misfires." The brain is responding to threats without understanding the situation because it has not filtered the entire situation – it believes it sees a threat, it reacts, and only minutes later does it comprehend it has made a mistake – usually when it is too late. This would explain road rage, says Fields, when a perfectly normal human being kills another because the brain is triggered into an angry response due to high stress, reacts savagely, and minutes later realizes the "threat" did not exist – it was only another vehicle cutting in a line or changing lanes without a signal. Fields notes "…the amount of crimes committed in a rage …" [508] are committed by the types of people who, friends and relatives will later say, "I never thought they could do this." These types of people fall into the mid-range on the ability spectrum.

These are the murders committed by people who will never kill again; the humans who "are like everyone else" until three variables have combined:

- The means (availability of a weapon)
- The decision (emotion plays no role)

---

[506] I should insert here, "the majority of…"
[507] Underwood, C. (2005)
[508] Cited in Goldhill (2018)

- Values (personal or professional)

In the case of Fields' "road rage" example, these three circumstances have come together so quickly that they do not enter the conscious mind. Desire has blurred all reasoning, stress has blurred common sense, and the three variables have not entered conscious thought. The road "rager" is acting on "auto pilot" now: they grab their weapon (sometimes it is the steering wheel), they gauge distance and speed to guide them in a decision, and the "opponent's" poor driving skills become personal. In seconds the "rager" has entered a zone. [509] When the "rager" emerges from this zone they might be shocked they committed murder, and no amount of apology can take that moment away.

Historian Christopher Browning (cited in Vronsky, 2007) studied one of the *Einsatzgruppen*, the action killing squads traveling the Soviet Union in 1941 to round up Jews in small towns and murder them *en masse*. Only 25 percent of these killers were Nazi party members; "they were ... reserve police officers ... ordinary Hamburg traffic cops." They were not indoctrinated by Nazi beliefs; they had not volunteered or were necessarily anti-Sematic. The killers were on temporary loan. Eventually, another way to exterminate *en masse* had to be devised, because these killing squads began to suffer what Vronsky labels "perpetration-induced traumatic stress": nightmares, suicide, drug abuse, a PTSD of "perpetrators of atrocities." [510] These *Einsatzgruppen* members were able to carry out mass murder because it was their duty, albeit not for an extended period; although they held the means to kill, the decision and values were short-lived or nonexistent.

The "Natural Ability to Murder" [511] can be demonstrated in a color chart: at the lowest end (in green, less likely to be dangerous) are those who refuse to take a life based on personal values, i.e. religious. [512] They might kill an insect or nuisance animal. On the highest end (red, most likely to be dangerous) i.e. "serial killers," who take a life without remorse, who do not view victims as human beings, who "crave" killing. These types of killers are less than one percent of all murders; FBI crime statistics reveal "there are approximately 15,000 murders annually; there are no more than 150 victims of serial murder in the U.S. in any given year." [513] Also in the red section are military action and law enforcement use of force; these killers have been trained how to successfully kill, and legally possess weapons used to take a life with the ability to use them skillfully. [514]

The largest faction of killers is inserted in between (yellow). These are people who can and will kill in a conscious act under the three variables. (means, decision, and values) Examples include:

- In work (a slaughterhouse, on the farm).
- Accidental
- Murder under the influence of drugs or alcohol.
- Attacking a threatening home intruder
- Crimes of passion

[509] In fighting dogs, it is called a "red zone." The author believes "red zone" can be applied to humans.
[510] Pp. 372-3
[511] See table in this text
[512] Example Desmond Doss, decorated American Army medic who refused to carry a weapon in WWII due to religious beliefs.
[513] Bonn (2014)
[514] Emotion plays no part in this spectrum.

- Revenge, retribution, payback for a perceived or true injustice.
- The degrees of murder (First, Second, Third degree)

Given what little is known of her background, the child Irma Grese was on the lower end (green) of the murder spectrum. She hated confrontation and ran from spats or mockery. She did not fight her schoolyard bullies. She cried when her brother was hurt and upset when her brothers teased her pet kitten. As a pre-adult beginning her career at Ravensbrück she quickly rose to the higher end of the spectrum as all three variables existed: Grese carried a whip or a gun (availability of a weapon) she wanted to kill[515]/was a sadist [516] (the decision), and through Nazi rhetoric she believed it was the right thing to do (values).

Grese slapped prisoners, a slap being a visual warning and an intimidation. Next, Grese used her shining boots and specialized whip to abuse prisoners. All three weapons kept her from direct contact. Women typically possess better lower body strength, and she aimed for vulnerable parts of the body. The camp prisoners were reduced to nonhumans moreso than when they arrived. These non-contact hits were degradating; they symbolized disdain. Eventually, Grese would advance to use of a gun; the gun would terrify and show power without being unholstered. It put even more distance between herself and the victim. As this use of forse escalated, so did her willingness to kill.

Anita Lasker – Walifisch survived the Holocaust to become a professional speaker, an author, and holds an an "Honorary" degree as Doctor of Divinity. She explains how Irma Grese turned from a simple village girl (green level) into a cold-blooded murderess (red level) so easily:

> You know, somebody like Irma Grese, how did she get into this position? She comes from a village somewhere. She's never heard of Jewish people and had a job somewhere... she was approached by someone who had tried to recruit people to work in concentration camps... she was offered a uniform, black boots, a dog, a gun, better pay... so, she ends up as a guard. Very proud to be in charge of other people. [517]

Renowned sociologist and author Ervin Staub explains that personality and circumstances affects a person's likelihood of assisting another person in need. "Harming and killing of others," writes Staub, can occur with "profound devaluation by a society or by an ideology adopted by the society." And "an evolution must occur … to lead to genocide." [518] A genocide, Staub explains, grows in steps. "Thoughts, feelings, and actions that do not change real conditions but at least help them cope with their psychological consequences." Examples of which occurred prior to the Holocaust:

- Devaluing certain groups- the longer the discrimination has occurred is more likely to turn.
- Scapegoating – a vulnerable self-concept, thus blaming others.
- Adopting ideologies – begins a strong respect for authority.

---

[515] It could also be said she wanted to appear brutal as brutal behavior gained attention and favor in this environment (values).

[516] Grese might not have "become a sadist" in the camps. See the section on "Sadism."

[517] Stubberfiled (2020)

[518] (2000) P. xi

- Joining new groups – organizations which exclude these certain groups are more likely to turn against the subgroup – in the case of the Holocaust, the "true" Germans turning on Jews." [519]

As each of the above occurs, the ability to kill increases. The above may occur as part of a whole puzzle to build the final picture. For example, in 1933 Germany:

April - Jewish businesses are boycotted.
May - Books written by Jews (and others not "state approved") are burned.
July - East European Jewish immigrants are stripped of German Citizenship.

As the discriminatory acts against the subgroups became more severe, the higher the kill drive became. Boycotting a Jewish business developed into beating, then killing, the Jewish owner.

Staub, a Holocaust survivor himself, believes one of the important parts of the puzzle is the reactions of bystanders – "active opposition by bystanders can reactivate the perpetrators moral values and also cause them to be concerned about retaliation."[520] Had shoppers and neighbors refused to boycott Jewish business on April 1, 1933, entering the shops *en mass* and ignoring the warnings painted on the shop windows, would there have been a May 10th book burning?

[519] Ibid, p. 5
[520] Ibid

CHAPTER 40
Sadism

"It could be several diagnoses that created evil in Irma Grese. 'Evil' is not a diagnosis here, but it sums her up."
- Rachael Bell, MS, MS, LPC and specialist in sexual deviant behavior

Grese embodied symptoms of several different diagnoses indicating comorbidity (two or more diagnoses), including paraphilic disorder, narcissistic disorder, and psychopathy.

Rachael S. Bell, MS, MS LPC of Bell & Associates, LLC is a licensed mental-health therapist with master's degrees in both clinical forensic and health psychology. Bell's vast experience in abnormal psychology and the legal system assists in her studies of abnormal human behavior. For more than a decade Bell was employed as a mental-health therapist in psychiatric hospitals and forensic institutes in Europe and the United States. "Irma Grese," Bell says with conviction, "was definitely a sadist." [521]

Cruelty, like the ability to murder, exists on a spectrum. For the *Einsatzgruppen* in the Browning study (see previous chapter) shooting a gun randomly into a group of strangers was the height of cruelty. To others, prolonged abuse, and torturing to the death – both components of Grese's behavior – were the pinnacle.

Sadistic sociopaths rose through the ranks of the Nazi party. The doctrine gave free range for sadistic behaviors unchecked. [522]

Sadism is defined as "the tendency to derive pleasure, especially sexual gratification, from inflicting pain, suffering, or humiliation on others." Rachael Bell explains, "a sexual sadist like Irma Grese gets overall pleasure from inflicting pain. She sexualized pain." Grese quickly moved through the ranks in the camp system *because* she was a sadist. "Imagine you're suddenly infused with all this power and control." Grese was surrounded by people who dared not fight back, who knew Irma Grese could easily end their life with a nod. "I am guessing she didn't feel a lot of control in her (younger years). Grese liked attention, power, control, and as a sexual sadist and surrounded by sadism – this sense of community – she rose through the ranks." [523]

Sadistic Personality Disorder (SPD), according to the DSM-III-R, is a "pervasive pattern of cruel, demeaning, and aggressive behavior towards others, which is directed toward more than one person and does not solely serve the purpose of sexual arousal."[524]

Rachael Bell believes this sadistic personality was also infused with other diagnosis. It is not possible to "do a full investigation on the case (of Irma Grese), but going by what little we know, and what we know about pathology, Grese was comorbid, meaning she probably would have been diagnosed with two or more diagnosis occurring simultaneously." If she could be tested and interviewed today, Grese would have revealed

---

[521] Personal interview, Rachael Bell, May 17, 2024
[522] True sadistic behavior, not an unpleasant or angry person
[523] Bell (2004)
[524] DSM-III-R (1987)

psychopathy - an extreme version of antisocial personality disorder (APD) – was probably histrionic, and definitely had a paraphilic disorder.

"Of course it's subject to dispute," Bell adds; from what is known Grese's personality, particularly in the court room, included a lack of remorse and guilt. Irma Grese did not understand these concepts. Psychopaths can tend to be pathological liars, lack empathy, and act callous; all symptoms Grese was reported to have. This makes it likely that she could have had psychopathy.

Consider the Belsen trial on October 17, 1945, when Grese was on the stand; the prosecutor noted how a girl from a small farm was so quickly promoted to the highest female position in a concentration camp. Was it because she was so cruel?

Irma Grese: "that is nothing to do with the dairy." [525]

Grese's environment was saturated with cruelty and the world of the concentration camps.

The psychopathy may have lain dormant in Grese's DNA but was manipulated by her later lifestyle. "Responses can change over time," Bell notes. The SS awoke that sleeping tiger.

Grese's sadism went beyond the "norm." A truly sadistic camp guard would have enjoyed whipping a prisoner to the ground but would not necessarily be sexually aroused. Sexual sadism is one example of a paraphilia.

> Paraphilic disorders:
>
> When an individual exhibits a propensity to engage in courtship or sexual behaviors considered extremely deviant of the norm, they may qualify for diagnosis of a paraphilic disorder. There is no universal agreement on the line between what is considered sexually deviant vs. atypical-but-normal sexual behavior, but the DSM-5 provides clear criteria for diagnosing sexual disorders. [526]

Psychopathy also involves narcissism, which Irma Grese displayed on numerous occasions: convinced she would be a movie star, visualizing herself as worldly, ensuring she looked good for the Belsen trial press, believing she would never receive a harsh sentence.

When "sexual arousal is dependent on pain and suffering" it is classified as *Algolagnic disorders*. "Sexual sadism disorder is a specific algolagnic disorder wherein sexual arousal occurs from the physical or psychological suffering of another individual;"[527] it is not the actual *act* of inflicting pain that arouses the algolagnic, but the pain the victim *experiences*. When Grese was beating a prisoner's breasts, she was enjoying how the slashes and bruises made the victim ache; it was not the whip in her hand and the damage she caused. "This is why she got off on watching prisoners in (the hospital). It was all about her" according to Bell. [528]

---

[525] Testimony of Irma Grese, Belsen Trial, day 27, 17 October 1945
[526] American Psychiatric Association. (2022) cited in Mayo, N.
[527] Ibid
[528] Personal interview with Rachael S. Bell, May 2, 2024

For this chapter, the author focuses on this definition of sadistic behavior and briefly touches algolagnic disorders.

Sexual Sadism

Dr. Lee Mellor is a recognized criminologist and acclaimed author on serial killers and sadistic behavior. Dr. Mellor disagrees with the hypothesis of Nazi Germany's influencing Irma Grese. "The Nazi regime did not create her," Dr. Mellor believes, "but gave her a space in which her pathologies could be enabled and fully expressed." Thus, Nazism did not *form* Grese but gave her *carte blanch* to act on her fantasies.

Dr. Lee Mellor finds Grese's fascination with the destruction of women's breasts interesting in her sadistic psyche. "I would like to know how she felt about her own breasts" he says when discussing this particular behavior. [529] What did that represent to her? Motherhood? Femininity? Sexuality? Grese may have been punishing herself through prisoners or punishing a symbol.

Dr. Mellor's hypothesis of Grese's desire to destroy women's breasts with torture and beatings "could be a perverse expression of intrasexual competition. She is destroying what she perceived as more attractive female competitors." Grese's focus on female breasts indicate she was destroying what she could not have – a means of punishing those who had "nice" breasts. This stems from an "overindulgent, and neglect by, her mother." Dr. Mellor explains how heterosexual male sadists focus on "breasts, genitalia, and buttocks" – this penchant for destroying these sex organs suggest Grese might have been bisexual, as were the rumors amongst the prisoners.

A few Holocaust survivors who witnessed some of Grese's sadistic cruelty would later express how Irma Grese appeared to become sexually excited when meting out certain punishments; how she focused on women's breasts (either underdeveloped or larger than average, depending on the witness) during medical care. She would beat and cut a buxom woman's bare breasts, then have the woman escorted to receive medical attention from a camp doctor. One source noted, while watching medical care of the abused woman, Grese watched the painful operations – none of the medical units carried anesthetics – "with cheeks flushed, swaying rhythmically and foaming at the mouth." [530]

Grese was also known to be sexually promiscuous, her behavior included sex with coworkers and sexual assault of prisoners, undressing in front of prisoners, and bragging to prisoners about her physical appearance. Both could be attributed to:

- Viewing prisoners as non-living objects
- An inflated ego
- True narcissism
- Poor sense of self boosted by bravado
- High functioning autism
- All or partial of dynamics listed here

Erich Fromm notes, "Sexual desire … is an expression of life … mutual giving … and sharing of pleasure." But sexual acts "… are characterized by the fact that one person

[529] Personal interview with Dr. Lee Mellor
[530] McKale, p. 43

becomes the other's object of contempt, of his wish to hurt, his sadistic desires affect his sexual impulses…" Fromm equates these types of sexual acts with the "attraction to power, to wealth, or narcissism (which) can arouse sexual desire." Fromm's definition of nonsexual sadistic behavior is "aiming at the infliction of physical pain up to the extreme of death (with) its object as a powerless being." [531]

Concentration camp female prisoners, who lived in constant fear, weak from starvation and illness, were ready-made victims for sadism. The sadistic behavior did not have to be physical; it could be mental – threats, promises with a potentially dangerous ending, the dichotomy of not following rules and never being punished at the cost of someone's life. Grese's game of throwing objects into the prohibited zones to watch prisoners be shot dead, of allowing a prisoner to escape selection only to call them back, flattering a prisoner nurse while holding a gun on her – Grese was entrenched in psychological sadistic acts as well as physical.

Human behavior is most clear in sexual acts "because it is the least learned behavior." [532] Sexual behavior reveals character traits – sadism, tenderness, anxieties. Thus, Irma Grese revealed her true character when she was beating and torturing others. As a modern example, serial killer Theodore Bundy was a sadistic necrophiliac, a pedophile, a rapist who tortured women by physical abuse, including beating, strangling, and biting. He told an interviewer his experience in the throes of murder. "You feel the last bit of breath leaving their body. You're looking into their eyes … (it makes you) God." [533] The ultimate authority, to take a life, the definitive sadistic high, made better by administering a measured, painful death. Multiple studies have revealed a sexual element to serial killing.

Sigmund Freud associated libido with cruelty. Libido being the driving force behind sadistic behavior, it is no wonder Grese became sexually aroused during a cruel act. She was in her early twenties, and – if rumor is truth – quite sexually active.

Dr. Lee Mellor believes Irma Grese "was a hypersexual as a means of coping with her own inner chaos – attempting to overcome feelings of worthlessness and dejection." Grese was "overcome(ing) these feelings (by using sex)" or observing acts that sexually excited her, for a "dopamine hit." The excitement of perverse sex and torture would cause a "rush" in Grese's body which made her feel powerful. "Once you combine (sadism with poor self-esteem), the sexual sadism makes sense." [534]

Emotional Sadism

Sexual sadism is deriving sexual gratification from inflicting pain, suffering, or humiliation; for the purpose of this discussion "emotional sadism" is deriving emotional gratification from the suffering of people (or, in some cases, animals.) Many studies have concluded serial killers began to practice torturing small animals such as birds, puppies, and kittens – helpless, vulnerable creatures where the torture was experimental but derived pleasure.

---

[531] (1992), electronic resource no pg. no.
[532] Ibid
[533] Michaud, S. (1999) P. 335
[534] Interviews with Dr. Lee Mellor, August 23 – 24, 2023

Sadism is not rare. Paulhus, D. L., and Dutton, D. G. (2016) have coined the term "everyday sadism" to refer to "largely acceptable forms of subclinical sadism that are prevalent in modern culture." As a society we have become inundated with "soft sadism" so that it is no longer recognizable, or it is socially acceptable. In the concentration camps, what today is appalling and sickening was "everyday sadism" – acceptable to many of the SS members and personnel, a standard of employment. Having "sport" was a form of everyday sadism. Threats of "turning into soap" or Grese's changing the prisoner's chosen for the gas chamber – any chance of causing mental anguish was normal to Irma Grese in particular. According to many prisoner's testimonies, and by today's standards, Grese, explains Rachael S. Bell, "was definitely a sadist who carried their enjoyment of hurting others into the sexual realm." In the last days of her work environment, Irma Grese was surrounded by stacks of corpses, prisoners dying all around her, and helpless people lying in waste. "I would guess she was aroused by that, too. Enjoying watching people in pain – just like when she enjoyed watching the surgeries without anesthetics, it was sexually arousing." [535]

One Holocaust survivor's experience is an excellent example of Grese's emotional sadism. Maurice Blik was four years old and a prisoner in Belsen when he became a victim of Grese's sadistic mental abuse. "Food wasn't very plentiful, and you protected what you had by sleeping with it under your head," he explains now. A four-year-old Maurice learned how to "read" people; "I got very good at figuring out when someone was going to die." Upon the prisoner's death, he would snatch their food as a matter of survival. Maurice was sitting on the hardwood floor of living quarters waiting on a prisoner to die so he could take their food when a blonde female guard in a resplendent uniform stepped into the barrack, leading a huge German shepherd on a leash. She spotted Maurice. She knew what he was doing. The guard pulled a big apple from her pocket and, not losing eye contact with the ragged child, began to consume the apple with relish, smacking her lips and grinning. Maurice knew to move or speak could mean death. His inner voice told him, "Don't let on you're frightened - if she doesn't get you, the dog will." When the apple was to the core, the guard spoke to the dog, and it sat. She unhooked its leash and set the core between its front paws. "And then she walked away" Maurice recalls. He stared at the apple core. "If I went for the core, I knew I was going to get it – either the dog would tear me apart or I'd get a bullet." The dog was snarling at him. "I knew dogs can smell fear." Upon the female guard's return, she grinned widely at the little boy, who had not moved, leashed her dog, then smashed the apple core into the floor with her boot, ensuring nothing was left. "I could tell she was entertained" Maurice explains now. The officer turned, dog on leash, and sauntered out, pleased with her sadistic game.

Years later, in a strange coincidence, Maurice would recognize this tormenter as Irma Grese from a photograph. Over eighty years old at this writing, Maurice Blik adds, "she was a vicious lady." [536]

[535] Interviews with Rachael S. Bell, May 2024

[536] Personal interview with Maurice Blik, November 18, 2023

Maurice Blik (wearing cap) with his sister, Clara. Maurice is two years old in this photo. Two years later, Maurice would be a Belsen prisoner where he was personally a victim of Irma Grese's psychological abuse. Both children survived. (Circa 1941. Location: Amsterdam. Photographer: unknown. Photo courtesy ©Maurice Blik. Used with permission.)

CHAPTER 41
Narcissistic Injury

"Trauma comes back as a reaction, not a memory."
- Bessel Van Der Kolk, MD, Trauma Research Specialist

In "The Mind of the Political Terrorist' (1991) Pearlstein discusses the concept of "narcissistic injury." Pearlstein postulates how "the specific intrapsychic and interpersonal aftermath most typically experienced by victims of narcissistic injury (is) narcissistic rage, the necessity for some form of narcissistic defense of the self and … some form of narcissistic aggression" (pp. 33-34).

Narcissistic injury refers to "the psychological damage that results when a child's narcissistic (i.e., self) needs for respect, understanding, and mirroring are defined." [537] Positive narcissistic development in children is developed by respect, understanding, and the message to the child that they understand the importance of self. Positive belief in oneself and self-assurance establishes, with a realistic understanding of capabilities, i.e. the child understands not everyone will enjoy their company, there are rules they must obey, and there are limits to what they are able to accomplish. Trauma in a family creates complications with coping skills and relationship issues. A dysfunctional family, such as one marred by argument and abuse, "creates" a personality of a child directly; for example, the child given the role of parent in families where the actual parent is unable or unwilling to act. The child's personality is affected indirectly: poor esteem, a distorted view of the environment, and inability to form healthy relationships can emerge in the child.

Not every abused child becomes an unhealthy adult. Some possess proper coping mechanisms and develop a healthy self, albeit damaged in some sense. However, numerous studies reveal a strong interrelation between childhood trauma and psychological damage. Millions of German children grew up in the era of Nazi Germany; a small percentage became brutal adults. Still, according to a study by Rios, et. al., a child experiencing early trauma (i.e., a suicide by a parent without "early resources" such as counseling) suffers psychological damage as do those with no "early resources." [538] Narcissistic injury is directly related to childhood trauma. [539]

There is no proof Grese did not receive counseling, but coming from a modest, agrarian family in a small town during this period it is highly unlikely she received professional assistance for coping skills, help in creating a sense of self, and thus taught skills to maintain healthy relationships. Witnesses (prisoners) in the concentration camp reported they dared not look Grese in the eye, avoiding her as much as possible due to Grese's explosive temper. A glance, a nod, a word - anything minor could set Grese into a frenzy and she would beat people close to death or shoot them. Grese moved from lover to lover inside the prison walls, occasionally using sex as a weapon (sadism, sexual assault).

We have learned Irma Grese suffered narcissistic injury from early in her life: [540]

[537] Miller, A. (1981) as cited in Rios (1993) p. 501).
[538] Figure 1, Rios et. al.
[539] See Table 3
[540] Based on the assumption all or most of the background of her childhood is true.

- She (may have been) raised in an environment of strife, with her parents arguing and fighting.
- Her mother committed suicide, and the "reason" for the suicide (the paramour) became part of Irma Grese's daily life.
- The message her mother "did not want her."
- The schoolyard became one of combat; Grese was "not wanted" on the playground.
- Her grades and social skills were poor.
- She became a flotsam in employment, with no solid work history. This might have been perceived as no employer "wanted" her.
- As she grew older, she experienced condemnation in the workforce- she was deemed "not good enough" for her dream job as a nurse.
- When she applied for a job in the concentration camp, she was sent away, told to try again later. While the justification was there – she was not old enough – Grese could have perceived the rejection as personal. (Recall she did not return immediately after turning 18 but waited.)
- Once hired, although she was part of the team, Grese had no friends.

There were many narcissistic injuries from her mother, and they continued into Irma Grese's adulthood. If the neighborhood gossip was correct, Berta Grese was not caring towards her children nor was she managing the household as she was expected, for whatever reason (mental illness, physical illness, etcetera). There are varying stories about how the household was run, but all of them included some discord. And then Berta Grese ordered her children to scrub their home clean and leave the house to go to the pub while she lay on the marital bed to kill herself. Berta placed her children in several precarious positions. The children would have thought they were going to fetch their father from the pub – another "normal day" only to return home to tragedy, guilt, profound sadness, and an incredible shift in the household dynamics.

Irma Grese and her siblings would have been highly affected by their mother's death, natural or no, and what transpired in the aftermath. A study by Runeson, et. al. on children exposed to parental death discovered "offspring who experience parental death are at increased risk for hospitalization for psychiatric disorders... as compared with offspring of alive parents, across all modes of parental death... the risk of offspring of suicide descendants were at greater risk for hospitalization." (p. 518) [541] The study also reveals "… the potency of exposure to parental suicide as a risk factor strongly depends on the age at exposure…" Rural children of the 1930s would not have been sent to a mental health facility to convalesce but would be expected to "pick up the reins" of their deceased parent's work and persevere.

A study by Shonkoff, et. al. [542] explains biological "memories" are created by suicide of parent, causing "weakening (of) physiological systems .... increased vulnerability to later morbidity and mortality ... more severe psychiatric disorder... early onset psychopathology... greater genetic liability for psychiatric disorder in offspring." (p. 521) Younger children are far more affected than young adults. It is highly probable that

[541] 2010

[542] Cited in Brent, et. al.

Bertha Grese's suicide, while aimed at punishing her husband, harmed her children more so. This is a supposition more than fact as no one truly knows what drove Bertha to drink hydrochloric acid (or whatever the chemical); she may not have thought it was poisonous and it could have been an act of attention – seeking behavior without realizing the lethality. Regardless, the suicide would influence the young Irma who, at thirteen, was at the cusp of childhood and into teenager years, when a young girl desperately needs an adult woman's advice or leadership.

By the time Irma Grese would have been placed in Ravensbrück, the environment and peer influence, coupled with the narcissistic injuries (physiological, psychiatric issues) of her childhood, Irma Grese was a timebomb.

Shonkoff's "increased vulnerability to later morbidity and mortality" is evident in Grese's letters to her family. Her letters to her siblings and parents carry similar messages:

- She will live forever in the hearts and minds.
- She is unafraid of death.
- She in a sufferer, though she does not say so directly.
- She is a great German.
- She will find peace in the other life, with a clear conscience and with pride.

Grese has made herself to be a martyr, but she has also made death into a sort of mystery, the answer of which she will know and embrace. She never mentions seeing her mother again in an afterlife (at least in the letters that exist) but stays to the above theme. Irma Grese received the death penalty, she cried mightily, she lost her appeal, and now she will die. Yet another narcissistic injury, and this one she has turned into her favor – Irma Grese created both a sacrificial lamb and a brave woman out of Irma Grese.

As Grese tirelessly beat a prisoner with her whip, boots, or truncheon, she might have been "beating" a representation for her narcissistic injuries. The prisoner, being female, representing:

- The mother Grese was punishing for leaving her at such an impressionable age, or
- The paramour for "causing" the suicide or replacing her mother so easily, or
- The girls in the schoolyard who rebuffed her.
- The BDM for not "allowing" her to initially join (misplaced blame).
- Her fellow comrades for not being her friend.

Almost twenty years of injury now manifested itself at the end of a whip and at the price of a human being's life. But it was the prisoner who died; the mother, paramour, and schoolgirls remained alive and safe. Thus, Grese had to "kill" the representative, again and again.

There were many narcissistic injuries from her father, and they continued into Irma Grese's adulthood. Her father appeared to be careless about his wife's suicide, marrying the mistress – the "reason" for her suicide – soon after the horrific death. He forbade his daughters to be in the "cool girls club" where popularity, a sense of tribe, and escape from home was there for the taking. Even when Irma Grese found work in a job where she belonged and enjoyed, making good pay, her father strongly disapproved of her life choices, beat her, and condemned her. (In Grese's opinion he beat her for her beliefs and not because of the broken doll or dangerous gun.) This injury manifested more rage in Grese, creating defense and aggression.

It is possible Grese donned the uniform as "pay back" for her father's indiscretions leading to her mother's suicide. She saw her father as liable for the discontented home life. Wearing the uniform and cruelty to others were against her father's wishes for his daughter and contradicted his personal beliefs. He was a Nazi party member, but so were others who joined for benefits and not idealism. Beating and abusing prisoners and being a true follower of the Nazi regime did not heal the narcissistic injury from her father, but it may have soothed it, if only for a while.

The men in the camps had been told females were their equal, but it was not always so in reality. Female guards were outnumbered by males, and the Nazi party remained male-dominant, where women were never allowed the highest positions in power, never allowed in the Nazi party except as "helpers," despite proving they belonged in this workforce. This would create yet another narcissistic injury. [543]

Young Irma Grese proudly entered work for her Nazi Germany only to find she was still in a man's world – not much different from the life she left – where the man was in charge and women had limited roles. Nazi law placed women in only a few roles, and a vicious camp guard was not one of them unless it became absolutely necessary. "We feel it is not appropriate when woman forces her way into man's world, into his territory," Adolph Hitler expressed in a speech to the National Socialist Women's organization. "Instead, we perceive it as natural when these two worlds remain separate." [544] Grese was not the Nazi dream of the perfect female - only aesthetically – she was brutal, never married, and had no children. She was the female second in command of one of the largest concentration camps in Nazi Germany before she was 23 years old yet reportedly not competent. She aborted at least one pregnancy. She had sex with the enemy. She was bisexual. [545]

Irma Grese sexually abused male prisoners. then sent them to the gas chambers. Rape is not a crime of sex but about power and control; the dominant issues in this offense, according to one study, are "power rape (sexuality used primarily to express power) or anger rape (use of sexuality to express anger)." [546]

These male victims feasibly represented the males who produced narcissistic injuries to Irma Grese:

- She was exulting power over her father, who had abandoned her.

[543] The purpose here is not to excuse Irma Grese's behavior nor go on a "wild goose chase" on what she may or may not have done, but to explore a reason for her unusual behavior given what is known.

[544] Becker, J. (2015)

[545] The attacks on the GLBT community ramped up when Hitler took power. Homosexual and SS fanatic Ernst Röhm was one of Hitler's most trusted friends, Chief of the SA, a ruthless man. Hitler had Rohm executed in 1934 as Röhm's homosexually became more open. Homosexuals – including suspected - were rounded up and sent to the concentration camps, labeled as criminals, sexual predators, and "undesirables." Grese would have known the Nazi ideology: Homosexuals were "evil." The belief that homosexuality could be passed on, like a virus. Homosexuals could not reproduce, therefor contributed nothing to the advancement of the Aryan Race. Irma Grese could have not served honorably had she been exposed as a lesbian, and would have been incarcerated.

[546] Burgess, W. et. al. (1977), *Rape: power, anger…*

- She was controlling and releasing her anger over the males surrounding her who, no matter how well she performed, would never accept her as a Nazi.
- She was punishing the Führer himself, who set boundaries on women, the women Irma Grese would never be; despite giving her life to the cause she would never be "good enough."

"You have to be somebody with real integrity not to abuse that power in the culture she grew up in," Holocaust survivor Maurice Blik observes now. [547]

[547] Interview with Maurice Blik, November 18, 2023

Pit of human ashes at Auschwitz I. Once a body was burned in the crematoria, prisoners would use mallets to smash the remains (such as bone). Truckloads of ashes would be dumped into a river, as filler, as fertilizer, and poured into pits. Irma Grese would have had a hand in creating these ashes as she sent people to the gas chamber, shot, beat them dead, or ordered the prisoners killed. (Circa: August 23, 2008. Location: Auschwitz I. Photographer: Jill Anne McCracken. Courtesy: Jill Anne Jill McCracken. Used with permission.)

***Kapos* preparing and placing bodies into the furnace.** Irma Grese, according to numerous witnesses, sent people to the gas chambers. This photo was posed for demonstration purposes. (Circa April 29-May10, 1945. Location Dachau. Photographer: unnamed Yugoslav prisoner. Photo courtesy the private collection of Ray Cook. Used with permission. These three images have been minimally altered for clarity.)

CHAPTER 42
Additional Factors to Consider

"The truth is rarely pure and never simple."
- Oscar Wilde

There are additional factors to consider in determining how Irma Grese became The Hyena of Auschwitz. As discussed, there is no "one" reason to any crime; there is no "simple" reason for how the Holocaust was created.

To say Grese hated Jews because of the SS is oversimplifying. There were numerous factors at work. The Holocaust worked because there was no one cause. Irma Grese and her ilk became who they were for the greater good of Germany, no *one* was totally responsible, bad behavior brought them recognition, and their life had desensitized them to death and destruction.

Loyalty to a Cause - "for Germany!"

German SS members (females as auxiliary) swore an oath to pledge eternal allegiance and unconditional obedience to Adolph Hitler and Hitler's appointees. This short, simple pledge bequeathed power over life, death, business, society, and education. Because it was a sworn alliance of obedience, it gave permission to destroy in the name of the Führer. The individual *man* was not burning a synagogue, shooting a Jewish child, or destroying Jewish – owned businesses, the *party* was committing these acts. In the name of the party, for the good of the country, a 'true" German could do anything – become God – and was never held personally responsible. Irma Grese had been taught in training at Ravensbrück: killing in the name of personal beliefs was not allowed; killing to advance the SS mission and protect Hitler's Germany was a *duty*. The initial mindset of *us* versus *them* began with this oath.

Germany had suffered great losses in WWI, both financially and emotionally. Soldiers who returned home suffering PTSD or were unable to work, who sought work in a time when there were no jobs, became beaten and hollow. Families lost their savings. The shame and lost pride hung like ugly clouds. Germany was a crumbling country that needed 1. To find a scapegoat and 2. A leader who would bring Germany back to thriving as a successful and prideful country.[548]

Disbursement of power - "____ made me do it."

Extermination of Jews and others in the camps was a carefully planned system, a disbursement of power, planned so that not one officer was responsible for the entire event. Auschwitz is a perfect example of how this aided the killing machine:

Step 1: A set of camp officers oversaw the removal of people from the cattle cars.

[548] An excellent discussion of this dynamic is included in E. Staub's book "The Roots of Evil." (2000). Cambridge Press.

Step 2: A group leader made selections as to who was to live and who would not survive.
Step 3: A different set of people (usually *Kapos*) would supervise the disrobing, delousing, haircutting – the preparation system for those chosen to live.
Step 4. Certain officers (with *Kapos*) oversaw directing the group into the gas chamber.
Step 5: Those in charge of dropping the Zyklon B were unconnected from them all.
Step 6: A detached officer would open the cover to a small window to ensure all the prisoners were dead.
Step 7: And finally, a separate group (*Kapos*) completed the body removal and dismemberment.

Prisoners were placed to labor in the crematoriums, removing officers from any "hands on" work with those marked for death and the dead. Prisoners were guiding the newly arrived prisoners along the walkway into the gas chambers, removing teeth and hair from the dead, dragging and placing bodies into the crematorium, removing the ashes from the fires, and ash disposal. It was a prisoner who would remove dead bodies during count or from other abuse.

By compartmentalization, the extermination of millions was not the fault of those uniformed individuals, but of a machine acting in accordance. Murder was conducted as an organization rather than as human beings.

Hitler himself blamed battle for ruining his social life; [549] he had missed theatre performances, concerts, and films because "this war is no convenience to me."[550] Towards war's end he laid blame on General Staff officers for losing the war and causing mayhem. He blamed Himmler for surrendering.

This "blame game" operated so well on all levels that millions of innocents were methodically murdered.

Many survivors recall the abuse of alcohol and drugs by the camp staff. Thus, another potential excuse for taking part in the killing machine, excuses already familiar to a substance abuser:

- I was drunk.
- I was high.
- I don't recall.
- I blacked out and when I came to…
- A substance (alcohol, etc.) made me do it.

By using this model, Irma Grese could never be responsible; she denied responsibility to death. She had acted in the name of Germany; she had worked as a cog in the wheel. She explained to her father and mother, "For I am doing my duty loyally for my Fatherland! Just as I and others did our duty…" [551]

[549] In truth, Hitler was not prevented of entertainment.
[550] Foreign News, *Time* (1945, October 8)
[551] K0snl

In 1969, United States comedian Flip Wilson introduced a character named "Geraldine" (Wilson in a woman's clothing), a saucy, fictional preacher's wife with a trademark catchphrase in telling a story. In one famous comedy routine, the fictitious preacher asks Geraldine why she committed forgery by signing his name to purchase an expensive new dress, Geraldine replies "the devil made me do it!" She then tells an elongated fib about "the devil" forcing her to walk down the street, peruse a shop window, fall in love with a dress, try it on, and write a hot check to purchase it. The humor is we knew "the devil" did not make Geraldine buy the dress, but it made for a good excuse because, her husband being a preacher, it is a plausible excuse. Geraldine can make herself believe a force larger than herself was in charge, forcing her to act against her will and commit a crime. Thus, Geraldine is blameless. The catchphrase became a cultural phenomenon.

Those accused of atrocities in the Nazi trials, including Irma Grese, employed the catchphrase "the regime/Hitler/Himmler/superior officers made me do it." For a long time, it worked – the "brainwashing" of young people by Hitler and the Nazi's rhetoric, the SS's implementation of all things Socialist, being surrounded in music, literature, social and education – the public believed, like Geraldine believed, it is possible to be seduced into doing something bad by unseen forces. Yet not all Germans became Nazis: some were hard-core supporters, some secretly worked against it, and most were unenthusiastic, believing in some but not all the dogma. Thus, blaming the crimes solely on the regime is not plausible.

Careful Creation of Leadership - the filtering of staff

Nazism was a carefully planned system, a filter, in leadership. Through "sifting" personnel, the unhealthiest aggressors like Irma Grese shifted to the topmost and placed in leadership roles. Those who could not rise to the extreme on the spectrum of murder stayed in the lower trenches. Recall some guards taking pity on prisoners, assisting the resistance, working as spies, or refusing orders to maim, torture, or kill.

Irma Grese had quickly sifted through the filter to act out her sadistic fantasies and behaviors to the *nth* degree. Because she was a sadist, because she was attempting to heal narcissistic injuries, she was able to climb the ladder to the highest rank available. It was said she had no pity, no shame, and no feelings for prisoners; according to her admissions she also had no friends and was communicating with few members in her large family. Without emotional ties, Grese was able to maim and mentally abuse without guilt. She was an easy target for Nazi leadership, and Nazi leadership was an easy draw to her.

Desensitization - murder as the norm

Katharina Hardy, survivor of Ravensbrück & Bergen-Belsen, said of her life as a prisoner: "Death, not life, was normal. Life was the exception." [552]

Irma Grese and the other staff in the concentration camps were what criminologist and serial killer expert Dr. Peter Vronsky call "State Serial killers." Vronsky explains the dynamics of working in the camps:

[552] Müller (2022)

- Conditioning to suppress empathy for the prisoners.
- Did not consider the prisoners as fellow mankind, but as objects.
- It was illegal for prisoners and guards to communicate privately.
- Killing was the norm at Auschwitz, as normal as riding a bicycle.
- "Fascist cult movements allowing the authoritarian personality type … to express themselves" in cruel and violent ways" towards "targeted groups." [553]

The "Authoritarian Personality Type" [554] features are:

- Rigid adherence to conventual values
- Submissiveness to authority figures
- Aggression towards "out" groups
- Opposition to introspection, reflection, and creativity.
- Preoccupied with power and "toughness."
- Destructive, cynical
- Believing dangerous conspiracies exist in the world.
- Exaggerated concern with sexuality

Irma Grese had been taught, from the first time she stepped foot into Ravensbrück, that empathy for prisoners was a weakness of the heart and mind. She had already felt the sting of weakness as a child, and the emotional pain it caused. Perhaps this mindset began as early as working at Hohenluchen, where she worshipped the lead physician SS - *Gruppenführer* Doctor Karl Gebhardt and observed vivisection on female prisoners from Ravensbrück. A lifetime of Nazi rhetoric certainly made her immune to seeing Jews and other "undesirables" as less than human beings, not to fraternize with – it was beneath her as a good German woman. Even when she was not on duty, Grese was amid death; she lived right on the cusp of dying prisoners, she walked through it daily, and it was the subject of work reports and daily talk.

She certainly had the personality for the work. The Nazi party had created "The Nazi Child" in Grese to ensure she became "The Nazi Adult." Irma Grese came from a humble background with little education and her dreams of becoming an instant movie star revealed she was unsophisticated. Grese was not particularly bright: she was breaking several important rules of the workforce and revealing a lack of maturity and introspection. Even her use of a childish nickname in a letter to her sister ("Irmikins") reveals much about her character. Regardless of the reason, Irma Grese was (allegedly) highly sexual, raping male and female prisoners, sending them to their deaths to keep the secret, slinking about the camps for sexual trysts with staff, and remaining at Belsen to be arrested because she was in love with an officer.

---

[553] ele, T, cited in Vronsky, P. (2007) pp. 392-93

[554] Erich Fromm and Alice Miller's work on authoritative roles reveal "individuals who grew up in the authoritarian culture of Germany would have trouble assuming responsibility for their own lives." (cited in Staub, E. 1989, p.29-30)

Estimated number of persons killed during Holocaust compared to major city populations

There is no way to know how many persons perished in the Holocaust, just as populations of major cities are estimated using best methods. The numbers below are accrued from valuable resources. However, this does give a somber glimpse: as an example, more Jews died during the Holocaust than the most recent censuses of San Francisco, California and Austin, Texas combined.

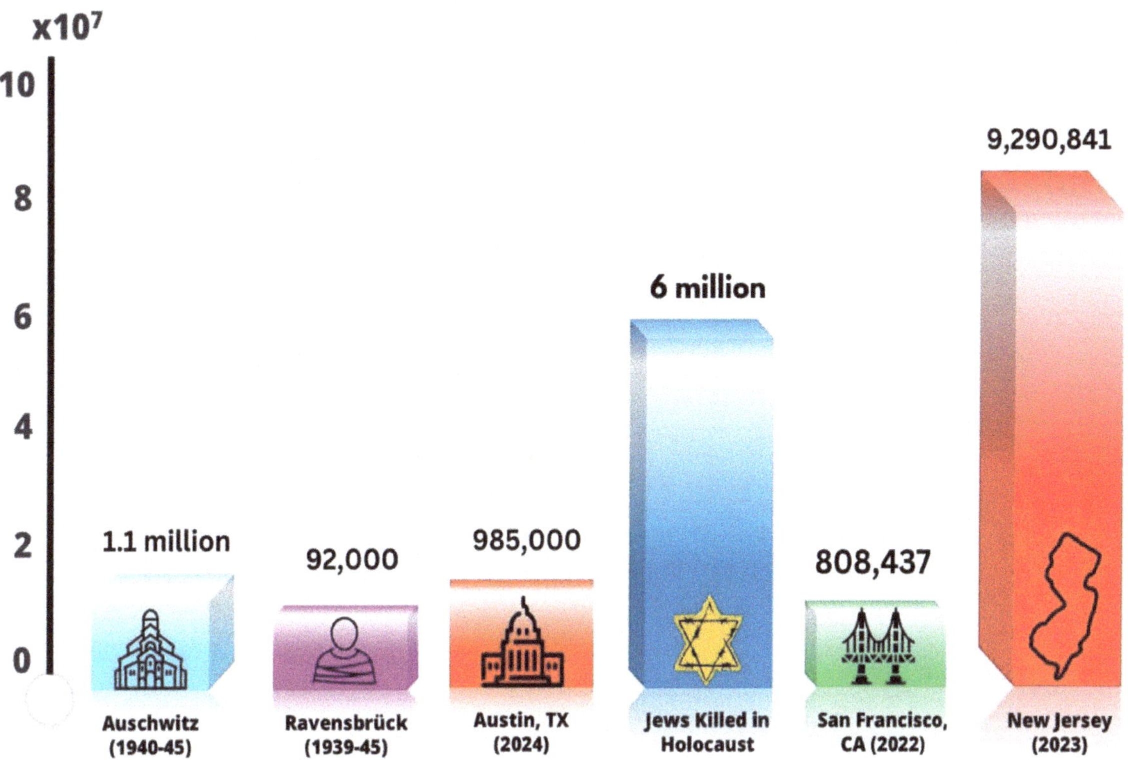

CHAPTER 43
The New Hyena

"There are very few people who are going to look in the mirror and say: The person I see is a savage monster. Instead, they make up some construction that justifies what they do."

- **Noam Chomsky, "How the World Works"**

Since her death Irma Grese has been recast by so many as something of a character, an archetype, or a superhero. She has been brought back to life in the media. Grese appears as a fantasy figure.

Over forty years after her death, Irma Grese makes headlines again. This time, she is in a black uniform and black boots, dressed somewhere between a Nazi guard and a dominitrex in *Angel: A Nightmare in Two Acts* a stage play written by Jo Davidsmeyer and directed by William Martyn. The play won several prestigious awards and ran in Bradenton, Florida. Davidsmeyer told the press "There is still a lot of interest in the Holocaust." She became interested in Grese because "Here was a young woman with charm and appeal, one who wasn't a raging lunatic but an ordinary person. How did she obtain so much power at such an early age? What drove her to do the things she did?" [555] The play won favorable reviews in the press. A new interest in Irma Grese emerged.

In 1975, Aeteas Film Produktions production company released a Canadian exploitation film called "Ilsa, She Wolf of the SS." The main character is a shapely white female with large breasts clad in a male Nazi uniform who commands a fictitious Nazi prison camp. The main character, a nymphomaniac who conducts sadistic experiments on male prisoners, is based loosely on both Ilse Koch and Irma Grese. The film became a cult classic. There have been numerous such characters in the media based on Irma Grese. These female characters are usually clad in leather, wearing the SS armband with WW2 German Allgemeine officer visor cap, and holding whips and guns with stiletto shoes or high-top leather boots, all based on this cult classic. [556]

Thus, Irma Grese has become an archetype – the "bitch" or the "slut" who is dangerous but enticing, using sex as a weapon. This made-up character has Aryan features, a perfect body, unrealistically large breasts, and is highly sexual. The crimes of torture and murder have been turned into fetishes; they hold power in part because their slaves give it to them. This characterization turns the Holocaust into a cartoon and the vicious camp guards into sexy superheroes. The purpose of the superhero is to create an extension of ourselves, the invincible being with special powers who can right the world's wrongs and is beloved for their good deeds. The enemies of the superhero are enemies to all – they desire to take away freedom and create mayhem. Superheroes give people something to believe in – something – or someone – to swoop in and save the day. While this "Nazi Female" character may or may not be a superhero in these movies or media, she is interesting; she represents the mixture of horror and sexuality, the ages-old genre that makes for popular consumption.

---

[555] Konesko, N. (1987). P. 29

[556] See also Peter Vronsky's Introduction in this book.

Irma Grese continues to have her champions, who steadfastly believe she was an innocent milk maiden forced into employment for the Nazis. Her champions trust their version of Irma had no part in selections, whippings, beatings, or any crime except being a woman caught in a Nazi world. Some insist Grese's nickname at Celle was *Stirb nicht* "Little Singer" because of her melodious voice as she sang while incarcerated. [557] She was tried in a "Kangaroo court," her supporters insist; the trial witnesses cannot be believed because they are prisoners of war, lying, or mistaken.. Grese supporters still insist that several "ugly" Jewish women lied on the stand in retaliation for Grese's good looks and charm.

Another myth surfaced when, in 1978, two MPs supposedly reported a new string of events:

> An army man named Ronald Cook was scheduled to be Grese's executioner. Regimental Sergeant – Major O'Neill was to assist. A Sergeant O'Hare and Corporal Rick Smith were to walk Grese to the gallows. O'Hare and Smith would be court martialed because they refused to lead Grese to be hanged. Ronald Cook refused to do his duty, but Major Jerome Burdik ordered Cook to conduct the hanging. Cook went home afterwards where he committed suicide.

There is even a "ghost story":

A local Jewish hangman was considered as Grese's executioner: Samuel Lutzheim. Grese threatened she would return in ghostly form if this Jew touched her.

On her last night, Grese sang German songs which she hummed on her way to the gallows in the morning. She charmed the American MPs who instantly became enchanted with her good looks. Hangman Lutzheim attempted to place a hood over her head, but Grese refused and became violent. Eschewing the hood, the Jewish hangman was forced to slap Grese repeatedly and force the noose over her head. The fight lasted over five minutes. Hangman Lutzheim had miscalculated the drop and Irma Grese hung, twisting in the air, until she suffocated; she took three minutes to die. Because she was the supervisor at Krema Three in Birkenau, her ghost haunted the building. On January 12, 1948, when Russians had taken over the area, Night Guard Harak Visen (the name varies) claimed to witness Irma Grese's ghost. A watchman known only as "Shem" refused to enter the building because of the ghost. The Russian army closed down Krema Three to quell the rumors. In 1992, the padlocks were broken, and five researchers were allowed overnight access, but fled the area soon after in fear.

Leni Riefenstahl, a German propaganda actress, announced she wanted to create a movie about this ghost, but the German government threatened her. The plan was dropped - Leni Riefenstahl did not wish to be arrested.

Irma Grese was called a hero and a martyr, an innocent falsely accused due to prejudice and greed. Jewish propaganda has brainwashed the public about Irma Grese's true nature and history…so now, her restless spirit haunts everyone…

---

[557] "*Stirb nicht*" in German means *"don't die."*

Like so many rumors, holding this ghost tale to light reveals all the impossibilities. The Krema Three photos used to accommodate this tale are proven to be of Krema Four. (The photograph was altered multiple times.) And it would not have been possible for the ghost Irma Grese to haunt Krema 3 because it was partially destroyed when she was employed at Auschwitz, and what little remained were destroyed just prior to the Nazis leaving the camp. There is no Krema Three to haunt. Multiple, official records are assurance Albert Pierrepoint was, indeed, the executioner. Irma Grese's famous "*Schnelle*!" is contradictory of a woman fighting a hood and noose, while receiving hard slaps to the face.

So continual myths, racism, fantasy, and Holocaust deniers and revisionists twist "The Hyena of Auschwitz," severely altering who she was, to the public.

This "New Hyena" is dangerous to history and demeaning to the millions of souls lost during the Holocaust. The new hyena turns the Holocaust into a cartoon and murder becomes a backdrop; the victims are forgotten in the background of the entertaining hyena character.

"I think (*Aufseherinnen*) were ordinary women doing diabolical things. I think that can happen anywhere."
- **Holocaust survivor and author Selma van de Perre [558]**

Auschwitz – Birkenau as it appears today. Irma Grese transferred here from Ravensbrück in March 1943. The same year, her father banned her from her family home. Grese would have walked through this entrance and passed these halls. She assisted in "selections" for the gas chambers, supporting in murder of an estimated 1.1 million people. [559] It was here she would become "The Hyena of Auschwitz." (Circa: August 23, 2008. Location: Auschwitz – Birkenau State Museum, Oświęcim, Poland. Photographer: Jill Anne McCracken. Courtesy of Jill Anne McCracken. Used with permission.)

[558] McGuinness (2021)
[559] Estimate by Holocaust historians, courtesy Auschwitz – Birkenau Memorial & Museum.

Recognitions

No author works alone. Research for this book could be particularly challenging due to language barriers, travel limitations, time, and subject matter. I am grateful beyond words for the people who took time to assist in the research, to ensure I get it right – or as close to as possible – and to honor the real people who suffered, endured, lived, and died through the most horrific time in history.

All persons hired to illustrate and format this book are minority small business owners. They are highly recommended. Contact them for assistance:
Cover art by Darasimi the Techartist. @bety_techartist on fiverr.com. Instagram – Darasimi arts. [560] Based on a concept by Judiht A. Yates.
Graphs artist: Design by Fareesa,@design_perfect (fiverr.com/design_perfect).
Editor: Zan Lee Duroy, ZanDuroy@gmail.com.
Photo enhancement: William Wiseman.
Artist: Nobe Studio, @nobeststudio.

With a special THANK YOU to Jamal Nasrullah, my patient and so very professional formatter. He is the best! Jamal Nasrullah (Whats app: +447915645877); https://acesse.dev/xESl4.

Please recognize the following people and their organizations. They work tirelessly to make it a better world:

(Alphabetically)

My translator and friend, Ann Marie Ackerman, J.D., amazing author, and researcher extraordinaire. Ann Marie wrote one of the best historical true crime books available. www.annmarieackermann.com.

Dr. Richard Adler, for your professional advice and assistance.

The Auschwitz-Birkenau Memorial & Museum, Former German Nazi Concentration and Extermination Camp, representing "a duty to remembrance and the education of future generations throughout the world." True heroes all. Auschwitz.org.
I particularly want to recognize Dr. Sylwia Wysińska for assisting with documents I could not have located elsewhere.

The group at Axis History Forum for allowing me to join and discuss this project, and for assisting me with research. This is an apolitical forum for discussion on the Axis nations and related topics with educated members. Forum.axishistory.com.

[560] Image of Irma Grese courtesy the Imperial War Museum, © Crown Copyright IWM.

My sister from another lifetime, Rachael Bell, MS, MS, LPC. I admire and cherish you. www.rbellcounseling.com.

Special thanks to Maurice Blik, British sculptor, author, and a wonderful gentleman, who told me, "Being a Holocaust survivor is a part of my life, but it isn't the only part of my life." www.MauriceBlik.com.

Christian Carlsen of the Stasi Records Archive. You assisted in making several month's research for images and their proper refences come to an end.

Christiane Botzet, Bundesarchiv, for taking the time to share the sources of images and documents.

Christine with Desert Island Discs, BBC, UK. https://www.bbc.co.uk/programmes /b006qnmr.

Magdalena Chomitkowska, a Poland-based historian of Irma Grese and Aufseherinen. Your knowledge is amazing. This would have been an entirely different book had you not contacted me. You lifted my spirits and did so much above sharing records and research. I am proud to have worked with you. I am proud to call you "friend."

Brian Clegg, science author, who writes "so many people find science dull and uninspiring. It shouldn't be. It's about how everything works." www.brianclegg.net.

In memory of and thanks to Raymond H. Cook, 3rd Army / US Army Ret., who landed on Normandy Beach, D-Day, and served his country from 1941-1945 as a Medic. Special thanks to his grandson Ray Cook, Jr. for sharing a part of history. Both are fine men.

Joanna Czopowicz, for an informative and interesting blog on the history of Ravensbrück. The subject is fascinating and never-ending. https://ssaufseherin.blogspot.com.

Dr. Dan Ellin, Archivist & Historical Consultant, International Bomber Command Central (IBCC) Digital Archive, University of Lincoln. Thank you for your assistance and going above and beyond in aiding an author from across the globe.

Dr. Susan Eischeid for your wonderful book on Maria Mandl. "Mistress of Life and Death" gives an account of how "normal" women became "abnormal" in their cruelty. This book is a treasure trove of information. https://seischeid.com.

Rodney Falk for taking the time to discuss his beloved mother. Rodney, I wish I could have met her. So many stories!

Tom Gillmor, Head of Content, Mary Evans Picture Library. Mary Evans Picture Library's core philosophy: "to make available and accessible wonderful images." www.MaryEvans.com.

Linda Gregg, TN. K9 Counselor. The *true* "dog whisperer." Facebook: "TN K9 Counselor."

Zachary Graulich, Director of Programs, Holocaust Memorial & Tolerance Center of Nassau for all the work your organization is doing to make a better society, to educate, and to keep those victims and survivors in our memories. www.hmtcli.org.

Jennifer Haynes of Invaluable Auctions for her assistance – you helped eight months of research come to an end, and you were cool with loud cats in the background during our phone calls.

Shannyn Johnson, Image Reproduction Technician, Canadian War Museum. I am thankful for your making online research so much easier.

Dan Jordan, Technical Information Specialist at the United States Holocaust Memorial Museum, The David M. Rubenstein National Institute for Holocaust Documentation for painstakingly searching Survivor Registry databases of over 210,000 survivors and their descendants.

"Sandra K" for being amazing and working with me. Thank you for rescuing animals! It would be wonderful to visit one day.

Alexandra Kosubek, German Federal Archives (Bundesarchiv) for walking me through the records department and providing invaluable assistance.

Sarah Kopelman-Noyes, Names Data Branch, Digital Assets Division, The David M. Rubenstein National Institute for Holocaust Documentation at United States Holocaust Memorial Museum. The Museum maintains the Benjamin and Vladka Meed Registry of Holocaust Survivors. You can download the registration form in various languages – go to https://www.ushmm.org/hsv.

Holocaust expert and historian Jill McCracken. I believe in serendipity. Your knowledge was such a boon to this book. Thank you for your willingness to share your expertise.

A hat tip to Dr. Lee Mellor, who always amazes me with his knowledge and travel stories. I'm lucky to call him friend and hot wings buddy. Meet him at www.LeeMellor.com.

Mr. Dave Moore, of WW2CollectorWorld.com, who assisted in seeking out information, I owe you a great deal of gratitude. Thank you for respecting history. I cannot give enough accolades for your work. What a great guy and what an amazing collection!

Amy Moorman, Director of Archives and Collections, Kaplan Feldman Holocaust Museum in St. Louis, Missouri. They have the "Change Begins with Us" program designed to empower St. Louis area visitors to work collectively to fight all forms of hate. https://stlholocaustmuseum.org.

Jason Murphy, Service Manager, National Library Online, National Library of New Zealand *Te Puna Mātauranga o Aotearoa* for information on photographs and copyrights.

Sylvia Naylor, Ph.D., Archivist, National Archives and Records Administration in College Park, MD. I so appreciate your response to my inquiry and your extensive search. You helped me locate records I believed lost forever.

Britta Pawelke, Museum Services – Photo Library, Ravensbrück Memorial, Brandenburg Memorials Foundation. The foundation encompasses history, educational programs, exhibitions, special events, research, and features ongoing collections. Thank you for sharing your time and going above and beyond to assist.
https://www.ravensbrueck-sbg.de/en/ .

Alexander Pearman, Archives, KZ-Gedenkstätte Dachau for assisting with records location.

Margaret Robinson, Speakers Bureau Coordinator, the Speakers Bureau at the Museum of Jewish Heritage—A Living Memorial to the Holocaust. I appreciate your willingness to assist.

Euan Roger, Remote Enquiries Duty Officer, The National Archives of the United Kingdom, for assisting an author in small town – USA. Thank you for taking the time.

Christian Rommer for your assistance and kindness.

Julia Rusakova, Yad Vashem. I appreciate all you do.

Cynthia Sandor, a talented author, whose webpage on the BDM is the best out there. Anything you want to know about the Hitler Youth is here. https://bdmhistory.com.

Monika Schnell, Employee in the scientific services department, Ravensbrück Memorial, Brandenburg Memorials Foundation. I so appreciate you. *Vielen Dank für deine Hilfe.*

Claudia Schelling, *Institut für Zeitgeschichte* for sending me in the right direction.

Kyra Schuster, Lead Acquisitions Curator, United States Holocaust Museum. Your quick response and assistance helped me with an important correction and educated several generations of two families.

Piotr Setkiewicz and Robert Placzek, Kierownik Biblioteki, Państwowe Muzeum Auschwitz-Birkenau w Oświęcimiu (Poland) – The International Center for Education about Auschwitz and the Holocaust for fact-checking to ensure I got it right. The additional information gave breadth to the story. www.Auschwitz.org.

Nancy Shanes, JewishGen Member Service Team and the members of JewishGen. JewishGen serves as the global home for Jewish genealogy. www.JewishGen.org.

Donella Thompson, Licensing Executive with Mirrorpix. Your patience is above and beyond. Your kindness is commendable. Mirropix shares the images that affect us most. https://mirrorpix.com.

The United States Holocaust Memorial Museum in Washington, DC Archives Department for assistance in locating items and information. Thank you for all you do. In 1996, you also unknowingly saved my sanity and played a part in keeping me alive. www.ushmm.org.

Dr. Karsten Uhl for all the work you do, and that you shared.

Peter Vronsky, whose work was my "go-to" as an undergraduate, graduate, and now my PhD. A fine writer and a good man. I am honored. www.petervronsky.org.

Torsten Zarwel, Bundesarchiv-Stasi-Unterlagen-Archiv, for assisting in image research.

Zan Lee DuRoy, my editor, and an amazing artist, confidant, sister-soulmate, and all things that define true friendship. Raise a glass to yet another ride. Instagram: @theamazingzan.

I would like to thank those who fought to liberate Auschwitz and other SS camps. So many heroes busted down the gates to freedom. You experienced hell and did your duty as a soldier and a human being. I salute you all.

And finally, my mother: always so proud to receive the first book printed; she will never hold this one. On June 30, 2024, she left us with a hole in our hearts that will never be filled. Mom, thank you for allowing me to be creative, for instilling in me the love of reading and writing, and for teaching me that "different" is not synonymous with "bad."

References

Abeyasekere, K. (2014, April 30). *British World War II veteran shares first-hand account of seeing concentration camp after*. U.S. Air Forces in Europe & Air Forces Africa.

https://www.usafe.af.mil/News/Article-Display/Article/748958/british-world-war-ii-veteran-shares- first-hand-account-of-seeing-concentration/.

A case study of Irma Grese: Constructing the "evil" and the "ordinary" through digital oral testimonies and written trial testimonies of the Holocaust survivors. *Kaleidoscope - Journal for the History of Science, Culture and Medicine.* 7(13), 529-541. https://doi.org/10.17107/KH.2016.13.529-541.

Adorno, T. (1950). *The Authoritarian Personality*. Harper & Row.

AICE. (n.d.). *Irma Grese*. Jewish Virtual Library. https://www.jewishvirtuallibrary.org/irma-grese.

Allan, Alexander Smith. (1991, March 4). *Oral History Interview with Alexander Smith Allan*. Interviewed by Imperial War Museum. United States Holocaust Museum. https://collections.ushmm.org/search/catalog/irn510809.

Allan, M. (22 September 1945). "*Handcuffed 'Beast' goes to Belsen.*" Daily Herald.

American Psychiatric Association. (2022). Diagnostic & Statistical Manual of Mental Disorders. (5th ed., text rev.).

"*Anwerbung und Ausbildung von SS- Aufseherinnen.*" All efforts were made to locate the source and dates of this handbook *Recruitment and Training of SS Aufseherinnen*. While some information on the booklet's origin is difficult to locate and copyright may not exist, it is a reliable source for the documents and photographs utilized in this book.

Axis History Forum (2002, March 11). *Irma Grese Photos*. (forum post by #30 Michael Mills). https://forum.axishistory.com/viewtopic.php?p=961691#p961691.

Baumel, J. T. & Laqueur, W. (2001). *The Holocaust Encyclopedia*. Yale University Press.

"Beast of Belsen, 9 Others to Die for Camp Deaths." (1945, 17 November). Toronto Daily Star.

"Beast of Belsen, Girl Sadist, Die on Gallows with 9 others." 1946. 15 December.) Washington Post.

"Belsen Woman Guard Weeps, Denies Guilt." (1945, October 17). New York Times.

"Beast of Belsen's widow arrested." (1946, August 26). *The Daily Telegraph*. p. 2.

"*Beast Dozes, Blonde Irma Titivates, Herta Smiles Now.*" (19 September 1945) Daily Herald.

Becker, J. (2015). The Cruelty of Nazi Women: An Examination of the War-time Trials of Irma Grese and Iise Koch. *New Views on Gender*, *15*, 52–58. Retrieved from https://scholarworks.iu.edu/journals/index.php/iusbgender/article/view/13614.

Belling, J. (n.d.) Irma Grese. [blog] http://www.whale.to/b/irma_grese.html.

Bellinger, J. (n.d.) "A German Girl's Heroic Death." The Website of Carlos Whitlock Porter. https://www.jrbooksonline.com/cwporter/heroic.htm?.

Belsen Death Camp Leaders Meet Justice, 35mm, 1.15 min., (Office of War Information: United News, 1945), National Archives and Records Administration, 208 UN 176.

"Belsen Girl Guard Blames All of SS." (1945, October 6). New York Times.

"Belsen Trial: Witness accuses Irma Grese." (1945, September 27). Liverpool Daily Post. P. 1.

"Belsen Woman Guard Weeps, Denies Guilt." (1945, October 17). New York Times.

Beemore, E. (2019, April 3). "Why German soldiers don't have to obey orders." History Online. https://www.history.com/news/why-german-soldiers-dont-have-to-obey-orders.

Bessel, R.; Lüdtk, A.; & Weisbrod, B. (2006). *No Man's Land of Violence. Extreme Wars in the twentieth century.* Wallstein.

Blakemore, E. (2018 April 3). Why German Soldiers Don't Have to Obey Orders. HISTORY. A& E Television Networks. https://www.history.com/news/why-german-soldiers-dont-have-to-obey-orders.

"Branded Victims see Beast of Belsen Swing," (14 December) *Toronto Star.*

"Blond Irma, Dressed up on Belsen Stand," *Toronto Star* (16 October 1945). Toronto Star.

Blau, Magda. (1990, June 11). "Oral History Interview with Magda Blau." Interviewed by L. Kuzmack. United States Holocaust Museum. https://collections.ushmm.org/search/catalog/irn504535.

Bonn, S. (2014, October 24). *5 myths about serial killers and why they persist [excerpt].* Scientific American. https://www.scientificamerican.com/article/5-myths-about-serial-killers-and-why-they-persist-excerpt/.

British Movietone. (1945). *Belsen Trials. AP.* Retrieved January 20, 2024, from https://newsroom.ap.org/editorial-photos-videos/detail?itemid=67479c44b5e9430e99c26188ef9c5787&mediatype=video&source=youtube.

"British Victim to Accuse the Beast." (18 September 1945). Daily Worker.

"British war veteran tells ITV News of the horrors he saw at Bergen-Belsen camp 70 years on." (14 April 2015). Itv.

Broszat, M. (1987). *Hitler and the Collapse of the Weimar Republic.* Berg Publishers.

Broszat, M. (1987). *The Hitler State: The Foundation and Development of the Internal Structure of the Third Reich.* Longman.

Brown, D. P. (1996). *The Beautiful Beast.* Golden West Historical Publications.

Brown, P.D. (2002). *The camp women: the female auxiliaries who assisted the SS in running the Nazi concentration camp system.* Mazal Holocaust Collection. Schiffer Publications.

Buber-Neumann, M. (2008). *Under Two Dictators*. Pimlico.

Bulow, L. (2004). *Irma Grese*. Hitler's Women - World War 2 - Irma Grese. http://www.auschwitz.dk/ Women/Grese.htm.

Burgess, W. Groth, A. N. Holmstrom, L.L. (1977). *Rape: power, anger, and sexuality*. American Journal of Psychiatry.

"Burying the bodies of (unknown) war criminals." Peter Clapham Collection, United States Holocaust Memorial Museum. Accession Number: 1994.A.0022.

Buss, D. (2006). *The Murderer Next Door: Why the Mind is Designed to Kill.* Penguin Books.

Bytwerk, R. (n.d.). *German Propaganda Archive of Calvin University*. Nazi stamps: 1933-1945. https://research.calvin.edu/german-propaganda-archive/stamps.htm.

Cahana, A. (1990, December 4). "Interview with Alice Cahana." Interviewed by L. Kuzmack. United States Holocaust Museum. https://collections.ushmm.org/oh_findingaids/RG-50.030.0051_trs_en.pdf.

Camurati, A. (2024, February 14). *Holocaust survivors share "Stories of strength" at Remembrance Forum*. The Island Now. https://islandnow.net/holocaust-survivors-share-stories-strength-remembrance-forum/.

Capital Punishment UK.com. (n.d.). "Hanged by the neck until dead!" The process and physiology of judicial hanging. https://www.capitalpunishmentuk.org/hanging2.html#causes.

Chindler, W. (2016). *Irma Grese - The Holocaust: The Incredible Life of Irma Grese and The Holocaust: The Intriguing Life and History of The Blonde Beast (Irma Grese, Auschwitz and the Holocaust, World War* 2). CreateSpace Independent Publishing Platform.

Chomsky, N. (2011). *How the World Works*. Real Story/Soft Skull Press.

Clark, E. & Larson, J. (2018). *Irma Grese: Hitler's WW2 Female Monsters Exposed.* CreateSpace Independently Publishing Platform.

Clark, T. (2012). The Beautiful Beast": Why was Irma Grese evil?" Working paper produced for the Department of Sociological Studies, University of Sheffield.

Cline, S. M. (2014). Women at work: SS *Aufseherinne* and the gender perpetration of the Holocaust. [Doctoral dissertation, University of Kansas].

Commentator unknown. (n.d.). World History's Execution of Irma Grese - The Hyena of Auschwitz - Nazi Guard at Auschwitz & Bergen-Belsen - WW2. YouTube. https://youtu.be/95F1k6YIh80?si=9fmnRpQSQswvrVNx.

Cosner, S. & Cosner, V. (1998). *Women Under the Third Reich.* Greenwood Press.

Crosbie, J. J. (2019, May 2). *The memory of Belsen – gathering the voices Scotland.* Gathering The Voices Scotland – Testimonies of Holocaust survivors who settled in Scotland. https://gatheringthevoices.com/the-memory-of-belsen/.

Croskery, W. (2011). Constructing the beastess: the trial of Irma Grese and the British press, 1945. [Master's Thesis, Nipissing University].

Dash, P. (1992 June 1). *Oral history interview with Paula Dash.* Interviewed by S. Tash. United States Holocaust Memorial Museum. https://collections.ushmm.org/search/catalog/irn509093.

Dawson, M. (2016, October 27). *After Hitler's pal died, Nazis recreated his injuries in a sick experiment.* New York Post. https://nypost.com/2016/05/08/the-women-tortured-by-nazi-doctors-and-the-american-heiress-who-saved-them/.

Dederichs, Mario (2009). *Heydrich: The Face of Evil.* Casemate Publishing.

DEGOB (National Committee for Attending Deportees). "SS Female Overseers in Auschwitz." (no date). Recollections on the Holocaust. Budapest. http://degob.org/index.php?showarticle=202.

Describes 'leg inspections' of Women at Belsen camp. (1945, 27 September). *The Maple Leaf.* UK.

"Diet Sheet for the prisoners of the Belsen Trial during the time 1 October – 7 October 1945." Peter Clapham Collection, United States Holocaust Memorial Museum. Accession Number: 1994.A.0022.

Dixon, I. (1992 January 12). Female SS Helpers. RMP World. https://www.redcap70.net/A%20History%20of%20the%20SS%. 20Organisation%2019241945.html/Female%20SS%20Helpers.html.

Ehrlich, Z. (1985, August 8). "Interview with Zdenka Ehrlich." Interviewed by CXW. Imperial War Museum. https://collections.ushmm.org/oh_findingaids/RG-50.149.0051_trs_en.pdf

"Eleven Belsen 'Beasts' hanged." (1945, December 15). The Daily Telegraph. N.P.

Encyclopedia Britannica. https://www.britannica.com/event/World-War-II.

Erpel, Simone. (2007). *"Im Gefolge der SS": Aufseherinnen des Frauen-KonzentrationsLagers Ravensbrück.* Berlin. pp. 59–71.

Eschebach, I. (1997). *'Das Aufseherinnenhaus. Überlegungenzueiner AusstellungüberSS-Aufseherinnenin der Gedenkstätte Ravensbrück', Gedenkstätten Rundbrief*, no. 75, pp. 1–11.

Feig, K. (1981). *Hitler's Death Camps.* Holmes & Meyer.

Fagence, M. (17 October 1945). *Laughed when accused of hair-curl trickery.* Daily Herald.

Fénelon, F. (1977). *Playing for Time.* Syracuse University Press.

Foreign News. (1945, October 8). *Time.* 36.

Fromm, E. (1992). *The Anatomy of Human Destructiveness.* Holt Paperbacks.

Gabbard, G. (1989). Two subtypes of narcissistic personality disorder. Bulletin of the Menninger Clinic. 53, 527-532.

Gaevert, T. & Hilbert, M. (2004). "Women As Booty." [film]. ARD Broadcasting.

Gentry, Caron E. & Sjoberg, L. (2007). *Mothers, Monsters, Whores: Women's Violence in Global Politics*. Zed Books.

Gilbert, G. (1995). *Nuremburg Diary*. Boston: DeCapo Press.

Goldhill, O. (2018, August 4). *A neuroscientist who studies rage says we're all capable of doing something terrible*. Quartz. https://qz.com/1348203/a-neuroscientist-who-studies-rage-says-were-all-capable-of-doing-something-terrible.

Goldner. L. (2011, March 9). *Oral History Interview on Video*. Interviewed by J. Rudolph and B. Catz. United States Holocaust Museum. https://collections.ushmm.org/search/catalog/irn44093.

Gonzalez, A., & Mosquera, D. (2011). Narcissism as a Consequence of Trauma and Early Experiences. *ESTD Newsletter*, *1*(2), 4–6.

Greenbaum, M. (1991, October 8). "Oral History Interview with Masha Greenbaum." Interviewed by S. Bradley. United States Holocaust Museum. https://collections.ushmm.org/search/catalog/irn513295.

Graf, M. (1989). *I Survived the Krakow Ghetto and Plaszow Camp*. Florida State University Press.

Grunwald-Spier, A. (2018). *Women's Experiences in the Holocaust*. Amberley Publishing.

"Guilt admitted by Nazi woman." (1945, October 06). The News and Observer.

Hájková, A. (2021 March.) "Between Love and Coercion: Queer Desire, Sexual Barter and the Holocaust," *German History* 39 no. 1.

Hamilton, R. F. (2014), *Who Voted for Hitler?* Princeton University Press.

Heinke, I. (2008). Female Concentration Camp Guards as Perpetrators: Three Case Studies" cited in O. Jensen and C.C.W.

Hellinger, M. (2021, September 11). *My strange connection with the most infamous female SS Guard*. The Sydney Morning Herald. https://www.smh.com.au/culture/books/my-strange-connection-with- the-most-infamous-female-ss-guard-20210908-p58pxw.html.

Herr, J. & T. (Ed.). (1987, September 19). *Oral history interview with Frederick Riches*. United States Holocaust memorial museum. https://collections.ushmm.org/search/catalog/irn510841.

Herrenkohl, R.C., Herrenkohl, T.I., Moyaln, C.A., Russo, M.J., Sousa, C., & Tajima, E.A. (2010, January 25). *The Effects of Child Abuse and Exposure to Domestic Violence on Adolescent Internalizing and Externalizing Behavior Problems*. ms, National Library of Medicine.

Hirst, R. (1945, September 17). *Kramer at trial chained to doctor*. Evening Standard.

Hohne, H. (1986). *The order of the Death's Head.* Ballantine Books.

HolocaustCentUK. (n.d.). *Female Hitler Youth.* The National Holocaust Centre and Museum. https://www.holocaust.org.uk/the-league-of-german-girls.

Holt, P. (1945, November 16). Beastress of Belsen felt “her duty to exterminate.” *The Daily Telegraph.*

Holt, P. (1945, November 18). “How did Irma Grese get like this?” *The Daily Telegraph.* Electronic copy, p. 2.

Hughes, T. A., & Royde-Smith, J. G. (2023, August 23). *World War II 1939 - 1945.*

Institutional repository oops. UNI-INFO - university newspaper. (n.d.). https://uol.de/en/bis/research- publishing/open-access/institutional-repository-oops.

Irma of Belsen smiled and waved. (25 September 1945). *Daily Mirror.* No page number.

Irma Grese. https://www.capitalpunishmentuk.org/irma.html.

Irma Grese breaks down at last. (28 September 1945). *Daily Mirror.* No page number.

Jakubovic, A. (2002, August 27). *Oral History Interview with Alice Jakubovic.* Interviewed by Dr. J. Ringelheim. Oral History, U.S. Holocaust Memorial Museum online. https://collections.ushmm.org/search/catalog/irn511521.

Jennings, R. (2015). *Irma Grese and Auschwitz: Holocaust and the secrets of the blonde beast.* CreateSpace Independent Publishing Platform.

Jewish Virtual Library. (No date). “Irma Grese (1923 – 1945).”

https://www.jewishvirtuallibrary.org/irma-grese.

Jones, L. (2014, November 14). *Eric “Winkle” Brown: The man who seemed not to notice danger.* BBC News. https://www.bbc.com/news/magazine-30039300.

Jones, R. (2012, July 9). *Oral History Interview with Ron WG Jones.* Interviewed by D. Little. Oral History, U.S. Holocaust Memorial Museum online. https://collections.ushmm.org/search/catalog/irn62052.

Josephs, L. PhD. (2015). Review of Traumatic narcissism: Relational systems of subjection. P*sychoanalytic Psychology*. Pp. 221-227.

Kaleska, N. (2016). Oral History Interview with Nina Kaleska. Interviewed by Linda G. Kuzmack. Oral History, U.S. Holocaust Memorial Museum online.

Kater, M.H. (2006). *Hitler Youth.* Harvard University Press.

Knoch, H. ed. (2010). Bergen-Belsen: Historical Site & Memorial. *Stiftung niedersächsische Gedenkstätten.*

Konesko, N. (1945, April 08). Young playwright’s Holocaust drama debuts Friday. The Bradenton Herald.

K0nsl. (2012, December 24). *Someone to remember: Irma Grese - 12-24-2012 - WNLIBRARY.* K0nsl’s Blog - http://K0nsl.org/blog.

https://www.yumpu.com/en/document/read/14887598/someone-to-remember-irma-grese-12-24-2012-wnlibrary.

Koslov, E. M. (2010). *L'Europe En Formation No 357 Automne 2010 Work, Violence and Cruelty An Everyday Historical Perspective on Perpetrators in Nazi Concentration Camps*, 29–51. https://doi.org/https://www.academia.edu/2032280/Work_Violence_and_Cruelty_An_Everyday_Historical_Perspective_on_Perpetrators_in_Nazi_Concentration_Camps?email_work_card=title.

Kornreich-Gelissen, R. (2015). *Rena's Promise: A Story of Sisters in Auschwitz.* Beacon Press.

Koester, R. (2011). *"Hugo Boss, 1924-1945. A clothing factory during the Weimar Republic and the Third Reich."* University of Munich.

"*Kramer Beams, Takes Notes*." (19 September 1945). Daily Worker.

"*Kramer's wife slapped."* (10 October 1945) Daily Mirror.

Kuzmack, L.G. (1990, January 3). Interview with Nina Kaleska. Oral History Testimony Transcript from videotaped interview #RG-50.030*0101, United States Holocaust Research Institute. https://collections.ushmm.org.

Kwiet, K. (2021a, May 20). *Kapos: Collaborators, perpetrators or victims?*. Sydney Jewish Museum. https://sydneyjewishmuseum.com.au/news/kapos/.

Lengyel, O. (1948). Five Chimneys (electronic copy). Madison, CT.: International Universities Press.

Lerner, B. (2020a, September 17). *The trial before Nuremberg*. Jewish Journal. https://jewishjournal.org/2020/09/10/the-trial-before-nuremberg/

"Letter from Irma Grese." (n.d.) Peter Clapham Collection, United States Holocaust Memorial Museum. Accession Number: 1994.A.0022.

Levi-Hass, H. (1982). *Inside Belsen*. Barnes & Noble Press.

Lewis, I. (2018). *Women in European Holocaust Films: Perpetrators, Victims and Resisters.* Palgrave Macmillan.

Lewysohn, L. (2018). *Reproduction of Die Zoologie des Talmuds* 1858. Translated from the original artifact. Wentworth Press.

Lilly, R. J. and Puckett, M.B. (1997). "Social Control and Dogs: A Sociohistorical Analysis," Crime and Delinquency 43.2: 123-147.

Long, B. (2021). *Photographing the Feminine: Aufseherinnen in Holocaust Photography and Popular Culture, 1944-2018.* [Unpublished master's thesis]. Carleton University.

Lustgarten, E. (1968). *The Business of Murder*. Charles Scribner's Sons.

Macintyre, B. (2016). *Rogue Heroes*. Broadway Books.

Mann, E. (1938). *School for Barbarians: Education Under the Nazis*. Dover Publications, Inc.

"Mass Murder, I'm Guilty, Belsen Head Girl Admits." (1945, October 5.) Toronto Daily Star.

Memorandum "Trial of 'Belsen' War Criminals." (04 September 1945). Peter Clapham Collection, United States Holocaust Memorial Museum. Accession Number: 1994.A.0022.

Merriam-Webster. (2023). *Holocaust definition & meaning*. Merriam-Webster. https://www.merriam-webster.com/dictionary/holocaust.

McRae, S. T. (2016). *Irma Grese: A True Account of the Holocaust's Deadliest Woman.* CreateSpace Independent Publishing.

Morris, Felicia (2011) "Beautiful Monsters," Legacy: Vol. 11: Iss. 1, Article 6. Available at: http://opensiuc.lib.siu.edu/legacy/vol11/iss1/6

Müller, J.M. (2024). *Defendant No. 9.* Books on Demand: Norderstedt.

Müller, S. (2022, December 16). *Holocaust survivor: "Bergen-Belsen is my home."* SWI swissinfo.ch. https://www.swissinfo.ch/eng/culture/-bergen-belsen-is-my-home-/48133338.

The National WWII Museum of New Orleans. (n.d.). Research starters: Worldwide deaths in World War II: The National WWII Museum: New Orleans. https://www.nationalww2museum.org/students-teachers/student-resources/research-starters/research-starters-worldwide-deaths-world-war

(N.d.). Retrieved February 2, 2024, from https://avalon.law.yale.edu/subject_menus/nca_v4menu.asp.

Mailänder, E. (2015, 05 February). The violence of female guards in Nazi concentration camps (1939 – 1945): reflections on the dynamics and logics of power. *SciencesPo (Encyclopédie des violences de masse).* https://www.academia.edu/30458984/The_Violence_of_Female_Guards_in_Nazi_Concentration_Camps_1939_1945_Reflections_on_the_Dynamics_and_Logics_of_Power.

Main Commission for the Investigation of German Crimes in Poland. (October 12, 1942 – May 4, 1945).

"Mass Murder, I'm Guilty, Belsen Head Girl Admits." (1945, October 5.) Toronto Daily Star. No page number.

Mayo, N. (n.d.). *Sexual sadism disorder DSM-5 302.84 (F65.52).* Theravive Counseling. https://www.theravive.com/therapedia/sexual-sadism-disorder-dsm--5-302.84- (f65.52).

Mears, C. (2020). A Social History of the Aufseherinnen of Auschwitz. [Doctoral dissertation, Kingston University]. https://eprints.kingston.ac.uk/id/eprint/50539/1/Mears-C-50539.pdf.

Memorandum "Trial of 'Belsen' War Criminals." (04 September 1945). Peter Clapham Collection, United States Holocaust Memorial Museum. Accession Number: 1994.A.0022.

Merriam-Webster. (2023). *Holocaust definition & meaning*. Merriam-Webster. https://www.merriam-webster.com/dictionary/holocaust.

McKale, D. M. (2012). *Nazis After Hitle*r. Rowman & Littlefield Publishers, Inc.

McGuinness, D. (2021, January 18). *Nazi Ravensbrück camp: How ordinary women became SS torturers*. BBC News. https://www.bbc.com/news/world-europe-55661782.

McNab, C. (2009). *The SS: 1923–1945*. London: Amber Books.

McRae, S. T. (2016). *Irma Grese: A True Account of the Holocaust's Deadliest Woman.* CreateSpace Independent Publishing.

Michaud, S. G. (1999). *The Only Living Witness: The True Story of Serial Sex Killer Ted Bundy.* Authorlink.

Montgomery, B. L. (n.d.). *Military Government - Germany; Military Court - War Crimes Death Warrant.* Irma Grese. https://www.capitalpunishmentuk.org/irma.html.

Move to make saint of Irma Grese. (16 April 1946). *Wanganui Chronicle*. Page 5.

Müller, S. (2022, December 16). *Holocaust survivor: "Bergen-Belsen is my home."* SWI swissinfo.ch.

https://www.swissinfo.ch/eng/culture/-bergen-belsen-is-my-home-/48133338.

Nazi Conspiracy and Aggression. (1946). Vol. 4 US Government. Retrieved February 2, 2024, from Yale Law School, Lillian Goldman Library "The Avalon Project." https://avalon.law.yale.edu/subject_menus/nca_v4menu.asp.

Nelken, H. (1996). *And Yet, I Am Here!* University of Massachusetts.

Nevala-Nurmi, S., & Nevala, S.-L. (2006). Girls and Boys in the Finnish Voluntary Defence Movement. *Ennen ja nyt - Historian tietosanomat*, *2006*(3-4), 1-15.

Noks, R. J. (2014, October 6). *Grese, Irma.* TracesOfWar.com. https://www.tracesofwar.com/articles/3841/Grese-Irma.htm.

North Shields Postman "delivered" blonde Irma Grese (1845, September 23). *Sunday Sun*. P.1.

Overview of Auschwitz and Cehei Ghetto. [Slideshow]. (no date). Candles Holocaust Museum & Education Center. Available at https://candlesholocaustmuseum.org/file_download/inline/a4f06920- 0fac-4d67-8ed2-ba566e8e2546.

Pearlstein, R. M. (1991). *The Mind of the Political Terrorist*. S.R. Books.

Pfughoet, A. (2024, March 22). *Lampshade from Nazi concentration camp is Human skin: Report | miami herald.* Miami Herald. https://www.miamiherald.com/news/nation-world/world/article287001900.html.

Phillips, R. (1949). *Trial of Joseph Kramer and 42 Others (The Belsen Trial)* William Hodge & Company.

Pierrepoint, A. (1974). *Executioner: Pierrepoint*. Goldstone Books.

Pine, L. (2010). *Education in Nazi Germany*. Berg Publishers.

Playfair, G. & Sington, D. (1957). *The Offenders: Society and the Atrocious Crime*. London: William Hodge.

RAF (oyal Air Force) Bomber Command 60th Anniversary. (24 August 2004). "Campaign Diary December 1943."

Ravenbrück concentration camp: History & overview. History & Overview of Ravensbrück. (n.d.). https://www.jewishvirtuallibrary.org /history-and-overview-of-ravensbr-uuml-ck.

Rees, L. & Talge, C. (Directors). (11 January 2005). *Auschwitz: The Nazis and 'The Final Solution*. [documentary]. BBC.

Ringelheim, J. (1996, June 3). Interview with Carola S. Steinhardt. Oral History Testimony Transcript from videotaped interview #RG-50.030*368, United States Holocaust Research Institute. https://collections.ushmm.org.

Ringelheim, J. (1996, July 16). Interview with Renita Laqueur. Oral History Testimony Transcript from videotaped interview #RG-50.030*370, United States Holocaust Research Institute. https://collections.ushmm.org.

Rios, P., Slyter, S.L. & Zamostny, K.P. (1993). Narcissistic injury and its relationship to early trauma, early resources, and adjustment to college. Journal of Counseling Psychology.

Runeson, B., & Långström, N. (2010). Psychiatric Morbidity, Violent Crime, and Suicide Among Children and Adolescents Exposed to Parental Death. Journal of the American Academy of Child & Adolescent Psychiatry.

Scanlon, A. (2011). Unsubstantiated Claims Surrounding Irma Grese. University of Amsterdam. https://www.academia.edu/2325346/Unsubstantiated_Claims_Surrounding_Irma_Grese.

Salomon, F. (1983, April 13). *Oral history interview with Frieda Salomon.* Interviewer not listed. United States Holocaust Memorial Museum. https://collections.ushmm.org/search/catalog/irn503448.

Sandor, C.A. "BDM History" website https://bdmhistory.com.

Sargent, J. (Director). (2003). Out of the Ashes. [Film]. Columbia Pictures.

Sassoon, A. (1985 October?). *Oral history interview with Agnes Sassoon.* Interviewer not listed. United States Holocaust Memorial Museum. https://collections.ushmm.org/search/catalog/irn510842.

Shephard, B. (2007). *After Daybreak: The Liberation of Bergen-Belsen, 1945*. Knopf Doubleday Publishing Group.

Schnurmacher, T. (2021, August 30). *Schnurmacher: How my mother's vanity saved her in Auschwitz*. The Canadian Jewish News. https://thecjn.ca/arts/books-and-authors/schnurmacher-how-my- mothers-vanity-saved-her-in-auschwitz/ .

Schultz, S. (1945, October 18). *Belsen blonde lashes back at prosecutor*. Chicago Tribune. P. 8.

Sentenced To Death (1945, Day unknown). *Leicester-Mercury*. Archived in the Charles Phillip Sharp Collection of the United States Holocaust Memorial Museum. Accession number Accession Number: 2004.664.3.

Stanisława Rachwałowa. (1945, 25 July). No. 26281, KL Auschwitz, files of the trial of Rudolf Höss , volume 3.

Szejnman (eds.) *Ordinary People as Mass Murderers: Perpetrators in Contemporary Perspectives.* Palgrave Macmillan.

Shefler, G. S. S. (2012, April 18). *Survivor lets go of rage, 67 years later.* The Jerusalem Post.

JPost.com. https://www.jpost.com/jewish-world/jewish-features/survivor-lets-go-of-rage-67-years- Later.

She flushed in court – Irma Grese sent thousands to gas chambers says witness. (1945, September 27). *The Gloucestershire Echo.*

Sofsky, W. (1999). *The Order of Terror: The Concentration Camp.* Princeton University Press.

SS-Hygiene Institute Vol 11a/b (271) and Log, SS Lager-Lazarett.

"SS Killed 4,000,000 at Oswiecim, Prosecutor Says at Kramer Trial." (1945, September 18). New York Times.

Staub, E. (2000). *The Roots of Evil: The Origins of Genocide and Other Group Violence.* Cambridge University Press.

Strebel, B. (2003). *Das KZ Ravensbrück. Geschichte eines Lagerkomplexes, Paderborn: Schoningh.*

Stubberfield, T. (Director). & Davis, M. (Supervisory Producer). (2020). Belsen: Our Story. [film]. BBC.

"Target Analysis." (August 1945). Flight 9.

Taylor, F. (2005). Dresden: Tuesday 13 February 1945. London, UK.

[TheUntoldPast]. (No Date). Digging Up Irma Grese. [Video]. YouTube. https://www.youtube.com/watch?v=KGmp-5KADrY&t=24s.

Testimony of Tadeusz Pietrzykowski against Rudolph Höss. (21 March 1947). Reprinted in "Chronicles of Terror." Witold Pilecki Institute of Solidarity and Valor.

Tillion, G. (1988). *Ravensbrück: An Eyewitness Account of a Woman's Concentration Camp.* Paris.

Tillman, R. (2022, February 15). Report: Hate crimes rose 44% last year in study of major cities. Spectrum news online. https://ny1.com/nyc/all-boroughs/news/2022/02/14/hate-crime-increase-2021-asian-american-.

Time. (1954, March 15). *Germany: Decent burial.* https://time.com/archive/6794838/germany-decent-burial/.

Treforest, Edda. "Oral History Interview with Edda Treforest." Interview by Robert Buckley. 21 May 1991.

Tristan, N. (2022). *The Hyena of Auschwitz: The Crimes of Irma Grese, The Beautiful Beast of Auschwitz*. CreateSpace.

Tyson, P. (n.d.). *Nova online | Holocaust on trial | the experiments.* PBS. https://www.pbs.org /wgbh/nova/Holocaust/experiside.html.

Underwood, C. (2005). Before He Cheats [Song]. On Some Hearts [Album]. Arista Nashville.

USC Shoah Foundation. (2012, May 17). *War Crimes Participant Norma Falk Testimony, USC Shoah Foundation.* [Video]. YouTube. https://youtu.be/yLmDE36tfns?si=CtgI4hTk0pJCcRTC.

United States Holocaust Memorial Museum. (n.d.). *Ravensbrück.* United States Holocaust Memorial Museum. https://encyclopedia.ushmm.org/content/en/article/ravensbrueck.

United States Holocaust Memorial Museum, Washington, DC. (n.d.). *Nazi Camps.* United States Holocaust Memorial Museum. https://encyclopedia.ushmm.org/content/en/article/nazi-camps.

Von de Grun (1980). *Howl Like Wolves: Growing Up in Nazi Germany.* Morrow.

Vronsky, P. (2007). *Female Serial Killers: How & Why They Become Monsters.* Penguin Books.

War Crimes Trials - Vol. II The Belsen Trial. 'The Trial of Josef Kramer and Forty-Four Others. http://www.bergenbelsen.co.uk/pages/trial/trial /trialdefencecase/trial_036_grese.html.

www.auschwitz.org, U. (2006, October 13). *Human Fat Was Used to Produce Soap in Gdansk during the War.* News / Museum / Auschwitz-Birkenau. https://www.auschwitz.org/en/museum/news/human-fat-was-used-to-produce-soap-in-gdansk-during-the-war,55.html.

Wieble, P. (1987, May 23). Cited in Plantar Studio Projektowe. (13 December). *Helene Grese: Faithful Sister. Interview From 1987!* Reprinted in https://ssaufseherin.blogspot.com/2019/12/helene-grese-wierna-siostra-wywiad-z.html.

"Weight check sheet, 14 October – 21 October 1945." Peter Clapham Collection, United States Holocaust Memorial Museum. Accession Number: 1994.A.0022.

Willmott, L. (2015, June 1). *The real "Beast of Belsen"? Irma Grese and female concentration camp guards.* History Today. https://www.historytoday.com/history-matters/real-beast-belsen-irma-grese-and-female-concentration-camp-guards.

Willis, C. (19 April 1945). "The kind of women who staffed concentration camps" *News Chronical.* London.

Winkler. (2014, September 8). *Shape shifting.* Jewish Journal. https://jewishjournal.com/commentary/opinion/133124/.

Author Judith A. Yates with Esther Litwin Loeb, to whom this book is dedicated. (Image is property of the author and any copy without authorization is a violation)

ABOUT THE AUTHOR

With over 45 years of experience in law enforcement and education, criminologist and award-winning author Judith A. Yates has written six nonfiction crime books, two fiction crime books, and one nonfiction travel memoir. She is the Editor of True Crime: Case Files magazine, and Director of Best True Crime Games, Books & Video LLC.

Ms. Yates has appeared as a consultant on A&E, the ID Channel, the Oxygen Network, and a multitude of local television programs and media. She is a highly regarded lecturer across the United States to include speaking engagements at the Henry C. Lee Institute Markle Symposium, the National Homicide Investigators Association, Texas Association of Private Investigators, The Federal Bureau of Prisons, and the Tennessee State Prison Annual Training.

Judith A. Yates' career has included investigations in civil and criminal cases, loss prevention management, custody, and federal law enforcement. She has also worked as a trainer and mentor for various local, state, and federal law enforcement and private organizations. She has over 15 years in education as a Program Chair and professor in Criminal Justice departments across Texas, Tennessee, and Kentucky. Ms. Yates was an instructor, and a member of the Emergency Response / Riot Control Team, annual trainers' team, mentor group, custody suicide prevention group, and Employee Club President with the Federal Bureau of Prisons.

Ms. Yates is currently completing her PhD in Criminology. She has attended specialized training throughout the country, including Wicklander-Zulwalski & Associates Interview & Interrogation, along with multiple cold case conferences and homicide investigators training and symposia. Ms. Yates has attended law enforcement schools in Texas, Tennessee, Georgia, New Mexico, and Maryland.

Judith A. Yates is a victim's advocate and has taught practical self-defense & crime awareness for over 35 years. She is a recognized expert on female crime as well as domestic violence. Ms. Yates has done volunteer work with domestic violence prevention organizations, missing and cold cases, and animal welfare. Ms. Yates resides on a small farm of rescued animals with her family. She is a left-handed Taurus and proud Texan with a phobia of alligators and admitted addiction to Coca-Cola in glass bottles.

Website: www.JudithAYates.com.

ABOUT Peter Vronsky, PhD

Peter Vronsky is completing his forthcoming book, tentatively titled American Werewolf: The True Story of the Torso Serial Killer Confessions (Berkley Books at Penguin Random House). This is Vronsky's firsthand account of a seven-year odyssey of interviewing serial killer Richard Cottingham. Peter Vronsky and his investigative partner Jennifer Weiss assisted law enforcement in closing nine cold case homicides Cottingham had perpetrated in the 1960s and 1970s.

Peter Vronsky's books and information can be found on his website:
www.petervronskybooks.com

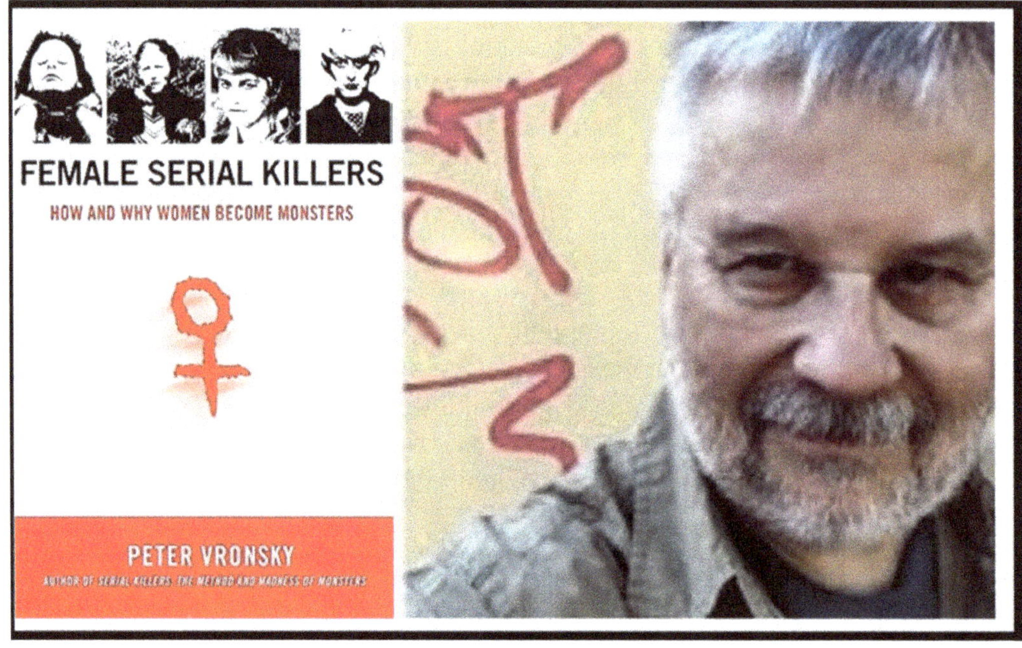

OTHER CRIME BOOKS BY JUDITH A. YATES

Available wherever quality books are sold – visit www.JudithAYates.com

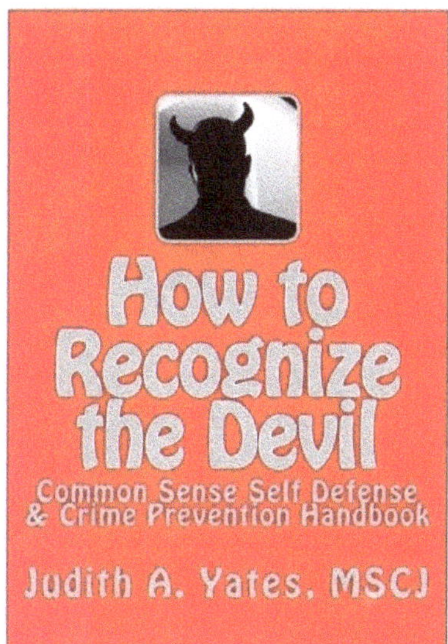

www.ingramcontent.com/pod-product-compliance
Lightning Source LLC
Chambersburg PA
CBHW080128270326
41926CB00021B/4394

* 9 7 9 8 2 1 8 4 8 6 7 5 4 *

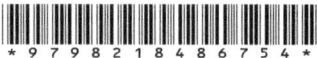